PROTEST POLITICS IN
THE MARKETPLACE

PROTEST POLITICS IN THE MARKETPLACE

Consumer Activism in the Corporate Age

Caroline Heldman

CORNELL UNIVERSITY PRESS   ITHACA AND LONDON

First published 2017 by Cornell University Press

Printed in the United States of America

Library of Congress Cataloging-in-Publication Data

Names: Heldman, Caroline, 1972– author.
Title: Protest politics in the marketplace : consumer activism in the corporate age / Caroline Heldman.
Description: Ithaca : Cornell University Press, 2017. | Includes bibliographical references and index.
Identifiers: LCCN 2017005004 (print) | LCCN 2017006422 (ebook) | ISBN 9781501709203 (cloth : alk. paper) | ISBN 9781501715402 (pbk. : alk. paper) | ISBN 9781501712111 (epub/mobi) | ISBN 9781501709470 (pdf)
Subjects: LCSH: Consumer movements—United States. | Consumption (Economics) —Political aspects—United States. | Social action—United States.
Classification: LCC HC110.C63 H45 2017 (print) | LCC HC110.C63 (ebook) | DDC 381.3/20973—dc23
LC record available at https://lccn.loc.gov/2017005004

Cornell University Press strives to use environmentally responsible suppliers and materials to the fullest extent possible in the publishing of its books. Such materials include vegetable-based, low-VOC inks and acid-free papers that are recycled, totally chlorine-free, or partly composed of nonwood fibers. For further information, visit our website at www.cornellpress.cornell.edu.

For Ian

The real power emerging today in democratic politics is just the mass of people who are crying out against the "high cost of living." That is a consumer's cry. Far from being an impotent one, it is, I believe, destined to be stronger than the interests either of labor or of capital.

—Walter Lippmann, *Drift and Mastery*, 1914

Contents

List of Illustrations   xi
Preface   xiii
List of Abbreviations   xvii

Introduction: Publicizing the Private Sector   1

1. A Consumer Revolution? Marketplace Activism
   since the Founding   25

2. "We Are the 99%": Contemporary Consumer Activism   54

3. "We Are Not a Mascot": Campaigns for Social
   and Economic Justice   74

4. "600,000 Bosses Telling Me What to Do": Campaigns
   for the Environment and Animal Rights   106

5. "Stop Serving Gay Chickens": Campaigns for Gender
   Justice and Lesbian-Gay-Bisexual-Transgender Rights   134

6. "Yes to Jesus Christ, No to *JC*": Campaigns for
   Conservative Causes   161

7. Who Rules? Corporate Power and Models of Democracy   189

Conclusion: Throwing Stones at Goliath   216

Notes   227
Index   273

Illustrations

1.1. Black residents walking, Montgomery
Bus Boycott, 1955   41

1.2. Counter sit-in at an F. W. Woolworth store,
Greensboro, North Carolina, 1960   43

2.1. Political engagement in the past year by Americans
younger than thirty   62

2.2. Cause marketing in millions from 2004 to 2014   66

2.3. Dollars spent on responsible investing in millions
from 1985 to 2015   68

2.4. Mentions of *divestment* in the *New York Times*
from 2004 to 2014   69

3.1. Confederate flag outside the South Carolina
statehouse, 2001   80

3.2. #BlackLivesMatter protest outside Macy's,
New York City, November 2014   90

4.1. Greenpeace spoof of a Kit Kat ad, 2010   112

4.2. Activist at a BP oil flood protest, Jackson Square,
New Orleans, 2009   114

4.3. Annual dolphin slaughter, Taiji, Japan, 2011   121

5.1. Altered CoverGirl ad protesting the NFL response
to domestic violence, 2014   142

5.2. National Same-Sex Kiss-In Day event, 2012   148

6.1. Sarah Silverman, comedian, displays her Jesus
Dress Up! magnet set, 2009   174

6.2. The Kraft "Let's Get Zesty" ad, 2013   175

Preface

This book is the culmination of two decades of work on consumer activism that began at Rutgers University in 1998. I have been writing about and presenting on the subject since that time, and it is a glorious, humbling experience to return to early academic work with fresh eyes, to marry a more developed intellectual sensibility with my first academic love—consumer activism.

When I started, my focus was on how women used consumer activism as a tool when they lacked power through formal political channels. I soon discovered that so little had been written on the subject that a narrow emphasis on gender was not sufficient to fill the large gap in existing research, so I broadened the scope.

Business scholars, historians, and sociologists had already "discovered" consumer activism, but I faced considerable resistance from political scientists who insisted that consumer activism was simply not political. As a consumer activist, I knew the political ramifications of this activity, and I sensed that it was becoming more important in the U.S. political landscape. I had chosen to study it because it was timely. Then, in 1999, the Battle in Seattle put consumer activism on the front page of the *New York Times,* and my battle to have consumer activism recognized as a political behavior became much easier.

In the intervening years, historians have published some first-rate books about U.S. consumer activism (e.g., Lizabeth Cohen, *A Consumer's Republic: The Politics of Mass Consumption in Postwar America*; Matthew Hilton, *Prosperity for All: Consumer Activism in an Era of Globalization*; and especially Lawrence Glickman, *Buying Power: A History of Consumer Activism in America*), but political science has been slow to the subject. I no longer have to convince most of my colleagues that this behavior is political, but oddly enough this book is the first to study the political and democratic implications of contemporary consumer activism in the United States.

My interest in consumer activism started when I was fourteen years old. I spent the summer working as a janitor at the local high school in order to purchase a used Commodore 64 so I could waste my days playing video games, as well as improve the reach of my consumer activism. Using a list from an animal rights magazine, I put my computer to use writing letters to companies that tested their products on animals. I was home-schooled, so I had the luxury of writing dozens of letters each week shaming these companies and pledging to not purchase their products unless they stopped testing on animals. (Of course my parents thought my printer activity was related to schoolwork, not activism.) I did not have the language for what I was doing (boycotting), nor was I aware of the long history of consumer activism or the many other people who were also engaging in it. All I knew that was that I wanted these companies to stop testing their products on animals and that my threat to withhold purchasing might give me some leverage.

Since that time, I have been active in many consumer campaigns. My frequent use of consumer activism provides insights into both its effectiveness and limitations, and my experience and training in electoral politics allows me to situate it within the broader political context. I also approach this subject with a business degree and years of experience working in the private sector in firms that were occasionally targeted by consumer activists. At one company, I developed the response protocol to consumer activism, which made me acutely aware of the risk posed by the unpredictability of (sometimes irrational) consumer activists.

I bring my knowledge as a practitioner of consumer activism, a corporate officer, and a political scientist to bear on this project, as well as my deep and abiding passion for the subject. This book was a long time in the making, and after all these years, I am thrilled to share it with you.

I am grateful to many people who helped me along the way. I am indebted to Richard Lau at Rutgers University for his rigorous critiques and unremitting encouragement. Rick persistently nudged me over the years to publish my work on this subject, and his faith in the project made it happen. I am very thankful to Jane Junn for funding my initial data collection and to Susan Carroll, Kerry Haynie, and Benjamin Barber—all at Rutgers—for their invaluable feedback that shaped the direction of the book.

This book would not have been possible without the thoughtful guidance of my editor, Michael McGandy, who improved the manuscript at every step. Michael made the process a joyful one with his creative ideas and enthusiasm. Julie F. Nemer's careful editing strengthened the manuscript, and Karen Hwa skillfully oversaw the revision process.

This book also benefitted greatly from reviewers. Lawrence Glickman offered keen insights on historical context and events that tremendously improved the project. I am indebted to him for furnishing the historical backbone of this book with his previous scholarship, and for investing the time to closely read my manuscript several times. Mark B. Brown was the first to suggest that I include a chapter on political theory, which I could not have done without his expertise and guidance on the subject. Andrew Murphy furnished helpful insights on political theory that took the project in new and necessary directions. Tony Barnstone was an early champion of the project who encouraged me to gather a decade of data to better understand patterns and trends. The contents of this book have also been shaped by students over the years. Rebecca Cooper, an Occidental College graduate, provided excellent editorial, formatting, and fact-checking assistance. Georgia Faye Hirsty, Erinn Carter, Clint Swift, and Sarah Oliver from Whittier College gathered background materials that enriched the book when they were undergraduates.

I am deeply grateful to Ian Breckenridge-Jackson for reading drafts and for managing the household while I worked long hours. In my absence, he managed to make all the cats love him more.

Abbreviations

AAF	Artists against Fracking
AAUW	American Association of University Women
AFA	American Family Association
AFL-CIO	American Federation of Labor and Congress of Industrial Organizations
AHA	American Humane Association
ALEC	American Legislative Exchange Council
ALF	Animal Liberation Front
ANWR	Arctic National Wildlife Refuge
ARM	Animal Rights Movement
BLF	Billboard Liberation Front
BP	British Petroleum
CARB	Citizens Against Religious Bigotry
CARM	Campus Anti-Rape Movement
CFA	Consumer Federation of America
CIW	Coalition of Immokalee Workers
COC	Color of Change
CORE	Congress of Racial Equality
CWA	Concerned Women of America
DAN	Direct Action Network
EII	Earth Island Institute
ELF	Earth Liberation Front
ERA	Equal Rights Amendment
ESG	environmental, social, and governance investing
FDA	Food and Drug Administration
FFRF	Freedom from Religion Foundation
FGRBC	Florida Gay Rights Buycott Campaign
FLOC	Farm Labor Organizing Committee
FMF	Feminist Majority Foundation
FOTF	Focus on the Family
FSC	Forest Stewardship Council
G8	Group of 8 (France, Germany, Italy, United Kingdom, Japan, United States, Canada, and Russia)

GJM	Global Justice Movement
GLAAD	Gay and Lesbian Alliance against Defamation
HRC	Human Rights Campaign
HSUS	Humane Society of the United States
HUAC	House Un-American Activities Committee
II	impact investing
IMF	International Monetary Fund
KFC	Kentucky Fried Chicken
LFTB	lean finely textured beef
LGBT	lesbian, gay, bisexual, transgender
LOHAS	Lifestyles of Health and Sustainability
LWS	League of Women Shoppers
MFA	Mercy for Animals
MMA	Media Matters for America
NAACP	National Association for the Advancement of Colored People
NAFTA	North American Free Trade Agreement
NBA	National Basketball Association
NCAI	National Congress of American Indians
NCL	National Consumers League
NFL	National Football League
NGLCC	National Gay and Lesbian Chamber of Commerce
NLWV	National League of Women Voters
NOM	National Organization for Marriage
NOW	National Organization for Women
NRA	National Rifle Association
OMM	One Million Moms
OWS	Occupy Wall Street
P&G	Procter & Gamble
PETA	People for the Ethical Treatment of Animals
PLW	Pro-Life Waco
PTA	Parent Teacher Association
PUSH	People United to Serve Humanity
SEC	Securities and Exchange Commission
SNCC	Student Non-Violent Coordinating Committee
SRI	socially responsible investing
Super PAC	super political action committee
TRP	The Representation Project
UCC	United Church of Christ
UFW	United Farm Workers

USAS	United Students against Sweatshops
USC	University of Southern California
USDA	U.S. Department of Agriculture
WAVAW	Women against Violence against Women
WTO	World Trade Organization

PROTEST POLITICS IN THE MARKETPLACE

PUBLICIZING THE PRIVATE SECTOR

In 2011, inspired by the success of civil disobedience in Tahrir Square during the Arab Spring, Kalle Lasn and Micah White organized a protest in the financial district of New York City to kick off what would become known as Occupy Wall Street (OWS). As a longtime consumer activist, Lasn had organized the international Buy Nothing Day, which urged consumers to avoid shopping on the two days after Thanksgiving, as well as TV Turnoff Week, which encouraged families to disconnect from electronic devices for a week.[1] OWS started with a humble encampment in Zuccotti Park and quickly grew into an organized community with about two hundred full-time occupants. It gained national recognition with the help of news coverage and the organizers' use of new technology (e.g., live streaming video and social media). Using the slogan "We are the 99%," OWS protesters criticized preferential governmental treatment of Wall Street over Main Street during the financial meltdown and protested growing economic inequality as well as undue corporate influence in politics and policymaking. The movement did not accomplish concrete policy change, but it did shift media focus away from the travails of the banks to the suffering of everyday Americans during the financial crisis.[2] At the height of the movement in October 2011, 59 percent of Americans said they agreed with the goals of the movement.[3]

OWS is the highest profile campaign in the contemporary era of consumer activism—the eighth era in U.S. history. This era emerged in the mid-2000s and is distinct in its use of various types of consumer activism, the sheer volume of activities, transnational focus,[4] and its use of social media. Social media quickly

1

spread news of OWS beyond New York City, and Occupy encampments sprang up in ninety-five cities across eighty-two countries.[5] Police closed Zuccotti Park and arrested over two hundred occupants in November 2011, and in the following two years, over 8,000 OWS protesters were arrested as they continued to stage protests and sit-ins at corporate headquarters, colleges and universities, banks, and board meetings.[6] Beyond direct action, the organizers called for a nationwide boycott of banks in response to new automated teller machine (ATM) fees, and they organized a Bank Transfer Day to get people to switch from their bank to a credit union. Over 75,000 people joined the Bank Transfer Day Facebook page, and credit unions saw their new-account traffic double.[7] OWS also used investment actions to achieve its goals.[8] The crowd-funding campaign Rolling Jubilee cancelled $15 million in consumer debt during its first year, and in 2012, OWS activists (and PNC Bank shareholders) attended the PNC Bank annual meeting to "confront the 1 percent directly."[9] OWS epitomizes the face of new consumer activism campaigns in that it involved thousands of decentralized actions from grassroots activists.

The purpose of this book is to analyze the democratic implications of consumer activism in the United States, both historically and in the contemporary era. This is the first book dedicated to questions of democracy and consumer activism, and I approach it through both normative and empirical lenses. This book is also the most comprehensive study of consumer activism in the United States to date, covering case studies of sixty-one consumer campaigns from 2004 to 2014. It is the first book to systematically study consumer activism in the social media age.

What Is Consumer Activism?

People who study consumer activism define it in different ways. I define *consumer activism* as citizen actions directed toward business entities to explicitly influence the distribution of social goods or social values. This definition is drawn from research on political participation because my book concerns the democratic implications of these actions. By doing so, I reveal deficiencies in the established conceptions of both political participation and consumer activism. But first, I must define what I mean by *politics* and *political participation*.

Mark Warren urges scholars to define *politics* in ways that clarify our normative investment in questions of democracy.[10] My goal in this book is to expand measures of democratic health by including nonstate forms of political engagement; thus, my definition of *politics* is expansive. In a broad sense, *politics* is the rules and practices established by humans to organize their lives. David Easton defines *politics* as conflict resolution through the "authoritative allocation of values" in society, whereas Harold Lasswell defines it as "who gets what, when, how," centering on resource allocation.[11] These two halves of politics—resources allocation and societal value—tend to align. The resources held by a group (e.g., Latinxs, women, or the working class) generally correspond with its members' sociopolitical standing because groups with higher social value are better able to extract resources from institutions. My definition of *politics* is the process of who gets what, when, and how in regard to societal resources and social value.

In terms of the *how*, scholars define *politics* as an exercise of power: a competition between people, groups, or states.[12] Robert Dahl, a democratic theorist, describes power as a relation among people in which a person can get another person to do something he or she would not otherwise do through varying degrees of persuasion, ranging from the use of a rational argument to physical force.[13] Power lies with the state through its authority to set the rules and then enforce them. The power to allocate resources and social value also lies with other entities, such as mass media, educational institutions, religious organizations, and businesses. My definitions of *politics* and *political participation* encompass both state and nonstate institutions that have the power to influence resources and social values.

For most of its history, mainstream political science defined *political participation* as electoral participation. In their 1972 classic, *Participation in America: Political Democracy and Social Equality*, Sidney Verba and Norman Nie characterize it as "those activities by private citizens that are more or less directly aimed at influencing the selection of government personnel and/or the actions they take."[14] To their credit, Verba and Nie also express interest in understanding broader attempts to "influence the authoritative allocation of values for a society, which may or may not take place through governmental decisions," but consider electoral actions to be a decent proxy measure for all political activities.[15] In their 1995 *Voice and Equality: Civic Voluntarism in American Politics*, the most comprehensive assessment of political participation in the United States to date, Verba, Kay Lehman Schlozman, and Harry E. Brady also define *participation* in narrow electoral terms, as actions that have "the intent or effect of influencing government action—either directly by affecting the making or implementation of public policy or indirectly by influencing the selection of people who make those policies."[16]

Electoral definitions of *political participation* assume that public policy is strictly a function of government. But we do not have to look very far to see that this is not the case. Corporations, churches, media organizations, and other politicized institutions are involved in both making and implementing public policy. For example, corporations influence elections through their contribution to political campaigns and interests, employee mobilization, and revolving doors. Corporations can also delay policy implementation through a variety of tactics such as foot-dragging, interpreting laws differently than intended, simply not abiding by policy guidelines, lengthy court actions, and relocating branches of the business to other countries to avoid compliance with U.S. laws.

Steven J. Rosenstone and John Mark Hansen provide a more inclusive definition of *political participation* as actions "directed explicitly toward influencing the distribution of social goods and social values."[17] This definition encompasses all citizen actions that overtly aim to change public priorities and the way public resources are shared. For example, producing a documentary film that explicitly seeks to raise the social value of transgender people is an act of political participation, as is a neighborhood campaign to reallocate local funds for snow plowing to pothole repair.

I borrow from Rosenstone and Hansen's definition of *political participation* and define *consumer activism* as citizen actions directed toward business entities to explicitly influence the distribution of social goods or social values. What makes these actions political, as opposed to just economic, is the end goal of affecting social goods and social values.[18] Social goods are shared public goods, such as clean water or tax dollars spent on public education. Social values are widely shared (largely unconscious) assumptions of what is important and right; guidelines for how individuals in a society arrange their priorities and make life choices. Most people have numerous interactions with business entities on a weekly basis, and although most of these interactions are not political, some are. For an action to be classified as consumer activism, its explicit aim must be to alter social goods or social values. The act can be individual or collective, as long as the end goal extends beyond personal interest to broader social interests.

My definition of *consumer activism* encompasses citizen action that targets the marketplace for political reasons as opposed to existing studies that center more narrowly on boycotting and buycotting (purchasing behavior that rewards companies for favorable practices or products). For example, Dietlind Stolle, Marc Hooghe, and Michele Micheletti define *political consumerism* as "consumer choice of producers and products based on political or ethical considerations, or both."[19] Similarly, Micheletti and Stolle define *political consumerism* as "the choice of producers and products with the aim of changing ethically or politically objectionable institutional or market practices."[20] These definitions revolve around people's decisions to consume (or not consume) particular products or services, whereas my definition revolves around the marketplace as the target for citizens who seek political change. Boycotting and buycotting remain the most popular types of consumer activism, but other tactics for altering business behavior that deserve attention have come to the fore in the past two decades, such as proposing an environmentally conscious shareholder resolution and occupying a business establishment to raise awareness of police brutality against black Americans. This book is the first to analyze the broader constellation of political actions in the marketplace.[21]

In defining *consumer activism*, scholars disagree about whether to consider individual actions along with collective actions. Lawrence Glickman, a historian, emphasizes collective action in his definition of *consumer activism* as "organized consumption, or, more often, nonconsumption that is collective, oriented toward the public sphere, grassroots, and conscious of the political impact of print or commerce."[22] He excludes individual actions, such as personal boycotts of stores or complaint letters to companies, because they lack the critical mass to influence business entities. I argue that most citizen actions, whether individual or collective, have limited impact on political outcomes, so effectiveness is not a useful criterion for inclusion. For example, one person's vote does not decide an election, and an individual letter to a member of Congress has little or no effect on legislation, but political scientists still consider both of these actions to be political because of the intent behind them. Furthermore, contemporary consumer activism is marked by its use of social media campaigns, which blurs the line between individual and collective actions. It is difficult to determine whether a person who reposts information about a boycott to shame a polluting company is engaging in an individual act or sees herself as part of a larger collective campaign. Glickman acknowledges that "the tradition of consumer activism is a political hybrid, then, taking many forms" and that contemporary consumer activism in the United States has evolved in new ways that require a broader definition to capture the complexity and richness of various tactics to hold businesses accountable beyond (non)consumption.[23] I consider individual acts to be consumer activism, as long as the acts go beyond individual self-interest to social goods or social values.

Types of Consumer Activism

There are many different ways to approach the study of consumer activism. Most studies examine the behavior of individual consumers, an approach that fails to capture marketplace actions other than (non)consumption. Other studies look at consumer movements, a lens than overlooks individual actions. To develop a more complete typology of consumer activism, I opt for a third approach: analyzing tactics. Citizens use four primary tools to hold businesses politically accountable: (1) (non)purchasing actions, (2) investment actions, (3) social media actions, and (4) direct actions.

(Non)Purchasing Actions

The first form of consumer activism, (non)purchasing actions, comes in two forms: boycotts and buycotts. *Boycotting* is avoiding buying products from companies to harm their reputation and profit margin; *buycotting* is purchasing products from companies to reward their favorable practices or products (also called *girlcotts, procotts, white listing,* and *reverse boycotts*).[24] The first recorded boycott took place in 617 CE in present-day Saudi Arabia, where two clans declared a boycott against a third clan to pressure it to withdraw its protection of a rival religious leader.[25] This boycott was not effective, and it came to an end within three years. In the fourth century CE, Athens threatened to boycott the Olympic games in response to an athlete's being fined for cheating. The threat was not successful in reversing the fine, and Athens did compete in the games that year. The next major recorded boycott effort took place a millennium later, initiated by colonists in the Boston Harbor, but it was another century before the term *boycott* was coined to describe these actions. The term *boycott* derives from 1880, when Irish peasants took action against Charles Cunningham Boycott, a British land agent.[26] After a bad crop year, local villagers effectively used a boycott to pressure him into reducing rents to an affordable level. Today, *boycott* is synonymous with *consumer activism*.

One of the best-known boycotts in the last generation targeted Nestlé from the early 1970s through 1984[27] to halt company sales of infant formula in less industrialized nations after a string of infant deaths. The boycott of Nestlé involved nineteen countries and was ultimately successful in getting the company to provide better labeling information. Consumer activists also staged the Boston Nestlé Party, an environmentally questionable dump of Nestlé products into Boston Harbor. The Nestlé campaign sent a message to all global companies about the willingness of U.S. citizens to hold corporations responsible for their actions overseas.[28] Activists also lobbied members of Congress, including Senator Ted Kennedy (D-MA), who publicly denounced Nestlé.[29]

Another classic boycott effort was a series of campaigns targeting U.S. companies doing business with South Africa with the goal of abolishing legal segregation (a.k.a. Apartheid) in the late 1980s. These efforts were led by a group of South African exiles living in London, and they quickly drew international attention and support from students, trade unions, and liberal political parties. Many U.S. companies halted their South African operations as a result of the boycott and divestment actions, including the Ford Motor Company and Apple Computers.[30] With the combined pressure from the global boycott, economic sanctions from the United States and United Kingdom, and a United Nations denunciation of Apartheid, the system was abolished in 1994 with the adoption of a new constitution. The Nestlé and South African boycotts put companies on notice that moral pressure of this kind was becoming "an increasingly important fact of business life."[31]

The first U.S. buycott started in the 1820s with Free Produce Movement, which encouraged people to purchase products made by free labor instead of slave labor. The strategy of this buycott was to limit the demand for slave-made products as a way to reduce or eliminate slavery. In the modern era, companies partner with political or social causes (cause marketing) to enhance their reputation and encourage buycotting. Examples include eco-labeling and partnerships with sympathy-inspiring causes such as domestic violence or breast cancer.[32] Some brands adopt a socially conscious identity, such as Ben & Jerry's Ice Cream (an assortment of liberal causes), The Body Shop (Fair Trade products and good labor practices), and TOMS shoes. Many Americans pay a premium to buy green, purchase organic products, buy Fair Trade, and purchase non-sweatshop-made products.

The most successful cause marketing campaign has been the Fair Trade Campaign, whose aim is to improve the environmental and working conditions of exporters in developing countries. Fair Trade products are one of the fastest growing global markets.[33] Certifying organizations, such as FairTrade International and Eco-Social, ensure that coffee, tea, bananas, and other consumer products meet certain labor and environmental standards. Fair Trade has become a popular buycotting tactic for U.S. corporations in the past decade.[34] Some national chains such as Starbucks and Whole Foods have become synonymous with Fair Trade products, and major supermarket chains throughout the United States offer Fair Trade items. Imports of Fair Trade products rose considerably in the past year, for example, coffee (32 percent), sugar (31 percent), cocoa (156 percent), produce (40 percent), and a slew of other products.[35] Approximately 60,000 retail locations sell certified Fair Trade products in the United States[36]

Smartphone technology now enables more boycotting and buycotting. Consumers can now walk down the grocery aisle and check on the labor, environmental, and social record of the companies that produce products using smartphone applications such as GoodGuide and Go Green. These applications have great potential to influence purchasing decisions because nearly two-thirds of adults in the United States have a cell phone, and half of cell phone users own smartphones with Internet access.[37]

Investment Actions

The second type of consumer activism entails investment actions: socially responsible investing, shareholder resolutions, and divestment. These actions attempt to bring about change by using preexisting mechanisms for share-holder input. Many social investment funds exist to cater to environmental, safety, health, labor, and other social justice concerns. For example, the Par-nassus Fund invests in companies that have a track record of respect for their employees and the environment. The Green Century Equity Fund screens companies for environmental responsibility. Domini Social Investments excludes "booze, butts and bets—alcohol, tobacco, and gambling stocks" and files shareholder resolutions on behalf of its clients. Amy Domini, the fund founder, couches her work in political terms when she states that "global com-panies are more powerful than governments," so consumers exercise political power through investing in ways they would not be able to through formal governmental channels.[38]

A second approach is shareholder resolutions that have come to play an important role in changing corporate actions around environmental, health, social justice, and workplace issues in the last decade. Politically oriented shareholder resolutions run the gamut of policy concerns. McDonald's implemented a sexual orientation nondiscrimination policy as a result of an organized shareholder action; Ford Motor Company and Nike endorsed a ten-point code of conduct for environmental responsibility; and a coalition of shareholders successfully persuaded Mitsubishi to abandon plans for build-ing a salt factory near a whale refuge in Mexico.[39] K.B. Homes, one of the largest home builders in the nation, responded to shareholder pressure about energy efficiency, and by 2010, 90 percent of its new homes were Energy Star qualified.[40] It is difficult to muster enough shareholder support to pass con-troversial resolutions, so some campaigns use media to get businesses to enact resolutions through public pressure.[41] For example, about a dozen major cor-porations, including Bank of America, were compelled to publicly acknowl-edge the growing gap between the rich and the poor in the United States in response to a popular but ultimately unsuccessful shareholder-resolution campaign to shine a spotlight on the pay ratio between company chief execu-tive officers (CEOs) and their lowest-paid employees. McDonald's stopped its use of Styrofoam containers because of a resolution from only 3 percent of its shareholders, and other fast-food restaurants followed suit.[42] Consumer activ-ism has led to a more environmentally sound, industry-wide, de facto public policy without government regulation.

A third investment action is divestment, an organized group exodus of inves-tors from a company or industry to protest its politics. In the 1980s, college stu-dents got hundreds of schools to sell their stock in companies that did business in South Africa under Apartheid. In the 1990s, students pressured their schools to pull investments from tobacco companies. Students today are urging schools to divest from the gun industry and from fossil fuels.[43] Divestment campaigns are a way to act locally with global consequences.

Social Media Actions

The newest form of consumer activism is online. Since the launch of Facebook in 2004, YouTube in 2005, and Twitter in 2006, activists have powerful new communication tools to shame or reward companies for their political stances and actions. Corporations have adapted by hiring social media experts for cause marketing and to protect against online brand threats. Social media have taken consumer activism to a new level in the past decade by making it easier for organized marketplace campaigns to reach more people.

Blogs are another online tool used by activists. For example, the feminist blogosphere (Ms. Blog, Feministing, Feministe, Jezebel, and hundreds of individual bloggers) can bring immediate, intense, and widespread attention to companies that engage in sexist marketing practices. One example of the potential for speed and effectiveness of social media consumer activism is a 2011 action against clothing retailer Abercrombie & Fitch. In March 2011, a feminist blog posted a short criticism of the company for marketing push-up bikinis for girls as young as seven years old. Within hours, it had been reposted on other Internet sites over five hundred times. Within twenty-four hours, multiple major news outlets had run stories about the bikini, and within a week, Abercrombie & Fitch had pulled the product from its website and stores with the following statement on the official company Facebook page: "We agree with those who say it is best 'suited' for girls age 12 and older."[44] The new social media age has revolutionized the ease and frequency of market campaigns, and given the potential for damage to their reputation, firms can be compelled to respond quickly.

In addition to social media tools and blogs, there are also a handful of social action petition sites. Change.org, the most popular petition platform, was created in 2007 and now boasts 10 million members.[45] They have had success with hundreds of consumer activism petitions. Change.org receives five hundred member-generated petitions a day, only a fraction of which gain traction, but those that do have the potential to change public conversation and policy. For example, in 2011, 175,000 people in 175 countries signed a Change.org petition compelling the South African parliament to create a task force to end "corrective" lesbian rapes.

Social media are an especially effective tool for holding corporations accountable because they can do significant reputational damage. In his longitudinal analysis of boycotts, Monroe Friedman finds campaigns that harm the reputation of the business are more likely to get a response from the targeted business than campaigns that do economic damage.[46] Naomi Klein also advocates the use of reputational damage as being important in holding corporations accountable for their behavior in her book *No Logo*.[47] The unpredictable, viral nature of social media campaigns has made it bad business to ignore consumer campaigns, and major corporations now have dedicated staff to respond to market campaign threats.

Direct Actions

Direct consumer activism comes in many forms, such as protests, sit-ins, teach-ins, picket lines, and culture jamming (e.g., defacing a billboard to change the message). Consumer protests are a staple of the antisweatshop movement that gained traction on college campuses in the late 1990s.[48] United Students against Sweatshops (USAS) has been at the forefront of continuous campaigns to force manufacturers to implement nonsweatshop employment practices. In 1999, students at Georgetown University staged an eighty-five-hour sit-in in the president's office to force the negotiation of the procedures for the production of university apparel. Similar protests took place that year at the University of Wisconsin and Duke University in response to "an economic war on the underpaid, overworked laborers who make the products that bear [university] logos."[49] Nike responded to the protesters almost immediately by releasing a list of its manufacturing facilities and promising improvements.[50]

College apparel and footwear manufacturers have improved factory conditions as a result of direct consumer activism.[51] In 2009, USAS and students from nearly ninety universities achieved their biggest victory when they succeeded in getting Russell Athletics, the largest U.S. producer of sportswear, to rehire 1,200 employees in a Honduran factory.[52] Russell had closed the factory to shut down union organizing, and students pressured their universities to sever their Russell contracts in response. Students took their actions beyond the quad by protesting during the National Basketball Association (NBA) finals in Orlando and Los Angeles, launching a Twitter campaign targeting Dick's Sporting Goods, and passing out fliers at Sports Authority locations. Russell's capitulation included a promise to not fight future unionizing efforts. Student consumer activism is behind the adoption by most retailers of manufacturing codes of conduct for safety and wages.[53] Student activism has also raised public awareness of the issue of sweatshops. Three-quarters of Americans say they will buy non-sweatshop-made clothing over clothing made in sweatshops if given the opportunity and if it is at a similar price, a reasonable expectation given that doubling the wages at sweatshops increases the average price of a garment by only 1.8 percent.[54]

Some types of direct action are extra-legal. Julia Butterfly Hill's action against the Pacific Lumber Company in northern California is an example of extreme consumer activism. Hill, an environmentalist preacher's daughter, set up residence on Luna, an ancient Redwood tree, to protect the surrounding stand of old-growth forest. During her stay on two platforms in the tree, Hill was visited by Joan Baez, a singer, and Woody Harrelson, an actor. She was also visited twice a week by her crew, who delivered food and supplies. Hill passed the time reading, talking on the telephone, and surviving the damp environs. "Hill was never truly dry during her two years in Luna."[55] The press nicknamed her "Madame Butterfly" for her tenacity. Hill climbed Luna on December 10, 1997, and did not come down until December 18, 1999, after the Pacific Lumber company agreed to preserve Luna and the surrounding tree stand for $50,000. Butterfly Hill also has permission to visit Luna with one-day advance notice.

The sometimes illegal tactics of the Earth Liberation Front (ELF) constitute extra-legal consumer activism. Founded in 1977, ELF maintains an updated website publicizing its recent activities. The first goal of the organization is to "inflict economic damage on those profiting from the destruction and exploitation of the natural environment."[56] ELF targets both corporations and governments, and the organization was responsible for an estimated six hundred acts between 1996 and 2002 that caused $43 million in property damage.[57] In 1998 ELF members set fire to a ski resort in Vail, Colorado, to protect a lynx habitat, causing damage to the tune of $12 million. In the early morning hours of August 1, 2003, ELF initiated the costliest act of environmental terrorism to date when its members set fire to a new unoccupied condominium complex in San Diego, causing damage to the tune of $50 million. The organization took credit for the act with a banner that read "If you build it, we will burn it," signed, "The ELFs are mad."[58] A few months later, the group torched 125 sports utility vehicles (SUVs) in Los Angeles County, targeting both dealerships and citizens. ELF members also spray-painted SUVs with the slogans "earth raper," "SUVs suck," and "fuck Hummer."[59] ELF was classified as the number one domestic U.S. terrorism threat in the early 2000s, and with the help of the post-9/11 Patriot Act, ELF was the subject of a multi-agency crackdown called Operation Backfire. After two years of surveillance and infiltration, fifteen ELF members were charged with arson and other crimes from 2005–2007, and all fifteen pled guilty.[60]

New Popularity of Marketplace Activism

Starting in the early 2000s, consumer activism surged to a level not seen since the organized Consumer Movement of the 1970s.[61] *Newsweek* identified this new trend in 2001: "The Big Idea after the cold war was to privatize the public sector. Now it's to 'publicize' the private sector—to get its wealth to work for social ends."[62] Rates of political boycotts and *buy*cotts have dramatically increased in recent decades, in both industrialized and less industrialized countries,[63] and organized consumer protests have become commonplace in the United States[64] This trend is evident in media coverage of consumer activism in the *New York Times* and the *Washington Post* from 1991 to 2010. Combined, these outlets published four stories on consumer activism in 1990, 20 stories in 1995,[65] and an average of 2,117 articles each year from 2000 to 2010.[66] Younger Americans in particular are participating in politics in new ways, forging new possibilities for political influence through the marketplace. Over half of Americans under 30 have engaged in political purchasing, and they are significantly more likely than their older counterparts to do so.[67] According to the *National Boycott Newsletter*, boycotts have increased markedly from about 30 per year in the 1960s to over 300 per year by 1990,[68] and over 500 annually in the 2000s.[69] Similar trends can be seen with all four primary forms of consumer activism, as discussed in chapter 2.

The examples of consumer activism I have provided so far all involve liberal causes, but conservative consumer activism has become commonplace in the last half century. As discussed in chapter 1, conservative consumer activism was first used in the 1850s to drive out Chinese workers and business owners during a national wave of Chinese exclusion, and was again used by whites to counter the Free Produce Movement later that century. Conservatives used Southern economic nationalism leading up to the Civil War, and a century later they employed counter-boycotts to slow the Civil Rights Movement. But conservative consumer campaigns rapidly multiplied from the 1970s on as a tool in the "culture wars." Today, conservative groups organize campaigns against corporate support for lesbian, gay, bisexual, and transgender (LGBT) rights, sexualized content in media, and gun rights. They have also organized effective counter-boycotts, for example, to reinstate Phil Robertson on the A&E reality show *Duck Dynasty* after his anti-gay comments. Consumer activism is not as widely accepted by conservatives as it is in liberal camps for political and religious reasons. Along political lines, the pro-corporate sentiment of Republicans conflicts with consumer activism because the market is seen as too valuable tool for freedom to be interrupted in this way. Along religious lines, some Christians take exception to boycotts as too coercive. Despite these concerns, consumer activism is used by a sizable number on the Right. This book is the first to systematically analyze the content, effectiveness, and democratic implications of conservative marketplace activism.

Marketplace Activism and Democracy

The purpose of this book is to look at the democratic effects of the newly popular consumer activism, a difficult task considering the lack of scholarly agreement on what constitutes democracy. The meanings and measures of democracy have long been contested by political theorists and philosophers.[70] In literal terms, the term *democracy* is derived from ancient Greek *demos* (people) and *kratos* (strength or power), which together form "rule by the people," as opposed to rule by aristocrats, monarchs, religious leaders, or bureaucrats.[71] Textbooks on U.S. government list the three primary pillars of U.S. democracy as political equality (exemplified in the maxim "one person, one vote"), political liberty (freedom from unnecessary or unlawful government intervention), and popular sovereignty (government authority derives from the consent of the people). This skeletal definition has been fleshed out by thousands of scholars since democracy was first practiced in Mesopotamia and Athens in fifth century BCE, but the pressure to craft a universal definition intensified after the collapse of the Cold War and the rapid spread of democratic systems across the globe. Although scholars have scrambled in the last two decades to come up with better definitions and measures of democracy, because these measures now serve as the basis for determining military and economic resource allocations,[72] a shared definition remains elusive. I present a working definition here that is drawn from the rich scholarship on democracy.

The academic debate on democracy is both normative and descriptive. In political theory, scholars have advanced three major normative democratic models: participatory, deliberative, and economic. Participatory democracy emerged in the 1960s as a critique of representative democracy (the idea that citizens could trust elected leaders to act in accordance with the will of the people). Under the participatory model, democracy requires that citizens exercise direct responsibility in political decision making through active self-governance. The deliberative democracy model gained academic purchase in the 1980s from constitutional and social theory scholars who concluded that citizen input into the decisions that affect their lives is a good first step but that a healthy democracy requires deliberation and debate prior to policy decisions being reached. Under the deliberative model, citizens discuss and debate public issues, and they shift their positions based on new information gleaned through dialogue with others. The economic model of democracy also materialized in academia in the 1980s. Political theorists argued that the United States cannot be considered a legitimate democracy until its economic institutions are democratized. Advocates of economic democracy maintain that employee participation, equal voting rights, and control over aspects of production that can be subject to collective decision making in the workplace are necessary for a truly healthy democracy. I return to these three normative models of democracy in chapter 7, but now I turn to empirical models to develop a measure of contemporary consumer campaigns.

Data-driven measures of democracy in political science are plentiful. In 2004, thirty political scientists from around the globe came together in Seoul, Korea, with the goal of generating a universal definition of democracy.[73] They were unable to agree on a definition, but they did agree on some basic components: free and fair elections, a multiparty system of government, an active civil society, independent media, an independent judiciary, and the rule of law. Similarly, David Campbell measures democracy using three dimensions: freedom, equality, and control by and of government.[74] He finds that Western democracies, including the United States, tend to score well on measures of freedom but less well on measures of equality due to wide economic gaps that lead to unequal participation and representation. Thus Campbell moves beyond the three pillars of democracy with his emphasis on the rule of law and economic equality, two additional components that I consider in building my measure of democracy.

There are three popular indices for measuring democracy: Freedom House, Vanhanen's Index, and The Democracy Index. Freedom House has published an annual *Freedom in the World Report* since 1941 that measures two dimensions: political rights (electoral processes, citizen participation, and the functioning of government) and civil liberties (freedom of belief and expression, the right to organize, rule of law, and personal autonomy). Vanhanen's Index measures democracy by examining levels of electoral competition and citizen participation. The Democracy Index, established by *The Economist*, builds on the Freedom House index with the ideas that freedom and democracy are not synonymous and that freedom is a necessary but not sufficient cause of democracy. The Democracy Index also measures electoral process and pluralism, civil liberties, government functioning, political participation, and political culture. These measures contribute new dimensions to the skeletal pillars of democracy. Specifically, they add measures of citizen participation, fair elections, and government responsiveness for consideration in crafting my measure of democracy.

Michael Coppedge and his colleagues generated a thirty-three-point index that measures six major types of democracy from the existing literature: electoral, liberal, majoritarian, participatory, deliberative, and egalitarian.[75] Electoral democracy refers to a system in which leaders vie for power through elections that involve a broad electorate and active media, written constitution, independent judiciary, and civil liberties. Joseph Schumpeter popularized electoral democracy in the literature over half a century ago, and since that time, democratic theorists have debated whether democracy is more than just a procedural ideal.[76] Liberal or pluralistic democracy is measured by the checks on government to prevent its encroachment on the rights of minorities. Majoritarian democracy, also known as responsible-party government, emphasizes the rule of the majority, the idea that the will of many should prevail over the few. Participatory democracy is the concept that direct democracy by the people is preferable, whenever possible; this approach emphasizes the importance of primaries, voting, citizen assemblies, public debates, and other citizen forums. Deliberative democracy theorists endorse policy decisions that are based on citizen deliberation rather than special interests, emotional appeals, or manipulation from politicians. Egalitarian democracy emphasizes political equality through equal participation, representation, protection, and public resources.

Jeremy Walden advocates a rights-based conception of democracy,[77] stating that democracy is not legitimate unless participation by the people, however indirect, is possible for all. "If some are excluded from the process, or if the process itself is unequal or inadequate, then both rights and democracy are compromised."[78] Henry Shue takes this argument a step further with his idea that, to meaningfully exercise their rights, citizens must have their basic subsistence and security needs met.[79] Coppedge's amalgamation of these various approaches to democracy adds many new dimensions for consideration, including active media, a written constitution, an independent judiciary, protections against encroachment on the rights of minorities, rule of the majority, and informed citizen deliberation.

I have identified another dimension of democracy that threatens political equality, political liberty, and popular sovereignty: corporate influence. As I discuss further in chapter 7, business holds a privileged place in politics. Corporations shape public policy, electoral outcomes, and even public opinion. Today's corporations have become *the* dominant institution in U.S. society, eclipsing the influence of the state, family, residential communities, and moral communities. Businesses have become integral to the creation of personal identity and societal meaning. They structure our time and produce societal norms through news and entertainment.[80] The advent of mass communication in the 1920s, television in the 1950s, and social media in the 2000s gives corporations unprecedented access to and influence in our lives. Three-quarters of Americans have regular access to the Internet,[81] and two-thirds have continuous Internet access through smartphones.[82] The average smartphone user reaches for his or her phone 150 times a day,[83] which means that most of us are constantly exposed to corporations advertising products, lifestyles, and values. Not surprisingly, the average American now sees a greater number of advertisements than ever before—around 3,000 a day compared to about 500 in 1971.[84] We are barraged by advertisements from television (through standard commercials and frequent product placements in programs), magazines, newspapers, and social media sites. We see advertisements when we leave the house on our digital devices, the sides of buses, and at our doctor's office. Corporations have become the dominant socializing institution for American citizens at the same time that they have gained greater power in the political sphere.

In the last half a century, corporations have become the most dominant force in politics and policymaking, as evidenced by their routinely favorable outcomes with elections, use of natural resources, technological development, product development, and working relations. Corporations have successfully deregulated and privatized efforts in every major public policy domain in recent decades.[85] In 2014, Martin Gilens and Benjamin Page, political scientists, conducted the first empirical test of "who rules" in the United States. They compared the influence of the average citizen, economic elites, mass-based interest groups, and business-oriented interest groups across 1,779 policy issues. "The central point that emerges from our research is that economic elites and organized groups representing business interests have substantial independent impact on U.S. government policy, while mass-based interest groups and average citizens have little or no independent influence."[86] In other words, corporate influence in the policy process trumps citizen influence, and this poses a serious threat to the political equality and popular sovereignty components of U.S. democracy, a threat that political theorists are only beginning to explore. In addition, some corporations wield their political influence in ways that limit political liberties. For example, the private prison industry successfully lobbies for sentencing laws that put more bodies behind bars for longer terms. The political power of for-profit firms comes at the expense of citizen interests and representative governance.

William Domhoff, a sociologist, finds that corporate elites came to dominate the policy process in the United States as a result of a rapid economic and population expansion at the turn of the previous century.[87] Whatever the reason, overbearing corporate power in politics threatens democracy by directing, limiting, and distorting citizens' voices and choices.[88] Corporate political influence contributes to what Mark Warren calls a "democratic deficit" in the United States, meaning that, even though the United States is classified as a democracy, several foundational democratic components are under threat.[89] David Vogel, one of the few political scientists to have a career-long focus on business power in the United States, proposes that business has gained such prominence in politics that citizens view corporations as a primary locus of political power.[90] Robert Dahl identified the corporate threat to democracy back in 1972,[91] but he did not envision just how powerful corporations would become in the lives of Americans and the political domain, or that the Supreme Court would validate this vast expansion of corporate influence with *Citizens United v. Federal Election Commission* (2010).

A more accurate measure of democracy should include a measure of corporate influence in the political process. It should also include a more nuanced consideration of nonelectoral forms of political participation, such as consumer activism, that serve as a check on corporate political power. This book contributes to a new line of democratic theory that examines the importance of citizen representation for democracy: the idea that political officials must be authorized by and accountable to those they represent.[92] Warren finds that, although advanced liberal democracies have failed to achieve the most basic representational component of democracy, "equal participation in collective decision making," the picture of growing citizen apathy in recent decades is more complex than a simple disaffection with political institutions.[93] Citizens have less faith in government institutions because they have become more critical of authority, are more aware of corporate influence in elections, are aware of the immense power of corporations to shape their daily lives, and do not trust government to represent their interests.[94]

This new awareness has contributed to a decline in participation in some arenas, but it has also inspired more nonelectoral participation, such as consumer activism. We are experiencing a shifting social and political landscape of democracy in which citizens are voting less but engaging more in political debates and decisions, for example, through collective groups targeting political elites and corporations in online forums.[95] Pippa Norris notes that this is a positive democratic trend because more citizens are engaged in elite-challenging activities than in previous decades.[96] These new nonelectoral forms of representation "are increasingly important to strengthening and expanding democracy" because this is where more Americans are expending their political time and energy.[97] Formal governmental institutions will always be important to politics, but a myopic scholarly focus on Congress, the presidency, and the courts has caused scholars to overlook domains in which politics, participation, and democracy are flourishing.[98]

In this book, I contribute to the burgeoning body of work that recognizes how political participation in nongovernmental domains is an increasingly important part of understanding and measuring democracy. To this end, I measure the democratic implications of consumer activism using the prominent dimensions that have been identified by scholars: political equality, popular sovereignty, political liberty, prevailing rule of law, economic equality, robust citizen participation rates, fair elections, active media, a written constitution, an independent judiciary, rule of the majority, protections against encroachment on the rights of minorities, and informed citizen deliberation. To these, I add the dimension of corporate influence.

My definition of *democracy* is a state with rule of law;[99] active and independent media; adequate economic equality to ensure robust, informed citizen participation; a written constitution; and an independent judiciary. This state is responsive to majority opinion, protects minority rights, maintains civil liberties for all, and is not beholden to business interests at the expense of citizen interests. My definition of *democracy* has two primary components: citizen contributions (democratic inputs) and contributions from political entities (democratic outputs). It requires that citizens be informed about pressing political issues and be equally able to enter the political sphere to voice their concerns based on that information. It also requires that political entities be responsive to citizen inputs in a transparent, systematic, and fair way.

The additional dimension of corporate influence extends the traditional definitions of *democracy* into the marketplace. The balance of citizen versus business interests is best measured by their relative access to public officials as well as laws and regulations that demonstrate a preference for profit over people. Democracy is weakened when business interests and frames dominate media content as a result of laws allowing media ownership to become concentrated in the hands of a few individuals. Uninformed or misinformed citizens are less able to distinguish their interests from the interests of business and are less able to advocate for their interests in the political sphere. Democracy is also weakened when business interests have superior influence in lawmaking as a result of campaign contributions and lobbying because lawmakers will logically be more beholden to these interests than the preferences of their constituents. Scholars must look beyond the traditional confines of government to the influence and practices of business entities to better measure the strength of democracy.

Turning now to a practical application of my working definition of *democracy*, I measure the democratic effects of marketplace activism using assessments of democratic inputs and outputs. I ask whether the action in question improves each of the following five democratic inputs:

1. Promotes robust citizen participation
2. Promotes political equality in participation and representation
3. Promotes the will of the majority
4. Promotes active media
5. Improves public discussion of policy issues

In other words, does a particular consumer action or campaign involve more people in political decision making, involve people in politics who were previously uninvolved, convey the majority's opinion to leaders, promote better media coverage of politics and policy, or get more people talking about a political issue? If the answer is "yes," the action or campaign in question improves democracy.

In similar fashion, I evaluate market campaigns using five democratic outputs, that is, the outcomes of political decisions. I ask whether the action or campaign:

1. Promotes political equality in state protection and public resources
2. Promotes corporate political accountability

3. Promotes government accountability to citizens
4. Protects against the encroachment of minority rights
5. Protects against government encroachment on civil liberties

That is, does the action or campaign encourage political and economic equality, hold business entities and governments accountable to the people, protect the rights of minorities, or protect against undue government interference in the lives of citizens? If an action or campaign advances any of these dimensions, it improves democracy.[100]

This ten-point measure of democratic inputs and outputs is suggestive of ways in which marketplace activism expands existing conceptions of democracy, but this instrument does not fully capture the texture and complexity of how marketplace activism contributes to or inhibits democracy. For example, although marketplace activism mostly expands the circle of democratic membership in the polity, on occasion it is used to suppress the political and economic participation of vulnerable groups, such as Chinese immigrants during the exclusion efforts in the 1800s and LGBT individuals in contemporary campaigns. I note this complexity where it arises.

Why Study Consumer Activism?

For academics and activists, the importance of studying consumer activism goes beyond its democratic implications. Political science is the academic field most interested in the study of power, but it has virtually overlooked challenges to corporate power in the United States. Loree Bykerk and Ardith Maney, political scientists, note that "despite a promising start, organized consumer activity at the national level was largely neglected as a research topic by political scientists in the 1980s,"[101] and this is still the case thirty years later. Samuel Barnes and Max Kaase, political scientists, first classified boycotts as a type of political participation in 1979,[102] but it took twenty years for consumer activism to be included in any national survey on political participation. In 2002, Scott Keeter et al. added consumer activism measures to *The Civic and Political Health of a Nation: A Generational Portrait* after pretest focus groups of young people indicated that a surprisingly large number were using their consumer dollars in political ways.[103] Lawrence Glickman, the first scholar to trace the long lineage of consumer activism in the United States, deems consumer activism "a significant, and understudied, strand of American political culture, a durable but flexible mode of political engagement."[104]

Consumer activism is a bellwether for the changing modes of political participation. In 2002, Keeter et al. set out to draw a comprehensive map of the different ways young people engage in politics, starting from the premise that contemporary wisdom in political circles had not kept up with new forms of civic engagement. The first stage of research involved a series of focus groups with young people in different parts of the country, and stories of boycotting came up with surprising regularity.[105] In the second stage of their research, Keeter et al. conducted several national surveys asking an exhaustive litany of questions about civic engagement; they concluded that "one dimension missing from most measures of political participation is consumer activism."[106] Keeter et al. identified three modes of political engagement or pathways that citizens can take to get involved in politics: (1) electoral engagement, (2) civic engagement, and (3) political voice. Electoral engagement includes activities that involve formal political channels, such as voting, making campaign contributions, and working for a campaign or political party. Civic engagement involves personal contributions to one's community through volunteering for local organizations, being active in a group or association, participating in charity events, and the like. Political voice is asserting oneself in the political realm through contacting influential decision makers such as government officials, media representatives, and corporations through canvassing, signing a petition, protesting, or engaging in consumer activism. This typology of political participation is useful in understanding where the consumer activism piece fits into the larger puzzle of electoral engagement. Citizens approach politics from many different angles that do not directly involve or interface with governmental bodies.

Researchers in Sweden, Denmark, Italy, and other European countries have been studying consumer activism since the 1990s. Although their understanding of who engages in this political behavior and why is well beyond our present understanding of this behavior in the United States, we cannot simply cut and paste the European findings into the U.S. context because Americans are uniquely situated in the marketplace. One fundamental difference is that, in socialist or democratic socialist countries, it is customary for the government to rally its citizens to boycott or buycott corporations, but in the United States, initiatives typically come from grassroots campaigns. The U.S. government does have mandated boycotts in the form of embargos, but this is distinct from European governments encouraging citizens to voluntarily boycott a company. Furthermore, consumer activism has a distinct legacy in the United States. It is part of the U.S. political tradition that began when colonists established it as a weapon of the weak in their fight for emancipation from Britain.[107] This tool afforded a band of mischievous colonists a high-profile way of protesting against an indifferent government, gave women political voice before they could vote, and enabled African American activists to launch a revolution. Our Framers conflated consumerism with democratic freedom in the founding documents and rhetoric, and this legacy continues today with calls for consumer patriotism. For these reasons, we need a robust study of consumer activism and democracy that is specific to the United States. This book is the first such study.

Another reason it is important to study consumer activism is to expand our knowledge of corporate political influence. Political scientists tend to overlook corporate power, both independent of and in relation to politics and government, and as a consequence, we tend to ignore direct citizen challenges to corporate power and practices.[108] There are a few notable exceptions, but as Scott Bowman writes, "the subject of corporate power has not received the attention it merits" and there is no political theory of the corporation as of yet.[109] Political science is in immediate need of a political theory of the corporation if we want to understand one of the major centers of power in U.S. politics.

Yet another compelling reason to study consumer activism is to further our understanding of the health of U.S. democracy—the main thrust of this book. Scholars who study political participation have lamented the steady decline in voting, trust in government, social capital, and political efficacy that started in the 1960s.[110] The chief concern is that citizens are less engaged in government, and that this weakens democracy, which requires fairly high levels of citizen input. A different picture emerges, however, when consumer activism is included in the tally of participation; and when both corporate influence and consumer activism are included in considerations of democratic health, we get a very different picture of the health of U.S. democracy.

This book also furthers our understanding of consumer activism by identifying and analyzing all the major peaks of consumer activity in the United States. This long view of consumer activism is invaluable for understanding the significance of this political tool, especially because everyday Americans know so little about its long and colorful history. Glickman notes that "it is a puzzle of the history of consumer activism that despite the fact that it has been a continuous strand in American politics, each successive generation of consumer activists tends to think it is the pioneering generation."[111] A longer historical lens moves us beyond this ahistorical pioneer imagining.

Plan of the Book

I begin this book with an analysis of seven distinct peaks of consumer activities in the United States from the American Revolution of the late 1700s to the Global Justice Movement of the 1990s. The history of American marketplace activism is the story of colonists, abolitionists, labor organizers, feminists, civil rights leaders, consumer safety advocates, economic justice activists, xenophobes, and racists using market channels to achieve political change. Consumer activism is an American tradition that has strengthened democracy at key points in U.S. history, with the exception of its infrequent use to suppress the rights of ethnic and racial minorities. Marketplace activism has mostly been employed by powerless and disenfranchised segments of society that lack access to and power in formal political channels. For example, black Americans used consumer activism more than all other groups combined during the twentieth century.

In chapter 2, I present an overview of the eighth (and contemporary) era of consumer activism in the United States, which started in the mid-2000s with the advent of social media. This is the first era in which activists used all four types of consumer activism: (non)purchasing, investment, social media, and direct action. Consumer activism in the current era is also distinct in its ease of use, transnational focus, effectiveness, and popularity. Americans have become more politically active through the marketplace in the past decade, and this has altered the way companies do business. I conclude that the current era of marketplace activism strengthens each of the ten democratic measures and that it also rewrites common knowledge about citizen participation. Citizens are participating less in electoral politics but more in nonelectoral activities such as activism in the marketplace.

I present original data in chapters 3–6, with a comprehensive assessment of the contemporary era of consumer activism using sixty-one case studies of campaigns from 2004–2014. This analysis is organized into campaigns for racial and economic justice, environmental and animal rights, gender justice and LGBT rights, and conservative causes. My case selection represents virtually all the major national consumer campaigns over the ten-year span of the study.[112]

In chapter 3, I examine fifteen prominent campaigns for racial and economic rights for people of color that involve racial discrimination, damaging stereotypes, and efforts to secure better working conditions. I find that almost all the campaigns for racial justice were effective in achieving their stated goal and that they strengthened different aspects of democracy by amplifying the political voices of the disenfranchised. These campaigns furthered the protection of minority rights and protection from encroachment on civil liberties.

In chapter 4, I study the democratic effects of thirteen market campaigns for environmental and animal rights that involve fossil fuels, pollution, deforestation, the killing of dolphins, and the treatment of animals on movie sets. Documentary filmmaking has played an important role in raising awareness about environmental and animal rights issues in the past decade. I find that these campaigns strengthened democracy in the United States by increasing participation, expanding public deliberation, and forwarding the will of the majority, especially pertaining to corporate decisions made in other countries. These campaigns also improved corporate accountability in areas regulated by the government, and in some cases, they improved accountability through new regulations.

In chapter 5, I examine thirteen campaigns to improve gender, sex, and sexuality rights. Organizers used consumer activism to advocate greater transgender representation in the media and to push for formal policy rights for LGBT individuals. These campaigns were generally effective in altering corporate behavior and public policy, and they improved democracy by putting policy issues on the agenda and increasing participation in and public deliberation concerning major policy issues such as family planning and same-sex marriage.

In chapter 6, I present a study of twenty conservative campaigns involving gun rights, the pro-life position on abortion, opposition to LGBT rights, and other culture war issues. Consumer activism continues to be mostly used by liberals, but since the 1970s, conservative organizations have organized marketplace activism with more frequency to fight against shifting societal values. Conservative campaigns strengthened democracy by increasing the overall rates of political participation and expanding public discussion of culture war issues. They also improved corporate political accountability. On net, the conservative use of consumer activism improved the health of democracy, but campaigns opposing LGBT rights weakened democratic inputs and outputs by curbing the rights and protections of this minority group.

In chapter 7, I apply normative democratic models to the marketplace. I examine when and how corporations came to assume a uniquely powerful position in U.S. politics by shaping public policy, electoral outcomes, and public opinion. Then I apply the participatory, deliberative, and economic models of democracy to consumer activism. I find that, in the face of overbearing corporate influence, consumer activism strengthens participatory democracy by advancing the rate of citizen participation and fostering self-governance. It also improves deliberative democracy by putting policies on the agenda and encouraging public discussion of policy issues. Consumer activism improves economic democracy by democratizing the corporate sphere through citizen activism. Compared to traditional forms of participation, I find that consumer activism is easier to engage in but that its effectiveness in bringing about systemic change is limited by its episodic, reactive nature.

In the conclusion, I summarize my findings about the democratic implications of marketplace activism. The contemporary era is unlike any we have seen in the past. New communication technologies have altered the balance of power between citizens and corporations in that everyday people can now press political claims through social media. Relatively high levels of consumer activism are part of a larger shift in political participation toward individualized civic activities at the expense of collective political action, and scholars must include consumer activism in measures of participation if they want to capture the full picture of political activity. When it comes to democracy, the United States is currently experiencing a democratic deficit because of the foothold corporations have acquired in politics in recent decades through the policy process, elections, hidden influence, and framing citizen interests.

Using systematic analysis of democratic outcomes from my case study analysis and application of normative models of democracy, I find that consumer activism generally strengthens U.S. democracy. Nevertheless, it also poses a threat to democracy by challenging popular sovereignty and turning political actors into marketplace actors in a way that diminishes civic notions of citizenship. Also, on rare occasions, it has been used to curtail minority rights (e.g., the exclusion of Chinese in the mid-1800s and the anti-LGBT campaigns in the 2000s). The broader point of this examination is that consumer activism has become a central form of political participation in the United States—and one with significant democratic implications.

A CONSUMER REVOLUTION?

Marketplace Activism since the Founding

On December 16, 1773, a band of about sixty colonists dressed in Native American garb boarded the *Beaver*, the *Eleanor*, and the *Dartmouth* in the Boston Harbor and dumped fifty tons of tea into its murky waters. The colonists, their nostrils thick with the smell of soot used to hide their identity as they stole aboard these ships, were sending a message to the British government through the marketplace, their last recourse against a geographically and politically distant body. The Boston Tea Party was one of many consumer activism campaigns during the Revolutionary period, the first era of consumer activism in the United States. The message of this consumer revolution was heard in the court of King George and has reverberated in the United States for over two centuries as successive generations of citizens have used protest politics in the marketplace.

My purpose in this chapter is to understand the democratic role consumer activism has played at various points in U.S. history. According to Lawrence Glickman, historian, "long before there was *consumerism* and well before there was the *consumer movement*, there was *consumer activism*,"[1] actions that use market channels to achieve political ends. It is a puzzling phenomenon that each successive generation of consumer activists think that they have discovered this political tool, but this is partly because so little has been written about its use over time. I draw from historians to describe seven eras of heightened consumer activism in the United States.[2] These eras are distinct periods of time, marked by high-profile consumer activities with a national scope. I do not attempt to fully catalog all consumer actions in the United States over time;[3] rather, I focus on eras of heightened activity to give the reader a sense of when and how this political tool has been used, and to what democratic effect.

I have identified seven historical eras of consumer activism: (1) the American Revolutionary Period (1790s), (2) the Free Produce Movement (1820s–1860s), (3) Chinese exclusion efforts (1870s–1900s), (4) the Progressive Movement (1890s–1920s), (5) the New Deal period (1930s and 1940s), (6) the Civil Rights and Consumer Movements (1960s and 1970s), and (7) the Global Justice Movement (1990s–2005). These dates are only suggestive because they fail to precisely capture the activities leading into and out of each period and between them. I argue that we are currently in the eighth era of consumer activism that began with the advent of social media in the mid-2000s.

With the exception of the Chinese exclusion efforts in the late-nineteenth century, these eras coincide with major social movements. Consumer activism is often used by individuals who lack access to conventional channels of power,[4] so its alignment with social movements is expected. Also, with the exception of the Progressive and Consumer movements, consumer activism has been used to achieve political goals that are not directly related to consumer rights or protections: freedom from a nonrepresentative government, the abolition of slavery, good government, the removal of Chinese immigrants, economic justice in the United States, gender equality, racial equality, and global economic justice.

Consumer activism has a unique history in the United States that predates the founding. American revolutionists were not the first to boycott goods, but their actions were novel in their mass mobilization and success.[5] It is an integral thread in the U.S. political tapestry, woven into our founding by the colonists' conflation of freedom and consumption, what Glickman labels "an American political tradition."[6] Consumer identity was ignited during the bloody struggle to establish the nation, and the marriage of political freedom and consumption was formalized by the Declaration of Independence. According to Chris Sunami, a philosopher, the phrase "life, liberty, and the pursuit of happiness" codified "Idealism, Materialism and Individualism into a unified whole."[7] Thomas Jefferson drew this statement from John Locke's *Second Treatise of Government,* in which Locke argued that "life, liberty, and estate" were natural rights to be protected by government.[8] Consumer identity has been entwined with ownership rights since the founding, and it has been a touchstone for defining democracy at the street level and for acculturating immigrants for two centuries since then. Consumption has historically offered new immigrants a quick way of assimilating in the United States, and Lizabeth Cohen, a historian, writes that, in the twentieth century, "consumer goods became innovative and often creative building blocks for the construction of different identities and new communities when the old ones were in decline."[9]

The First Era: The American Revolution

James Axtell, a historian, documents the first era of consumer activism in the United States. The seeds of consumer identity were planted as early as the 1690s. They would later blossom in the form of boycotts in service of the Revolutionary War nearly a century later. Early colonial leaders aligned virtuous citizenship with virtuous shopping habits to serve the political good of the whole. Axtell labels this period the first consumer revolution because so many colonists conflated consumption with good citizenship. Consumer identity was a necessary, but not sufficient, cause for the revolution. According to Timothy H. Breen, a historian, the American Revolution was the result of a misunderstanding on the part of British officials and citizens about colonial wealth.[10] British citizens believed the hyperbolic portrayals of affluent colonial life that appeared in popular publications, and British leaders enacted new taxes to capitalize on this (mostly fictitious) rapid expansion of wealth.[11] These "fables of abundance" were based on a grain of truth because colonial women had started the trend of conspicuously consuming European fashion and the invention of mass marketing created new imaginary needs that expanded consumer demand.[12] This new demand was tenuously based on credit for most citizens of the New World, and as the debts came due, the fear of "economic enslavement" prompted a colonial movement against the cultural influence of the "Baubles of Britain."[13] Colonists believed that British officials were purposefully trying to "keep Americans poor, marginal consumers just able to pay the rising taxes."[14] When the British government imposed the Stamp Act to assert its power over the colonies, it transformed private acts of purchasing into public political acts. The ensuing Revolutionary War was a war for independence, but it was also about defending the burgeoning national consumer identity and the ability of individuals to participate in the marketplace without hindrance.

Breen writes that, with their livelihood under threat from British taxation, colonists were drawn together with a common political identity developed "through a discussion of the meaning of goods."[15] The colonies formed a national identity through public dialogue around the boycott, one based on imagining the colonies as one commercial entity to counter British overreach in politics and the marketplace. The colonists' response to British taxation was also shaped by the conflation of good citizenship and consumer identity. A virtuous citizen was synonymous with a citizen who strategically curtailed her or his consumption for the greater political good. Colonists boycotted the Stamp Act on and off from 1765 to 1770 by deliberately not purchasing goods requiring stamps. Because polling had yet to be invented, no data exist on the rates of participation in the boycott of British products, but historians are confident that a vast majority of colonists participated in the market-based efforts aimed at winning national sovereignty from the motherland. Local merchants were instrumental in organizing these boycotts, and they quickly became "the distinctive signature of American political protest."[16] According to Breen, revolutionary boycotts were a novelty because "no previous popular rebellion had organized itself so centrally around the consumer."[17] Glickman writes that "the revolutionaries became the first in a long line of Americans to link consumption—or its withdrawal—and politics."[18]

The colonists had many shared identities leading up to the American Revolution: Christians, lovers of liberty, farmers, and merchants. But according to Breen, it would not have succeeded without the shared identity wrought by consumerism that brought the thirteen colonies together.[19] Consumer identity was more intensely felt in the urban northeast than by the Southern whites or slaves. The influence of consumer activism during the founding is hard to measure because it was the first spark in a firestorm of political actions, but it was an effective spark. In 1774, the Continental Congress established a network of local bodies to enforce the British boycott throughout the colonies. This action culminated in the Declaration of Independence in 1776, and although the British boycott was not solely responsible for the colonies' breaking away from England, it played a key role by applying political pressure through the marketplace. It is hard to imagine the American Revolution taking place at the time and in the manner that it did without a massive outpouring of consumer activism that facilitated a shared (consumer) identity.[20]

In terms of democratic inputs, I ask whether the action (1) promotes robust citizen participation, (2) promotes political equality in participation and representation, (3) promotes the will of the majority, (4) promotes active media, and (5) improves public discussion on policy issues. Consumer activism during the American Revolution increased the overall rates of political participation in that residents from every colony were swept up in passing nonimportation agreements and boycotting British goods. The colonists were the first group to establish consumer activism as a "weapon of the weak against the strong."[21] Because this activism required large numbers to be effective, it gave many people a voice in public affairs who otherwise would not have had one. Up and down the Atlantic seaboard, citizens signed nonimportation agreements at local town gatherings. Whether or not they were male or landowners, they shunned the consumption of British tea, sugar, stamps, paper, glass, and other consumer products. This constituted a radical extension of political participation beyond white, landowning men, a move that was heavily debated in certain quarters because it was the first time white women were "allowed" a political voice. As in later periods, women's role as primary purchaser in the household allowed them power in pursuing political agendas prior to gaining suffrage.

Consumer activism during the founding also promoted equality of participation and representation because these actions were a response to the failure of the British government to adequately consider colonial input and interests. The end goal was to establish better democratic representation in the colonies. These actions contributed to their ultimately breaking away from England and instituting a more representative political system that immediately benefitted the democratic representation of property-owning white men. Most Americans would wait over a century to see even a modicum of political equality because the American Revolution did not significantly change the political, social, or economic lives of Native Americans, blacks, women, or indentured servants.[22] For example, the women who were on the front lines of the sugar and tea boycott efforts were not granted rights under the Constitution.

Consumer activism during this first era also improved democracy by furthering the will of the majority to gain independence from England.[23] Boycotts were an effective way to convey widespread colonial resistance to British officials. Consumer activism during this era did not explicitly promote active media, but it did improve public deliberation about what was best for the colonists in terms of governance and policy. Shared actions in the marketplace encouraged the recognition of shared interests and unified the deliberations around those interests. Colonists discussed taxes, political representation, and boycotts in public gatherings, and newspaper circulars on the subject were widely read. The Boston Tea Party stirred public discussion around colonial power and representation, especially in light of the British response of shutting down the Boston Harbor. Consumer activism leading up to the American Revolution improved democracy by allowing colonists a voice through the marketplace that they did not have in formal political channels.

My five-part measure of democratic outputs asks whether the action (1) promotes political equality in state protection and public resources, (2) promotes corporate political accountability, (3) promotes government accountability to citizens, (4) protects against the encroachment of minority rights, and (5) protects against government encroachment on civil liberties. Consumer activism during the founding had profound democratic effects on four out of the five measures (the boycott did not protect the rights of minority interests). These actions forced public resources to be distributed in a fairer manner by establishing a more representative government. Boycotts and direct consumer actions were also responses to breaches of civil liberties in the enforcement of the Stamp Act, in which British inspectors used warrantless searches to enter homes looking for contraband. Consumer activism also improved corporate political account-ability by targeting companies that were complicit in colonial tax schemes. For example, the Boston Tea Party targeted the East India Company (EIC) when the British government tried to enforce the EIC monopoly on tea in the colonies by assisting the company to undercut local tea merchants. In short, consumer activism improved citizens' democratic voice and equality during the founding.

The Second Era: The Free Produce Movement

Glickman was the first scholar to note that consumer activism was used through-out the nineteenth century and the first to identify a second era of consumer activism in the Free Produce Movement.[24] This market campaign encouraged people to purchase products made by free labor instead of slave labor. Glickman documents that "from harvesting raw materials, to producing, distributing, and marketing goods, free produce entrepreneurs sought to develop alternatives to an economy that, even in the Northern United States, was thoroughly intertwined with the system of slave labor."[25] The Free Produce Movement was initiated by free blacks in collaboration with white Quaker abolitionists to "buy for the sake of the slave."[26] The idea was that "if there were no consumers for slave-produce there would be no slaves."[27] The movement had support from prominent activ-ists, including Harriett Beecher Stowe, Frederick Douglass, and Lucretia Mott. Glickman finds that the Free Produce Movement was the first major boycott in the United States that targeted business practices directly, one that quickly spread through publications and word of mouth.

The first Free Produce store opened in 1826 in Baltimore, and before the demise of the movement in the 1850s, activists opened more than fifty other stores in eight states.[28] Free Produce stores competed with other general stores, although their wares were often of a lower quality. Some consumers wore the less fashionable apparel as a badge of honor to indicate their activism, much like Prius drivers today,[29] but for others, the styles were simply not worth the sacri-fice. Free Produce activists also used visually compelling exposés that juxtaposed products with images of human suffering involved in their production. White, Southern nonintercourse associations formed in response to the Free Produce Movement and ran boycotts to buttress the Southern slave economy and weaken the slave-free economies of northern states.[30] This was the first known case of conservative consumer activism in the United States.

The Free Produce Movement fizzled within a few decades due to issues in the supply chain, low demand for products that were costlier and less attractive, and consumer concerns that products were not truly free of slave labor. As with many social movements, its decline was also the result of internal movement disputes. Despite its short life and market ineffectiveness, the Free Produce Movement, according to Glickman, gave Americans a new template for contemporary consumer activism by framing purchasing in moral terms, and unlike consumer activism during the revolutionary period, the Free Produce Movement characterized purchasing as a politically empowering tool that aligned good citizenship with making the "right" purchases rather than abstaining. The movement also cast consumers as the primary moral actors of the burgeoning republic rather than producers. It heightened notions of consumer sovereignty by exposing the interconnectedness of the market and consumers' participation in slavery through purchasing slave products.

Consumer activism during the Free Produce Movement improved democracy by raising the overall rate of political participation to include citizens who were denied the vote. Women of all races and African American men joined abolition efforts through their patronage of Free Produce stores during a time when they were denied access to the vote. Free Produce consumer activism also furthered the political equality of free black Americans, who could participate in the abolition struggle in a way that was less likely to elicit violence from racist whites than would direct activism. This movement did not promote active media, but it improved democracy by promoting public deliberation about good citizenship and the role consumers played in upholding slavery. Free Produce consumer activism extended democracy by politically engaging Americans who had little voice in formal politics and by pushing for new laws for minorities who had few formal rights. These stores were also a way for concerned citizens in the North to voice their concern about state policies in the South, into which they had no direct means of input.

Free Produce consumer activism also advanced democratic outputs by mediating the encroachment on the rights of minorities, in this case, slaves and free people who were denied voting rights, a basic requirement for full citizenship. It offered a channel for political action that was otherwise closed to these citizens. Consumer activism during this era also furthered political equality in state protection through its aim to abolish slavery. Activists used market channels to send a message to citizens and lawmakers that the rights and liberties afforded to free people in the United States should be extended to enslaved people.

Consumer activism during the Free Produce Movement also improved democratic outputs by increasing corporate political accountability. Activists introduced ethical consumption as a competitive factor in retail, and they put direct market pressure on retailers that sold slave-made goods. Consumer activism during this era also mediated government encroachment on civil liberties—namely, slavery, a state-sanctioned practice that was legal in many states until ratification of the Thirteenth Amendment in 1865. The policy impact of this short-lived consumer moment was limited, but its impact on consumer consciousness and the use of market channels for political means was long. It improved political equality by offering a relatively safe way for free blacks in the North to get involved with abolition efforts, strengthened popular sovereignty by amplifying the political voices of free blacks and women who lacked voting rights, and furthered political liberty by challenging state-sanctioned slavery in the South.

The Third Era: Chinese Exclusion

In the 1850s, white workers used consumer activism to drive out laborers from China who worked in gold mining, farming, and construction. These consumer activists used openly racist rhetoric in their campaign against what they called the "yellow peril"—an influx of Chinese immigrants they feared would lower wages for all workers. Jean Pfaelzer, an English professor, documents how white workers used boycotts, rallies, property damage, and physical violence to drive out Chinese workers; organized labor and political support aided their bigoted efforts.[31] Government officials passed a series of taxes and fees on Chinese workers and businesses, as well as laws that segregated schools and housing, and prohibited Chinese intermarriage with whites. In 1882, Congress approved the Chinese Exclusion Act, the first law to limit the immigration of a specific ethnic group. This act allowed only limited immigration from China, and it barred all Chinese nationals already living in the United States from gaining citizenship. The Chinese Exclusion Act was twice renewed by Congress, and it was not repealed until 1943.

Leading up to the Chinese Exclusion Act, white workers used a variety of tactics to drive out Chinese laborers. The Supreme Order of Caucasians and the Anti-Coolies Association[32] orchestrated a campaign to blackball Chinese businesses and Chinese workers in the 1870s. Glickman notes that a newspaper at the time described it as "the most gigantic boycott ever known in this country."[33] Residents of Eureka, California, forcibly removed Chinese immigrants by torching their businesses.[34] Residents of Truckee, California, used a less violent boycott approach to ethnic cleansing.[35] The Truckee approach was seen as a gentler, more socially acceptable way to force Chinese immigrants to leave, so it was adopted by other cities in California, Oregon, and Nevada. The California Anti-Chinese Non-Partisan Association organized a statewide petition to ban Chinese workers, and in 1891, the Boot and Shoemakers White Labor League joined with the Farmer's Alliance to call for a national boycott of shoes made by Chinese laborers. The Workingman's Party coupled boycotts with violent demonstrations in major West Coast cities, and many Chinese nationals were forced to flee to other states for safety. Unfortunately, safety proved elusive.

As Chinese immigrants moved east in search of work, discriminatory laws and boycotts followed them. In Butte, Montana, in 1884, the trade unions organized a boycott of Chinese businesses, and fearful whites managed to drive out most of the Chinese residents of Butte. A decade later, white residents boycotted again to remove the remaining Chinese residents, but this time Chinese residents pushed back. A group of Chinese merchants sued for the loss of business in *Hum Lay et al. v. Baldwin* (1896), and in a surprising move, the court ruled in their favor, which put a stop to the boycott and required white organizers to pay damages to Chinese business owners. Nevertheless, this legal victory did not slow the national trend of boycotting to exclude Chinese immigrants from the labor and business markets.[36] In 1886, the Central Labor Union of New York called for a boycott of Chinese labor to prevent laborers driven out of the western states from moving east.[37]

As with previous marketplace campaigns, Chinese laborers organized a boycott of the boycotters.[38] According to James Bradley, an investigative journalist, they called on officials in China to boycott U.S. products in protest of the state-sanctioned mistreatment of Chinese immigrants, and from 1904 to 1906, these efforts cut U.S. exports to China by more than half.[39] The boycott of U.S. products had widespread national support from residents of all walks of life in China, and merchants played a crucial role by refusing to stock U.S. goods. Chinese nationals and merchants living in Thailand, Japan, and the Philippines also joined the boycott. Delber McKee, a historian, notes that the Chinese boycott of U.S. products quietly disappeared in 1906 after President Theodore Roosevelt pressured Chinese officials to put an end to it.[40] These counterboycott efforts were ultimately not successful in overturning the discriminatory laws or putting an end to the violence faced by Chinese immigrants during this dark chapter in U.S. history.

Consumer activism during this era presents a democratic challenge.[41] In terms of democracy, boycotts of Chinese laborers and businesses in the United States increased overall rates of political participation by getting residents more involved in local political efforts, and it also increased public discussion on immigration and labor policy. The boycotts also amplified the will of the majority in towns and cities across the United States, which improved democracy. However, this marketplace activism was clearly anti-democratic in its aim to ethnically cleanse the nation. Consumer activism during this era diminished political equality in participation and representation by politically silencing and driving out Chinese immigrants, and it lessened equality in state protection by framing Chinese immigrants as "other," less than and not worthy of state protection in the face of violence. The boycotts of Chinese immigrants also encroached on the rights of minorities to immigrate to, work in, and open a business in the United States, and they infringed on the civil liberties of Chinese immigrants by ignoring the *Hum Lay et al. v. Baldwin* decision against conspiring to injure or destroy Chinese businesses. The Chinese exclusion boycotts increased political participation for white Americans, but at grave democratic expense to Chinese immigrants. Consumer activism has occasionally been used in ways that diminish and suppress democracy and outputs, as seen in this era and in the previous era with Southern boycotts to curb abolition efforts.

The Fourth Era: The Progressive Movement

The next era of consumer activism coincides with the Progressive Movement, from 1880 to 1920, when middle-class Americans attempted to clean up government and corporate practices through more citizen input into politics and the government regulation of business. Lizabeth Cohen writes that reformers were responding to the perceived "dangers of an industrializing, urbanizing, and politically corruptible twentieth-century America" after muckraking journalists exposed widespread political corruption, for example, the bribery and graft of Boss Tweed's Democratic Party Tammany Hall in New York.[42] Citizens used boycotts and direct consumer action with frequency in response to inflated prices, defective products, and political leaders who were unresponsive to encroaching corporate power. As Glickman documents, the term *boycott* was used for the first time during this era,[43] and while the ground was made fertile for periodic consumer activism during the Founding, it sprang roots during this era and grew as the presence and political power of corporations expanded throughout the twentieth century.[44]

Michael Sandel, a political theorist, notes a cultural shift between producers and consumers during the Progressive era because Americans were struggling to find a shared identity that would transcend ethnicity, class, and occupation in the newly nationalizing economy.[45] As with the American Revolutionary period, citizens once again found unity through consumption. Progressive reformers capitalized on the struggle for identity and developed a new mass politics based on the shared consumer experience of high prices and shoddy products. Robert Mayer, a business professor, finds that "progressivism in general and consumerism in particular can be interpreted as attempts on the part of both society and individuals to reconcile the traditional American values of thrift, restraint, refinement, and concern for one's fellow citizens with increasing affluence afforded by an industrial society."[46] Consumerism patched the gap between self-interested affluence and altruistic republican citizenship by establishing consumption as a positive activity, if done ethically.

Consumerism was also crucial for assimilating new immigrants during the Progressive period. Andrew Heinze, a historian, writes that "In the sphere of consumption, virtually all newcomers to America discovered an opportunity for social advancement that often eluded them in the domain of production."[47] In their places of employment, new immigrants were at the bottom of the ladder but in the arena of consumption, they could culturally mingle through the display of material products. Cultural assimilation and identity through consumption were particularly salient for eastern and southern European immigrants, millions of whom immigrated between 1880 and 1914 to escape abject poverty and persecution. This was particularly true for Jewish immigrants who came to the United States from European countries to escape anti-Semitism. According to Heinze, "the unique attitude of Jews toward America motivated them to view items of consumption as foundation stones of American identity."[48]

During the Progressive Era, boycotts were often employed by politically marginalized people who lacked power in formal political channels. Working-class Jewish women organized a boycott against the high cost of kosher meats in New York in 1902.[49] In 1910, a labor union in Cleveland organized a meat-free month to protest the high cost of meat in the city. Working-class women organized cost-of-living boycotts in major cities, including Kansas and Baltimore, to protest the rising cost of everyday household items.[50] African Americans also used boycotts during the Progressive Era to fight Jim Crow laws. Between 1900 and 1907, activists organized boycotts of segregated street cars in over twenty-five cities in the South to protest a spate of state laws put into place after the Supreme Court upheld "separate but equal" in *Plessy v. Ferguson* (1896).[51] These actions did not achieve the end of Jim Crow, but they established boycotts as a legitimate tactic in the continuing struggle for racial equality that would culminate in the Civil Rights Movement later in the century.

Grassroots activists were able to pass significant policy reforms during the Progressive Era through consumer activism. Muckraking journalists raised public awareness about the ills of growing corporate power through investigative journalism, which in turn inspired consumer actions. Upton Sinclair exposed unsanitary meat packing practices in *The Jungle* (1906), which prompted public outcry and the establishment of the Pure Food and Drug Act and the Meat Inspection Act. Ida Tarbell exposed the monopolistic practices of the Standard Oil Company, which sold oil below market price to drive out its rivals and then inflated the price once the company was the only game in town. Samuel Hopkins Adams uncovered the fraud involved in patented medicines, and Ida B. Wells wrote pieces on Jim Crow racism, the lynching of black men, and corrupt railroad companies. Consumer pressure secured passage of the Interstate Commerce Act (1887) and the Sherman Anti-trust Act (1890) to rectify an imbalance of power between producers and consumers.

Consumption became a distinctly gendered practice in the late 1800s when shopping became synonymous with "women's work," so it is only fitting that women led most of the consumer actions of the Progressive Era. Housewives protested rising prices in cities across the country[52] and boycotted to improve working conditions for their husbands.[53] The National Consumers League (NCL) was formed in 1899 to lower prices and improve workplace safety and compensation.[54] Founded by prominent social reformers Jane Addams and Josephine Lowell, the NCL was headed up by Florence Kelley to mobilize female purchasing power and offer expert advice on safe and ethical purchasing.[55] Against the backdrop of overwhelming complexity in the newly industrial world, the NCL stressed the prominence of the consumer in economic and political life. The idea was that consumers possessed great power in the new economy if they were aware of this power and used it in political ways. For example, the White Label Campaign encouraged women to purchase undergarments with a special label verifying the ethical production practices. According to Kathryn Kish Sklar, a historian, women accomplished what men could not in terms of consumer policy during the Progressive Era through sustained marketplace activism.[56] Women had been important political players in previous eras of consumer activism, but the Progressive Era saw the development of a distinctly female culture of pressing political concerns through consumer activism.

Progressive Era consumer activism strengthened democracy through higher rates of citizen participation in politics, giving women a persuasive voice in politics before they were granted the right to vote in 1920. Similarly, African American men who technically had the vote but were barred from voting through the Jim Crow laws also engaged in politics through the marketplace in this era. Boycotts were a unique tool to challenge the Supreme Court decision to uphold segregation in *Plessy v. Ferguson* because the political and legal avenues had been exhausted. Consumer activism promoted the will of the majority to have access to safer products made in an ethical fashion. Consumer activism was propelled by investigative journalism that improved public discussion by raising awareness of issues with monopolies, unsafe products, and misleading advertising.

Progressive Era consumer activism was especially effective in improving democratic outputs. It protected against infringement on the rights of minorities by allowing people of color and women alternative political tools to push back against discriminatory policies and business practices. It also improved corporate political accountability by shining a light on unethical practices and government complicity in corporate exploitation. Progressive reformers put government transparency and corporate accountability on the national policy agenda through boycotts and direct consumer actions. In response, lawmakers passed sweeping good governance and corporate accountability reforms. Marketplace activism during this era also mediated against the government encroachment of civil liberties by pushing back against state-sanctioned racial segregation. Considered in the whole, these actions strengthened democracy by raising the volume of the political voices of women and African Americans of all genders, improving popular sovereignty by including the political voices of those without a vote (women) or voice (African Americans), and improving political liberty by pushing back against state adoption and enforcement of Jim Crow laws.

The Fifth Era: The New Deal

A decade after the Progressive Era waned, consumer activism surged again during the New Deal period, which commentators at the time referred to as the New Deal for consumers.[57] The term *consumer movement* first appeared in public discourse during this era to describe a growing number of organizations and community leaders making overt appeals to citizens as consumers.[58] This era started with the 1927 publication of *Your Money's Worth* by Stuart Chase and Frederick J. Schlink, which awakened the U.S. public to the conflict between corporate profit motives and consumer interests. By 1939, *Business Week* reported that "the consumer movement has spread like wildfire across the country in the past decade and it's gaining in force every day."[59] Business leaders lamented the threat of the consumer, and political leaders welcomed the renewed marriage of citizenship and consumerism because it gave them leverage in regulating and taxing big business. Glickman notes that "the 1930s was perhaps the only decade in American history when commentators could speak of 'consumer society' as a potentially radical force."[60]

According to Jean-Christophe Agnew, a historian, consumer activism was a logical response to the Great Depression because "depressions and wars are by definition moments of crisis, moments when a society is potentially open to radical definitions of its political, social, and economic foundations."[61] The first four eras of consumer activism were citizen uprisings dominated by colonists, abolitionists, xenophobes, and housewives respectively, but politicians led consumer activism during the fifth era. Kathleen Donohue, a historian, documents how President Franklin D. Roosevelt advanced the idea that citizens have a state-guaranteed right to private consumption and "freedom from want."[62] Roosevelt's theme was depicted in a well-known Norman Rockwell painting published in the

Saturday Evening Post. Cohen notes that "freedom from want" is defined "not as a worker with a job, not as government beneficence protecting the hungry and homeless, but rather as a celebration of the plentitude that American families reaped through their participation in a mass economy."[63] Consumption during the New Deal had become as American as a store-bought apple pie.

Cohen identifies a second prominent message from political leaders during this era: mass consumption would ameliorate the economic crisis and bring about "a more democratic and egalitarian America for all its citizens."[64] Politicians encouraged people to spend and consume in order to "fix" the economic crisis and address inequality, the latter having reached its highest level in U.S. history during the Great Depression. Leaders also galvanized national identity and pride with the idea that the triumph of democracy over communism and fascism lay in the hands of consumers who bought products. This "consumption as empowerment" message was reminiscent of the Free Produce Movement and the Progressive Era, but it was more effective in piercing national consciousness during the fifth era because the appeal was coming from prominent political leaders.

During this era, most white Americans heeded the call to purchase for the national welfare and income equality, but African Americans continued to use boycotts to push for civil rights. Consumer activists organized "Don't Buy Where You Can't Work Campaigns" that opened business doors to black Americans. These campaigns brought "tremendous economic pressure to bear on local white capitalists, while favoring black businesses wherever possible, turning familiar strategies of economic self-help and self-sufficiency into a new kind of mass politics."[65] The first campaign took place in Harlem where activists used boycotts and protests to successfully pressure employers to hire African American workers.[66] In the wake of this success, activists organized similar campaigns in Newark, Baltimore, Chicago, Washington, DC, Cleveland, Detroit, and Los Angeles. In Chicago, the "Use Your Buying Power as You Use Your Ballot" campaign used boycotts to get white-owned businesses to hire black employees and serve black customers. Previously, black leaders such as Booker T. Washington and Marcus Garvey had been pushing for black-owned businesses as an alternative to racial segregation and discrimination, and these combined efforts eventually forced many local white-owned businesses to hire black employees. Preachers in cities across the United States played a critical role by spreading the word about the "Double Duty Dollar" from the pulpit: "Patronize your own, for that is the only way we as a race will get anywhere."[67] The "Buy Black" efforts employed during this era are still in use in black communities today.

Women of all races were especially involved in consumer activism during the fifth era. Black and white women organized local groups to work on rent control and affordable food, and the more formal Housewives Leagues ran strikes and boycotts of meat shops that charged exorbitant prices in the Depression economy. The NCL shifted its focus to consumer protection, and many local branches established consumer cooperatives as shopping alternatives. The League of Women Shoppers (LWS) was formed during this era to encourage women to use their purchasing power to improve working conditions, and U.S. housewives flocked to the organization with the help of celebrity spokespeople. They were joined by other established women's organizations in their consumer activism, including the American Association of University Women (AAUW) and the National League of Women Voters (NLWV). Similar to the Progressive Era, women were often the key leaders of boycotts against inflated food prices and unsafe products during the New Deal. In 1939, *Business Week* reported that "it is these organized women's groups that constitute the real strength of the consumer movement."[68] The efforts of housewives were so effective that some businesses organized against them with public (dis)information campaigns and faux consumer organizations meant to malign the movement.

Many New Deal initiatives were passed in response to housewife consumer activism, including the Home Owners Refinancing Act (1933) to make home ownership more affordable and the Food, Drug, and Cosmetic Act (1938) to improve consumer safety. This was the first era in which consumer activism resulted in widespread de facto policy decisions from businesses, establishing citizens as the watchdogs of consumer protection in the marketplace. Depression Era consumer activism came to an abrupt end when corporate opponents and commentators successfully portrayed these efforts as "communist" in the context of the Red Scare. Led by the House Un-American Activities Committee (HUAC), the Red Scare spread fear that communists were infiltrating the U.S. government.

New Deal consumer activism strengthened democracy through higher rates of participation, equality in participation, and representation for African Americans, who used boycotts to push for economic empowerment and an end to employment discrimination. Women's political voices were also amplified through housewives' leagues that used boycotts to pass policies to improve consumer rights and safety. Consumer activism during this era also enhanced democracy by promoting majority opinion that consumers should be protected and treated fairly in their dealings with businesses, and it inspired a national conversation about what rights and protections citizens should be afforded in their relations with businesses. Marketplace activism also inspired public discussion around the role of U.S. consumers in international relations.

Consumer activism during the Great Depression strengthened democratic outputs by protecting against encroachment on the rights of minorities. Black activists were able to gain employment concessions from local businesses in major cities throughout the United States that were not afforded them by law.

They were able to achieve de facto policy reforms, such as the hiring of African American workers, through the marketplace that could not be achieved through formal political channels. Activism in the marketplace also encouraged greater corporate political accountability when businesses were targeted for their inflated prices and discrimination, and housewives and black activists effectively politicized businesses through boycotts. Consumer activism also contributed to greater government accountability during this era in the passage of major consumer rights and safety legislation. In sum, Depression Era consumer activism strengthened political equality by giving a political voice to black Americans and women of all races to forward their concerns in the marketplace and political channels, and it improved popular sovereignty by making government officials and corporations more beholden to the will of the people.

The Sixth Era: The Civil Rights and Consumer Movements

The sixth era of consumer activism in the United States coincided with the overlapping Civil Rights (1955–1968) and Consumer (1960–early 1980s) movements. The sixth era is distinct in its sheer volume of consumer activism, the establishment of powerful consumer lobbies at all levels of government, and the mainstreaming of consumer activism in the lives of millions of Americans. It is the first era in which activists used investment actions such as divestment, shareholder resolutions, and socially conscious investing.

Civil rights activists used boycotts, buycotts, and direct consumer actions to overturn segregation laws and to lean on state and local officials to comply with federal desegregation laws. Consumer activism was used more frequently by African Americans during the sixth era than at any previous time in U.S. history, and with greater success than in any other period.[69] Activists boycotted business establishments, organized sit-ins at lunch counters in the South, and stole from stores believed to be price-gouging black people who had limited mobility in the inner cities. Bus boycotts throughout the South exemplified African American efforts to bring about political change through the marketplace. Aldon Morris, a sociologist, points out that buses were targeted because transportation was seen as a public issue, not a "private misery."[70] Claudette Colvin was the first person arrested for resisting segregation on a public bus in Montgomery, Alabama. Colvin's act of defiance was downplayed by local civil rights leaders because she was a pregnant teenager at the time, and they wanted a more "respectable" person to be the face of the boycott. The refusal by Rosa Parks, a longtime activist, to give up her seat to a white man in 1955 launched the Montgomery Bus Boycott and made national headlines. Parks had been the stalwart head of the Youth Division of the Montgomery National Association for the Advancement of Colored People (NAACP). She had refused to give up her seat several times, but this was the first time she was arrested.

The Montgomery Bus Boycott was launched the same year that activists called for a boycott of the state of Mississippi, the place where Emmett Till, a fourteen-year-old Chicago teen, had been murdered by racists; public photos of his mutilated face in an open casket sent waves of shock through the nation. After one successful day in which 90 percent of African American riders boycotted the bus system in Montgomery (figure 1.1), organizers recognized that this could be a landmark effort for advancing civil rights, so they recruited Dr. Martin Luther King Jr. to be the spokesperson of the boycott. While in Montgomery, King also organized a boycott of downtown stores that discriminated against blacks.[71] Local government officials unsuccessfully tried to stop this boycott with police harassment and grand jury charges of conspiring to carry out an illegal boycott.[72] Ted Ownby, a historian, finds that African Americans had the spending power to make boycott actions sustainable and effective throughout the South.[73] Their efforts in Montgomery ended after thirteen months, when the Supreme Court ruled that the segregation of public transportation was unconstitutional.

FIGURE 1.1   Black residents walking, Montgomery Bus Boycott, 1955

As with the counterboycotts during the Free Produce Movement, Southern whites organized buycotts to patronize businesses targeted by civil rights boycotts. For example, when the NAACP organized a Don't Buy Segregation campaign in Jackson, Mississippi, in 1965, white shoppers came from all over the state to shop in the city. Ownby documents that the atmosphere was festive—a "big party" for white people.[74] Even though they were frequent, these one-day buy-in efforts by whites were not enough to counter the sustained activism of civil rights activists using the marketplace to advance their cause.

Prominent civil rights organizations also used direct consumer action in the struggle for civil rights. The Congress of Racial Equality (CORE) and the Student Non-Violent Coordinating Committee (SNCC) organized peaceful lunch-counter sit-ins to force desegregation (figure 1.2). In 1960, four first-year students from the North Carolina Agricultural and Technical College staged a sit-in at a segregated Woolworth's lunch counter in Greensboro. The manager refused them service but allowed them to stay at the counter until the store closed. The next day, over twenty black students from local colleges joined the protest. The manager again refused the students service, so they spent the day studying, surrounded by heckling and jeering white racists. This was not the first sit-in of the Civil Rights Movement, but it was the most prominent. By the fifth day, over 300 protesters had joined the sit-in, and local television and print media outlets were covering the story. The public attention it received inspired similar nonviolent consumer actions at private and public facilities throughout the South, including lunch counters, theaters, libraries, and swimming pools. These sit-ins forced F. W. Woolworth to reverse its position on segregation after seeing a 30 percent drop in sales.[75] The Greensboro Four were served a meal at the same Woolworth's lunch counter six months after their initial sit-in.

In his *Letter from Birmingham City Jail*, Dr. Martin Luther King Jr. situated the sit-ins within the historical context of the freedom promised by the Founders, as a freedom defined through consumption: "One day the South will know that when these disinherited children of God sat down at lunch counters they were in reality standing up for the best in the American dream and the most sacred values in our Judeo-Christian heritage, and thusly, carrying our whole nation back to those great wells of democracy which were dug deep by the founding fathers in the formulation of the Constitution and the Declaration of Independence."[76]

The Freedom Rides were another direct consumer action during this era. The passage of desegregation laws was not enough to put Jim Crow segregation to rest in the South, so CORE and the SNCC organized interstate bus rides to challenge the noncompliance of the Southern states with the Supreme Court ruling in *Boynton v. Virginia* (1960), which ruled that segregated buses, restrooms, and waiting rooms in bus terminals were unconstitutional. Activists used

FIGURE 1.2   Counter sit-in at an F. W. Woolworth store, Greensboro, North Carolina, 1960

direct consumer action because the federal government was not stepping in to enforce compliance.[77] They organized Freedom Rides with white and black riders together to challenge the de facto segregation. The first group of Freedom Riders left Washington, DC, on two buses bound for New Orleans in May of 1961, but they never made it to their destination.[78] The riders faced minor violence in Virginia, and extreme violence in North Carolina, South Carolina, Alabama, and Mississippi. In Anniston, Alabama, local law enforcement worked with the Ku Klux Klan to brutalize the riders. A mob slashed the tires of one bus and nearly succeeded in burning the protesters alive with a firebomb. Klansman beat riders on a second bus and left them in various states of consciousness. The riders continued on to Birmingham, Alabama, where they again faced violence when they stepped off the bus. Despite the mob brutality, another group of Freedom Riders left from Nashville headed to Alabama a few days later. They were attacked with iron pipes and baseball bats outside Montgomery, and local racists singled out white "race traitors" for particularly brutal attacks. All told, the Freedom Riders organized over sixty rides with approximately 450 riders. Most of these activists were arrested in Jackson, Mississippi. Some of the violence was captured in photographs, which drew national media attention and public outrage at the inaction of the federal government. President John F. Kennedy put pressure on Southern governors to protect the Freedom Riders, and he directed the Interstate Commerce Commission to enforce desegregation on public buses moving across state lines. Consumer activism in the form of riding busses was crucial to this desegregation campaign.

The Civil Rights Movement was a well-organized response from black communities to the daily experiences of humiliation and violence due to the Jim Crow laws in the South,[79] but consumerism played a role in spreading racial angst beyond the South. Television sets has become relatively inexpensive by the early 1960s, and most working-class Americans were suddenly privy to sanitized visions of white middle-class life. Popular shows such as *I Dream of Jeannie* portrayed white-picket fences, spacious homes with modern appliances, and expensive cars as the U.S. norm. These images were daily reminders of the exclusion of black Americans from middle-class consumption, and a forceful reminder that blacks remained second-class citizens who were socially and economically prohibited from full participation in the marketplace. Protesters took to the streets in the Watts neighborhood of Los Angeles, California, in 1965 and in Newark, New Jersey, in 1967 to protest the black exclusion from full (consumer) citizenship. As Amiri Baraka, a poet, testified about the Newark protests to a government commission, "The poorest black man in Newark, in America, knows how white people live. We have television sets; we see movies. We see the fantasy and reality of white America every day."[80] Social, economic, and political racial inequalities persist today, but the Civil Rights Movement brought about rapid radical change through the near demise of Jim Crow and the passage of the Civil Rights Act (1964) and the Voting Rights Act (1965). Direct consumer action was one tool in a movement with a hefty activist toolkit.

The use of consumer activism by civil rights groups improved democracy and outputs during this era. It increased the overall rates of political participation by providing Americans who were excluded from voting because of Jim Crow with tools to apply political pressure. Boycotts, buycotts, and direct consumer actions amplified the voice of black Americans in politics and thus promoted policy equality in participation and representation. Actions in the marketplace also improved public discussion on issues of racism by raising awareness of the persistent inequalities and brutality that blacks faced at the hands of their fellow Americans and law enforcement officials. Sit-ins and Freedom Rides brought about greater political equality in state protection by forcing the federal government to enforce state compliance with the desegregation laws and protect activists. It mediated against encroachments on the rights of minorities by pressuring government officials to enforce laws meant to protect minorities and made the government more accountable to African Americans at the same time that it encouraged corporate political accountability. Private companies across the South desegregated their facilities in response to the threat of boycotts and direct actions, and they were no longer able to use local tradition to flagrantly violate federal law. Consumer activism during the Civil Rights Movement also mediated against government encroachment on civil liberties by exposing alliances between the Klan and local officials, and by diminishing police violence against African Americans. Similar to the American Revolution, the success of the Civil Rights Movement was contingent on the use of consumer activism.

At the same time that President John F. Kennedy was providing begrudging support for the Civil Rights Movement, he reinvigorated the Consumer Movement with his 1962 Consumer Bill of Rights, which established a right to safety, information, choice, and representation. Kennedy framed consumers as a special interest group when he stated they "are the only important group [that is] not effectively organized, whose views are often not heard."[81] Kennedy had used this message in earlier campaigns, and voters liked it so much that he adopted it as a pillar of his 1960 presidential run. Once in office, Kennedy advocated sweeping consumer regulations on pesticides, meat, and pharmaceuticals, as well as other product safety requirements that we take for granted today.[82] He required all executive agencies to appoint a special assistant to protect the interests of consumers,[83] and he created a Consumer Advisory Council to implement the Consumer Bill of Rights. Kennedy was killed before he had a chance to see his consumer rights platform realized, but Lyndon B. Johnson continued the work by creating a new executive post of Special Assistant for Consumer Affairs position, a post that President Richard Nixon later made a permanent part of the cabinet. Johnson appointed Esther Peterson, a fierce consumer advocate, to this position.[84]

Within a decade of the implementing of Kennedy's Consumer Bill of Rights, the Consumer Movement was institutionalized through hundreds of organizations that were formed at the national, state, and local levels to advocate consumer rights and protections. The most powerful consumer lobby, the Consumer Federation of America (CFA), was established in 1968. By the mid-1970s, the CFA had over 200 regional consumer organizations, and hundreds of similar groups formed around specific policy issues.[85] Publications and public forums were vital in raising public awareness about product safety issues. The readership of *Consumer Reports*, a magazine featuring corporate exposés and the latest research on product safety, grew to nearly 4 million in the 1970s.[86] Another national organization, the Consumers Union, raised public knowledge about prescription drugs, warrantees, life insurance, and many other issues through grassroots community forums. Rachel Carson's book *Silent Spring* (1962) raised awareness about the health and environmental effects of widespread pesticide use that led to the U.S. government ban of the use of the pesticide DDT a decade later.[87]

Ralph Nader, the best-known U.S. consumer activist, came to the fore during the sixth era. As a young lawyer, he left his law practice in Connecticut and hitchhiked to the U.S. capital to advocate for consumer concerns.[88] Nader worked with a group of young activist attorneys, affectionately called Nader's Raiders, to lobby for national product safety legislation and corporate accountability. Nader's scathing critique of the auto industry in his book *Unsafe at Any Speed* (1965) led to national auto safety legislation and the creation of the National Highway Traffic Safety Administration. Nader also formed the powerful consumer lobby Public Citizen that wields influence in Washington politics today. Its motto is "defending democracy, resisting corporate power."

Nader and others raised awareness about the distinct and often competing interests of producers and consumers during the Consumer Movement by exposing the routine corporate practice of placing profits over people. According to national Harris polls, by the late 1960s a majority of Americans believed that people such as Nader were necessary to "keep business on its toes."[89] This position was so commonly accepted that the Boy Scouts of America created a merit badge for consumer purchasing that could be earned by studying consumer laws, writing to a legislator, or analyzing corporate practices. Nader reinvigorated public awareness of the politics of consumption, but he was by no means the first consumer activist.

As in the previous eras of consumer activism, women played a prominent role as consumer activists during the sixth era. In 1966, local housewives organizations orchestrated a national supermarket boycott to bring down prices that involved over 100,000 consumers in 21 states.[90] Women also organized boycotts to change incomprehensible freshness codes in supermarkets and to allow women access to credit.[91] Monroe Friedman, a psychologist, conducted a survey of local price-boycott leaders during this period and found that all of the sixty-four leaders were women—young, mostly white, well-educated, middle-class homemakers.[92]

The Women's Movement brought issues of "manipulative consumerism" to the forefront during the sixth era with a high-profile feminist revolt against images of rigid gender roles that promoted high standards of consumption.[93] In *The Feminine Mystique* (1963), Betty Freidan wrote that "the perpetuation of housewifery, the growth of the feminine mystique, makes sense (and dollars) when one realizes that women are the chief customers of American business. . . . The really important role that women serve as housewives is to buy more things for the house."[94] The National Organization for Women (NOW) called for product boycotts during congressional hearings on discrimination against women in Washington, and House member Edith Green (D-OR) announced her own personal boycott during the hearings: "I have made a personal resolve not to buy certain products advertised by ridiculing women; and I would hope that (women's groups) would really carry on a systematic boycott of products that in their advertising depict the woman as a supercilious idiot. This is what happens in a lot of the TV commercials. I see it and I think this is by design. We have gone past that stage."[95] Consumer boycotts became commonplace during this era for people of color and women of all races striving to combat racial and sexual inequality, but feminist boycott efforts had a distinct class (middle- and upper-class) and race (white) bias. Also, during this era, the female leadership of the movement that had been so prominent during the Progressive and New Deal eras was eclipsed by mostly male leaders of national consumer nonprofits. Consumer activism because its own distinct movement and became mainstream at the same time that men assumed the public reins of leadership.

The Consumer Movement was extraordinarily effective in passing twenty-five major consumer laws. Citizens demanded greater government intervention in consumer protection as the physical distance between consumers and producers widened, and this legislation gave the federal government an enhanced role in regulating a vast array of consumer products. The principle of caveat emptor ("buyer beware") that defined the business–consumer relationship until the middle half of the previous century, slowly eroded during the twentieth century with the adoption of a spate of laws intended to protect consumers from corporate harm and manipulation.

The Consumer Movement waned with Ronald Reagan's pro-corporate presidency,[96] the success of Big Business in defeating a congressional bill to establish a permanent Consumer Protection Agency, and opponents' intentional feminization of the movement through framing and rhetoric (e.g., "angry housewives," "consumer hysteria," and "the politics of the pantry"), despite a move toward mostly male leadership.[97] Nevertheless, the movement altered the fabric of politics in the United States. Robert Mayer, a professor of family and consumer studies, writes that the Consumer Movement "so transformed institutions and consciousness that many pro-consumer actions now occur as a matter of course and without fanfare," and Friedman concludes that the corporate environment is now highly politicized.[98] Political purchasing and investment actions became a normal part of U.S. consumption in the sixth era.[99]

In terms of democratic effects, the Consumer Movement was long on political leadership, lobbying, litigation, and the establishment of nonprofit organizations but short on grassroots activism. Aside from a handful of boycotts organized by housewives to bring down prices and feminists to protest the misrepresentation of women in the media, movement leaders used formal political channels and the courts to gain concessions. The biggest contribution of the Consumer Movement to democracy was its production of a new level of citizen awareness and consumer entitlement that permanently politicized the marketplace.

The Seventh Era: The Global Justice Movement

The seventh era of consumer activism in the United States started with the contentious Battle in Seattle in 1999 that evolved into the Global Justice Movement (GJM). The GJM has its early roots in the struggle to prevent the 1994 passage of the North American Free Trade Agreement (NAFTA), but the Battle in Seattle put the movement on the public's radar.[100] The GJM has brought hundreds of thousands of protesters together in the past decade, and activists continue to protest gatherings of the World Trade Organization (WTO), Group of 8 (G8), World Bank, International Monetary Fund (IMF), and the Summit of the Americas. GJM organizers have also created alternative summits on global justice to coordinate global activism around issues of corporate power.

GJM participants oppose U.S. neoliberal policies that they consider to be the cause of many social, political, and economic ills in the developing world.[101] The primary tactic of this "movement of movements" is direct consumer activism in the form of protests outside corporate–government gatherings. With roots in Latin American activism and previous protests in Lima (1975) and Germany (1988), the GJM held Seattle protests that shut down the WTO proceedings. In the decade following the Battle in Seattle, similar gatherings occurred in fifty-nine cities at meetings of the G8, WTO, World Bank, and IMF to press for environmental policy change, economic justice, and human rights. In addition to protesting outside of meetings, movement participants also gather once a year for the World Social Forum at different locations across the globe. According to its 2001 charter, "The World Social Forum is a plural, diversified, non-confessional, non-governmental and non-party context that, in a decentralized fashion, interrelates organizations and movements engaged in concrete action at levels from the local to the international to build another world."[102] The World Social Forum is the organizing hub for the movement,[103] and attendance grew steadily for a decade, reaching a high of 75,000 participants in Senegal in 2011. U.S. activists organized two U.S. social forums in Atlanta (2007) and Detroit (2010) that attracted 15,000 attendees each.[104]

Jackie Smith, a sociologist, proposes that this is the first era of consumer activism with a transnational focus,[105] and indeed, ideas of global citizenship and new communication technologies have made transnational consumer activism more frequent. But the Free Produce Movement and the Japanese silk boycotts from previous eras also had a transnational focus. The seventh era is distinctive in its use of social media as an organizing tool because it was simply not available in previous eras.

The heavily transnational focus of the GJM would not have been possible without new communication technologies. Online technology was behind the success of the Battle in Seattle and many other well-attended protests because coordination of the thousands of groups involved in these events required a private rapid means of communication. The goal of the Seattle protest gathering, established by the Direct Action Network (DAN), was to shut down the WTO meeting. The gathering was achieved after tens of thousands of planning and training hours on the part of thousands of volunteers. Training camps were established to teach classic civil disobedience techniques such as human blockade formation, rappelling (to hang banners on buildings and other tall objects), and lockdown techniques that link protesters to each other through plastic tubing. Dan Solnit, an organizer, toured the West Coast in the months leading up to the WTO meeting to recruit participants. He used extensive e-mail outreach.[106] Several websites operated around the clock to connect participants and provide up-to-date information about events. The Internet revolutionized the effectiveness of consumer actions because most campaigns require a broad base of vocal consumers.[107] John Vidal, a social movement scholar, finds that most grassroots organizations now depend on online means to "motivate, activate and communicate their uncensored messages."[108]

The GJM is still active, but, according to Agnieszka Paczynska, a conflict studies professor, its profile and public buy-in declined after critics aligned their concerns about capitalism with the terrorist attacks of 9/11.[109] Organized labor withdrew from the GJM post-9/11 for fear of being seen as anti-American, and the loss of the alliance with Big Labor has hampered the ability of the movement to draw the large crowds of protesters necessary for direct consumer actions. Also, some GJM activists shifted their attention from trade policies to anti-war efforts when the U.S. military went into Iraq and Afghanistan.[110] The number of organized protests has declined from a high of ten in 2001 to an average of four per year from 2005 to 2013.[111]

Although the seventh era is waning, the influence of the GJM has been significant. Robert Edwin Kelly, a political scientist, documents how consumer activists were able to get seats at the table of the World Bank and the IMF to reform contentious debt-relief programs for less-developed nations.[112] GJM activists have also made labor and environmental considerations a standard part of international trade agreements. GJM actions have effectively shifted environmental and labor rights paradigms globally using boycotts, direct actions, and social media campaigns.[113]

In terms of democratic inputs, consumer activism during this era increased the overall rate of political participation by establishing forums and direct consumer actions that have attracted hundreds of thousands of participants to date. GJM consumer activism also improved political equality in participation and representation because, according to Gary Coyne, a sociologist, and his associates, the movement participants were more diverse than the U.S. population and than the voting population in terms of race.[114] GJM consumer activism therefore amplified the political voices and concerns of traditionally underrepresented people. It also promoted active media through the use of online blogs and other forms of communication to raise awareness of issues of global exploitation. Consumer activism during this era also strengthened democracy by improving public discussion on policy issues, namely, globalization and the effects of U.S. consumption on the labor practices and living conditions of people in other counties. Many Americans now have a global consumer consciousness that simply did not exist prior to the GJM. The movement used direct consumer activism to raise public awareness and dialogue about the effects of trade agreements on environmental and labor rights.

Consumer activism during the GJM era also increased democratic outputs by protecting against the encroachment on the rights of minorities, namely, the rights of minorities in less-developed countries that are affected by U.S. political and corporate practices that they have little or no say about. Like the colonists who fought against political decisions made on their behalf without their input, GJM participants struggle against corporate and trade policies that affect residents in other countries who lack formal political representation. Transnational consumer activism improves democratic outputs by holding corporations and business entities such as the WTO and the World Bank accountable for the political consequences of their decisions. Prior to the GJM, the typical American was unaware of the existence of these organizations and their effects on less-industrialized countries. Consumer activism during this era also promoted greater government accountability by applying pressure to agencies that previously operated in the international arena with little public scrutiny. GJM consumer activism strengthens political equality by getting underrepresented Americans involved in activism and giving people outside of the United States a voice in policy decisions that affect their lives. Consumer activism during this era also improves popular sovereignty by holding quasi-governmental organizations that implement trade policies more accountable to the people affected by their decisions.

In this chapter, I describe seven distinct eras of consumer activism in U.S. history, beginning with the American Revolution and ending with the GJM. During the first era, colonists formed a shared identity through consumerism and found a common purpose through consumer activism. Breen finds that the American Revolution would not have been successful without a shared consumer identity to bring the thirteen colonies together against the British.[115] The second era, during the Free Produce Movement, had the aim of abolishing slavery. It established the idea of purchasing for political ends rather than just abstaining. During the third era of consumer activism, white people very effectively used boycotts to ethnically cleanse Chinese businesses and laborers from the United States, and during the fourth era, a new mass politics emerged around the shared consumer experiences of shoddy unsafe products and inflated prices. During the fifth era, political leaders asked citizens to think of themselves as both the "guardians of the marketplace" and "saviors of democracy." The sixth era coincided with the overlapping Civil Rights and Consumer movements, and the marketplace became a crucial tool for advancing racial equality and consumer protection and safety during the era. The messages of the Consumer Movement were woven into our national identity in such a way that consumer activism has become an everyday practice for many Americans. The seventh era of consumer activism started with the Battle in Seattle in 1999, which evolved into the GJM. This era demonstrates the transnational nature of contemporary consumer activism and the effective use of new media technologies.

In the late 2000s, we entered the eighth era of consumer activism, marked by the emergence of social media technologies that have multiplied the number and frequency of national organized consumer campaigns. Social media have also changed the way activists organize against corporate interests. In the remainder of this book, I describe this new era and analyze its democratic implications.

This brief look at the history of consumer activism shows that these actions have, for the most part, strengthened democracy at key points in U.S. history. Consumer activism increased the overall rate of political participation in all seven eras by supplementing and supplanting electoral participation. In many of the eras, activism in the marketplace also improved political equality in representation and political outcomes by amplifying the voices of the politically disenfranchised. Consumer activism advanced the interests of the majority during the American Revolution against an unresponsive government, during the national Chinese exclusion movement against the perceived threat of "yellow peril," and during the Progressive and Consumer movements in opposition to expanding corporate power. In every era, consumer activism increased discussion on major policy issues of the day.

Consumer activism strengthened democratic outputs by promoting political equality in state protection and public resources during the American Revolution regarding British taxation, and actions against slavery and Jim Crow racism during the Free Produce, Progressive, New Deal, and Civil Rights movements.

Consumer activism improved business political accountability in every era by pressuring business entities to consider the political implications of their practices through boycotts, direct consumer actions, nonimportation agreements, and divestment. It also improved government accountability during virtually every era, as evidenced by the passage of new laws and better enforcement of existing laws pertaining to representation, consumer protection, and the rights of black Americans and women of all races.

The glaring exception to consumer activism's improving democracy and outputs is the Chinese exclusion era. Although consumer activism during this era raised overall rates of political participation and furthered the economic interests of the white majority, it also eroded the civil liberties of Chinese immigrants and reduced equality in state protection and public resources. Boycotts were an effective way to abolish the rights of Chinese minorities during this era, just as they were effective in furthering the rights of African Americans and women of all races during other eras. Consumer activism has rarely been used to curtail civil liberties and rights, but it is an equally effective tool to achieve anti-democratic ends.

Consumer activism has been an especially important political tool for women, who have historically engaged at higher rates than men due to their status as the primary purchasers in the household.[116] Women are in a prime position to know more about the variety, availability, relative price, and quality of products—information that increases the likelihood of practicing political consumption.[117] Women hold unique power as consumers in U.S. society, and they are generally familiar with this power, making or influencing the purchase decision in over 80 percent of consumer sales.[118] Women in the United States have historically used market channels when they lacked formal political power, which is still evident today in the vast underrepresentation of female legislators at the local, state, and national levels. "Through such direct action techniques as [boycotting], demonstrations, picketing, and leafleting, [women] have made their voices heard in the marketplace and the halls of government."[119] This was especially true under female leadership during the Progressive and New Deal periods, but it was less true when male politicians and consumer leaders took the literal and figurative reins of consumer activism in the Consumer Movement of the 1970s and beyond.

David Vogel, a political scientist, writes that consumer activism has also been an important political tool for African Americans, who participated in more organized consumer actions than all other groups combined during the twentieth century.[120] Consumer activism has been instrumental in the uneven, unfinished decline of overt racism, through boycotts and sit-ins in particular. This was particularly true during the height of the Civil Rights Movement, when activists pushed for desegregation as well as social, political, and economic equality of opportunity. Consumer activism was a powerful political tool for protesters in light of the tacit and sometimes overt government endorsement of racial segregation. "[M]uch of the history of the civil rights movement can be viewed as a series of direct confrontations between a minority group and an inequitable marketplace."[121]

Consumer activism has been a part of U.S. political tradition as early as the American Revolution, and since that time, Friedman finds that "the boycott has been used more than any other technique in the U.S. to promote and protect the rights of the powerless and disenfranchised segments of society."[122] The history of U.S. consumer activism is the story of colonists, abolitionists, labor organizers, feminists, civil rights activists, consumer safety advocates, economic justice advocates, and racists using market channels instead of or in addition to governmental channels to achieve political change. It is a political tool that has been used by diverse, sometimes opposing, interests since the Founding—a unique U.S. political tradition.

The analysis I have presented in this chapter also indicates that marketplace activism produces a distinct type of political participation, one that is often messy, in that it is decentralized and often reactive. It holds little resemblance to the mostly orderly acts of casting a vote, writing a check for a political candidate, or volunteering for a political party. Episodes of intense marketplace activism are driven by activists focused on a single issue about which they care passionately. It is often desperation that propels activists to use market channels rather than governmental channels, and in doing so, they challenge the popular sovereignty of the political regime. In this sense, marketplace activism can be seen as a complement to governmental activism, one that improves the accountability of the latter.

"WE ARE THE 99%"

Contemporary Consumer Activism

The intensity of consumer activism on both sides of the political aisle surrounding Donald Trump's presidency is unlike anything we have seen in U.S. politics. Trump renamed his eponymous hotel chain Scion in October of 2016 because bookings from those opposed to his political views had fallen off.[1] That same month, Shannon Coulter, a small business owner, launched the #GrabYourWallet boycott of Trump brands and companies that carry Trump family merchandise.[2] Coulter was incensed by Trump's recorded comments about grabbing women by their nether regions, so she set out to make a political statement through the marketplace. Nearly three dozen companies are on the #GrabYourWallet list, and to date, at least seven retailers have dropped Ivanka Trump products, including Nordstrom, Neiman Marcus, and Shoes.com.[3]

Anti-Trump activists also launched a boycott of New Balance shoes after a company spokesperson told a reporter, "With President-elect Trump, we feel things are going to move in the right direction."[4] This statement inspired Andrew Anglin, a well-known neo-Nazi blogger, to declare New Balance the "Official Shoes of White People."[5] Liberal consumer activists took to social media in droves to post pictures and videos of them lighting New Balance shoes on fire with the hashtag #boycottnewbalance.

In the months after the election, Trump supporters organized numerous boycotts of companies with leaders who opposed Trump.[6] GrubHub CEO Matt Maloney sent an email to his employees the day after the election stating that the company would not tolerate actions or words demeaning minorities and immigrants, even though it "worked for Mr. Trump."[7] After this memo leaked to the press, #BoycottGrubHub trended on Twitter and the company's stock fell 5.1% in one day.[8] PepsiCo CEO Indra Nooyi told a reporter that "our employees are all crying" over Trump's win, and #BoycottPepsi was quickly added to the conservative boycott agenda.[9] Trump supporters also organized #DumpKelloggs after the food conglomerate caved to liberal consumer activism and stopped advertising with Breitbart, a right-wing news blog.[10]

The travel ban Trump proposed in the first month of his presidency led many to engage in marketplace activism. On the liberal side, 200,000 Uber users deleted their accounts when the company lowered its prices to JFK airport after taxi drivers declared a strike at the airport to protest the ban.[11] Uber was seen by some as trying to break the strike. The hashtag #DeleteUber trended on Twitter, and Lyft, Uber's biggest competitor, donated $1 million to the American Civil Liberties Union to capitalize on the political moment and attract new customers. Conservatives boycotted Starbucks (#BoycottStarbucks) after CEO Howard Schultz denounced Trump's ban and pledged to hire refugee workers.[12] The hashtag #BoycottBudweiser trended around the time of the Super Bowl in response to an ad depicting the immigration of the company's founder to the United States. The ad was perceived by some as critical of Trump's travel ban.[13]

The flurry of marketplace activism around Trump's presidency, and the Occupy Wall Street movement a few years earlier, epitomize the eighth era of consumer activism that emerged in the mid-2000s. The current era is distinct in terms of the sheer volume of activity and the use by activists of all four types of consumer activism: boycotts, investment actions, direct actions, and especially social media. In this chapter, I analyze the democratic implications of the primary types of marketplace activism after first examining when and why consumer activism went mainstream to better understand why it is so popular today. I conclude with a discussion of how contemporary consumer activism rewrites the debate about participatory decline. In short, Americans are still engaging in politics, but they are moving away from electoral politics and toward protest politics in the marketplace.

Consumer Activism Going Mainstream

Peaks of high-profile consumer activism come and go, but an underlying shift has taken place in the United States since the 1970s, marked by the widespread adoption of everyday consumer activism that has transformed the political landscape so that Americans now use these tools with regularity as a result of intensified consumer citizenship,[14] and more recently, social media. Consumer activism has gone mainstream as a result of the rise of mass consumer culture that has empowered consumers; the shift to post-industrialism that has caused people to be more concerned about their political, economic, and social footprint in the marketplace; and new networked campaigns that have made consumer activism easier to engage in.

Mass Consumer Culture

The historian Gary Cross and the sociologist Juliet Schor agree that, since the 1950s, the United States has been *the* consumer culture, defined as a "society of goods . . . a choice, never consciously made, to define self and community through the ownership of goods."[15] The history covered in chapter 1 illustrates that consumption has always been a central component of American political identity.[16] John Kenneth Galbraith, economist, notes that Americans have always used consumption to define freedom, personal happiness, social status, and shared identity but that consumerism as *the* overriding feature is a relatively new development in American culture, made possible through the development of mass marketing, the Progressive Era, and the advent of mass communication.[17] Jackson Lears, a cultural and intellectual historian, writes that mass marketing was adopted in the 1850s and that within fifty years materialistic values had taken root through the skillful creation of new desires and needs.[18] In response, consumer values became deeply entrenched during the Progressive Era to mend the conflict between self-interested materialism and altruistic republican citizenship.[19] The political philosopher Michael Sandel writes that "although they did not view their movement in quite this way, Progressives reformers who urged Americans to identify with their roles as consumers rather than producers helped turn American politics toward a political economy of growth and distributive justice whose full expression lay decades in the future."[20] Cross concludes that mass consumer culture blossomed around the time of the Progressive Era but that its roots did not grow deep until after World War II in response to growing relative affluence and the expansion of the mass marketing of goods and social values through new communication technologies such as the television.[21] Cross observes that consumer values won out over other values because they had been linked to core elements of American identity since the founding: "Consumerism succeeded where other ideologies failed because it concretely expressed the key political ideals of the century—liberty and democracy—and with relatively little self-destructive behavior or personal humiliation."[22]

According to the political scientists Lance Bennett and Robert Entman, the rise of mass consumer culture has profoundly altered the ways in which citizens relate to each other and to societal institutions.[23] The new citizen consumer thinks of him- or herself as an entitled consumer in every relationship, whether it is with corporations, government, other institutions, or fellow Americans.[24] An attorney friend once told me that lawyers wake up in the morning and view each moment of their day through a legal lens. Analogously, in mass consumer culture Americans wake up in the morning and view each moment of the day through the lens of an exchange in which they are on the receiving end, an orientation that is inherently antithetical to conventional civic engagement. President Kennedy's 1961 inaugural clarion call, "Ask not what your country can do for you—ask what you can do for your country," has been turned on its head to "What can my country (and everyone else) do for me?" Sandel finds that the citizen participant of yesteryear has been replaced by the citizen consumer of today in a way that redefines democracy.[25] He argues that Americans of all political leanings have an "impoverished" sense of citizenship and community that leaves us frustrated with government because we, as consumer citizens, harbor unreasonable expectations of what government can do. Lizabeth Cohen shares these concerns and labels the new political order a "consumer republic" in which business interests dominate politics, policy decisions, and virtually every aspect of American lives.[26] Mass consumer culture comes with a high political price tag as more Americans evaluate their government through a consumer lens: a steep slide in voting and a plummeting trust in government. At the same time, the consumer orientation makes Americans more empowered in the marketplace and thus more likely to engage in consumer activism, which counters some of the negative effects of consumer citizenship identified by Sandel and Cohen.

This consumer empowerment is grounded in the idea that Americans have a right to consume because consumption equals freedom. This idea has been with us since the American Revolution, but mass media has made this feeling more intense and uniform since World War II.[27] Consumers feel powerful with the choice of 30,000 products in an average supermarket,[28] and the cliché that the "customer is king" gives us a sense of importance and control in our otherwise overworked, hectic existence. The 1959 "kitchen debate" between Vice President Richard Nixon and Soviet leader Nikita Khrushchev reinforced the idea that democratic freedom was synonymous with consumer choice for a television audience. These world leaders debated the merits of capitalism over a kitchen table in a replica of a house with the latest amenities that the average American could (supposedly) afford. The recreational and time-saving devices in the home were intended to signify the fruits of capitalism, and during the debate, Nixon overtly equated American freedom with consumer choice: "Diversity, the right to choose, the fact that we have 1,000 builders building 1,000 different houses is the most important thing. We don't have one decision made at the top by one government official."[29] Cohen points out that Nixon was the first political official to endorse consumerism as freedom in the television age, solidifying and empowering the citizen consumer.[30] In Nixon's words, "The United States comes closest to the ideal of prosperity for all in a classless society" through the free purchase of goods, including homes, the latest fashions, and cars—"what freedom means to us."[31]

Two decades later, President Jimmy Carter's "malaise" speech was widely denounced because it was anathema to personal and national identity based on consumption: "In a nation that was proud of hard work, strong families, close-knit communities, and our faith in God, too many of us now tend to worship self-indulgence and consumption. Human identity is no longer defined by what one does, but by what one owns. But we've discovered that owning things and consuming things does not satisfy our longing for meaning. We've learned that piling up material goods cannot fill the emptiness of lives which have no confidence or purpose."[32] Pundits and the public criticized Carter's speech for misplacing blame. He had dared to critique consumerism, calling on Americans to reject their "worship [of] self-indulgence and consumption" because it led to "fragmentation and self-interest."[33] He challenged Americans to tighten their belt of consumption for the prosperity of the nation, a call reminiscent of the American Revolution but one that did not fit with new conceptions of virtuous citizenship. Carter's words fell on hostile ears because it was a direct challenge to consumer citizenship. He was calling for an outdated type of citizenship, one that was seen as a threat to Americans' freedom (to purchase).

The entrenchment of the idea of consumption as freedom was made apparent again in 2001 when President George W. Bush responded to the terrorist attacks of 9/11 with a plea to the public as "consumer patriots" to go shopping to pull the United States out of its economic slump.[34] Americans were also encouraged to boycott post-9/11 as a display of their patriotism. In 2003, conservative cable news personalities called for a boycott of French products in response to French opposition to U.S. military action in Iraq. Restaurants across the country renamed their French fries "Freedom Fries" (including the congressional dining room), and a boycott of French wine caused a 13 percent drop in sales within six months.[35] The French government Tourist Office estimates that the boycott resulted in a loss of $500 million in U.S. tourist dollars alone.[36]

Consumer citizenship enables us to feel free in periods of economic expansion, even when our civil rights and liberties are being seriously challenged by legislation. For example, the U.S.A. P.A.T.R.I.O.T. Act, considered by many constitutional scholars to be the biggest rollback of civil liberties in U.S. history, passed in 2001 with virtually no public discussion. Imagine the public outcry over the passage of a hypothetical U.S.A. S.H.O.P. L.E.S.S. Act, that would curtail consumer choice in the marketplace. Consumer citizens would take to the streets over such an infringement on liberty and the American way of life.

The Post-Industrial Shift

The rise of mass consumer culture in the 1950s empowered consumers, but this necessary cause was not sufficient to bring about the mainstreaming of consumer activism that occurred in the 1970s and accelerated in the mid-2000s. Another causal factor is the post-industrial shift. The post-industrial shift of the 1970s raised public awareness of the political, social, economic, and environmental effects of consumption. According to Ronald Inglehart, a political scientist, post-industrialism is characterized by higher relative levels of affluence, education, and income; a shift from manufacturing to service sector work; and the rapid expansion of mass communication, which started in the 1970s.[37] Jeremy Mitchell notes that, during this time, consumer values rapidly and widely accepted as affluence grew, product offerings exponentially increased, and consumers had more leisure time than ever.[38] The post-industrialist shift also brought the ability to look beyond daily subsistence concerns to higher-order needs, as defined by Abraham Maslow's Hierarchy of Needs.[39] Monroe Friedman observes that in the 1970s, the content of boycotts evolved from primarily economic and labor issues to higher-order issues, such as racial justice and environmentalism. The relative affluence enjoyed by millions of Americans enabled them to "go beyond survival concerns to wrestle with quality-of-life issues."[40] The Consumer Movement, Women's Movement, and Environmental Movement all demonstrate that citizens are looking beyond daily subsistence to larger quality-of-life issues.

On the surface, the post-industrial shift to higher-order and more altruistic thinking appears to run counter to the materialistic values of consumer culture, but U.S. citizens hold both sets of values simultaneously and with ease.[41] In fact, marketers commonly use post-industrial values to sell products and services using anti-consumerist, anti-materialist ad campaigns, for example, Sprite's "Image Is Nothing" appeal in the late 1990s. This highly successful campaign made Sprite one of the top-selling sodas. In a similar vein, Volkswagen introduced its updated version of the Beetle in 1997 with commercials that rebuked modern materialism and, without irony, presented its product as an alternative to consumption. In 2003, Amy Cortese, a *New York Times* journalist, labeled the phenomenon of higher-order purchasing Lifestyles of Health and Sustainability (LOHAS)—"the biggest market you've never heard of."[42] LOHAS includes 68 million Americans with $230 billion in spending power who "worry about the environment, want products to be produced in a sustainable way and spend money to advance what they see as their personal development and potential."[43] The consumers making up this market respond to marketing messages from companies that share their values, and they are willing to pay more for products and services that reflect these values. In other words, marketers have effectively branded consumption as the ultimate form of self-actualization and aligned good citizenship with shopping. LOHAS consumers are self-actualizing, coupling materialism and post-industrial values.

New Networked Movements

Consumers who are empowered and self-actualizing engage in higher rates of consumer activism. These two trends explain consumer activism's going mainstream starting in the 1970s, but the rapid adoption of social media in the mid-2000s took consumer activism beyond normal behavior to "cool." The rates of consumer activism have steadily increased since the 1970s, but they surged in the 2000s as the result of new online organizing tools that made this form of activism easier and more attractive.[44]

Starting in 2004, online organizing has played a significant role in both shaping anti-corporate public sentiment and putting pressure on companies to alter their products or practices.[45] Online organizing has produced what Manuel Castells, a sociologist, identifies as new networked movements—decentralized, leaderless movements in which activists come together around shared problems and goals through new communication technologies.[46] Social movements have always involved some sort of network, but the new communication technologies have taken networking to a new level. Since the 1990s, U.S. activists have used online means to hold corporations responsible for their actions across the globe, through the springing up of networked movements such as the Arab Spring and OWS.[47] The new networked movements have better potential to hold institutions accountable than previous movements because activists can organize under the radar and do not have to rely on the mainstream media to shape the terms of the debate.[48]

The networked nature of contemporary protest politics means that there is access to real-time information about corporate practices and products, and that a single individual can more easily initiate or participate in a market campaign, resulting ultimately in higher rates of consumer activism. Social networking sites (such as Facebook, Twitter, Instagram, and Tumblr), blogs, and petition platforms make it simple to share information about a corporation and to quickly organize a petition, boycott, or protest.

On the other end, the new communication technologies make consumer activism more effective by conveying a unified message to corporations faster, and therefore corporations are more likely than ever to respond with speed.[49] For example, in 2013, it took mere weeks for Chip Wilson, Lululemon founder, to step down from his company after publicly stating that "some women's bodies just don't actually work" for wearing the yoga pants made by the company. His resignation came after three online petitions called for women to boycott the high-end athletic apparel brand and activists took to Twitter with the hashtag #TooFatForYogaPants.[50]

Online organizing also makes consumer activism "cool" because it provides a public space to perform good citizenship. Activists can post about a petition or boycott on social media sites where friends, family members, and associates can see their activities and reinforce their good deed with a "like" or retweet.[51] For Americans with access to the Internet, networked activism is easy to engage in, requiring little more than the click of a button to sign a petition, share a link, or make a donation. Some scholars are critical of the contribution of online activism, referring to it as "slactivism" or "arm chair activism,"[52] suggesting that, although an activist may care about a social cause, she or he is not willing to work very hard for it. As I explore further in chapter 7, it is true that online activism requires little in the way of time and resources, but this is precisely what makes consumer activism more effective than ever. A mass of people can come together around a pressing concern quickly and in such a high-profile way that the targeted corporation cannot ignore their demands. If we take seriously the idea that corporations are political brokers and de facto policymakers that require political accountability, then the high rates of online consumer activism described here are a significant new form of grassroots activism.

Social media has moved political participation away from collective campaigns and toward more individualized actions in advanced post-industrial societies such as the United States[53] Many Americans engage in political purchasing, investing, online campaigns, and even direct actions without being a part of a formal campaign. Similar to the previous GJM era, contemporary consumer activism also transcends class, race, and even national boundaries. For example, people in the United States are boycotting to improve the lives of Indonesian garment workers, children working in factories in Vietnam, and Chinese workers being mistreated in the U.S. territory of Saipan. Consumer activism is a way to express domestic good citizenship and to demonstrate global good citizenship,[54] especially if one can do so in a public way online.

Rates of Consumer Activism

Consumer activism comes in four primary forms: political purchasing actions (boycotting and buycotting), investment actions (responsible investing, shareholder resolutions, and divestment), direct actions (consumer protests, culture jamming, and vandalism), and social media campaigns. Boycotts have always been the most popular form of consumer activism in the United States. Investment actions started in earnest in the sixth era, and social media actions started in the mid-2000s.

Political (Non)Purchasing

Rates of political purchasing have shot up since the 1970s in advanced industrialized nations and less-industrialized nations for reasons already discussed.[55] In the United States, the number of organized boycotts went from about thirty per year in the 1960s to three hundred per year by 1990 and to thousands per year today.[56] Boycotts are typically organized by labor groups, organizations representing the interests of people of color, religious groups, environmental groups, and feminists. In other words, most of these campaigns reflect politically liberal interests. About one out of every five Americans (18 percent) boycott each year, and 23 percent buycott.[57] Political purchasing is far more popular with younger Americans than it is with older Americans. Nearly 60 percent of people younger than thirty have boycotted at some point in their lives and 40 percent have boycotted in the past year (see figure 2.1).[58]

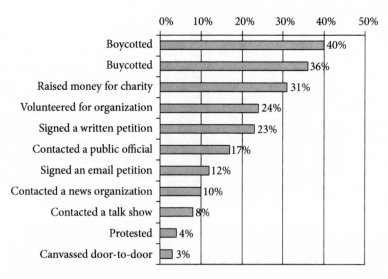

FIGURE 2.1 Political engagement in the past year by Americans younger than thirty. Data provided by the Center for Information and Research on Civic Learning and Engagement.

It is interesting that consumer activism is popular with young Americans during a time when their electoral participation has reached an all-time low. Compare this rate to the voting rate, a mode of participation that has declined 15 percent among young people since 1972.[59] Lance Bennett writes that "as traditional outlets such as voting are increasingly seen as less-relevant ways to effect change, consumer power is taking hold with young people as a viable form of political expression."[60] People born in the 1970s and later have come of age in a world increasingly defined by brand names, a global consciousness, and heightened consumerism.[61] Their consumer activism outpaces other forms of civic and political engagement, including fund-raising for charity, volunteering for an organization, and contacting a public official (see figure 2.1).

Most existing research conflates consumer activism with boycotting, so this is the type of consumer activism for which we have the most data. Aside from age, the same demographic variables that predict electoral participation also predict political purchasing. Rates of boycotting vary by race, ideology, and education. Liberal, educated, white Americans are more likely to engage in political purchasing than other Americans. It is interesting to note that even though women have led consumer activist efforts in previous peaks,[62] and they have historically "complemented on the consumption side of the economic coin their husbands' activities on the production side,"[63] no gender gap exists today in the United States. A gender gap does persist in Italy, Britain, Japan, and Denmark.[64] Another finding of interest is that income is a potent predictor of electoral participation but not of political purchasing.[65] Americans across the economic strata spend their money to achieve sociopolitical ends.

Although white Americans are more likely to practice political purchasing, this is still a very popular tool for civil rights organizations that represent people of color. The NAACP, Operation PUSH (People United to Serve Humanity), the Rainbow Coalition, and Color of Change (COC), frequently use boycotts to push for civil rights, and African Americans' buying power is currently growing at a faster rate than the national average.[66] Reverend Jesse Jackson notes the effectiveness of these tactics as an alternative to more formal political participation for African Americans: "We have the power, nonviolently, just by controlling our appetites, to determine the direction of the American economy. If black people in thirty cities said simultaneously 'General motors, you will not sell cars in the black community unless you guarantee us a franchise here next year and help us finance it,' GM would have no choice but to comply."[67] More recently, Kweisi Mfume, former representative (D-MD) and recent head of the NAACP, observed that "sometimes at the end of the way, economic action becomes the only action with teeth."[68] The liberal bent of consumer activism in the United States also exists in European countries.[69]

In addition, conservative boycotts are not uncommon. Bill O'Reilly, the former top-rated host at Fox News, frequently calls for boycotts. After 9/11, he organized a four-year boycott of the French for "their actions in the UN and their approach to the Iraq situation in general."[70] His website lists the companies to boycott, including Bic, Cartier, and Grey Goose Vodka. In 2003, after Pepsi featured Ludacris, a rapper, in its commercials, O'Reilly asked viewers to boycott the company for its use of a "gangsta rapper." O'Reilly stated that "gangsta rap" glorified violence, drug use, and the degradation of women. In 2014, O'Reilly called for a boycott of Mexico for jailing a U.S. marine on weapons charges and because of its record on human trafficking.[71] The Heinz ketchup company, owned by Theresa Heinz Kerry (wife of former presidential candidate John Kerry) was the focus of an organized boycott by Republicans during the 2004 presidential election and beyond.[72] As I explore further in chapter 6, consumer activism is more popular than ever with conservative pundits, preachers, nonprofits, and leaders.

The rates of participation in boycotts also vary by consumer empowerment. People who feel entitled in the consumer-producer relationship are more likely to boycott and buycott than others.[73] As with electoral politics, higher levels of education, political interest, and civic duty lead to higher rates of consumer activism. Consumer activism is also positively correlated with political distrust, meaning that people who have lower levels of trust in formal government are more likely to engage with politics in the marketplace.[74] Benjamin Newman and Brandon Bartels, political scientists, paint a complex picture of the contemporary consumer activist:

> The American political consumer is someone who is educated, interested in politics, and feels a strong sense of duty to engage in political life, but does not necessarily place his or her trust in government and elected officials as a means of achieving all of his or her policy goals. The political consumer is relatively young and likely possesses a high level of general discontent. The political consumer is someone who tends to embrace informal and individualized forms of engagement with political and social issues and groups. Last, the political consumer is someone who has a high level of civic initiative and is willing to expend a good deal of effort in engaging in participatory acts.[75]

Not surprisingly, people who think consumer activism is effective are also more likely to use it.[76] Aaron Bush, a twenty-eight-year-old Seattle resident and avid consumer activist, articulates this point well: "I guess I see it as being in some ways more powerful than voting. To me it's a more direct, active way to promote what you believe in."[77] Consumer activism is a form of lifestyle politics, individualized, informal citizen actions that stress "politicizing the personal."[78]

For most activists, consumer activism is simply another tool in an already full civic engagement toolbox, but for a few, consumer activism is their only tool. Consumer activists are more likely to vote and protest than other Americans,[79] so consumer activism typically complements rather than supplants electoral participation. With this said, about 50 percent of young Americans are disengaged from electoral politics, and of this group, one-third engage in consumer activism.[80] This means that for about 15 percent of young Americans, consumer activism is their sole political tool.

Political purchasing actions are generally effective. Major boycotts cause stock values to significantly decline in the months following the action,[81] and often affect the reputation of companies for years in ways that are difficult to quantify. According to Monroe Friedman, about one boycott out of four achieves its desired change in corporate practices.[82]

Business scholars have identified the factors that increase boycott success. At a minimum, the problem driving the boycott has to be defined and severe. Nebulous issues such as racism are too broad to compel corporations into action, whereas racial profiling by certain merchants is actionable. In addition, successful boycotts cannot require much in the way of psychological or financial costs to the consumer.[83] If suitable alternatives exist to the targeted product (such as bread, gas, or fast food) or company, then less consumer effort is required, thus increasing citizen participation in the boycott and its relative success. Media attention, public demonstrations, and celebrity involvement[84] all improve the effectiveness of boycotts, so it is no surprise that market campaigns often combine political purchasing with direct action. Brayden King, a business scholar, finds that media attention affects the corporate bottom line through a decline in stock.[85] His analysis concludes that being organized by more formal organizations, such as a well-established nonprofit group, increases the likelihood that a boycott will be successful and that larger corporations with good reputations are better targets because media attention will be more damaging. "The disruptiveness of boycotts depends on the ability of boycotters to draw media attention and on the selection of ideal target organizations."[86]

On the buycott side, many companies now use cause marketing to encourage consumers to buy their products by aligning with causes. Bruce Burtch, the father of cause marketing, is credited with the phrase, "do well by doing good," which emphasizes the mutual benefit to the conscience of the customer and the corporate bottom line. For example, Altria (formerly Phillip Morris) makes charitable contributions to align its deadly product (cigarettes) with domestic abuse prevention and Meals on Wheels. Ben and Jerry's Ice Cream is widely known as an environmentally and socially conscious company, having little to do directly with the ice cream the company produces. Yoplait yogurt teamed up with Susan G.

Komen for the Cure on its "Save Lids to Save Lives" campaign. Singapore Airlines is affiliated with the nonprofit organization Doctors Without Borders. American Express promotes the idea of shopping at local vendors with its Small Business Saturday ad campaign. The Product Red campaign, launched in 2006, is the largest cause marketing campaign to date; The Gap, Apple, and a host of other companies teamed up with The Global Fund in its fight against AIDS, tuberculosis, and malaria worldwide. In the last two decades, the amount of money that businesses have spent on cause marketing has gone from about $120 million in 1990 to over $1 billion today.[87] Figure 2.2 shows the rapid increase in cause marketing expenditures over the last decade to promote buycotting.

Whereas boycotts are generally organized and episodic, buycotts are more individualized and constant because they reward a corporate practice rather than trying to change it. Four out of five Americans say they would switch to a brand associated with a good cause if the price and quality matched the product they currently use.[88] Buycotting is especially appealing to Americans under the age of thirty who are more likely to purchase from cause campaigns (37 percent, compared to 30 percent of older Americans), and are more likely to encourage others to support a socially responsible corporation (30 percent, compared to 22 percent of older Americans).[89] To survive the new normal of consumer activism in the social media age, corporations have to project a positive image by partnering with causes while simultaneously avoiding perceptions of impropriety that might attract a boycott.

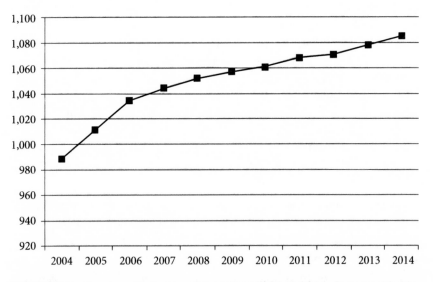

FIGURE 2.2 Cause marketing in millions from 2004 to 2014. Data provided by the Annual IEG Sponsorship Reports.

Investment Actions

Citizens are now placing political pressure on corporations through investments and shareholder resolutions to a degree that is unparalleled in U.S. history. Shareholders can engage in responsible investing, propose a resolution to change corporate practices, or divest from companies to gain political concessions—all these actions have experienced remarkable growth in the 2000s. Nine out of ten investors say they consider corporate social responsibility in their investment decisions.[90]

The first investment action, responsible investing, comes in three primary forms: socially responsible investing (SRI), which screens companies for socio-political aspects; impact investing (II), which involves projects with a sociopolitical outcome; and environmental, social, and governance (ESG) investing, which entails purchasing stock in companies with superior performance because of these factors.[91] With SRI, investors can avoid companies that profit from gambling, alcohol, tobacco, pornography, contraception, and a multitude of other offensive products or services. Impact investors purchase stock in companies or funds that have a measurable positive environmental or sociopolitical effect, for example, a private equity firm that builds affordable housing in Brazil or a fair trade fund that invests in organic coffee companies in Ecuador. ESG investors flock to funds that identify corporations that are profitable because of their good environmental, labor, or governance practices. All three types of responsible investing have increased tenfold since the 1980s, and account managers now offer them as a matter of course.[92] Today, $1 out of every $8 under professional management is invested in responsible investment funds.[93] As figure 2.3 shows, responsible investments have gone from a $40 billion annual enterprise in 1985 to over $6 trillion in 2015.

Socially responsible investors are more likely to be young, female, and less wealthy than other investors.[94] These investors believe that corporate, social, and environmental performance matters as much as financial performance. They also believe corporations have an obligation to serve both their shareholders and the broader society.[95] Socially conscious investors are similar to those who boycott and buycott, with the exception that they are more likely to be female. Young educated people are also more likely to use this political tool than older Americans. The demographic factors that predict SRI differ from the factors that predict engagement in electoral politics. Older Americans with higher incomes are more likely to vote, but the opposite is true of SRI.

Another form of investment action is to propose a shareholder resolution to change corporate practices. Investors who own at least $2,000 of company stock are allowed to propose resolutions, and about half of all resolutions proposed in the past decade have involved social or environmental concerns.[96] Investors

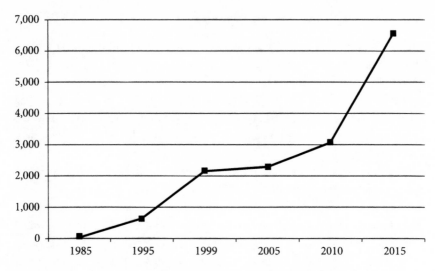

FIGURE 2.3   Dollars spent on responsible investing in millions from 1985 to 2015. Data provided by the Social Investment Forum.

who either propose or vote for resolutions based on socially responsible goals currently control $1.2 trillion.[97] Consumer activists have been using shareholder resolutions since the 1970s, when the Securities and Exchange Commission (SEC) deemed political resolutions acceptable, but their use has increased considerably in the 2000s, from 150 in 2001 to 417 in 2014.[98] The most popular resolutions in 2014 were about political spending, climate change, other sustainability concerns, diversity issues, human rights, and the treatment of animals.[99] As shareholder resolutions have become more common, they have also become more effective. In 2005, only 3 percent of socially conscious resolutions gained the 30 percent support required for consideration by a corporate board, but today, one out of every three resolutions achieves the necessary threshold.[100] This new effectiveness can be attributed to their more frequent use and greater sophistication.[101] The most successful resolutions involve corporate transparency concerning political contributions, antifracking measures, climate change, and workplace discrimination.

Divestment campaigns are another type of investment action. They emerged in the sixth era of consumer activism during the 1970s. Divestment campaigns seek to alter corporate practices for sociopolitical reasons through a mass defection of the investors. For example, Kodak shareholders successfully used divestment in the 1980s to protest the involvement by the company in the South African Apartheid regime.[102] More recently, the global fossil fuel divestment campaign has compelled over eight hundred institutions, including universities

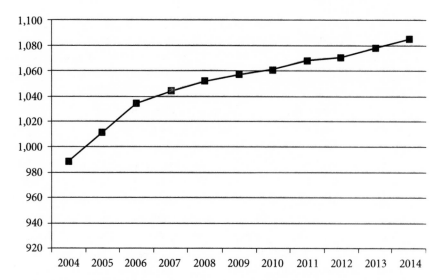

FIGURE 2.4 Mentions of *divestment* in the *New York Times* from 2004 to 2014

and churches, to divest from companies and funds involved in fossil fuels. The momentum for this campaign is building, as evidenced by a steep rise in institutions divesting from fossil fuels from 74 in 2013 to 181 in 2014.[103]

Quantitative data do not exist on the rate or effectiveness of divestment campaigns, so I use a blunt proxy measure of mentions of the word *divestment* in the *New York Times* to measure their rate and public attention. During the 1990s, *divestment* was mentioned an average of thirteen times per year. As figure 2.4 shows, mentions of *divestment* had a sharp upward trend in the 2000s that began with major national antifracking, gun control, and climate change campaigns. By 2014, *divestment* was mentioned over a thousand times per year in the newspaper. An analysis of the corporate response finds that 42 percent of consumer product companies that divested did so because of shareholder activism in 2014.[104]

Social Media Actions

Virtually all contemporary consumer activism campaigns use social media. The widespread adoption of online technology in the mid-1990s and the invention of social media platforms in the mid-2000s have allowed consumer activists to organize in ways that were previously impossible and to reach wider audiences for market campaigns. Online organizing was the reason that officials so vastly underestimated the number of protesters who would attend the Battle in Seattle in 1999. With the advent of social media sites dedicated to online activism, the mid-2000s saw a veritable explosion in the number and success of market campaigns.[105] Corporations are paying more attention to consumer activism because social media provides unprecedented opportunities for consumers to complain about and organize against them.[106] A 2013 Cone survey found that consumers are increasingly using social media to spread negative news about companies.[107]

The advent of online activism has improved the efficiency and effectiveness of campaigns in the marketplace.[108] Organizers now gain results in weeks or even days using social media as opposed to the months or years required in previous eras of consumer activism.[109] The recent Change.org campaign around "pink slime" illustrates the speed and effectiveness of consumer actions that gain traction on popular activist sites. In 2012, a Texas blogger, Bettina Elias Siegel, brought attention to the long-debated use of what Jamie Oliver, a celebrity chef, characterized as "pink slime" in school lunches and other meat.[110] "Pink slime," called lean finely textured beef (LFTB) by the meat industry, is an amalgam of animal by-products treated with ammonia or citric acid that used to be used mostly in pet food. In 2004, the Food and Drug Administration (FDA) approved it for limited human consumption, and producers started adding it to ground beef. By 2012, 70 percent of ground beef sold in U.S. supermarkets included LFTB filler.[111] "Pink slime" had previously received attention from major media sources (the *New York Times* and ABC News), but it was Siegel's use of social media that put pressure on the U.S. Department of Agriculture (USDA) to stop using the filler in school lunches. Siegel created a Change.org petition that received over 100,000 signatures in its first four days (and went on to garner over 350,000 signatures). Nine days into the petition, the USDA announced that it would give schools the option of whether they wanted to serve "pink slime" in their meat.[112]

Direct Consumer Actions

Direct consumer actions include protests, sit-ins, teach-ins, picket lines, culture jamming, street theater, vandalism, and a host of others tactics whose aim is to raise awareness of the sociopolitical effects of corporate behavior. In recent decades, organized consumer protests and demonstrations have become commonplace in the United States[113] For example, thousands of Americans participated in protests throughout major U.S. cities in the months following the 2010 British Petroleum (BP) oil spill on the Louisiana Gulf Coast, which killed eleven people and discharged nearly 5 million gallons of oil into the ocean. These protests were prompted by the perception that BP could have done more to prevent this human and environmental disaster. Collective actions were organized outside BP gas stations and city halls, and the protests I attended in New Orleans and

Los Angeles involved marches that wove through the cities, humans dressed up as birds for a "die-in," and people covered in what appeared to be oil.

Culture jamming was also part of the consumer activist repertoire when BP billboards were defaced with oil to make a statement about the culpability of the company in the disaster. Culture jamming is the act of altering or hijacking media or products to change their meaning. This can involve altering images on billboards, bus stops, the sides of busses, and other public spaces. The Billboard Liberation Front (BLF) invented culture jamming in 1977, and over the years, it has altered hundreds of billboards to protest the cigarette industry, government wiretapping, war, state-sanctioned torture, the food conglomerate McDonalds, and the use of human growth hormones in beef cows. Culture jamming is particularly effective today because the message can reach a wider audience when it is shared online. For example, in 2001 Nike offered customized lettering on its running shoes, so Jonah Peretti (who went on to found Buzzfeed) ordered a pair with the word *sweatshop* stitched into the sneaker. This consumer action was intended to raise awareness of ongoing Nike labor practices overseas, and it did. Nike refused to print the *sweatshop* shoe, and the ensuing e-mail exchange quickly circulated online, garnering national media attention.[114] As I demonstrate in subsequent chapters, today's consumer activists typically incorporate all four types of consumer activism into their campaigns.

Democratic Implications

Pippa Norris, a political scientist, writes that protest politics have moved from the margins into the mainstream.[115] The rising rates of boycotting, buycotting, responsible investing, shareholder resolutions, divestment actions, and direct consumer actions confirm that consumer activism has become a mainstream form of protest politics in the U.S. context. This has important implications for democracy, especially in light of the decline in voting.

Voting, the hallmark of political participation, has seen double-digit declines in the United States since 1960, and even though the 2008 presidential election caused presidential voting to spike up to nearly 60 percent of the eligible electorate, turnout continued to decline in subsequent elections.[116] Voter turnout in 2014 was the lowest it had been in seventy-two years, with less than half the eligible electorate participating.[117]

In 1978, David Brody, a political scientist, introduced the paradox of participation: the voting rate was declining at the same time that education and income (two variables that usually improve voting likelihood) were increasing.[118] Political scientists have offered several explanations for this decline: lower feelings of "external political efficacy," that is, the belief that one's participation matters in politics; older Americans not passing their civic-mindedness on to their children and grandchildren; the declining role of political parties as providers of political cues; and the erosion of social capital, the "networks, norms, and social trust that facilitate coordination and cooperation for mutual benefit."[119] Robert Putnam finds that social capital "has been shrinking for more than a quarter of a century" and that this recent erosion is washing away the exceptional U.S. political bedrock of civic engagement through churches, unions, parent-teacher associations (PTAs), civic groups, and fraternal organizations that determine levels of political participation.[120] Putnam concludes that television and other forms of mass communication have radically "privatized" the way we spend our leisure time and that this, in turn, has caused social capital and conventional political participation to shrink.[121] Television in 2001 absorbed over half of the average American's disposable free time, a significant increase since 1965.[122]

I argue that Putnam gets it half right. Television has privatized Americans' leisure time in ways that erode social capital, but television is also the single largest transmitter of consumer citizenship that erodes social capital and electoral participation.[123] Harry Boyte, a philosopher, attributes widespread ignorance of basic facts about U.S. politics to the consumer model of citizenship that has replaced an ethos of active citizenship. According to Boyte, Americans used to view themselves as practical agents in a civic world, working together to solve collective problems; but now, as citizen consumers, people have discarded previous notions of civic responsibility. Boyte and Benjamin Barber conclude that the new model of consumer citizenship threaten the very core of democracy because it disconnects people from the polity and inhibits both the desire for and practice of self-governance.[124]

With all the hand wringing about the decline in electoral participation, most scholars have overlooked one crucial fact: modes of participation are not simply falling, they are shifting.[125] Citizens have made a dramatic shift toward more individualized civic activities, such as boycotting, at the expense of collective political action.[126] In *Democratic Phoenix*, Norris finds that electoral engagement has been replaced by newer types of participation, including online activism, networked social movements, and transnational policy networks. "Political energies have diversified and flowed through alternative tributaries, rather than simply ebbing away."[127]

Participation is shifting away from formal governmental channels in favor of market channels. Mass consumer culture simultaneously planted the seeds of participatory decline and produced the pesticide of consumer activism to counter it. This arrangement calls into question the scholarly attention paid almost exclusively to electoral modes of participation and limited measures of democracy that fail to account for activism outside the electoral arena. Consumer activism in the contemporary social media era is "putting the roots back in grassroots"[128] in a way that strengthens political equality, political liberty, and popular sovereignty.

In this chapter, I have examined how consumer activism became a mainstream political activity starting in the 1970s, as a result of the rise of mass consumer culture and the shift to post-industrialism. The United States is a nation that defines personal, group, and national identities in terms of the purchase and consumption of a dizzying array of products. New networked social movements have caused rates of consumer activism to accelerate in the 2000s. We are currently in a new era of consumer activism—the eighth era—one that emerged in the mid-2000s as a result of social media. This era is characterized by its mainstream nature, transnational focus, networked organizing, and use of all four types of consumer activism. In the past decade, boycotting, buycotting, socially responsible investing, shareholder resolutions, divestment actions, and direct consumer actions have all experienced a steep increase. Widespread consumer activism has important implications for democracy. While engagement in electoral politics has been declining since 1960, more individualized actions, such as consumer activism, have increased. Citizens feel less empowered in their relationship with the government but more empowered in their relationship with business. They are increasingly turning to market channels to express their political voice—a voice that has become more effective in recent years as social media technology has made consumer actions more plentiful and effective.

"WE ARE NOT A MASCOT"

Campaigns for Social and Economic Justice

In 1965, grape pickers orchestrated a consumer action against grape growers to protest decades of low wages and poor working conditions. Filipino American farmworkers united with Mexican American farmworkers during the strike and formed the United Farm Workers of America (UFW). This collaboration was crucial in the success of the strike because it preempted producers from using racial division to break the strike, as they had done several times in the past.[1] The UFW action initially drew attention from civil rights organizations, church activists, and students. Cesar Chávez's 300-mile march from Delano to the state capital brought in public support. The UFW was joined in its strike by unionized longshoremen in the Bay Area, who refused to unload the grapes that came to their docks, leaving tons of grapes to spoil in their crates.[2]

Chávez also enlisted the American people in the fight and referred to them as "our greatest court, our court of last resort."[3] He called for a grape boycott, and hundreds of union organizers travelled across North America to tell their stories to support it. According to a 1975 Lou Harris Poll, at its height 17 million Americans were participating in the boycott. White middle-class families across the country sided with poor workers of color in California simply by abstaining from purchasing grapes. The boycott was an unmitigated success, and in 1970, in the face of mounting public pressure and plummeting grape sales, the management signed its first union contract that ensured better pay, medical benefits, improved protections against pesticides, and the provision of fresh drinking water and toilets in the fields.

Organizers had been fighting for their rights in the fields for nearly a century before the UFW campaign, but every previous action had been defeated until a mass boycott action was employed. Many children born in the 1960s and later were raised in households where boycotting for social justice was a common activity, but the grape boycott was the first such effort in the new age of mass media. The grape boycott followed the long tradition of consumer activism as a "weapon of the weak" for those who lack access to and power in formal political channels. It was the first prominent campaign for racial and economic justice for people of color in the mass media era, and it served as the blueprint for subsequent campaigns in its use of direct consumer actions, boycotts, and media pressure.

In this chapter, I analyze the democratic implications of contemporary consumer activism campaigns aimed at achieving social, economic, and political justice for people of color. The Montgomery Bus Boycott and the lunch counter sit-ins discussed in chapter 1 are examples of consumer activism for racial or economic justice. Economic inequality is a primary manifestation of racial inequality, so campaigns that address low wages and poor working conditions for people of color are also campaigns for racial equality.[4]

I analyze campaigns of the last decade, from 2004 to 2014. This period coincides with the advent of social media since Facebook was formed in 2004 and Twitter and Tumblr were launched in 2006. To identify cases, I used Lexis-Nexis and the search terms *boycott* and *consumer activism* in three national newspapers: the *New York Times*, the *Washington Post*, and *USA Today*. It is common for researchers to use newspapers for identifying consumer actions, and selecting national publications generates a politically and tactically diverse set of boycotts that are in the public eye.[5] My analysis does not include regional actions or actions that did not receive national news attention because online technology has led to an explosion of consumer actions in the past decade, which made it impossible to track every campaign or semi-organized action. My search netted 8,970 articles that mentioned *boycott* or *consumer activism*. From this list, I identified actions that targeted corporations or business entities, originated in the United States, had a national focus or base of support, and involved a racial or economic justice issue.

I found fifteen market campaigns that fit these criteria from 2004 to 2014. Some of these boycott actions started before the period in question, and a few are still active today. For each of the campaigns, I describe what problem prompted the action, who was involved, and what tactics they used to give the reader a sophisticated understanding of contemporary consumer activism. Of the fifteen campaigns in this chapter, twelve had the aim of improving the lives of people of color in the United States and three originated in the United States but sought to improve the lives of people in other countries. I describe the U.S.-based cases first. The campaigns are diverse in their aims, their strategies, and the people involved. Some were a response to stereotypical representations of people of color, and others attempted to improve employment conditions or overturn racial profiling. Their common core is that they used consumer activism to achieve justice for people of color.

In terms of tools, activists employed all four types of consumer activism. All fifteen campaigns used boycotts, eleven used social media, nine used direct action, and five used shareholder and investment actions. All the campaigns initiated after 2010 employed social media as a tool, which is the new normal for contemporary consumer activism campaigns. Most of the campaigns were effective in achieving their stated goal, and all furthered democracy by expanding opportunities for participation and amplifying the political voices of the disenfranchised.

Market Tactics for Racial and Economic Justice in the United States

Twelve market campaigns for racial and economic justice for people of color in the United States made national news from 2004 to 2014. I begin with the long-standing boycott of the Washington Redskins, which heated up in recent years, and then wrap up this section with a short-lived national boycott of McDonald's over an employee's treatment of an elderly Korean customer in Queens, New York.

The Washington Redskins Campaign

Since the late 1980s, over two hundred Native American and civil rights organizations have called for the Washington Redskins football team to change its name because they believe that it promotes a harmful ethnic stereotype. This is a market campaign proper. Suzan Shown Harjo of the National Congress of American Indians (NCAI) organized the first protest outside a Redskins game in 1988, and she has been the titular leader of the movement since.[6] By 1992, over 2,000 marchers gathered outside the Super Bowl game in Minnesota, waving signs that read "Repeal Redskin Racism," "We Are Not a Mascot," and "Promote Sports Not Racism."[7] Activists have protested every year since, with pressure intensifying in recent years.[8] In 2013, a group of over sixty religious leaders in Washington, DC, sent a letter to the, Roger Goodell, the National Football League (NFL) commissioner, asking him to change the name, but the owner, Dan Snyder, defended its use, citing "tradition." That same year, the DC City Council unanimously condemned the name and sent a letter to Goodell to stop using this "racial slur."[9]

According to a 2014 poll commissioned by the NFL, 71 percent of Americans supported keeping the name.

After years of unsuccessful protests, activists began using boycotts targeting the corporate partners of the Redskins. For example, in 2014, the Osage Nation in Oklahoma initiated a boycott of FedEx, and the United Church of Christ (UCC) passed a resolution asking its members to boycott Redskins games and merchandise until the team changes its name.[10] The UCC has over 5,000 churches with 1 million members nationwide, so this was an important strategic coup for boycott organizers. In 2014, shareholders filed a resolution with FedEx for it to clarify how its association with the Washington Redskins has affected the reputation of the company, but the chief executive officer (CEO) refused to issue a clarification.[11] In September 2014, the Oneida Tribe of Wisconsin asked FedEx to reconsider a stadium naming-rights agreement with the Redskins, but 99 percent of the shareholders voted to continue working with the team.[12] Activists have also used social media outreach, including a Moveon.org petition that collected over 7,000 signatures, a Change.org petition with just under 1,000 signatures, and a Care2.org petition with over 8,000 signatures.

To date, consumer activism has not been effective in changing the Redskins name, but it has raised awareness of the controversy and given a political voice to Native Americans who oppose the use of the name but lack the necessary formal political power to determine how corporations use their culture and heritage. This campaign is unlikely to be effective because it does not reflect the will of a majority of Native Americans. In May 2016, the *Washington Post* published a poll showing that nine out of ten Native Americans were not bothered by the use of the term *Redskins* by the team.[13]

The Mt. Olive Pickle Campaign

In 1999, the Farm Labor Organizing Committee (FLOC) organized a boycott of the Mt. Olive Pickle Company, the second largest pickle producer in the United States. This was a market campaign proper in that its aim was to change the political behavior of a specific company. FLOC was formed by Baldamer Valasquez, a migrant worker, in response to the terrible working conditions he and his family experienced as farmworkers. Valasquez grew up in the Rio Grande valley of Texas and migrated with his family to Ohio every year to harvest pickles, sugar beets, and berries. As a teen, he was incensed by the mistreatment of migrant workers, and he dedicated his life to improving theirs. He founded FLOC in 1967, and in 1969, he became the first person in his family to earn a college degree.

Valasquez's early efforts in the 1970s were not effective, but he ran a successful boycott against the Campbell Soup Company in the early 1980s that doubled migrant workers' wages, secured better housing, and established a corporate grievance process. This campaign was successful because FLOC used media shaming, a tactic he also used in subsequent campaigns. In the Mt. Olive campaign, FLOC wanted to improve migrant workers' squalid living conditions and prevent their deaths from heat and exposure to pesticides. These pickers were mostly migrant guest workers from Mexico and Guatemala who came to the states each year during produce season. The ultimate target of the boycott was the cucumber growers, but FLOC targeted Mt. Olive to compel the company to put pressure on its suppliers to offer better wages and working conditions.

FLOC was able to raise awareness of migrant workers' conditions with heart-wrenching cases that made the news. For example, in 2001 Urbano Ramirez left his wife and five children in Mexico to migrate for a job in the fields of North Carolina. He woke at the crack of dawn on June 26 to pick cucumbers for a Mt. Olive supplier, but after lunch he wandered off in a delirious state. No one went to look for him, and no one filed a missing person's report. His body was found in the nearby woods ten days later, and the Department of Labor fined the cucumber farmer $1,800 for failing to provide water to the workers. In 2003, Mamerto Chaj Garcia was working for a Mt. Olive supplier when he started experiencing stomach pains. He asked his boss for help but was told that he should just take some aspirin. After he collapsed from the pain, Garcia was taken to a hospital for surgery on a burst appendix. He was fired without cause a few weeks later. These stories put a human face on the problem.

FLOC found support from over three hundred diverse organizations, including the National Council of Churches, the American Federation of Labor and Congress of Industrial Organizations (AFL-CIO), and Black Workers for Justice and Solidarity. In addition to calling for a boycott of the company, activists gathered outside supermarkets across the country to call for the removal of Mt. Olive pickles from the shelves. This pressure caused the Kroger supermarket chain to remove Mt. Olive products from over 130 stores. Students were also active in the Mt. Olive boycott efforts. For example, students from the Progressive Alliance at Duke University successfully banned Mt. Olive products from the cafeteria. The United Methodist Church urged its members to abstain from Mt. Olive products during the boycott, even though church member Bill Bryan, the Mt. Olive president, lobbied against the church action.

This consumer activism campaign achieved its goals. In 2004, FLOC reached an agreement with the Mt. Olive Pickle Company to raise wages 10 percent over three years and to offer a 3 percent price bump to farms that offered worker's compensation.[14] At the press conference to announce the agreement, Velasquez noted the role of the media in exacting reputational damage: "The company is tremendously relieved to have the boycott ended. They were getting tired of all the negative publicity."[15] Mt. Olive claimed that the boycott did not hurt its bottom line much but that the potential reputational damage from the negative attention was a point of concern. Bryan commented, "I'm one pickle packer who is glad to be out of a pickle today." FLOC gained considerable power as a result of the boycott, and the organization went on to negotiate better labor conditions with growers of Christmas trees, tobacco, and other produce in North Carolina. This national boycott effort gave voice to migrant guest workers, who have limited political power in the United States, and like the grape boycott, this campaign saw middle-class Americans working to better the lives of indigent people of color simply by abstaining from purchasing their favorite pickles.

The Confederate Flag Campaign

In January 2000, the NAACP, a civil rights organization that is an advocate for the rights of people of color, initiated a tourism boycott of South Carolina to protest the flying of the Confederate flag in front of state offices. The aim of this campaign was to change the actions of the state; it used market tactics rather than a market campaign proper. State Senator and Pastor Darrell Jackson first pushed for the removal of the flag in 1992. In 1994, a majority of state senators voted to remove it, but the state House of Representatives allowed the bill to die. The issue came up again in 1995 and 1997, but these attempts were met with organized opposition from within the government as well as veterans and historical groups.

The NAACP used a variety of campaign tactics. It called on travelers and associations to avoid the state until the flag was removed and partnered with other organizations to boycott the state. Over forty associations supported the boycott, including the Seventh Day Adventist Church, the Black Bikers, and the Association of State Democratic Party Chairs.[16] Many travelling sports teams also boycotted the state, and South Carolina lost opportunities to host tournament basketball games and a bowl game because of the participation by the National Collegiate Athletic Association in the boycott. The New York Knicks cancelled a preplayoff camp in South Carolina to show support for the boycott, and Serena Williams withdrew from a tennis tournament in South Carolina. In 2007, Steve Spurrier, a South Carolina football coach, made headlines when he publicly stated, "I realize I'm not supposed to get into the political arena as a football coach, but if anybody were to ask me about that damn Confederate flag, I would say we need to get rid of it."[17] Beyond the boycott, union members and NAACP activists marched each year outside the state capital building. Since 2010, organizers used social media tactics to shame the state under the hashtag #boycottSC.

FIGURE 3.1   Confederate flag outside the South Carolina statehouse, 2001

The economic impact of the flag boycott was immediate. In the months after the boycott was called, North Carolina saw a $2 million increase in business as boycotters moved north.[18] Within a year of the start of the boycott, South Carolina officials voted to move the flag from the top of the capital building to a nearby monument honoring Confederate soldiers (see figure 3.1). This gesture was not deemed sufficient by the NAACP, so the boycott continued.

In the first few years of the boycott action, organizers were successful in getting city officials throughout South Carolina to remove the flags. They also threatened a secondary boycott of the Holiday Inn, so the hotel chain removed the flags outside of their Southern locations. In response, the grass-roots Southern Patriot Group against Holiday Inn organized a counterboycott to protest the removal of the flags. The group established a website to spread the word about the counterboycott: "We will drive all night or sleep in the car if necessary. We will demonstrate true Southern grit by eating peanut butter sandwiches, if necessary, rather than partaking of Holiday Inn's Sunday buffet."[19] Other conservative groups rallied to keep the Confederate flag flying, including the Sons of Confederate Veterans, who held annual rallies in support of the flag. A few outspoken political leaders in the state also staunchly defended the flag when the boycott started, including Representative Joe Wilson (R-SC, who also gained national notoriety when he heckled President Barack Obama by yelling, "You lie" during the 2009 State of the Union speech) and state Senator Glenn McConnell (R), who deemed the removal of the flag "cultural genocide" and told the press, "this state is not going to succumb to economic terrorism."[20]

In 2009, state Representative Chip Limehouse (R) called for an end to the boycott, stating that it had hurt the state economically. Fifteen years into the boycott, momentum slowed,[21] and the Harlem Globetrotters returned to the state for the first time since the boycott was called. Then, on June 17, 2015, avowed white supremacist Dylann Roof entered the Emanuel African Methodist Episcopal Church in Charleston and gunned down nine black people. He later told authorities that he was trying to ignite a race war. Roof is a Confederate flag aficionado, and his actions renewed attention to the flag boycott. Within a matter of weeks, lawmakers voted to remove the flag. A few days prior to its official removal, Bree Newsome, filmmaker and activist, scaled the pole and removed the flag as an act of civil disobedience. The NAACP officially ended the boycott at its annual conference in July 2015.

The Taco Bell Campaign

In 2001, the Coalition of Immokalee Workers (CIW), a group representing mostly indigent, undocumented immigrant tomato pickers in southwest Florida, called for a boycott of Taco Bell to put pressure on its suppliers for better wages and safer working conditions.[22] This was a market campaign proper because it directly targeted a business. In the years leading up to the boycott, the CIW had assisted federal investigators in uncovering cases of indentured servitude, workplace injuries, and unlawfully low pay on tomato farms. When CIW initiated the boycott, workers were earning $50 for picking 2 tons of tomatoes, a rate that had not changed in thirty years.[23] CIW was started by Lucas Benitez, a Mexican migrant worker who had come to the United States to work in the fields when he was seventeen years old. He came to organizing through anger at having witnessed and experienced verbal and physical abuse.

Benitez mobilized several migrant communities in Immokalee—Mexican, Guatemalan, and Haitian workers.[24] They met in a room in a local church and soon became a force for better working conditions in the local farming community. Benitez and his fellow organizers quickly realized that they would have to target national companies to bring about structural changes in the supply chain. They identified Taco Bell as their target. The boycott attracted considerable support from church leaders and students, including the National Council of Churches, which represents 50 million churchgoers worldwide. Students at twenty-one colleges removed or blocked Taco Bell from their campus, and they created over three hundred chapters of "Boot the Bell" on campuses across the United States

The CIW used direct consumer action in addition to the boycott. A group of Immokalee workers travelled to the company headquarters on a Taco Bell Truth Tour, stopping in fifteen cities along the way to rally support for their cause. Workers organized three community-wide work stoppages that crippled the fast food industry in the South, and they staged high-profile hunger strikes that attracted media attention. Celebrities such as Martin Sheen lent their support, which raised the national profile of the campaign.

In 2005, with the assistance of former president Jimmy Carter, the CIW was able to successfully negotiate a code of conduct with Yum! Brands, the parent company of Taco Bell, to prevent its suppliers from engaging in indentured servitude. The agreement also raised wages 1¢ per pound of tomatoes, adding as much as $7,000 per year to the average worker's pay, a raise that is almost enough for workers to reach the national poverty level. This agreement was announced at a press conference at the headquarters Yum! Brands in Louisville, Kentucky, in March 2005. CIW activists had marched to the company headquarters to protest, but instead they became the audience for this important announcement. After the success of the CIW action against Taco Bell, it secured similar agreements with McDonald's, Walmart, Burger King, Subway, Whole Foods, Chipotle, and other major tomato purchasers. The CIW was successful because its demands were clear and it applied economic pressure on as well as public shame to a well-known brand. This coalition offered a political voice to a group that has almost no formal political power: poor, mostly undocumented, migrant workers in the United States. Similar to the UFW in the 1960s, the CIW used a boycott to gain concessions that were not obtainable through strikes or protest actions.

The CIW went on to enact its Fair Food Program, a collaboration of workers, farmers, and major retail chains, including Subway, Walmart, and McDonalds, in which brands agree to fair wages and working conditions throughout their supply chain. In 2015, the CIW was awarded the Presidential Medal for Extraordinary Efforts Combating Modern-Day Slavery.

The Great American Boycott

On May 1, 2006, the Great American Boycott organizers called on immigrants and their allies to avoid buying, selling, or working with businesses or schools in the United States. This May Day boycott was a response to growing anti-immigrant sentiment, a way to demonstrate the extent to which everyone relies on the work of undocumented immigrants. The aim of this campaign was to shift public opinion as well as influence lawmakers, and it used market tactics rather than a market campaign aimed at a business. This event was organized by a small group of activists in Los Angeles who were inspired by the efforts of Cesar Chávez and others in the 1960s. News of the boycott-protest spread quickly through social media, and labor unions, immigration advocacy groups, and religious groups in Los Angeles soon joined the efforts.[25] The actions were intended to protest the Minutemen, an anti-immigrant group, as well as a congressional bill making it a felony offense to be or to aid an undocumented person in the United States. According to Jesse Diaz, one of the leading coordinators of the boycott, "People are ready for a boycott . . . to use their power as consumers to send a message to the Senate and the Minutemen, and whatever other anti-immigrant group, that we will no longer tolerate their attacks."[26] Diaz was born in Los Angeles in 1964, and as a child, he was exposed to the Chicano empowerment movement that was percolating in the city. The poverty, discrimination, and racism he experienced as a child and young adult propelled him into political organizing later in life.[27] Diaz, along with Javier Rodriguez, a labor organizer, hosted a series of meetings with Father Estrada from La Placita Church and Angela Zambrano from the Central American Resource Center to plan the logistics of the boycott. Rodriguez was born in Coahuila, Mexico, in 1964, the son of a labor organizer. He was deported from the United States as a child and experienced struggle and discrimination when he later returned to the United States without documentation. Rodriguez became politicized in 1965 when he attended a rally against police brutality, and has worked on behalf of undocumented immigrants since that time.

Some natural allies of the boycott effort were not initially on board because the idea of a national boycott was daunting. The UFW, for example, was skeptical that a small group of organizers in Los Angeles could raise enough awareness to make the boycott effective. Then, on January 17, 2006, Rodriguez published an opinion piece in *La Opinión*, the largest Spanish language newspaper in the

United States, calling for mass demonstrations and a boycott on May Day. Within two weeks, more than one hundred regional and national organizations had signed on to participate with their members. Organizers used political purchasing, direct actions, and social media (including a website, Facebook page, and Twitter account) to spread word about the action.

On the day of the Great American Boycott, hundreds of thousands of protesters took to the streets in seventy U.S. cities. In Los Angeles, 500,000 protesters marched downtown, and in Chicago, 400,000 activists turned out to march.[28] Labor unions and Latin American countries joined the boycott in solidarity with U.S. activists, and stores closed in New York, Los Angeles, and Chicago because they were understaffed. "Lettuce, tomatoes and grapes went unpicked in fields in California and Arizona, which contribute more than half the nation's produce, as scores of growers let workers take the day off."[29] Truckers in Los Angeles and Long Beach took the day off, and meatpacking companies such as Tyson Foods and Cargill closed their plants for the day due to their heavy reliance on immigrant workers. The economic effects of the boycott were minimal, but it raised public awareness of the U.S. reliance on undocumented workers. The congressional bill making it a felony to be undocumented in the United States did not pass, but it is not clear what role the boycott action played in its failure. The Great American Boycott achieved its goal of raising awareness of our reliance on immigrant labor.

The Cristal Campaign

In July 2006, Jay-Z, rapper and record company CEO, called for a boycott of Cristal, a $300-per-bottle champagne popularized by its frequent mentions in rap songs.[30] This was a market campaign because its organizer focused on a specific business. Jay-Z was responding to a magazine interview in which Frederic Rouzaud, the Cristal managing director, said the company was not happy about the attention his product received from the hip-hop community: "What can we do? We can't forbid people from buying it. I'm sure Dom Perignon or Krug would be delighted to have their business."[31] Jay-Z interpreted Rouzaud's comment as a racist attempt to distance Cristal from black Americans who had made Cristal a hip-hop household name.

Beyond calling for a boycott, Jay-Z removed the references to Cristal in his songs from his live shows and encouraged other artists to do the same. New York club owners saw a drop in Cristal sales in the months following the boycott, but overall, it had little economic effect because the United States accounts for only 15 percent of the Cristal market.[32] Jay-Z's efforts did effectively sever the alliance between Cristal and hip-hop that he had helped to create, and artists no longer refer to this bubbly in their songs.

The Love Guru Campaign

In summer 2008, Rajan Zed, a Hindu religious leader, called for a global boycott of Mike Myer's movie *The Love Guru* because he believed it mocked Hinduism.[33] This was a market campaign proper because its goal was to change the political actions of a business entity. Zed, an Indian immigrant, is a longtime activist for interfaith acceptance and serves as the president of the Universal Society of Hinduism. He gained national recognition when he delivered the first Hindu prayer to be offered at the U.S. Senate as a guest chaplain invited by Senate majority leader Harry Reid (D-NV) on July 12, 2007. He used this national platform to speak out against the portrayal of Hinduism in *The Love Guru*. Zed was soon joined in the boycott by the Conference of Catholic Bishops, some prominent Jewish rabbis, Presbyterian ministers, Buddhists, and Native American and civil rights leaders. Rabbi ElizaBeth W. Beyer called on all Americans to boycott *The Love Guru*: "It is unfortunate that the comedy jabs at a culture of which many Americans are not familiar. It leaves viewers with a distorted, sexually flagrant parody.... In the case of this movie, we owe it to our Hindu friends to speak out against this misleading sham. Gross distortions of another culture do not lead to improved relations, tolerance and understanding. They lead towards disrespect. Please join me in a boycott of this movie."[34] Zed used social and mainstream media to spread the word, and he organized a petition that received over 5,000 signatures. *The Love Guru* bombed at the box office and was gone from theaters after just five weeks. Zed credited the boycott for the failure of the film, but its 14 percent rating on the popular film-rating site Rotten Tomatoes undoubtedly played a part. As one reviewer put it, "*The Love Guru* movie may be more offensive to fans of humor than it is to Hindus."[35] The distributor of the film, Paramount Pictures, did not comply with demands to stop the sales of the DVD, but the speedy reaction from religious leaders around the world sent a strong signal to those in the film industry that they should be more careful when depicting religion and religious leaders.

The Boycott Arizona Campaign

In 2010, immigrant rights activists called for a boycott of the state of Arizona for passing state Senate Bill (SB) 1070. This was a campaign that used market tactics to influence lawmakers rather than a market campaign proper. SB 1070 requires residents to carry proof of citizenship at all times and gives law enforcement officials the power to verify immigrant status during police stops. The law also imposes penalties for people who aid undocumented people in the state. Critics of the law say that it encourages racial profiling, but supporters respond that it does not allow law enforcement officers to stop people based solely on race.[36]

SB 1070 made national headlines that spurred protests across the nation and a boycott of the state of Arizona.

On May 1, exactly four years to the day of the Great American Boycott, protesters took to the streets in over seventy cities across the United States to protest SB 1070.[37] Arizona Representative Raúl Grijalva (D-AZ) was the first to publicly call for a boycott of his state, and the cities of San Francisco, Los Angeles, Oakland, Minneapolis, Denver, Seattle, and others soon followed suit by barring their employees from work-related travel to Arizona.[38] Some cities also divested from companies headquartered in Arizona. A handful of organizations cancelled major events in the state to protest the law, including the American Immigration Lawyers Association and the World Boxing Council. Zack De la Rocha, the singer of the popular band Rage Against the Machine, called for a musicians' boycott of the state. Dubbed The Sound Strike action, De la Rocha convinced many prominent musical acts to boycott Arizona, including Kanye West and My Chemical Romance.

In a "social-media era in which protesters can organize at the drop of a tweet,"[39] activists used online tools to gather boycott supporters. Within days of the passage of SB 1070, a boycott petition and three "Boycott Arizona" Facebook pages were created that received support from over 20,000 people.[40] In response to the boycott, Tea Party activists called for a buycott of the state, encouraging people who supported the law to visit Arizona and patronize its businesses.[41] In an attempt to stop the boycott, the Arizona Hotel and Lodging Association set up the Facebook page "Don't Boycott AZ Tourism" to raise awareness of the effects of the boycott on the 200,000 Arizonians employed in the tourism industry.

Boycotts are nothing new to Arizona, a state that lost hundreds of millions of tourist dollars in the 1980s when the governor cancelled Dr. Martin Luther King Day, but the size of the SB 1070 boycott was not anticipated by public officials. According to Michele Reagan (R), a state representative who signed the bill, "The majority of us who voted yes on that bill, myself included, did not expect or encourage an outcry from the public. . . . Nobody envisioned boycotts." Even though a poll indicated that a majority of Americans supported Arizona's immigration law two years after its implementation passed, the minority voices of undocumented residents and their allies were amplified by the boycott action.[42]

The Boycott Arizona campaign was a leaderless, grassroots, online, networked campaign, the effectiveness of which is hard to measure. In the first few years of the boycott, many tourists and dozens of conventions went elsewhere.[43] The boycott cost the state an estimated $141 million dollars in the first six months of the boycott,[44] but the effects were soon muted by a rebounding economy in the state. The author of the law, Russell Pearce (R), was voted out of office in a wave of anti–SB 1070 sentiment, and business leaders came together to effectively counter similar proposals by the state legislature. Glenn Hamer, the president of the Arizona Chamber of Commerce and Business, stated that "there was simply no way to expect that level of reaction. . . . It's now clear to the mainstream business community that there are consequences to going it alone on immigration."[45] Most provisions of SB 1070 were overturned in the courts, but the "show your papers" provision was upheld, and 100,000 Latinos left Arizona in the year after the law was passed.[46] The long-term effect of the Arizona boycott is damage to the reputation of the state.[47] The boycott was clearly effective in raising awareness of the issue and letting state leaders know that their policy actions have consequences. It also was a way for undocumented people without a formal political voice to express their opposition to the policy and for those with a minority opinion on the subject to exert political influence.

The Barneys and Macy's Campaign

In 2012, Reverend Al Sharpton and other civil rights leaders in New York called for a joint boycott against Macy's and Barneys for racially profiling black shoppers, which is also referred to as "shop and frisk."[48] This was a market campaign proper that sought to change the political practices of retailers, and the action came after a stream of incidents that were covered in mainstream media. In 2012, Constant Quedraogo, a young black man, was detained by Macy's store security for attempting to return items he had previously purchased.[49] A year later, Art Palmer was detained and questioned after he made a purchase at Macy's in New York. Later that month, two undercover New York police detectives detained Trayon Christian at Barneys after he purchased a $350 Ferragamo belt. A few months later, Kayla Phillips was stopped by security officers outside Barneys after purchasing a $2,500 designer handbag.[50] They questioned whether she had stolen the credit card she had used to purchase the purse. The incidents gained national attention when Rob Brown, an actor best known for his work on HBO *Treme*, was detained and walked through Macy's in handcuffs after purchasing a watch for his mother.[51] After learning of these alleged incidents of profiling, Sharpton spearheaded the boycott. Sharpton, who started as a child preacher touring with gospel great Mahalia Jackson and later worked as James Brown's tour manager, has been advocating for black Americans most of his life. Reverend Sharpton is now a former media host and White House advisor who uses his considerable public capital in high-profile cases of racial injustice. For the Macy's and Barneys boycott, Sharpton mobilized thousands of concerned New Yorkers to march in response to the incidents, and he asked everyone to boycott these retailers until they changed their policies for catching shoplifters. Sites across the blogosphere joined in with calls to boycott the retailers, including Feministing and Jezebel.

Barneys and Macy's would not provide any information about the economic impact of the joint boycott, but both retailers quickly established new policies for detaining customers. They also wisely slowed the protest momentum by meeting with black leaders and capitulating to their policy demands as soon as the boycott action went public. A few years later, the retailers settled lawsuits brought by customers who were racially profiled. (In an interesting twist, Jay-Z was targeted by an unsuccessful Change.org petition that received 59,000 signatures to compel him to cut his ties with Barneys.)

The joint market campaign against Barneys and Macy's successfully altered the way both companies treat people of color in their stores, and other major retailers followed suit. The reputational threat posed by the joint boycott was enough to radically alter the way black Americans are treated by major retailers. Consumer activism was used to obtain better corporate compliance with existing federal antidiscrimination laws.

#BlackLivesMatter Boycotts

The #BlackLivesMatter movement has employed two major boycott actions: a boycott of the American Legislative Exchange Council (ALEC) for its stance on "stand your ground" laws and the Black Friday boycott (on the busiest shopping day of the year) after Officer Darren Wilson was found not guilty in the shooting death of Michael Brown in Ferguson, Missouri.[52] The #BlackLivesMatter campaign was created in 2012 by Alicia Garza, Patrisse Cullors, and Opal Tometi, three black queer women who coordinated across coasts.[53] Garza, who lives in Los Angeles, devised the hashtag that would become the campaign name with the Facebook post: "Black people, I love you. I love us. Our lives matter. Black Lives Matter."[54] Prior to this campaign, Garza had worked on campaigns for domestic worker rights, antiracism, and antiviolence against trans* and gender nonconforming people. Cullors, who lives in Oakland, California, is also a lifelong social justice advocate. As a child, she witnessed family members experience police brutality, and this inspired her to work on law enforcement accountability initiatives.[55] Tometi, the daughter of Nigerian immigrants, is a writer based in New York. She had worked as an immigrant rights organizer prior to creating most of the social media infrastructure for #BlackLivesMatter.[56] Social media facilitated movement organizing across a great distance. Consumer activism is one of many tools used by the movement.

#BlackLivesMatter started in the wake of the verdict in the trial of George Zimmerman, a neighborhood watch volunteer.[57] Zimmerman shot and killed seventeen-year-old Trayvon Martin in the housing complex where Martin's family lived in Florida. Martin was walking home from a convenience store where he had just purchased an Arizona Ice Tea and a bag of Skittles. Zimmerman assumed that Martin intended to engage in criminal activity, so he followed Martin, had a physical struggle, shot, and killed the teen. After a lengthy trial that riveted the nation, Zimmerman was found not guilty. The #BlackLivesMatter campaign is critical of the structural racism that persists in the United States, especially as it manifests in the killing of unarmed black people by law enforcement and vigilantes. This campaign is not a market campaign proper; rather, it is a campaign that uses market tactics. Busloads of riders travelled from New York to Ferguson, Missouri, in 2014 after Officer Wilson shot Brown. Hundreds of protests have taken place in cities and towns across the United States to protest police brutality toward black Americans since 2012. Campaign organizers are amassing support employing boycott actions and social media, through the use of Facebook, Twitter, Tumblr, and other web pages. The organizers of #BlackLivesMatter set up a Tumblr page to encourage activists to share ideas, information, and tactics with one another.

In response to the Martin shooting, #BlackLivesMatter and the liberal advocacy group, Color of Change (COC), called for a boycott of ALEC, the conservative lobbying organization responsible for promoting the "stand your ground" gun laws in multiple states that probably emboldened Zimmerman to shoot Martin. COC had unsuccessfully called for a boycott of ALEC over its promotion of voter ID laws that disproportionately affect people of color, but it had gained little traction for the action until the Martin shooting.[58] After a petition signed by over 100,000 people, a phone campaign directly involving ALEC companies, and intense social media pressure, over thirty companies withdrew their support from ALEC, including Walmart, Intuit, Kraft, the Coca-Cola Company, Procter & Gamble, GM, Amazon.com, Wendy's, and the Bill and Melinda Gates Foundations. More than fifty legislators also cut ties with ALEC. According to Gabriel Rey-Goodlatte, COC chief strategist, "Because of this campaign and others, corporations are increasingly sensitive to the way they can be held accountable for their associations. Companies may be taking a second look at many of their relationships, and this presents a huge opportunity to challenge corporate involvement in politics and policy across many issue areas."[59]

In 2014, #BlackLivesMatter protesters called for another boycott of Black Friday (the busy shopping day after Thanksgiving) in response to the grand jury decision not to indict Officer Wilson.[60] On that day, protesters gathered outside of big retail stores such as Walmart in dozens of major cities. In Oakland, California, about twenty people chained themselves to the door at a subway station heavily used by holiday shoppers, and three hundred activists protested at a mall in San Francisco. In New York, a crowd gathered outside Macy's (see figure 3.2). The aim of these direct consumer actions was to raise awareness of persistent

FIGURE 3.2   #BlackLivesMatter protest outside Macy's, New York City, November 2014

racism on a day dedicated to shopping. As a Chicago protester, Heather Loring-Albright, put it, "getting the best sales is just silly when people's lives are being wrecked every single day."[61]

The Black Friday boycott had some economic success, leading to an 11 percent drop in sales compared to the previous year, even with a rebounding economy.[62] The broader #BlackLivesMatter campaign has pushed for policy reform, and to date, about a dozen bills have been introduced in Congress to increase police accountability. The Death in Custody Reporting Act was introduced in 2013, requiring states to keep track of the number and circumstances of people who die in police custody and for attorney generals to analyze this information.[63] The #BlackLivesMatter campaign has also raised public awareness to the point that the police and vigilante killings of other unarmed people, which would have otherwise gone virtually unnoticed, now appear in the national headlines. These includes the deaths of Eric Garner, a forty-three-year-old father of six with asthma, who was killed by an officer using an illegal chokehold in July of 2014; twenty-two-year-old John Crawford, who was shot in Walmart by police for handling a BB rifle he had picked up off the shelf in August 2014; Ezell Ford, a twenty-five-year-old man who was shot in the back by an officer in Los Angeles in August 2014; Dante Parker, a thirty-six-year-old newspaper reporter who was misidentified, was arrested, and died from injuries from a Taser while in police custody in Victorville, California, in August 2014; twelve-year-old Tamir Rice in Cleveland who was shot by police while playing with a toy gun in November 2014; and Walter Scott, who was shot in the back by Officer Michael Slager after a traffic stop, who then planted a Taser near his body in South Carolina in April 2015 (a case that came to light because a hidden bystander recorded the shooting). #BlackLivesMatter put these issues on the national agenda, and the campaign continues to pressure officials using a variety of tactics, including consumer activism.

The Food Network–Paula Deen Campaign

In 2013, Paula Deen, cooking-show host, also known as "the butter queen," admitted in a deposition for a workplace discrimination suit that she used the n-word in the past and had allowed bigoted behavior to take place in her restaurants. The campaign against her was a market campaign proper because it took aim at The Food Network for political reasons. According to the lawsuit, in reference to planning a "true southern plantation-style wedding" for her brother, Deen told her employees, "Well, what I would really like is a bunch of little niggers to wear long-sleeve white shirts, black shorts and black bow ties, you know in the Shirley Temple days, they used to tap dance around." No one person or organization initiated the boycott, but some celebrities spoke out in ways that probably mobilized viewers. Wendy Williams, the host of a popular daytime television talk show, told viewers, "[Paula Deen] seems to think that it's okay. It's not okay. It just goes to show you money doesn't buy you class, it only exposes who you really are. Stupid is as stupid does." Jackée Harry, a sitcom star; Reverend Sharpton; and Whoopi Goldberg chastised Deen for her use of the n-word and nostalgia for the pre–Civil War era. Some celebrities also defended Deen's use of the n-word, including Howard Stern, shock jock; O. J. Simpson; and Stacey Dash, a conservative commentator. The celebrity back and forth on social media raised the profile of this leaderless consumer campaign.

When the deposition documents came to light, Deen gave a widely watched interview on the *Today Show*, imploring the audience to forgive her and stating that she does not consider herself to be racist. This appeal did not silence the critics, and in the face of boycott pressure and a Twitter campaign that reappropriated the hashtag #PaulaDeenTVShows, companies that did business with Deen quickly cut ties, including Walmart, Caesars Entertainment (which operated four Deen-themed restaurants), Home Depot, Target, QVC, Sears, and Kmart.[64] Calls to boycott The Food Network and Deen's corporate sponsors were very effective in sending the message that racism in the workplace would not be tolerated by the network.

In response, Deen's supporters made a strong stand against her firing. They organized a counterbuycott, and as a result, sales of Deen's cookbooks soared during the controversy.[65] Deen supporters also called for a boycott of The Food Network to put pressure on the company to rehire the popular host. Multiple Change.org petitions were posted within days of the controversy, garnering between 700 and 38,000 signatures. On Facebook, the "We Support Paula" page had nearly 600,000 "likes," mostly from Southern white women.[66] Deen's departure from The Food Network caused its ratings to slump,[67] and in 2014, Deen launched The Paula Deen Network to which subscribers can tune in for $10 a month. All told, the boycott efforts against Deen were symbolically but not economically effective because she continues to profit from her successful cooking enterprise. The Food Network's firing of Deen did send a strong message against racism, but the network suffered economic consequences for taking this stand.

The McDonald's Campaign

In December 2014, Korean American leaders called for a national boycott of McDonald's after an employee struck a Korean customer with a broomstick at a restaurant in Queens, New York.[68] This was a market campaign proper, directed at a business entity. James Jin Kim, a sixty-two-year-old patron, complained about the slow service at the restaurant, and in response, Rooshi Sajjad, an employee, hit him with a broomstick that barely missed his head. Protesters gathered outside of the Queens McDonald's after the release of the video, and an Internet campaign ensued.[69] The *Korean Times* and the *New York Times* ran stories about the tension between McDonald's employees and older Korean Americans who frequented the establishment and stayed for hours, often ordering only a cup of coffee. This incident epitomizes a cultural clash; Korean traditions dictate elderly people should be treated "like gold." As Young Jin Kim, the chair of the Korean American Business Council of New York put it, "Respecting elders is particularly serious and important," a reverence that supersedes business interests.[70]

Christine Colligan, the leader of the Korean Parents Association of New York, spearheaded the boycott efforts. Colligan had emigrated to the United States from Korea in 1983 to work as a translator for an equestrian school in New Jersey. She was the middle child in a family of nine, and her father worked on the first car ever created in Korea (fashioned from scrap metal from U.S. army jeeps). As head of the Parents Association, she organized teacher appreciation days, parenting workshops, and a teacher exchange program. The McDonald's action was Colligan's first foray into activist politics. She has continued along the activist path, and in 2016, she organized a campaign in support of Seongsoo Kim, an elderly man who was beaten by an unknown assailant in a New York hospital.

The McDonald's boycott failed to put even the slightest dent in sales at that Queens location where the incident occurred, let alone the daily U.S. sales of the company; however, the company had to consider the potential damage to its reputation. In response to the campaign, McDonald's changed its franchise seating policies. State representative Ron Kim (D) brokered an agreement for extended seating hours for Korean American patrons and sensitivity training for employees. This market campaign raised awareness about the mistreatment of older people of color in this fast food establishment, and it improved corporate compliance with federal antidiscrimination laws.

Market Tactics for Racial and Economic Justice Outside the United States

U.S. activists organized three market campaigns aimed at racial/economic justice for people of color in other countries from 2004 to 2014 that generated national attention and participation. All three campaigns used boycotts and social media tools to achieve their goals for workers in Honduras, China, and Bangladesh.

The Russell Athletics Campaign

In 2009, USAS enjoyed their biggest achievement when they forced Russell Athletics, the largest U.S. producer of sportswear, to rehire 1,200 employees in a Honduran factory.[71] This was a market campaign proper that sought to change the political business practices of the company. Russell had closed the factory to put a stop to union organizing, and in response, students at ninety universities convinced their schools to sever campus contracts with Russell Athletics. Founded in 1997, USAS is the largest student-led labor organization in the country, boasting over 250 campus affiliates. USAS mobilized students to advocate for poor workers of color in another country through consumer activism in the United States. Beyond a boycott, students engaged in direct action by protesting outside the National Basketball Association (NBA) finals in Orlando and Los Angeles. They also started a Twitter campaign targeting Dick's Sporting Goods, a major Russell Athletics retailer, and passed out fliers detailing the union-busting efforts outside Sports Authority locations across the country. A small group of enterprising students also went to the residence of Warren Buffett, the owner of Russell's parent company, but he was not home. They delivered a letter to Russell Athletics signed by sixty-five members of Congress citing "severe violations" of labor rights.

This case was a rare example in which direct economic pressure compelled action as opposed to the more common path to effectiveness—damage to a reputation through media attention. All told, the campaign cost Russell Athletics $50 million in lost sales. Russell Athletic officials signed an agreement promising not to fight future unionizing efforts at other factories, reinstated all 1,200 employees, awarded them $2.5 million in back pay, and reestablished all union rights. This unprecedented victory in antisweatshop activism cut across race, economic, and national lines because mostly white students of economic privilege were the advocates for the interests of poor workers of color in Honduras.

The Apple Campaign

In February 2012, the activist organization Sum of Us collaborated with Change.org to deliver over 250,000 petitions to Apple stores in six cities protesting the working conditions of people of color at the FoxConn factory in southern China.[72] This was a market campaign proper, whose aim was to change Apple production practices. A month earlier, the *New York Times* had exposed working conditions that included employees working long hours with no breaks, their exposure to dangerous chemicals, and the repetitive nature of the work leading to suicides.[73]

Sum of Us is a new breed of activist organizations. It is a virtual group that has no central office and only a tiny staff scattered across the globe, working on their laptops from home and coffee shops.[74] This online organization has 4 million members who also use their laptops to engage in consumer activism to hold corporations accountable for environmental pollution and disasters, food prices, global financial crises, and the like with the tagline "fighting for people over profits." Sum of Us was founded by Taren Stinebrickner-Kauffman, an Australian American activist and the daughter of two professors. Her father, Bruce Stinebrickner, a political science professor, coauthored a textbook with Robert Dahl, a famed political theorist known for his work on the democratic effects of corporate power. Stinebrickner-Kauffman's organization has a staff of about twenty-five web-savvy activists who coordinate consumer campaigns with a radical systemic critique. Their website states that "corporate injustices are largely left to continue unabated. But the world doesn't have to be this way. And here's the secret. We own the corporations that are causing these problems. They rely on us to buy their products. They count on us to buy their stock. They need us to work for them. They need us to continue to elect governments that let them get away with murder. We are SumOfUs.org, and we're not going to take it anymore."[75] In addition to the Sum of Us members' work on Foxconn, unaffiliated grassroots consumer activists also created multiple Facebook pages, such as "Apple Boycott" and "Boycott Apple," in response to revelations about the FoxConn working conditions. Concerned private individuals crafted over twenty petitions on the Change.org platform alone.

The economic impact of this short-lived boycott was probably nil because the company was enjoying historic profits of nearly $40 billion in annual profits, but Apple, which presents itself as a fresh, hip, and socially conscious corporation, immediately responded to the threat to its brand. The company paid $250,000 to join the Fair Labor Association and performed an audit of human rights conditions at all of its 229 partnering facilities, which uncovered that one-third were not in compliance with hazardous waste handling and 62 percent were not in compliance with the maximum work-hour policy.[76] Apple and FoxConn agreed to raise the minimum wage and cap the workweek at forty-nine hours at the facility. Apple funded much of the costs for improving wages, reducing overtime, increasing the number of annual audits, and hiring more workers to keep up with demand without taxing employees.[77] Consumers did not have to actually abstain from purchasing Apple products because the threat of a boycott was enough. This campaign shows the impressive power of U.S. consumers as advocates for the interests of people in other countries who are suffering as a result of the business practices of U.S. firms.

The Bangladesh Factory Campaign

In 2014, consumer activists were able to secure better conditions for factory workers in Bangladesh after a long struggle. This was a campaign that used market channels to bring about policy change rather than a market campaign proper. Working conditions in Bangladesh had been cause for concern for U.S. retailers for years, and in November 2012, a fire caused by "unpardonable negligence" at the Tazreens Fashion factory in Bangladesh killed 112 people.[78] Workers at this factory were manufacturing clothing for Sears, Walmart, The Gap, H&M, and other retailers. In the months leading up to the fire, workers had staged protests and demonstrations demanding better wages. On the night the fire broke out, more than 1,000 employees were working overtime to fill orders for various international clothing brands. The fire started on the ground floor, where fabric and yard were illegally stored without fireproofing. The building lacked an outdoor fire escape and a sprinkler system, and none of the fire extinguishers were working. Managers had ordered workers to ignore the other labor rights organizations created by the Bangladesh Fire and Building Safety Agreement, requiring independent inspection of factories.[79] This agreement would have protected the 4 million workers—mostly women—who worked in the 4,500 manufacturing facilities in Bangladesh, but retailers refused to sign on because they did not want the expense and legal liability.

In April 2013, the Rana Plaza garment factory collapsed in Bangladesh, killing 1,127 people. One day before the collapse, an engineer who inspected the facility issued a dire warning that the building was unsafe after finding cracks in the building from shoddy construction with the addition of new floors.[80] The building was owned by Mohammad Sohel Rana, a local political leader who wielded power in the region with impunity through threats and violence. A media crew had filmed the cracks in the Rana Plaza building the day before the collapse, but Rana ordered workers to return to the building the following morning. The building collapsed as workers came in for the morning shift. After the collapse, the cofounder and president of the National Garment Workers Federation of Bangladesh, Amirul Haque Amin, created a Change.org petition to compel major retailers to compensate the families of workers who died in the collapse, and the petition gathered 95,000 signatures. Amin's interest in worker rights started when he was a college student at the University of Dhaka in the 1980s, when he volunteered with an international trade union and witnessed worker abuses. Amin had been fighting for better working conditions in Bangladesh factories for over three decades using conventional organizing tools and with limited success. He turned to an online petition platform for the Rana Plaza action—his most effective work to date. International outcry was swift, and in the U.S., consumer activists took to the streets to protest retailers that profit from unsafe manufacturing in Bangladesh on the backs of the poor, mostly women of color.

Within a year of the Rana collapse, over seventy global brands had signed the Bangladesh Fire and Building Safety Agreement, including Target, Macy's, J. C. Penney, and Kohl's. Students organized at Duke University, New York University, Columbia University, Cornell University, Georgetown University, and other schools to work only with retailers who had signed the agreement. The Bangladeshi safety accord ensures the inspection of five hundred facilities each year and allocates money for inspections and repairs.[81]

The Gap and Walmart refused to sign the safety accord because it was not "financially feasible."[82] Instead, they came up with their own plan that had weaker accountability provisions.[83] These two companies then became the target of a consumer activism campaign involving social media shaming, a boycott, and direct action.[84] Organizers created Facebook pages such as "Enough Is Enough: Boycott Gap and Walmart." USAS created the websites Walmart-DeathTraps.com and GapDeathTraps.com, encouraging consumer activists to deliver letters to the stores and to organize demonstrations outside these retail locations. A Change.org petition urging The Gap and Walmart to sign the safety accord gathered 101,000 signatures. Consumer activists across the United States organized protests outside The Gap and Walmart stores that intensified as summer 2013 wore on. Staff from the Bangladesh Center for

Worker Solidarity went on an End Death Traps speaking tour throughout the United States to encourage consumers to put pressure on Walmart and The Gap to sign the safety accord through boycotting. To date, these retail giants have not signed the accord.

The United States is experiencing a renaissance in manufacturing, partially as a result of intense pressure from networked consumer activists because companies that profit from outsourcing face risks to their reputations if something goes wrong in the supply chain. Retailers are increasingly choosing to locate manufacturing closer to home.[85] The networked character of consumer activism has created an environment in which retailers will pay more up front for better assurance that their brand is safe. One example of this is Disney's complete withdrawal of production from Bangladesh after the Rana factory collapse, and its previous withdrawal of manufacturing from Pakistan, Belarus, and Ecuador for poor factory conditions. Worker rights organizations do not recommend companies' withdrawing from countries that fail to establish and enforce safe and fair working conditions because this would lead to the collapse of local economies that would ultimately hurt workers; but Disney's decision to pay much higher production costs for its merchandise to protect its brand speaks to the effectiveness of networked consumer activism.

The consumer activism around the Bangladesh fire and building collapse was successful in pressuring many major retailers to sign the Bangladesh safety accord. It also effectively raised public awareness of clothing purchased in the United States and factory conditions on the other side of the globe. Nevertheless, an Action Aid survey of workers who survived the Bangladesh collapse a year later found that half had difficulty paying their rent, two-thirds had issues buying food, and three out of four had not been able to return to work because of their injuries.[86] On the one-year anniversary of the Rana collapse, thirty protesters picketed outside Walmart in Chicago, encouraging the company to sign the Bangladesh safety accord.[87] The market campaign to reform Bangladesh factory working conditions was an unequivocal success in terms of bringing about its stated goal of policy reform, but it is also an important reminder that new policies are sometimes not enough to address inequalities.

Campaign Effectiveness

Most of the campaigns for racial and economic justice analyzed in this chapter were successful. In theory, success can be measured in many different ways: by measuring the number of participants, the politicizing effects on participants, or the rise in public awareness. In practice, with decentralized, often leaderless

TABLE 3.1 Effectiveness of racial and economic justice campaigns

CAMPAIGN	EFFECTIVE?
Apple-Foxconn	Yes
Arizona	Ongoing
Bangladesh factories	Yes
#BlackLivesMatter-ALEC	Ongoing
Cristal	No
Great American Boycott	Yes
Macy's-Barneys	Yes
McDonald's	Yes
Mt. Olive Pickle	Yes
Paula Deen–The Food Network	Yes
Russell Athletics	Yes
South Carolina	Yes
Taco Bell	Yes
The Love Guru	No
Washington Redskins	Ongoing
Effectiveness = 83%	

movements, it is impossible to measure the number of participants in consumer campaigns. Likewise, it is difficult to quantify the level of public awareness raised by a campaign. Survey data could illuminate the politicizing effects on participants, but this would require generating a representative sample of participants, which is not possible given the nebulous nature of these campaigns. For these reasons, I used a more direct measure of effectiveness: whether or not the campaign achieved its stated goal. Table 3.1 shows which campaigns achieved their goals, which did not, and which are still ongoing.

Three campaigns are ongoing: Boycott Arizona; the Washington Redskins campaign; and the Black Friday #BlackLivesMatter boycott, which has become an annual tradition. The Boycott Arizona campaign is considerably quieter than it was a few years ago, the #BlackLivesMatter movement still has steam, and activists show no signs of slowing their efforts to remove the *Redskins* name. For the ongoing campaigns, it is simply too early to evaluate their effectiveness. Two campaigns were unmitigated failures. The Cristal campaign was unsuccessful in putting a dent in corporate profits or getting the CEO to retract his statement, and *The Love Guru* campaign did not halt DVD distribution.

Ten of the remaining campaigns were effective in bringing about their desired goals. All the domestic and foreign campaigns for better working conditions were successful (Mt. Olive Pickle Company, Taco Bell, Apple, Bangladesh factories, and Russell Athletics). The campaign targeting Russell Athletics in Honduras reopened a factory and secured better wages and unionization, the actions concerning Bangladesh brought about a new international factory agreement, and the boycott of Apple led to immediate changes in labor policies at Foxconn. The two campaigns to mitigate biased customer treatment were also effective (Macy's-Barneys and McDonald's). In terms of racist remarks, the Cristal campaign was not successful, but efforts against Paula Deen were effective. The high success rate of market campaigns for racial and economic justice reported here is at least partially a function of the way I selected my sample. Campaigns that receive national media attention are, by definition, already successful in getting the message out in mainstream media, which increases the likelihood they will achieve their campaign goal.

Democratic Implications

Each of the market campaigns in this chapter strengthened U.S. democracy by improving multiple democratic measures. Table 3.2 reports the democratic

TABLE 3.2 Democratic contribution of racial and economic justice campaigns

CAMPAIGN	DEMOCRATIC SCORE (0–10)
Apple-Foxconn	5
Arizona	9
Bangladesh factories	5
#BlackLivesMatter-ALEC	7
Cristal	3
Great American Boycott	6
Macy's-Barneys	6
McDonald's	6
Mt. Olive Pickle	4
Paula Deen–The Food Network	4
Russell Athletics	5
South Carolina	6
Taco Bell	5
The Love Guru	4
Washington Redskins	4
Average = 5.26	

score for each campaign, ranging from 0 (no democratic inputs or outputs) to 10 (high democratic inputs and outputs). Actual scores range from 3 (the Cristal campaign) to 9 (the Arizona campaign), with an average score just over 5. This score is a blunt measure of democratic influence, a simple count of the different ways in which the campaign improved democratic inputs and outputs. We can conclude that all the campaigns improved multiple aspects of democracy, and on average, market campaigns for racial and economic justice strengthened five measures of democracy out of ten measured.

These campaigns expanded opportunities for political participation by furnishing an outlet for people without access to formal political channels (e.g., undocumented immigrants), making political participation easier, by providing a tool to achieve concrete policy outcomes with corporations that would not be possible via electoral politics, and by allowing people in the United States to exercise political pressure to change corporate practices in other countries. It is important to point out that, beyond empirical democratic measures, these campaigns vary in terms of involvement and the level of citizen engagement. For example, the Apple boycott gained traction quickly through social media use, which is a low involvement activity, while the Mt. Olive Pickle company mobilized student activists to remove Taco Bell from their campus, which was a more involved activity. These decentralized, often leaderless campaigns also varied in terms of how many people were mobilized. No hard data are available on how many people were involved in each campaign, but it is safe to say that the boycott of *The Love Guru*, for example, involved fewer people than the #BlackLivesMatter Black Friday boycott.

Promotes Robust Citizen Participation

The campaigns examined in this chapter increased overall rates of political participation because they offered an easy way for people to get involved without having to engage with the complex and often inaccessible formal policy process. Consumer activists were able to put political pressure on business entities by boycotting or signing a petition, which are types of activism that require little in the way of political knowledge or effort compared to casting a vote or lobbying a public official. These market campaigns also expanded political participation by providing an outlet for people who are disenfranchised from formal electoral politics, such as undocumented residents of Arizona and migrant workers with the Mt. Olive Pickle and Taco Bell campaigns. These market campaigns also expanded participation by pressing political concerns that are not easily addressed through the formal policy process. For example, the campaigns targeting Mt. Olive Pickle and Taco Bell effectively raised wages for employees, a result that would otherwise have required a multistate campaign for legislation to change farming industry regulations and enforcement. Instead, organizers were able to mobilize consumer activists to apply surgical pressure to the offending companies to bring about change in more targeted and efficient ways. These market campaigns also increased participation by allowing people in the United States to directly advocate on behalf of workers in other countries in a way that is not possible via electoral politics.

Promotes Political Equality in Participation and Representation

Market campaigns for racial and economic justice in the past decade have also improved democracy by promoting political equality in participation and representation. These campaigns gave voice to the politically voiceless—undocumented people affected by the actions of the Mt. Olive Pickle Company, Taco Bell, and the state of Arizona. Undocumented people and allies came together to protest the treatment of noncitizens with the Great American Boycott campaign, a political statement that could not have been made through formal electoral politics. In a similar fashion, consumer activists in the United States improved conditions for workers in Honduras, China, and Bangladesh, who lack formal standing in U.S. politics. Domestically, the #BlackLivesMatter campaign and consumer efforts against McDonald's, Macy's, and Barneys promoted political equality in participation and representation by giving a voice to the concerns of racial minorities who are not being adequately protected by corporate antidiscrimination laws.

People of color have historically engaged in electoral politics at a significantly lower rate than white people,[88] but market campaigns targeting companies for racial justice help to close that participation gap. In a similar vein, consumer activism against *The Love Guru*, the Washington Redskins, and the Confederate flag in South Carolina was a way for Indian Americans, Native Americans, and black Americans, respectively, to protest racial discrimination in the absence of laws preventing it. Consumer activists use free speech in the marketplace to counteract disparaging stereotypes protected under free speech laws.

Promotes the Will of the Majority

None of the market campaigns examined in this chapter promoted the will of the majority. Campaigns for racial and economic justice often push against the existing social and economic order. The concerns of marginalized groups, such as migrant workers and Native Americans, rarely draw the attention or public support of the U.S. majority.

Promotes Active Media

Most of the campaigns in this chapter promoted more active media by putting issues on the agenda that were not being covered by mainstream outlets. In three cases—Apple, the Bangladesh factory collapse, and the Paula Deen controversy—investigative journalism sparked marketplace activism, but for the remaining twelve campaigns, media coverage followed the activism. Most of the market campaigns in this chapter also advanced more active media by creating alternative media coverage through social media. The Boycott Arizona, #BlackLivesMatter, and Taco Bell campaigns were particularly effective in bringing alternative narratives to media coverage through their use of social media tools.

Improves Public Discussion on Policy Issues

All the consumer activism campaigns analyzed in this chapter improved public discussion on policy issues. Mass participation in market campaigns translated into a greater discussion and awareness of the meaning and significance of the Confederate flag, working conditions in the farming industry, the treatment of black and Korean customers at chain stores, portrayals of racial minorities in branding and popular culture, and the impact of U.S. corporate policies on workers in other countries. Social media has become a popular way to share information and spur public discussion about policy issues in a lively, activist way that is undoubtedly more appealing to many Americans than electoral politics or formal means of political discussion. Social media consumer activism lets people participate in policy discussions on their own schedule from the comfort of their home or on the go through their smartphone with friends and groups online. Consumer activism hinges on shaming business entities, and with the advent of social media, this is more possible than ever.

Promotes Political Equality in State Protection and Public Resources

The campaigns in this chapter improved racial equality by affecting the way the state protects people and allocates resources. People of color are profiled, harassed, and imprisoned at much higher rates than white Americans as a result of racial bias on the part of store security, police officers, prosecutors, and juries.[89] This systemic bias is unlawful because it establishes unequal justice in a country where the Fourteenth Amendment to the Constitution mandates that citizens receive equal protection under the law. The boycotts of McDonald's and the joint boycotts of Barneys and Macy's pressured these corporations to better enforce existing laws prohibiting discrimination. In a similar vein, the #BlackLivesMatter campaign is using market tactics to put pressure on the state through market channels to end unlawful policing practices. The aim of the campaigns against the states of Arizona and South Carolina was to overturn racial discriminatory laws to bring about equality in state protection.

Promotes Corporate Political Accountability

Campaigns for racial and economic discrimination in the past decade also strengthened U.S. democracy by improving corporate accountability in areas that are currently regulated by the state. The actions against Mt. Olive Pickle Company, Taco Bell, Russell Athletics, Apple, Bangladesh factories, and Paula Deen–The Food Network succeeded in achieving higher wages, safer working conditions, and better treatment of workers of color. As previously noted, the campaigns targeting Barneys, Macy's, and McDonald's held these corporations accountable for their discriminatory treatment of customers, and these public efforts put pressure on other companies to improve their practices as well for fear of facing a similar public shaming campaign. Other market campaigns checked corporations for the ways in which they represent people of color that are offensive but not unlawful, including boycotts of *The Love Guru*, Cristal, the Washington Redskins, and the states of South Carolina and Arizona. Consumer activism is a vehicle for holding business entities accountable for their political actions when the state tacitly or actively endorses problematic practices.

Promotes Government Accountability to Citizens

A few campaigns in this chapter used market channels to improve government accountability. Boycott organizers in the Arizona and South Carolina campaigns used consumer activism to directly target governments to improve their accountability to the people after exhausting legislative and legal channels. These actions are liable to be less effective than targeting business entities because only a fraction of state revenue comes from tourist dollars, so there is less of an imperative to protect the brand. Furthermore, although corporations can respond to threats from consumer activism in a rapid manner through a centralized CEO, state decision making is decentralized in the hands of many lawmakers and other concerns often override prudent state branding decisions.

Protects against the Encroachment of Minority Rights

Some of the campaigns examined in this chapter improved democracy by pro-tecting against the encroachment on the rights of minorities. Consumer activ-ism aimed at Barneys, Macy's, and McDonald's protected the rights of racial minorities to receive equitable customer treatment, free from racially motivated profiling and detainment. The #BlackLivesMatter campaign is a struggle to pro-tect the rights of racial minorities to be treated equitably in the eyes of the law. Campaigns targeting the Mt. Olive Pickle Company, Taco Bell, Paula Deen–The Food Network, and the Great American Boycott pushed back against the racially discriminatory treatment of people of color in the workplace. Poor workplace conditions are entwined with race because people of color are more likely to face discrimination, lower wages, and less safe working conditions than white people.[90]

Protects against Government Encroachment on Civil Liberties

Two of the market campaigns for racial and economic justice in the past decade improved democracy by mediating against state encroachment on the civil liber-ties of people of color. The boycott against the state of Arizona blew the whistle on a law that essentially permits racial profiling. This law is still in place, but the boycott raised awareness of the potential discriminatory effects of the law, which may diminish use of the law for racial profiling. There is no way to measure how the law might have been enforced without all the public attention it has received, but it is safe to say that police officers cannot racially profile with impunity when allies across the nation are watching. In similar fashion, the #BlackLivesMatter organized after George Zimmerman's vigilante shooting of Trayvon Martin in Florida. The police shooting of Michael Brown in Ferguson, Missouri, and the dozens of police shootings of unarmed black people that have happened since have put this topic on the national policy agenda. Legislatures across the country have proposed over sixty new bills to protect the civil liberties of people of color, including new body cameras and racial sensitivity training for officers. Few of these bills have actually been passed,[91] but over time, public attention to this issue will translate into fewer people of color being profiled, harassed, and shot by officers of the state.

Fifteen consumer activism campaigns aimed at racial and economic inequality made national news in the past decade. Most of these campaigns were effective in achieving their stated goals of improving wages and working conditions; put-ting an end to racial profiling by police and retailers; removing offensive images or stereotypes involving people of color; and raising awareness around the mistreatment of immigrants, migrant workers, and undocumented workers of color in the United States and other counties. These market campaigns fortified democracy in the United States by increasing participation in politics, promoting political equality in representation and state protection, improving discussions on public policy issues, improving government and corporate accountability, and protecting the rights and civil liberties of minorities. As has been the case throughout U.S. history, market campaigns opened new channels for political participation that attracted people who lacked access to formal political channels. Consumer activism continues to be a "weapon of the weak," a tool for those who are disenfranchised to have a voice in politics and policy. Social media have made consumer activism a much more powerful tool in the continuing struggle for racial/economic justice for people of color.

"600,000 BOSSES TELLING ME WHAT TO DO"

Campaigns for the Environment and Animal Rights

In 1986, the Earth Island Institute (EII) launched a national boycott to halt the common practice of intentionally netting dolphins to lure the tuna fish that swim beneath them.[1] This common technique had resulted in the deaths of many dolphins from drowning. The EII specifically targeted the three largest tuna brands for the boycott: Heinz (Starkist Tuna), Bumble Bee Seafoods, and Van de Kamp (Chicken of the Sea). The EII shamed these companies with ads featuring schoolchildren and celebrities. By 1990, the EII had established a new "Dolphin Safe" tuna label, adopted by Congress, that became the new industry standard.[2] Today, the EII International Marine Mammal Project enforces this law through a tuna oversight program that monitors fishing vessels, tuna canneries, ports, and storage facilities for over seven hundred companies.[3] The Dolphin Safe boycott effectively banned dolphin killing for 90 percent of the world's tuna markets.

The Dolphin Safe campaign was an early part of a growing trend toward greater concern for animal treatment in the United States, originating in the late twentieth century. The Animal Rights Movement (ARM) was formed in the two decades following the 1975 publication of the seminal book by the Australian philosopher Peter Singer, *Animal Liberation: A New Ethics for Our Treatment of Animals.*[4] ARM participants use boycotts, social media campaigns, divestment, and direct actions, including extra-legal actions (e.g., vandalism and arson), to challenge animal testing, factory farming, and the use of animal fur in apparel. Support for the ARM has increased significantly this past decade. The number of Americans who believe that animals should be given the same rights as humans has increased from 25 percent in 2003 to 32 percent in 2015, and the number of vegetarians has grown from 1 percent in 2009 to 5 percent in 2016.[5]

The Environmental Movement emerged in the 1970s, at the same time as the ARM, and because both causes involve the impact of humans on the natural world, the two movements share a great overlap in communities. Public support for environmental protection has grown significantly in the past four decades, and the tenets of the movement have become a permanent part of the national political agenda.[6] About half of Americans care "a great deal" about the pollution of drinking water, rivers, lakes, and reservoirs, and one-third are concerned about climate change.[7] Environmental activists have used consumer activism along with lobbying to pass major environmental bills at the national level, including the Clean Air Act, the Clean Water Act, and the Endangered Species Act.

The most extreme forms of consumer activism have involved environmental protection and animal rights. The Animal Liberation Front (ALF) and the Environmental Liberation Front (ELF) are two radical organizations with overlapping membership that target companies directly. The mission of ALF is to end "the 'property' status of nonhuman animals"; the ELF seeks to "defend and protect the Earth for future generations by means of direct actions."[8] Both of these groups routinely engage in extra-legal consumer activism to advance their causes.[9] From 1990 to 2010, ALF and ELF perpetrated more than 150 criminal acts against corporations, such as mailing envelopes to corporate executives with razor blades laced with rat poison; throwing pies in the faces of CEOs; and committing vandalism and arson at labs known to conduct animal testing, factory farms, circuses, fishing vessels, new housing developments, and the Bureau of Land Management and the Forest Service.[10] In 2002, the FBI put ALF and ELF at the top of its domestic terrorist threat list. This was a controversial decision because ALF and ELF actions cause property destruction rather than posing a threat to human life, and the FBI was later found to have engaged in the improper monitoring of activists.[11] Although most animal rights and environmental activism is not as extreme as the tactics used by ALF and ELF, it still poses significant risk to corporations that are concerned about preserving their image because public support is on the side of nonhuman animals and environmental protection.

In this chapter, I analyze the democratic implications of contemporary market campaigns for animal rights and environmental protection from 2004 to 2014 using the methodology described in chapter 3. Thirteen market campaigns fit the criteria for study. These campaigns employed all four primary types of consumer activism, but direct action was more common than in the campaigns for other causes. Out of the thirteen campaigns, eleven used direct actions, ten used boycotts and social media tools, and three used shareholder actions. I find that these campaigns improved democracy by increasing participation, public discussion, and corporate accountability. I also find that documentary films have been a popular instigator of consumer activism campaigns for environmental protection and animal rights.

Environmental Protection Campaigns

The Stop Staples Campaign

In July 2001, two nonprofit organizations, Forest Ethics and the Dogwood Alliance, kicked off a boycott against Staples, the office-supply store, to urge the company to stop selling products made from old-grown forests.[12] Forest Ethics is a Canadian organization that got its start in 1979 when a group of environmentally conscious residents on Vancouver Island organized to block a logging company from clear-cutting on a nearby mountain range. Dogwood Alliance was founded in 1996 to fight for the environmental interests of communities in the southern United States. The organization was cofounded by Cielo Sand and Denny Haldeman. Sand is an artist and organic farmer who grew up in the woods of Indiana and got involved in forest preservation as a young adult. Haldeman, an off-the-grid carpenter from Tennessee, has been active in forestry preservation issues for four decades.

The Stop Staples campaign was a market campaign proper because it sought to change the practice of a market entity. Old-growth forests are stands of trees that attract and provide habitat for a diverse wildlife, in turn increasing the biodiversity of the forest because of their considerable age. *Biodiversity* refers to the variety of living things in an ecosystem, and greater biodiversity is linked to longer sustainability of an ecosystem. The Stop Staples campaign started against the backdrop of a fierce decade-long policy debate about the preservation of old-growth forests. President Bill Clinton ignited the debate in 1993 with his Forest Conference and the subsequent locking up of large swaths of old-growth forests in the Pacific Northwest.[13] A decade later, consumer activists demanded that Staples stop selling products made from old-growth trees sourced from countries outside the United States.

The campaign kicked off with a national day of action when activists lined up outside over one hundred Staples stores to protest the company and raise public awareness of deforestation. For the next few years, environmental activists teamed up with college students across the nation to protest on college campuses and outside of Staples locations, circulating petitions, writing letters to local newspapers, and distributing educational leaflets in public locations.[14] Staples first responded by denying that it was using products made from old-growth timber and dismissing consumer activism as a legitimate political strategy. A Staples spokesperson said the company was being unfairly targeted: "Typically, what activist groups do in this day and age is go after the market place. And the typical strategy is to target the largest company within that sector because it's high profile."[15] In response, activists published an investigative report in 2002 confirming that Staples suppliers were sourcing from the ancient Canadian boreal forest and old-growth stands in Indonesia.[16]

After three years of direct consumer activism and boycott pressure, the Stop Staples campaign was able to claim victory in March 2004. The activists secured an agreement that Staples would stop using old-growth products, and that 30 percent of its paper products would be made from recycled materials. This agreement shifted practices industry-wide. Staples started purchasing products that were certified by the Forest Stewardship Council (FSC), which in turn put pressure on timber companies and pulp producers to change their practices.[17] The FSC now certifies products for all the major office-supply chains, and recycled paper products have become the industry norm.

The Kleercut Campaign

In November 2004, the environmental group Greenpeace started a consumer activism campaign targeting Kimberly-Clark for its use of old-growth forest in its Kleenex, Scott, Viva, and Cottonelle production. This was a market campaign proper because organizers called for a change in the practices of a market entity. The company was sourcing from suppliers that were clear-cutting the Canadian boreal forest, the largest remaining old-growth forest in North America. The process of clear-cutting removes all the trees in an area, which in turn devastates the ecology of that area, as opposed to sustainable selective cutting.

Greenpeace was founded in 1971 by Jim Bohlen, a U.S. navy veteran, and Dorothy and Irving Stowe, a married Quaker couple, all Canadian activists. Bohlen was an engineer who worked on a U.S. missile program before immigrating to Canada to protest the U.S. nuclear position in the Cold War. Dorothy Stowe had worked as a socialist organizer during college in Rhode Island, and Irving Stowe was a Yale-trained lawyer who had protested the war. After their marriage, they both took the surname *Stowe* in honor of author and abolitionist Harriet Beecher Stowe. The three activists were frustrated by the glacial pace of existing environmental organizations, so they created an organization based on pacifist direct action.

Greenpeace called for a consumer boycott of the Kleenex brand because of its high profile. More than seven hundred businesses, as well as twenty-two colleges and universities, boycotted or divested from the parent company of the brand, Kimberly-Clark.[18] Campaign organizers also used creative direct action to raise public awareness of their cause, such as sneaking into an annual shareholders' meeting and replacing a scheduled PowerPoint presentation with informative slides about the environmental record of Kimberly-Clark. Organizers planned over 1,000 protests, including one that locked down the company facility in Knoxville, Tennessee.[19] Creative activists also snuck into commercial shoots for Kleenex products to share facts on camera about the environmental destruction caused by the company, and others slipped fliers with "wiping away ancient forests" into boxes of Kleenex in retail locations.[20]

After five years of sustained pressure and boycott participation from an estimated half a million Greenpeace members, Kimberly-Clark caved to the pressure of consumer activism in 2009. The corporation agreed to use only timber approved by the FSC and pledged to use recycled materials for 40 percent of its products in North America.[21] The company introduced a new line of recycled products that appealed to environmentally conscious consumers.[22] The Kleercut campaign used boycott pressure, creative direct action, and some shareholder activism to put pressure on this industry leader, and in doing so, the activists set the standard for the industry.[23] This action was relatively unique in that Greenpeace enlisted hundreds of other business entities to stop using Kimberly-Clark products; some of these businesses undoubtedly aligned with the environmental group to avoid a boycott themselves.

The ExposeExxon Campaign

A coalition of environmental groups initiated a boycott of ExxonMobil in 2005, protesting efforts by the oil giant to debunk the scientific consensus that climate change is human-made and to protest its push for oil and gas exploration in the Arctic National Wildlife Refuge (ANWR),[24] the largest public wilderness in the United States. This was a market campaign proper because the efforts centered on a single business entity to change its political position, although the attention it garnered may have also influenced lawmakers. The campaign targeted ExxonMobil, the world's second largest oil company because of its record on environmental issues (which was worse than its competitors) and its outspoken criticism of the scientific findings that humans are responsible for climate change. At the time of the boycott, ExxonMobil was funding over forty public policy groups whose aim was to cast doubt on the concept of human-made climate change.[25]

The ExxonMobil boycott was the first time in consumer activism history that most major environmental organizations came together to target one company, including the Sierra Club, Defenders of Wildlife, the Natural Resources Defense Council, the Union of Concerned Scientists, the U.S. Public Interest Group, and

Move-On.org. This coalition was motivated to take action because the groups had essentially been locked out of policy discussions in Washington, DC, with a Republican-controlled White House and Congress.[26] With this combined effort, these groups mobilized hundreds of thousands of members to divest from and boycott the company. ExposeExxon also set up a website and used social media to promote its cause. Activists created an online petition specifically to stop the drilling in ANWR, which received over 35,000 signatures. Consumer activists also used direct action by protesting outside ExxonMobil gas stations across the United States. Celebrities joined everyday activists in chaining themselves to gas pumps. Nevertheless, ExxonMobil eventually responded to the campaign by digging in its heels. Representatives asserted that the company did recognize the dangers of climate change and that it was committed to investing in technology and research to lower greenhouse emissions.[27]

The ExposeExxon campaign was not effective in altering the behavior of ExxonMobil. The company initially experienced a statistically significant drop in stock value as a result of the boycott,[28] but in the last three months of 2005, profits rebounded. ExxonMobil made $9.9 billion, mostly through a hike in retail prices, and posted historic profits for the year.[29] Company lobbyists intensified their efforts to open ANWR for drilling, and President Obama signed a law allowing drilling in the Arctic in May 2015. The ExxonMobil CEO, Lee R. Raymond, was replaced by Rex Tillerson in late 2005, and Tillerson, who would go on to serve as Donald Trump's secretary of state, was even stauncher than his predecessor in publicly challenging climate-change science and funding policy groups for that purpose.[30] The ExposeExxon campaign channeled activism toward the company during a time when environmental groups had little influence in Washington, but the goals of the campaign were nebulous and ultimately not achieved.

The Nestlé Palm Oil Campaign

In 2010, Greenpeace targeted the food retailer Nestlé to stop deforestation in Indonesia during the process of palm oil production.[31] This was a market campaign proper because it targeted a market entity to change its practices. After just eight weeks of Greenpeace pressure, Nestlé came up with a new policy promising zero deforestation in its palm oil supply chain, to be enforced by the oversight group Forest Trust. This swift response was probably the result of Nestlé's experience being the target of the world's longest running boycott for its milk products, as well as the creative use of the media by Greenpeace to shame the company. Although activists did protest outside Nestlé headquarters, their most effective tactic was a spoof of a Kit Kat candy advertisement that went viral and was seen by nearly 1.5 million people (figure 4.1). In this video, a bored office worker bites

FIGURE 4.1   Greenpeace spoof of a Kit Kat ad, 2010

into a Kit Kat bar only to find that it is the finger of an orangutan, one of the species endangered by the clear-cutting of forests in Indonesia for palm oil production. Organizers also targeted Nestlé's Facebook page with excoriating comments about its rainforest destruction.

The demands of the Nestlé Palm Oil boycott were met before a national consumer boycott truly got underway. The success of this campaign is attributable to consumer activists' creative use of social media to raise awareness.[32] The company initially responded by trying to remove the video, but given this impossibility, they capitulated to the Greenpeace demands in a matter of months rather than years.[33] Nestlé also created a new social media crisis management department to respond to similar threats in the future.[34] This consumer activism campaign was an unmitigated success in achieving its goals, and thanks to social media, achieving them in record time.

The British Petroleum Campaign

In 2010, after an underwater oil spill off the coast of Louisiana killed eleven people and spewed nearly 5 million barrels of oil into the ocean, environmental organizations and grassroots activists organized a boycott of the oil giant, British Petroleum (BP).[35] This was a market campaign proper that sought to change the practices of BP, although the attention it received probably influenced lawmakers as well. Several national organizations immediately called for a boycott: Public Citizen (a consumer watchdog group founded by Ralph Nader), Democracy for America (a Vermont-based group founded by Howard Dean, former Democratic National Committee chair and presidential candidate), and the Sierra Club (a conservation organization founded in 1892 that elected John Muir, a mountaineer, as its first president). The Sierra Club held a press conference to announce its boycott with the Reverend Jesse Jackson, a prominent civil rights activist who had been on the balcony of the Lorraine Motel with Dr. Martin Luther King Jr. when he was shot. The response from established environmental organizations was to be expected, but the grassroots activism around the BP boycott was remarkable.

Lee Perkins, a freelance videographer from Shreveport, Louisiana, started the Boycott BP Facebook account that went on to garner nearly 700,000 "friends."[36] The page called for a boycott of BP "until the spill is cleaned up!" In an interview with Diane Sawyer on ABC News, Perkins, in a deep Southern drawl, admitted that, although he occasionally recycled, he did not consider himself an environmentalist until this action: "I now see the error of my ways." Perkins became the spokesperson for Gulf Coast residents whose lives were affected by the spill: fishermen, fisherwomen, and those who worked in the tourism industry. When asked how he had organized the campaign, Perkins told Sawyer, "I've got 600,000 bosses telling me what to do, so I listen."[37] He shared the Public Citizen online petition, which asserted that consumers would no longer tolerate the abysmal record of safety and environmental disasters of the company.[38] In 2010, Lady Gaga and other performers from the Mayhem Festival joined the boycott. Creative vandals also made a statement about the oil spill by dumping oil or oil-like substances on BP signs at numerous gas stations in the United States.

Millions of Americans participated in the boycott, venting their frustration at BP for yet another preventable environmental disaster. This action effectively reduced profits in retail gas stations across the country, especially at stations that were targeted by protesters at the pumps.[39] Station owners experienced losses from 10 to 40 percent in the months following the BP spill, and in response, the parent company set up a program to compensate retailers for their losses through direct payments, reduction in credit card fees, and assistance with advertising costs.[40] BP suffered a minor financial setback with the reimbursement costs, the dip in stock value, and some local retailers dropping their BP label. The more severe damage was to its reputation, a loss that would probably have occurred regardless of the organized boycott. Three years after the catastrophic spill, 41 percent of Americans held a favorable view of the company, compared to 43 percent who held an unfavorable view.[41]

The BP boycott campaign goal of getting the company to quickly restore the Gulf Coast was achieved. BP spent $42 billion cleaning up the region and reimbursed merchants and employees for the loss of business and income, respectively.[42] Public outcry certainly played a role in the rapid and generous response

FIGURE 4.2 Activist at a BP oil flood protest, Jackson Square, New Orleans, 2009

of BP to the spill (figure 4.2), but the Obama administration also put pressure on the oil company. The White House passed three major administrative rulings to prevent a similar spill from occurring in the future.[43] It is impossible to isolate the effects of the consumer activism from the White House pressure, but it is safe to say that combined they caused BP to act both affirmatively and quickly to clean up the Gulf Coast.

The Artists against Fracking Campaign

Most Americans had never heard of fracking, a shale gas extraction process, before Josh Fox's 2010 investigative documentary *Gasland*. This was a campaign that used market tactics to influence legislators rather than a market campaign proper aimed at business entities. In the film, Fox examines whether the boon in fracking is safe and concludes that fracking poses significant health and safety risks. Fox, a theater major from Columbia University, became politicized around the issue of fracking when his family was offered a sum of money to allow a fracking line on their land in northern Pennsylvania. In his quest to learn more about the practice, he spoke with residents throughout the area who had experienced fracking, and his activism was born through these personal testimonies.

Since *Gasland*, the oil industry and environmentalists have locked heads in a debate about whether fracking is harmful, and research on the subject is new and emerging. A 2014 review of health-related studies on fracking found that it contaminates nearby air and drinking water with chemicals that have been linked to birth defects and cancer.[44] The Seismological Society of America has confirmed that fracking is directly linked to earthquakes because the process involves drilling deep into the surface of the Earth and fracturing shale rock formations to let natural gas escape.[45] Activists have responded to this relatively new environmental threat with consumer activism. In the United Kingdom, the grassroots Frack Off campaign targets business entities and governmental bodies with the goal of outlawing fracking altogether. In 2011, activists stormed drilling sites to hang antifracking banners, an action that was timed to coincide with the Shale Gas Environment Summit in London. In the United States, Mark Ruffalo, an actor, formed the nonprofit Water Defense to fight against industrial contaminants, and in 2010, Yoko Ono and Sean Lennon started Artists against Fracking (AAF) after an oil company started fracking near their upstate New York home. AAF now has over two hundred celebrity members who use their star status to raise awareness of the issue.

The goal of the AAF campaign is to raise public awareness about the effects of fracking so that citizens can put pressure on lawmakers and activists to ban it. In 2013, residents in a fracking region in Pennsylvania gave Ono, Lennon, and Susan Sarandon a tour of fracking sites that included a demonstration of polluted tap water (which caught fire when lit), point pollution emitted near homes, and a broken fracking well that residents suspected was causing illness in the area. AAF chronicled this trip in a video that has received nearly 30,000 views to date. The release of the video was accompanied by a call-in and an online letter-writing campaign targeting Governor Andrew Cuomo, urging him to ban fracking in the state. The governor unexpectedly banned fracking in late December 2014, in response to the activism and mounting science showing the harmful effects.[46] In summer 2015, Maryland became the third state to ban fracking in response to research and activism on the issue, behind New York and Vermont (a symbolic gesture because Vermont does not have natural gas reserves).[47]

AAF is now lobbying to ban fracking throughout the United States. To fund their cause, they have released an antifracking album called "Buy This Fracking Album" that features Bonnie Raitt, Pete Seeger, and other top-name artists. Consumer activists have attempted to ban fracking or fracking-related activities in over four hundred communities across the United States, with mixed success.[48]

For example, activists in Denton, Texas, engineered the first fracking ban in the state, but their success was short-lived when the state legislature passed a ban on local bans to reverse the Denton vote and similar votes in the future.[49]

The antifracking campaign in the United States has extended well beyond the efforts of AAF, but this organization was crucial in raising national public awareness of the issue. The organization accomplished its short-term goal to ban fracking in New York. Instead of calling for a boycott of or divestment from companies that frack, AAF used its celebrity to raise awareness of the issue through social media and put pressure on lawmakers to pass public policy regulating these companies. This unique strategy was effective in achieving the goals of the AAF campaign.

The Go Fossil Free Campaign

In 2011, the nonprofit 350.org organized the Go Fossil Free Campaign to target the top polluting companies in the world. 350.org describes itself as "building a global climate movement" and derives its name from livable CO2 levels (below 350 parts per million) recommended by climate scientists.[50] This is a market campaign proper because it targets business entities directly.

Go Fossil Free was founded in 2008 by a group of friends, including environmental Bill McKibben, an activist and author of *The End of Nature* (1988), the first book on climate change written for a lay audience. McKibben grew up in a political family and witnessed his father getting arrested during a protest of the Vietnam War. Later, after graduating from Harvard University, McKibben dedicated his life to the environmental cause in response to the overtly anti-environmental positions staked out by Ronald Reagan during his presidency.

Go Fossil Free targets the top two hundred fossil fuel producers because the burning of carbon-based fuel produces carbon dioxide that traps heat in the atmosphere and raises the global temperature. This global warming has been linked to extreme weather events, a rise in the sea level, and the habitat loss and subsequent extinction of several species. India Coal tops the 2015 list of the top fossil fuel polluters in the world.[51] The short-term goal of the campaign is to reform fossil fuel production processes to capture as much CO2 as possible, and the long-term goal is to shift to alternative, sustainable, nonpolluting energy sources, such as solar, wind, and water power. After more than four decades of failed public policy on climate change, these high-profile environmentalists turned to consumer activism in an attempt to create new de facto energy policies through the marketplace.

Former vice president Al Gore released the popular documentary film *An Inconvenient Truth* in 2006, which raised public awareness and salience of the issue of climate change. The Go Fossil Free campaign capitalized on public momentum from the documentary as well as new social media organizing tools. The primary tool of the campaign is divestment; activists are encouraged to run local campaigns that focus on specific institutions (e.g., universities, religious institutions, and retirement funds) to get them to freeze new fossil fuel investments and divest from funds that include fossil fuel bonds and public equities within five years. Campaign organizers explicitly reference the divestment from South Africa in the mid-1980s to end Apartheid as their inspiration for using this tactic. The campaign has received endorsements from President Obama and other world leaders, who have publicly encouraged people and companies to divest from top polluters.

The first institution to divest was Swarthmore in 2011, and to date, thirty-two colleges and universities in the United States have divested.[52] At Georgetown, the Board of Trustees voted to divest after two and a half years of sustained pressure from student activists, who used marches and a petition to make their point. Similar tactics are being used on campuses across the country. Tulane University students occupied their president's office to protest fossil fuels, Harvard University students blocked the main entrance to the administration building, and students at Tufts University engaged in a march and a sit-in at the president's office. Go Fossil Free has become the new student movement for the next generation.

Go Fossil Free is a popular student movement, but campaign support has come from many institutions worldwide, including the National Council of Churches and twenty-two other religious institutions. Public and for-profit entities have also divested from fossil fuels, for example, the prestigious Rockefeller Brothers Fund and nineteen other foundations. Two U.S. counties and twenty-two cities have divested from fossil fuels, and the Go Fossil Free campaign has reached far beyond U.S. borders. Hundreds of campuses in Canada and throughout European countries have joined the campaign, including Oxford University.[53] In June 2015, Norway became the first country to divest its pension fund from fossil fuels.

This campaign is ongoing and has experienced some success in its first four years. From 2011 to 2015, the Dow Jones coal index fell 86 percent, meaning that coal stocks are worth less, and the massive coal producer Peabody Energy listed the divestment campaign as a threat to share prices in its annual report.[54] The decline in coal stock value was mostly accomplished through the stigmatization of coal rather than actual loss of market share because most of these divesting institutions have only a fraction of their investment holdings in fossil fuels.[55] The goals of Go Fossil Free are lofty and will take years of sustained pressure to accomplish because they require a paradigm shift in the way companies operate and people consume energy.

Animal Rights Campaigns

The Kentucky Fried Cruelty Campaign

In 2005, Reverend Al Sharpton, political commentator and MSNBC host, and Russell Simmons, rap mogul, joined forces with the People for the Ethical Treatment of Animals (PETA) in calling for a boycott of Kentucky Fried Chicken (KFC) to protest the mistreatment of the 750 million chickens the company processes each year.[56] This was a market campaign proper, aimed at the leading industry offender.

PETA was founded in 1980 by Ingrid Newkirk, a British American who as a child had lived in India and volunteered with her mother in Mother Teresa's leper colony. It was there she learned that it did not matter who suffered but how they suffered. Newkirk dedicated herself to animal protection after she failed to save the life of a dog who had been bound and beaten behind her family home in New Delhi. Alexander Fernando Pacheco cofounded PETA. An experience in a meat-packing plant during college sparked his interest in animal rights, and on summer breaks, he worked on the antiwhaling ship *Sea Shepherd*. Simmons, the cofounder of Def Jam Records, is a prominent vegan who speaks out against animal abuses in factory farming. His activism also extends to racial disparities in drug-sentencing laws and to promoting same-sex marriage, and he spent several days in Zucotti Park as part of the OWS protest.

The KFC Cruelty campaign called for more room per chicken in factory farms, the adoption of a process that puts chickens to sleep before slaughter, and the banning of hormones that cause the birds to collapse under their own weight. PETA had been pushing for better poultry industry standards for years prior to joining forces with Sharpton and Simmons, but Yum! Brands, the parent company of KFC, was unusually resistant to this activism. According to Newkirk, they were "by far the most stubborn corporation we have attempted to work with."[57] (As discussed in chapter 3, Yum! Brands, the parent company of Taco Bell, had previously been the target of a successful boycott from the Coalition of Immokalee Workers to improve wages and working conditions for tomato growers, so this was not its first time at the boycott rodeo.) PETA targeted KFC because it is the fast food industry leader in poultry use.

The Kentucky Fried Cruelty campaign employed all four types of consumer activism. The first strategy was for PETA to involve celebrities (including Paul McCartney, Jenna Jameson, and Alice Walker) to promote the boycott using free media and social media. Sharpton and Simmons received top billing, given their status as black opinion leaders because KFC markets heavily to African Americans. In addition to the boycott, PETA used direct action outside KFC stores across the country, documenting the abuse of chickens by KFC suppliers. PETA also produced a series of videos about KFC chicken cruelty, such as the *KFC Torture Camp* video that was viewed more than 200,000 times. PETA produced investigative footage by sending members undercover in factory farms to document the abuses. All told, the Kentucky Fried Cruelty campaign involved over 12,000 protests in front of KFC establishments, some with prop cages, staged chicken slaughtering, and burning effigies of Colonel Sanders.[58] In 2008, PETA activists in swimsuits sat in "scalding tanks" of "bloody" water in public places in Philadelphia and Baltimore to demonstrate that chickens are often scalded to death in the hot water meant to remove their feathers. PETA activists also purchased stock in Yum! Brands and proposed a shareholder resolution to improve animal treatment by KFC. This shareholder action failed to generate much support among shareholders, but it did attract free media attention.

After five years of boycotting, divestment, and direct actions, KFC Canada agreed to hold suppliers to the PETA production standards, and the company also added a vegan chicken substitute to their menu.[59] PETA claimed victory for the campaign in Canada, but Yum! Brands has not altered its practices in the United States. Campaign organizers are still using the boycott, direct consumer actions, shareholder actions, and social media to keep pressure on KFC to improve its treatment of chickens.

The Canadian Seafood Campaign

In 2005, the Humane Society of the United States (HSUS) led a boycott against seafood from Canada, urging that country to stop its annual seal hunt.[60] This is a campaign that uses market tactics to influence government policy rather than a market campaign proper. The Canadian government authorizes the hunt each year, which results in the killing of approximately 200,000 seal pups. During each hunt, seals are impaled and cut open with large metal hooks. Their pelts are used for luxury items, but most of the meat is thrown away.[61] The annual seal hunt brings in only about 5 percent of the annual income of fishermen and women, so HSUS targeted seafood exports to the United States to gain more leverage for the boycott.

Fred Myers, Helen Jones, Larry Andrews, and Marcia Glaser founded the HSUS in 1954 to stop animal cruelty. Myers, the central figure, was a journalist who grew up in Missouri, where his father ran a newspaper stand. Myer's worked as the editor of the American Humane Association (AHA) magazine prior to starting HSUS, and his writings became increasingly more radical to the point that he faced heavy censorship from the AHA board. Myers abruptly left the AHA when the organization declined to take a stance against the growing use of animals in biomedical research, and three other staff members left with him.

The Canadian seafood campaign made use of a boycott and social media to stop the annual hunt. HSUS has a webpage dedicated to the campaign where individuals and commercial businesses (restaurants, grocery stores, and seafood suppliers) can sign a pledge to boycott Canadian seafood. In the seven years of the campaign, more than 6,500 businesses and 800,000 individuals have signed the pledge, including many celebrity chefs and "conscious" retailers such as Whole Foods and Trader Joes. The HSUS also started a Change.org petition that garnered nearly 100,000 signatures and made a series of widely shared graphic videos showing seals being clubbed and gored to death. HSUS makes it easy for individuals to avoid establishments that serve Canadian seafood with a free app that checks for seal-friendly businesses.

In the first year of the campaign, the boycott caused an estimated $100 million drop in Canadian seafood sales,[62] and within five years, seafood exports from Newfoundland, Canada, dropped 44 percent.[63] Momentum for the campaign remains relatively strong,[64] but it lost some steam in 2013 when Anthony Bourdain, a celebrity chef, publicly called out the forty-two chefs who had signed the pledge to boycott Canadian seafood.[65] He argued on Twitter that the seal slaughter was an integral part of the economy and culture of the Inuit and other First Nations people, and that to ban the slaughter altogether would have devastating economic consequences.

Boycotts mostly derive their power from public shaming and potential reputational loss, as opposed to actual economic loss. The Canadian Seafood Boycott is unusual in that it has resulted in both economic and reputational loss. In 2014, the World Trade Organization upheld the ban on seal pelts in effect in thirty-four countries, including the United States, and the public outcry over the killing of seals was significant in passing this legislation.[66] The Canadian seafood boycott is still in effect with moderate momentum, and it has dramatically reduced the seafood exports to the United States. The seal hunt is smaller now—about 50,000 seals per year—and it is no longer economically viable for those who participate in it. The Canadian government subsidizes the hunt, but 71 percent of Canadians oppose these subsidies.[67] Campaign organizers have pledged to continue their efforts until the seal hunt has stopped altogether.

The Cove Campaign

In 2009, the Academy Award–winning documentary *The Cove* revealed the slaughter of 20,000 dolphins and other porpoises off the coast of Japan each year for consumption.[68] This is a campaign that uses market tactics to influence government policy rather than a market campaign proper that targets specific business entities. The star of the film, Ric O'Barry, was a dolphin trainer for the

Flipper television show for years before becoming an advocate for dolphin rights. He went from training dolphins to advocating for them when one of his *Flipper* dolphins, Cathy, died in his arms in what O'Barry believed was a suicide. According to O'Barry, dolphins are not automatic air breathers, so they can end their life whenever they choose to by not taking a breath. Cathy chose to not take her next breath, and there was nothing O'Barry could do to revive her. In 1970, he founded The Dolphin Project, but the release of *The Cove* nearly forty years later launched the cause into global consciousness.

The first half of *The Cove* demonstrates that dolphins are highly intelligent, complex creatures with a rich emotional life. The second half of the film shows their annual slaughter for food and other commercial uses (figure 4.3). The filmmakers used underwater cameras and microphones disguised as rocks to gather graphic footage of the dolphin slaughter. The film raised awareness and inspired a worldwide movement against this annual dolphin hunt in Taiji, the only place where such hunting still takes place on a large scale.

The Cove campaign capitalized on viewer outrage by allowing people to send a text to sign up for action alerts before they left the theater. This new organizing means is used frequently in consumer activism campaigns today. In terms of tactics, the campaign has primarily used social media to shame Japanese companies to stop the hunt and to put pressure on the Japanese government to better regulate dolphin killing. Members receive text message and email alerts when

FIGURE 4.3   Annual dolphin slaughter, Taiji, Japan, 2011

organizers need a mass of people to sign a petition, call government officials, or send letters. *The Cove* campaign organized a petition directed at President Obama, Vice President Joe Biden, and Kenichiro Sasae (the Japanese ambassador to the United States) demanding that the Japanese government stop the annual dolphin slaughter in the Taiji Cove. The petition has received over 1 million signatures. O'Barry delivered these signatures to the White House in April 2015. Kathleen Kennedy, the U.S. ambassador to Japan, deemed the dolphin killings inhumane.[69] The Sea Shepherd Conservation Society has teamed up with TakePart to stream live video footage of the dolphin hunt each year in Taiji Cove. They also use Twitter to send frequent updates to activists across the globe.

In the years since *The Cove* was released, Japanese officials have condemned the film and consistently defended the hunt in Taiji Cove as "tradition."[70] The Japanese press does not cover the controversy, and the release of the film has been blocked in Japan, a move that has limited the effectiveness of potential boycott efforts because most of the porpoise products are sold in Japan.[71] Despite those obstacles, international attention generated by the film caused Taiji fishermen to release seventy dolphins from their first catch the year *The Cove* was released,[72] and the number of dolphins and porpoises killed in the Taiji Cove has declined each year since. Overall, dolphin killings went from about 2,000 annually when the film was released to under 1,000 six years later.[73] The mission of the campaign is to end to the dolphin hunt altogether, so the campaign continues today. In January 2016, O'Barry was arrested and detained for nineteen days by Japanese officials for taking a side trip during his previous trip that the Japanese government claimed was unauthorized by his passport. Officials deported O'Barry and banned him from returning to Japan for five years.

The Hobbit Campaign

After reports that three horses and over twenty chickens, sheep, and goats died on set in 2012, PETA called for a boycott of *The Hobbit*.[74] This was a market campaign proper because it centered around one film production company. Whistleblowing animal wranglers who were working on the film reported to PETA that negligence has been the biggest cause of animal deaths (because the animals were kept on farms with sinkholes and steep cliffs). The identities of the whistleblowers are not known.

Peter Jackson, the filmmaker, responded to the whistleblower complaint with denials. There was "no mistreatment, no abuse," and he called PETA a "very radical organization" to discredit the campaign.[75] Jackson told reporters that the animal wranglers went to great lengths to ensure animal safety on set, and the agency responsible for ensuring animal safety told reporters that no animals had died during filming. Jackson also confirmed that they could not ensure animal safety when they were not working on set. According to PETA officials, the death toll for animals working on *The Hobbit* was the worst they had seen in the industry and sending a strong message to these filmmakers would, in turn, send a strong message to Hollywood that activists are actively monitoring for potential animal mistreatment. The boycott inspired an investigative report by the *Hollywood Reporter* into the practices of the AHA, the organization responsible for awarding the "No animals were harmed in the making of this film" statement that rolls at the end of movie credits.[76] In response, the AHA pledged to change the way it oversees animal treatment in the industry.

PETA used a boycott, social media, and direct action tactics in their campaign against *The Hobbit*. It asked people to avoid seeing the film in theaters and initiated an online letter-writing campaign to convey the activists' dismay directly to Jackson. Activists across the globe protested outside theaters on opening night, but these efforts did not have a significant economic effect on *The Hobbit*. It opened to rave reviews and the highest box office returns for a December film opening ($87.4 million).[77] If the goal of the PETA campaign was to raise awareness of animal abuse on *The Hobbit* set, they achieved this goal through news media coverage of the shocking claims. If their goal was to put the film industry on notice that activists are monitoring their animal treatment, this goal was probably achieved as well because the campaign was so high profile.

The SeaWorld Campaign

The 2013 documentary *Blackfish* inspired a massive outpouring of consumer activism against the popular SeaWorld theme park. The film accuses SeaWorld of mistreating its killer whales (orcas), and raises ethical and safety questions about keeping orcas in captivity. This is a market campaign proper because it targets the practices of a business entity.

Blackfish centers on the story of Tilikum, a SeaWorld orca involved in the deaths of three people. The film opens with footage of Dawn Brancheau, a trainer and Tilikum's last victim, whom he dragged underwater in front of an audience at the end of a "Dinner with Shamu" show in 2010. *Blackfish* has been seen by over 20 million people, and it continues to be one of the top-viewed documentaries on streaming services several years after its release.[78] *Blackfish* has inspired grassroots consumer activism against SeaWorld, but the activism is far less organized than the campaign accompanying *The Cove*. *Blackfish* filmmakers did not initially establish a campaign to capitalize on viewer dismay, and the "Take Action" tab on the *Blackfish* website sends readers to other organizations for ideas of actions to take.

After the initial box office success of *Blackfish*, PETA and the Sea Shepherd Conservation Society capitalized on new public awareness from the film to organize actions. Sea Shepherd was started in 1977 in Vancouver, British Columbia, by Captain Paul Watson to disrupt the annual baby harp seal harvest in eastern Canada, and since that time, he has made two hundred activist voyages. In 1978, Captain Watson hunted down the notorious pirate whaling boat *Sierra* and rammed it out of commission. As a young adult, Watson worked with the Canadian Coast Guard, protested with the Sierra Club against nuclear testing, and was an early and active Greenpeace member. His more violent approach conflicted with the Greenpeace dedication to nonviolence, so he left the organization to start his own. Watson's activism is featured in the Animal Planet series *Whale Wars*.

PETA and Sea Shepherd have used legislative tactics and consumer activism to target SeaWorld. In 2014, they successfully lobbied the San Francisco Board of Supervisors to pass a historic resolution banning the captivity of orcas, whales, and other porpoises due to their intelligence, complex emotional capacity, and their high stress and mortality rates in captivity.[79] Lawmakers in New York have proposed a *Blackfish* bill to ban keeping captive orcas in parks, and Congress passed sweeping legislation to better protect captive mammals. Activists are pushing for a national law to outlaw the captivity of these animals.

In terms of consumer activism, grassroots organizers set up a petition to pass the Orca Welfare and Safety Act that would make keeping captive orcas illegal, and it has received over 1.5 million signatures to date. Another 1.2 million Americans have pledged to boycott SeaWorld until the park releases its orca whales and "empties their tanks." Grassroots activists also targeted celebrity performers who were scheduled to play at a SeaWorld park in Florida the summer after the release of *Blackfish*. Most of the artists cancelled their performance and pledged support for the boycott, including the Beach Boys and Pat Benatar.[80] Activists also used direct action by staging hundreds of protests outside SeaWorld theme parks and publicly shaming the company at high-profile events such as the Rose Bowl Parade in Pasadena, California, where seventeen people were arrested in a protest.

SeaWorld leadership felt threatened enough by direct consumer activism that it planted an employee as an animal rights activist for years to gather intelligence about planned protests and other activities.[81] This employee, Paul McComb, protested outside SeaWorld theme parks, protested the SeaWorld float at the Thanksgiving Day parade in New York in 2013, and was even arrested by police during the Rose Parade protest in California. News of McComb being a plant caused further reputational harm to SeaWorld.

Blackfish and consumer activism had an immediate economic impact on Sea-World. Park attendance dropped 5.6 percent, the stock value dropped from $26 to $16 per share within a year,[82] and Standard & Poors downgraded the credit rating of SeaWorld.[83] The company responded by hiring a new CEO and investing $10 million in an ad campaign to promote company efforts to rehabilitate orcas.[84] SeaWorld also pledged $11.5 million to conservation efforts for orca whales in the wild and has established an independent oversight group of scientists to oversee its orca program. Nevertheless, the crisis management public relations did not work. In 2015, the company reported an economically catastrophic 84 percent profit loss.[85]

The ultimate goal of the campaign around *Blackfish* was to ban the captivity of orca whales and other similarly situated sea creatures. The campaign caused extensive reputational and economic harm, and it achieved its goal in March 2016 when SeaWorld announced that it would stop breeding killer whales and phase out its killer whale shows in San Diego, Orlando, and San Antonio over the next three years.[86] The company issued a public statement confirming that the market campaign was instrumental in its decision: "Why the big news? SeaWorld has been listening and we're changing. Society is changing and we're changing with it," the company said. "SeaWorld is finding new ways to continue to deliver on our purpose to inspire all our guest(s) to take action to protect wild animals and wild places."[87]

The DiGiorno Pizza Campaign

In 2014, animal rights group Mercy for Animals (MFA) targeted DiGiorno Pizza after an undercover video surfaced showing farmworkers at one of its suppliers engaging in animal cruelty toward cows.[88] More specifically, the farmworkers kicked and stabbed the cows, and dragged them by ropes. Within a matter of days, this video went viral and was replayed by mainstream news organizations. The dairy supplier immediately fired two of the workers and removed another from contact with animals. Four dairy workers were later charged with eleven counts of animal cruelty. This was a market campaign proper because it sought to change the practices of a business entity.

MFA was started in 1999 when a rural Ohio high school student, Nathan Runkle, witnessed a fellow student smashing a piglet's head against the wall in an agriculture class. Runkle was inspired to activism when he learned that this was a standard practice for farmed piglets. MFA has used surveillance technology to expose factory farming and rodeo practices through undercover investigations across the country.

For the DiGiorno campaign, MFA demanded that the company adopt meaningful animal protections for all dairy suppliers that included zero tolerance for mutilation and abuse, and humane care for cows who have to be put down. They targeted the company with a boycott and a Change.org petition that drew over 66,000 supporters, and within six months, the campaign claimed victory. DiGiorno Pizza cut ties with the dairy supplier where the animal cruelty took place, and its parent company launched a "strenuous audit program" in ninety countries to ensure humane animal treatment.[89] MFA called this the "most comprehensive and far-reaching animal welfare policy of its kind."[90] After the success of this campaign, MFA launched the Slice of Cruelty campaign to raise awareness about other cases of animal cruelty at dairy suppliers for major pizza brands, including Pizza Hut and Domino's. The MFA campaign against DiGiorno achieved its campaign goal quickly through a shocking investigative video and a well-organized social media campaign.

Campaign Effectiveness

Most of the market campaigns for environmental protection and animals rights examined in this chapter achieved their goals. As shown in table 4.1, five out of the thirteen campaigns are still underway: Go Fossil Free, Artists against Fracking, Kentucky Fried Cruelty, Canadian seafood, and *The Cove*. Although it is too

TABLE 4.1   Effectiveness of environmental and animal rights campaigns

CAMPAIGN	EFFECTIVE?
Artists against Fracking	Ongoing
BP	Yes
Canadian Seafood	Ongoing
DiGiorno Pizza	Yes
ExposeExxon	No
Go Fossil Free	Ongoing
Kentucky Fried Cruelty	Ongoing
Kleercut	Yes
Nestlé Palm Oil	Yes
SeaWorld	Yes
Stop Staples	Yes
The Cove	Ongoing
The Hobbit	No
Effectiveness = 75%	

early to tell whether these five will be successful, it does appear that Artists against Fracking will ultimately achieve its goals given its early success. The KFC campaign is seven years old and has lost momentum; it is unlikely to be successful, especially considering that KFC agreed to alter its chicken treatment in Canada but not the United States. The Canadian seal hunt still happens on an annual basis, but the kill numbers have been drastically reduced; campaign momentum has dissipated because of this moderate result.

Six of the remaining eight campaigns achieved their goals. The Stop Staples and Kleercut campaigns effectively stopped these corporations from using old-growth timber. Consumer activists got Nestlé to stop deforestation for palm oil extraction, and the DiGiorno boycott improved animal treatment in the global supply chain of the company. The BP campaign kept public pressure on the company after the oil spill until it cleaned up the Gulf Coast and properly compensated people for their losses. The SeaWorld campaign achieved success in early 2016 when the company decided to ban orca breeding and phase out killer whale shows. Two campaigns had mixed results. The ExposeExxon campaign failed to stop Arctic drilling or shift the company position on climate change. *The Hobbit* boycott did not affect the success of the film, but it did send a strong message to the film industry of what might happen if animals are mistreated

Documentary films have become the new tinder to spark consumer activism campaigns involving environmental and animal rights concerns. *An Inconvenient Truth, Gasland, The Cove*, and *Blackfish* were all important in inspiring consumer activism campaigns in this study. Morgan Spurlock's 2004 *SuperSize Me* was the first documentary film in the social media age to have a strong political impact. It documented Spurlock's health issues after eating food exclusively at McDonald's for a month. One day before the film was released, McDonald's added a "Go Active" menu to its offerings, and after the film inspired a national debate about fast food and nutrition, the company removed supersized options from its menu altogether. Other fast food chains followed suit by offering healthier options; that is, *SuperSize Me* effectively changed practices industry-wide. This documentary set the precedent for how documentary films can mobilize people to achieve concrete outcomes such as healthier menu options in restaurants that are disproportionately frequented by poor Americans. Videos in general are more prominent in sparking contemporary consumer activism as social media makes it easier to share the outrage. The Nestlé Palm Oil and DiGiorno campaigns were effective because an ad spoof and an undercover video documenting animal abuses, respectively, went viral. Shocking images have become de jure for contemporary consumer activism around animal rights and environmental issues.

Democratic Implications

All the campaigns analyzed in this chapter improved democracy. As shown in table 4.2, the campaigns improved five democratic measures on average. The Artists against Fracking campaign had the greatest effect on democracy, followed by the BP, ExposeExxon, and Go Fossil Free campaigns.

Environmental and animal rights campaigns improved political participation and public discussion on policy issues such as climate change; deforestation; fracking; and the treatment of animals in the wild, on factory farms, and during film shoots. All these campaigns improved corporate accountability for actions and decisions that have policy consequences.

Promotes Robust Citizen Participation

All the campaigns examined in this chapter increased overall rates of political participation because they encouraged citizens to engage in purchasing behavior, direct actions, shareholder actions, and social media campaigns with a political aim. Some campaigns provided an outlet for political voice when formal political power was limited by geography. For example, consumers in the United States were able to halt deforestation in Canada with the Stop Staples and Kleercut campaigns and in Indonesia with the Nestlé Palm Oil campaign. The Go Fossil

TABLE 4.2 Democratic contribution of environmental and animal rights campaigns

CAMPAIGN	DEMOCRATIC SCORE (1–10)
Artists against Fracking	7
BP	6
Canadian Seafood	4
DiGiorno Pizza	4
ExposeExxon	6
Go Fossil Free	6
Kentucky Fried Cruelty	4
Kleercut	4
Nestlé Palm Oil	5
SeaWorld	5
Stop Staples	4
The Cove	4
The Hobbit	4
Average = 4.8	

Free campaign uses U.S. investment dollars to change the actions of the top-polluting companies, almost all of which are located in other countries. Ongoing campaigns are using consumer activism to end the hunts of seals in Canada and dolphins in Japan, and *The Hobbit* boycott involved the treatment of animals in New Zealand. Activists in the United States have no formal political standing in these countries, so consumer activism is the ideal tool for changing corporate practices that are not regulated by the U.S. government.

Five of the campaigns in this chapter focused on domestic concerns, most of which involved the immediate protest of a corporate action. Consumer activists went after BP directly following the massive oil spill in the Gulf Coast, targeted fracking in New York after the release of the *Gasland* documentary, and took swift action against farm animal abuse that was caught on tape in the DiGiorno Pizza case. Consumer activists also responded swiftly to *Blackfish* with the aim of getting SeaWorld out of the business of housing live sea mammals. The KFC campaign has been the least successful of the domestic campaigns, although it proved effective in Canada. All these campaigns increased citizen participation by providing nonelectoral outlets to express citizen outrage.

Promotes Political Equality in Participation and Representation

None of the campaigns reviewed in this chapter improved equality in participation and representation, although animal rights activists may disagree with that statement because many see their work as providing a voice for the voiceless. Similar to advocates for young children, individuals with disabilities, and other groups that face challenges with self-advocacy, some animal rights activists see themselves as speaking for animals who suffer and feel pain but do not have a voice, political or otherwise. Humans are the accepted unit of analysis for determining the health of democracy in the United States, but activists have successfully added animal rights and protections to the constitutions of Switzerland and Germany.[91] In this sense, animal rights activists may argue that campaigns for animal rights improve the equality of representation if animals are included in the consideration.

Promotes the Will of the Majority

Most consumer activism campaigns push a minority position in the face of the majority opposition and lack of access to formal political power, but a few of the campaigns in this chapter forwarded the will of the majority. The BP campaign was one of these exceptions because the nation was glued to its television sets during the eighty-seven days the company took to cap the well, and three-quarters of Americans considered the spill a "major environmental disaster."[92] Eight out of ten Americans rated the response by BP negatively, and 64 percent supported criminal prosecution of company executives in the months following the spill. The Go Fossil Free and ExposeExxon campaigns also furthered the will of the majority because most Americans support the curbing of pollution that contributes to climate change.

Promotes Active Media

Virtually all the market campaigns discussed in this chapter promoted democracy through more active media because they put policy issues on the media agenda that would otherwise be overlooked. This is a given because public shaming is such an effective tool in getting businesses to alter their behavior. The Stop Staples Campaign revived media attention to issues of preserving old-growth forests through protests at Staples locations, and the Kleercut campaign produced alternative media in the form of a spoof ad campaign that received mainstream media coverage. Greenpeace used a similar tactic with the Nestlé Palm Oil boycott by creating a shocking spoof ad that went viral.

Marketplace activists made ANWR a household name through social media efforts and protests that were widely covered in the press, as did Go Fossil Free and the campaign against fracking. The same can be said for all the animal rights campaigns that informed the public of animal slaughter and abuse that would have otherwise gone unnoticed in mainstream media coverage. Marketplace activists blew the whistle on the mass slaughter of seals and dolphins, and the mistreatment of animals on movie sets, in factory farms, and at amusements parks. Animal treatment is not a popular topic in the mass media, but these campaigns were able to draw media attention using shocking documentaries, viral videos, and protest actions.

For one campaign, the relationship between the media and activism was reversed; that is, active media produced the action. Investigative reporting of the BP oil leak led to marketplace activism against the company, and a series of high-profile reports on the initial failure by BP to quickly and fairly compensate those affected is what drove continued marketplace activism.

Improves Public Discussion on Policy Issues

All the consumer activism campaigns in this chapter improved public discussion on policy issues. Citizens debated climate change, fracking, and deforestation. They learned about corporate practices in other countries and how this affects local animal and human populations, and has larger long-term effects, such as global warming. Citizens learned about standard factory farming practices and debated the ethics of animal treatment. From unethical dairy farming practices to harvesting dolphins, most of the campaigns in this chapter put their concerns on the policy agenda, and every campaign raised awareness of the policy issue though public information and debate.

Promotes Political Equality in State Protection and Public Resources

Some of the environmental campaigns of the past decade improved the equality of state protection and resource allocation. Artists against Fracking locked up most of the Marcellus Shale to protect against water and air pollution as well as earthquakes. Celebrities used their media power to advocate for rural, often poorer residents who lacked political power or stock options to stop oil companies from drilling near their homes. The Boycott BP campaign put pressure on the company to clean up the Gulf Coast and compensate people for their losses. Without sustained public attention and pressure, the tens of thousands of small business owners and employees in the fishing industry would have had less bargaining power with BP. The Go Fossil Free campaign is using divestment to restrict fossil fuel emissions to protect people from catastrophic changes in the atmosphere—changes that will affect poorer countries the most.[93] Perhaps this is why so many advanced industrialized nations, including the United States, have done so little to date to curb greenhouse emissions. This Go Fossil Free campaign improves democracy by forcing powerful global companies, including those in the United States, to lower their emissions sans strong international sanctions to do so.

Promotes Corporate Political Accountability

Campaigns for the environment and animals rights also strengthen U.S. democracy by improving business accountability in areas that are currently regulated by the state. Two campaigns improved oversight of companies that were deforesting in other countries as a way to circumvent restrictions against cutting of old-growth forests in the United States. All the animal rights campaigns called for stronger enforcement of existing animal cruelty regulations in factory farming, filming, and amusement parks.

Promotes Government Accountability to Citizens

A few campaigns used market channels to improve government accountability. The Boycott BP campaign forced better government oversight of off-shore drilling, and the antifracking campaign led to new legislation in the state of New York. The *Blackfish* campaign led to a mandate in San Francisco against dolphins in captivity.

Protects against the Encroachment of Minority Rights

Although none of the market campaigns for animal rights directly protect minority rights (in that nonhuman animals do not have recognized rights in the U.S. political system), some of the environmental campaigns promote minority rights. The ExposeExxon campaign to prevent oil drilling in ANWR seeks to protect the largest Alaskan caribou herd on which the 7,000 members of the Gwich'in Nation rely for their livelihood. The caribou would be driven from the ANWR refuge by the noise if drilling were allowed. ExposeExxon is a struggle to preserve the environment and the culture and economy of this Native American tribe.

Similarly, although the chief focus of the Nestlé Palm Oil boycott is orang-utan protection, the campaign also involves the rights of marginalized people in Indonesia who are being forcibly displaced by palm oil plantations. Furthermore, some farmers adjacent to palm plantations have lost their livelihood because the chemicals used in production have polluted the soil and water. To date, the palm oil industry in Indonesia is responsible for approximately 5,000 land conflicts, and poor rural residents have little power to stand up to international corporate interests.[94] The use of U.S. consumer power to change the behavior of global companies when it comes to deforesting for palm production also protects the rights of marginalized peoples in Indonesia.

Protects against Government Encroachment on Civil Liberties

None of the environmental or animal rights campaigns in this chapter involved government encroachment on civil liberties.

In this chapter, I have analyzed thirteen animal rights and environmental protection campaigns from 2004 to 2014 and found that most used boycotts, direct action, and social media in their market campaigns; only three used shareholder and divestment tactics. All the campaigns launched in 2010 and later used social media, a prerequisite now for campaigns that reply on a broad base of support. Visual media have become an important part of contemporary consumer activism campaigns. Some of the campaigns in this chapter began with a revealing documentary, while others gained momentum through videos that went viral. Almost all these campaigns were successful in achieving the goals they set out to accomplish. About half the campaigns have come to a close, and only two failed to accomplish their goal.

The consumer activism campaigns for animal rights and the environment that I have analyzed here improved democracy by increasing participation and public discussion. Some campaigns also forwarded the will of the majority and allowed U.S. activists to exercise political power over corporate decisions made in other countries. These campaigns also improved corporate accountability in areas regulated by the government and, in some cases, improved accountability through new regulations. All told, in the past decade, millions of Americans protested outside businesses, signed petitions, boycotted, divested, and used social media to shame corporations in the name of environmental protection and animal rights. The use of unified consumer activism gave citizens a powerful political voice to alter corporate practices with policy implications.

"STOP SERVING GAY CHICKENS"

Campaigns for Gender Justice and
Lesbian-Gay-Bisexual-Transgender Rights

In 1992, gay rights activists called for a boycott of the state of Colorado after voters passed a constitutional amendment allowing employers to discriminate against gays and lesbians. A coalition of Lesbian-Gay-Bisexual-Transgender (LGBT) organizations called for consumers to boycott travel to and products from the state (e.g., Coors, Samsonite, and Celestial Seasonings).[1] Some organizations cancelled conventions and meetings in the Centennial state, and the cities of New York and Los Angeles posted an official travel ban for government employees. The hit 90s television show *Frasier* relocated from Denver to Seattle because of the boycott. Colorado state lost approximately $40 million in the convention and tourism business until the state Supreme Court ruled the amendment unconstitutional in 1994 and the boycott was suspended.[2]

In this chapter, I explore the democratic implications of thirteen national consumer activism campaigns for gender justice and LGBT rights that took place from 2004 to 2014. These campaigns used market channels to challenge sexist media, expand access to contraceptives, reduce domestic violence, and protest antigay laws and the corporate leaders who support them. All the campaigns I analyze in this chapter are part of the culture wars, conflicts between older, more traditional values and newer, more morally and sexually liberal values. Because the public is deeply divided on culture war issues, they instigate passionate debate, as evidenced by the many cases in this chapter that produced potent counterboycotts.

I begin this chapter with an overview of feminist and LGBT consumer activism in the decades leading up to my period of analysis. I then examine five feminist and eight LGBT campaigns, describing who initiated each campaign, why it was started, who was targeted, the tactics used, the length of the campaign, and whether it was successful. All these campaigns used boycotting and social media tools to press their cause, and seven used direct action as part of their efforts. None of the campaigns for gender or LGBT rights used divestment as a tactic. I conclude that these campaigns were more effective than not and that they advanced democratic ideals by increasing participation, discussion, and corporate accountability. Most of these campaigns also reflected the will of the majority at the same time that they protected the rights and furthered the interests of minorities.

Feminist and LGBT Campaigns, 1970s–2000s

Consumer activism has been a popular tool for feminists starting with the second wave of the Women's Movement in the 1970s.[3] For example, in 1974 Women against Violence against Women (WAVAW) organized a boycott of Warner Communications to reform the routine industry practice of using advertising imagery depicting violence against women. This boycott effort did not have an economic effect, but WAVAW effectively shamed the industry into adopting a formal prohibition on violence against women in advertising (that has been only loosely enforced). The National Organization for Women (NOW) also used boycott threats to address sexism in advertising more broadly. By the late 1970s, the National Advertising Review Board was pushing companies to consider whether their ads stereotyped, degraded, or infantilized women based on the threat of a NOW boycott. Feminists also used consumer activism to promote the Equal Rights Amendment (ERA), a proposed constitutional amendment allowing that "equality of rights under the law shall not be denied or abridged by the United States or by any State on account of sex."[4] In 1977, NOW organized a boycott of states that had not passed the ERA, and in 1979, the state of Missouri sued over the boycott on antitrust grounds. The Supreme Court upheld the right of NOW to boycott states under freedom of speech protections, and the Democratic Party pledged to pull funds from candidates who did not support the ERA.[5]

Feminist consumer activism was relatively quiet during the Reagan years, but in 1989, Sinead O'Connor, a musical artist, called for a boycott of the television show *Saturday Night Live* to protest the appearance of Andrew Dice Clay, an explicitly sexist comedian, as a guest host. The following year, a group of prominent feminists, including Gloria Steinem, called for a boycott of Knopf for publishing *American Psycho*, a book by Bret Easton Ellis that graphically chronicles an investment banker's killing of women. In the early 1990s, feminists used consumer activism to urge the French drug manufacturer, Roussel-Uclaf, to release the patent for the RU 486 abortion pill to producers in the United States.[6] The company was reluctant to do so because it anticipated a powerful boycott from pro-life groups, but it relinquished the patent when the Feminist Majority Foundation (FMF) organized a boycott of Roussel-Uclaf subsidiaries in the United States

The third wave of feminism washed ashore in the mid-1990s, focusing on "fashion, sexuality, celebrity, and consumerism."[7] Feminist activism in general, and feminist consumer activism in particular, dropped off during this period as many young women embraced what previous waves of feminism had identified as oppressive trappings of patriarchy—a focus on dress and appearance, and a celebration of women's objectification as empowering rather than sexist. This wave of feminism also shifted the focus from systemic and institutional sexism to individual rights and micropolitics in a way that deprioritized organized action.[8] This hegemonic brand of feminism was less critical of consumerism and the influence of corporations, and therefore less conducive to pressing feminist concerns in the marketplace.

In the mid-2000s, the United States saw its fourth wave of feminism emerge in the new feminist blogosphere with tech-savvy vocal young people harnessing the power of online communications to push against sexism and for a redefining of gender, sex, and sexuality norms. Fourth-wave feminism still uses the individual orientation and micropolitics of the third wave, but its span and analysis are more systemic, given the global reach of online activities. Fourth-wave feminists are avid users of online consumer activism to the point that they have created new activist applications and mobile technology to hold corporations accountable.

Gay rights activists started using consumer activism in earnest in the early 1990s. The first LGBT boycott was the previously mentioned Colorado campaign. Florida passed a similar law a year after Colorado, and LGBT activists established the Florida Gay Rights Buycott Campaign (FGRBC) in response. The FGRBC produced a list of businesses that had chosen to maintain a standard of nondiscrimination based on sexual orientation, despite the absence of a legal obligation to do so. The campaign also distributed thank you cards for activists to send to businesses to inform the companies that they were being targeted for the buycott. The FGRBC was not able to get the law rescinded, but the outpouring of business support resulted in the establishment of a de facto antidiscrimination policy among businesses.[9] Since that time, consumer activism has been an important arrow in the quiver of activists for gaining partner benefits, same-sex marriage, and better representations of LGBT individuals in the media.

Gender Justice Campaigns, 2004–2014

The Flush Rush Campaign

In March 2012, organizers launched a boycott campaign against Rush Limbaugh, a popular radio talk show host, after he called Sandra Fluke, a law school student and birth-control advocate, a "slut" and a "prostitute" on air. Limbaugh was responding to a speech Fluke had given to House Democrats the previous week in which she extolled the importance of mandating employer contraceptive coverage in national health care. Limbaugh personally criticized Fluke in his rebuttal: "What does it say about the college co-ed Susan Fluke [sic], who goes before a congressional committee and essentially says that she must be paid to have sex, what does that make her? It makes her a slut, right? It makes her a prostitute. She wants to be paid to have sex. She's having so much sex she can't afford the contraception." For the following two days, despite the negative press he was drawing because of these remarks, Limbaugh continued to make similar comments about Fluke. He also stated that Fluke was "having so much sex, it's amazing she can still walk." He followed up with the suggestion that female students at Georgetown should use aspirin between their knees as birth control—a not-so-subtle suggestion that they should be abstaining from sex.[10] The result, Flush Rush, was a market campaign proper, one aimed at changing the behavior of a business entity. Liberal media watchdog organization Media Matters for America (MMA) joined with Flush Rush and #StopRush to boycott Limbaugh in response to these comments.[11]

MMA launched in 2004 with the mission of monitoring media outlets for "conservative misinformation."[12] As a young professional, David Brock, MMA founder, was a conservative journalist and author whose work was used to discredit Anita Hill and launch an investigation of President Bill Clinton in the Paula Jones case. Brock became a staunch progressive after publishing a piece in *Esquire* magazine titled "Confessions of a Right Wing Hit-Man"[13] in which he apologized for his shoddy investigative reporting.

MMA spent over $100,000 running radio ads in eight major cities encouraging people to contact Limbaugh's sponsors and express their concern about his comments. The ultimate goal of the campaign was to get Limbaugh off the air through sponsor attrition. Clear Channel radio, the owner of most of Limbaugh's affiliate stations, pledged its support for the talk show host as soon as the boycott was announced. To support the boycott, activists crafted many petitions that received thousands of signatures, and organizers ran a social media campaign to shame corporations that bought ad time on Limbaugh's show. The Flush Rush social media campaign got a kick start when a single Reddit member, who goes by the name of Jaybercrow, put out a plea for action that made it to the front page of the site. Reddit members took to multiple social media platforms to express their dismay, and some activists posted scathing reviews on sponsor websites and business sites such as Yelp.

In the first few weeks of the boycott, over thirty radio station affiliates replaced Limbaugh's show and he lost forty-five ad sponsors, including Allstate Insurance and TurboTax.[14] Limbaugh denied that the boycott had an economic effect, but the CEO of Cumulus radio admitted that the boycott cost his company and other affiliates millions of dollars in lost revenue that year, and the Wall Street Journal Radio Network suffered such substantial losses that it went out of business in the first few weeks of the boycott.[15] Radio giant Dial Global suffered a loss of $98 million in 2012 that it attributed partially to Limbaugh's comments.[16] Even though the boycott fell out of the news within a month of Limbaugh's statements, it continues to affect overall industry ad revenues. Norman Pattiz, the CEO of Courtside Entertainment, told an industry group that a "tremendous chunk of advertising revenue was wiped out in terms of support for national talk radio programs" by the Flush Rush campaign.[17] Some sponsors that dropped Limbaugh stopped advertising on radio altogether. The Flush Rush campaign is unusual in that, although it wreaked severe economic havoc, the boycott was not enough to achieve the campaign goal of getting Limbaugh off the air.

The GoDaddy Campaign

In 2013, The Representation Project (TRP) organized a boycott of Internet provider GoDaddy.com for its portrayal of women in its advertising. TRP is a nonprofit organization affiliated with the popular documentary *Missrepresentation* (2011) and with the mission of raising awareness of how gender stereotypes hurt everyone.[18] This was a market campaign proper because its goal was to change the political practices of GoDaddy, a business entity. TRP built a social media campaign to combat sexist media, and GoDaddy was its first target because the company had built its name recognition by cutting through the advertising clutter with racy ads. Their most viewed ads revolved around jiggling "GoDaddy Girls" and Danica Patrick, a racecar driver, in the nude.

TRP was founded by Jennifer Siebel Newsom, an actor and director. She grew up in the upscale Bay Area town of Sausalito and earned her MBA from Stanford. Newsom worked in the nonprofit sector for a global environmental coalition before moving to Hollywood to pursue an acting career. She had moderate success as an actor, appearing in such shows as *Mad Men* and *Strong Medicine*. She became politicized around gender issues in her early thirties when she was pregnant with her first daughter, inspiring her to create *Missrepresentation*. TRP created a mobile app called #NotBuyingIt with which users can connect with like-minded people, and identify and tag ads or other content as sexist.[19]

For example, one user posted a photo of an aisle in Toys 'R Us with frilly pink toys for girls and violent toys in camouflage for boys, using the #NotBuyingIt hashtag. During the 2013 Super Bowl, consumer activists sent over 7,500 tweets directed at GoDaddy with the hashtag #NotBuyingIt to protest an ad showing a swimsuit model making out with a stereotypical nerdy guy to represent the "sexy" and the "smart" sides of the brand. GoDaddy contacted TRP after the Super Bowl and pledged not to use stereotypical or hypersexualized images of women in ads for the next Super Bowl. CEO Blake Irving publicly stated that the GoDaddy ads were "on the edge of inappropriate" and promised to use less polarizing content in the future.[20] During the 2014 Super Bowl, GoDaddy featured Patrick as a bulked up body builder, and its 2015 ad featured a man working late at the office.

The GoDaddy campaign had no economic effect on the company—it actually added more accounts as a result of the controversy—but it was effective because the #Notbuyingit campaign branded the company as sexist. The organizers achieved their campaign goal quickly and are now targeting American Apparel, Victoria's Secret, Carl's Jr., and other prominent brands with the #NotBuyingIt social media app.

The Beverly Hills Hotel Campaign

In 2014, the Human Rights Campaign (HRC) joined forces with the FMF and other gender and LGBT groups to launch a boycott against the historic Beverly Hills Hotel to protest the politics of its owner, Hassanal Bolkiah, the sultan of Brunei. Earlier that year, the sultan had approved the gradual adoption of Sharia law in Brunei, including capital punishment for same-sex couples and legalizing rape in marriage if the wife is older than thirteen. This was a campaign that used market tactics to change governmental practices overseas rather than a market campaign proper.

HRC is the largest LGBT advocacy organization in the United States. It was founded in 1980 by Steve Endean, the first gay rights lobbyist in the country (registered in Minnesota). Endean dedicated his life to LGBT advocacy after experiencing sexuality discrimination in his pursuit of politics. He was a self-described Midwestern Catholic boy who believed that his quest for gay rights was his calling from God. Endean died of AIDS-related complications in 1993, but his life work lives on in the HRC. The FMF was founded by Eleanor Smeal in 1987. Smeal became politicized around feminist issues as a young mother when she encountered problems obtaining childcare. She held leadership positions with the League of Women Voters and NOW before starting her own nonprofit. She is credited with coining the term *gender gap*, which is now widely used.

The HRC and the FMF were joined by many celebrities, including Oprah Winfrey and Jay Leno, in their boycott of the Beverly Hills Hotel and other hotels owned by the sultan. Sir Richard Branson of the Virgin Group also joined the boycott with the promise not to patronize any of the sultan's hotels. A representative for the HRC told reporters, "Our campaign is to make these hotels nuclear-radioactive and they will quickly become shadows of their former selves"[21] so that the sultan would sell the hotel.

Organizers used boycott and direct action tools to press for their cause. In the first month of the boycott, over a dozen organizations moved their galas and conventions to other locations, including the Motion Picture & Television Fund and the Gill Action Fund. John Legend, a musician, cancelled a scheduled performance at the hotel. Lost meetings and social bookings cost the Beverly Hills Hotel over $2 million in lost revenue.[22] In addition to economic loss, the Beverly Hills Hotel has lost its pristine reputation as a glamorous getaway for a long list of famous and wealthy individuals (including Marilyn Monroe), a branding loss that will be difficult to restore because celebrities are leading the cause.[23]

Campaign organizers kicked off the boycott with a massive protest outside the hotel that drew international media attention. The sultan of Brunei did not respond to this or subsequent protests outside this famed hotel. A year after the boycott, small groups of protesters still gather outside the hotel most days of the week to hold signs and wave at passing cars, but some celebrities have returned to the hotel.[24] Angelina Jolie and Brad Pitt patronized the pink hotel in early 2015, and Russell Crow works out in the gym when he is in town. The boycott has faced stiff criticism from some celebrities for harming employees in Los Angeles in the name of helping oppressed people 8,000 miles away in Brunei. Kim Kardashian penned a blog post questioning the validity of the boycott and protests, to which Billy Polina, an organizer responded, "Miss Kardashian needs to know that in Brunei she would have been flogged for having a baby out of wedlock."[25]

The campaign against the Beverly Hills Hotel received worldwide media attention and was even discussed at the United Nations.[26] This was the first time in U.S. history that the actions of the leader of another nation were taken to task through consumer activism targeting corporate holdings in the United States. The boycott was rare in that it inflicted measurable economic damage, but to date, the sultan shows no signs of divesting from his Hollywood icon or reversing his decision to implement Sharia law in his country.

The National Football League Boycott

In February 2014, NFL player Ray Rice was physically violent toward his soon-to-be wife, Janay Palmer, at a casino in Atlantic City. Rice and Palmer were both arrested and charged with assault. A week later, celebrity news program *TMZ* stirred public outrage when it released a surveillance video of Rice dragging Palmer out of an elevator. A few months later, NFL Commissioner Roger Goodell suspended Rice for two games to punish him for this violence. Following the press conference to announce this decision, the Ravens Twitter account sent out a message blaming Palmer (now Janay Rice) for the role she had played in the violence perpetrated against her.

One month after this press conference, *TMZ* released another part of the surveillance video showing the violence that Ray Rice had meted out in the elevator, and again there was a national outcry, but this time it was much louder. Within hours of the release of the video, Goodell suspended Rice claiming that he had not previously seen the entire footage. But investigative reporters found that the NFL had received the entire video five months prior,[27] meaning the NFL had a public relations crisis on its hands. Women make up 45 percent of the 150 million NFL fans and represent the largest demographic for NFL financial growth,[28] so the league was in a precarious economic position for its light sanctions against Rice for domestic violence. This was a market campaign proper, one targeting the NFL to change its approach to players who perpetrate domestic violence.

The NFL boycott was initiated by many different activists instead of an organization or a unified coalition. Keith Olbermann, ESPN commentator, and a host of writers and political leaders called for a boycott of the NFL until Goodell fired Rice and was permanently banned from the NFL. For Olbermann, not boycotting means "we become accessories after the fact."[29] Feminist activists used social media shaming tools to call for Goodell's removal and more stringent NFL penalties for players who perpetrate domestic violence. NOW called for Goodell's removal, and the hashtag #BoycottNFL started trending. This controversy also sparked the #WhyIStayed hashtag, a national online discussion of why women often stay in situations of domestic abuse. UltraViolet, a new feminist organization, paid for a banner to be flown over an NFL game that said, "Goodell must go." A Care2.org petition calling for Rice's suspension for an entire year received nearly 25,000 signatures.

CoverGirl, "the official beauty sponsor of the NFL," became the target of a secondary boycott. The CoverGirl-NFL relationship had been developed to appeal to the large female viewership of the league. Activists barraged the official CoverGirl Facebook page and tweeted at the company to sever its ties with the NFL. An activist digitally altered a CoverGirl ad to include a black eye on the model (figure 5.1).[30] This image went viral, giving CoverGirl an economic black eye, but the brand decided to maintain its affiliation with the NFL.

The NFL also faced pressure from other corporate advertisers, such as FedEx and Marriot Hotels. The advertisers were quick to issue statements that they were watching the NFL response closely. PepsiCo issued a statement saying,

FIGURE 5.1   Altered CoverGirl ad protesting the NFL response to domestic violence, 2014

"Domestic violence is completely unacceptable. We are encouraged to see the NFL is now treating this with the seriousness it deserves."[31] Anheuser-Busch released a statement criticizing the NFL for its handling of the Rice case, and the Radisson Hotel chain withdrew its NFL sponsorship. These sponsors were preempting a secondary boycott against their own companies.

A year into the boycott, Goodell was still the commissioner and Rice was suspended, not banned, from playing football. The NFL released a statement touting a new domestic violence policy, but as some noted, it was not new or binding.[32] Goodell established a six-game suspension for future incidences of domestic violence with consideration for mitigating factors. In other words, the suspension can be as long as the NFL commissioner decides. For second offenses, players are to be banned indefinitely, but they can apply to be reinstated after one year. These "new" rules did not constitute a substantive policy change or a zero tolerance policy, as Goodell had claimed. It is possible that the boycott will give the NFL pause the next time it considers sanctions, but this market campaign did not lead to strong policies against domestic violence or the removal of those who had fumbled Rice's case.

The Hobby Lobby Campaign

Arts and crafts store Hobby Lobby faced a boycott in July 2014 when it challenged a new mandate to provide contraception in its employee healthcare coverage, with a case that went all the way to the Supreme Court. Over seventy other companies filed similar legal challenges, but Hobby Lobby received the most attention from activists because its name led the Supreme Court filing.[33] This was a market campaign proper because it sought to close down a company for its political stance on birth control. The Supreme Court ruled that corporations can choose not to provide contraceptive coverage to their employees based on religious beliefs, and activists immediately responded with a boycott.

George Takei, *Star Trek* actor and LGBT activist, was the first to call for this action through his popular blog, and he was joined by the nonprofit organization Freedom From Religion Foundation (FFRF), UltraViolet, and individual organizers across the country. FFRF, the largest nontheist organization in the United States, was founded in 1972 by Anne Nicol Gaylor and her daughter Annie Laurie Gaylor. In the late 1960s, Anne was a prominent pro-choice activist in Wisconsin, and her daughter Annie joined her in these efforts. In 1977, they led a campaign to recall a judge after he made comments blaming a rape survivor for her rape. This mother-daughter team also organized protests against gun violence and in support of other progressive issues prior to Anne Gaylor's passing in 2015.

UltraViolet is a women's advocacy organization that was founded in 2012 by Nita Chaudhary and Shaunna Thomas. The organization was named after the color that symbolizes the struggle for women's and LGBT rights in the United States. Within two months of its founding, UltraViolet had 300,000 members. Prior to cofounding the organization, Chaudhary had been a director at MoveOn. org, the largest online activist community in the world. Thomas was previously the executive director of the progressive nonprofit P Street Project. She became politicized when she worked on the 2004 presidential election.

For the Hobby Lobby campaign, FFRF, UltraViolet, and a network of grassroots activists worked in loose coordination. They established a Facebook group with over 18,000 members, and 207,000 people signed an online petition organized by liberal news source, The Daily Kos. The petition framed opposition to the Supreme Court ruling in terms of women's reproductive freedom: "Five male justices on the U.S. Supreme Court have ruled in favor of Hobby Lobby, allowing the company—and all other 'closely-held' corporations—to use religion as an excuse to interfere with their employees' medical decisions. But that's only the beginning of the company's well-laid plans for a theocracy. The good news is, you can use your dollars to shut this whole thing down."[34] UltraViolet used direct consumer action by staging light brigades outside Hobby Lobby stores in seven major cities in the weeks after the ruling. This organization also produced a humorous video with puppets to dispel myths about contraceptive coverage that was viewed over 40,000 times.

In response to the boycott, supporters of the Hobby Lobby decision staged a counterbuycott. They organized Hobby Lobby Love Day on July 3, 2014, encouraging people to patronize the store and show support for its politics. Bristol Palin, the daughter of Sarah Palin, former Alaska governor and vice presidential candidate, wrote a blog post encouraging people to shop at Hobby Lobby and post photos on social media: "No matter what your photo says, buying something at Hobby Lobby will send a strong message. Thank you for having the guts to stand up to an overreaching President who's trying to re-make America into his own image."[35] The hashtag campaign #ReligiousFreedom was used by counterboycotters over 10,000 times in the weeks following the Hobby Lobby decision.

The Hobby Lobby boycott action lacked unity of effort and a clear goal, but the public supported the cause. A Reuters-Ipsos poll found that only 35 percent of Americans agreed with the Court decision on Hobby Lobby and that a majority opposed allowing companies to decide whether to provide contraceptive coverage for their employees.[36] The Hobby Lobby boycott was further complicated by the fact that so many other companies had the same stance on contraception as Hobby Lobby, but a boycott of over seventy businesses and brands was unwieldy. Furthermore, Hobby Lobby shoppers tend to be older conservative white women, and few of the younger liberal activists participating in the boycott had shopped at the store to begin with.[37] If activists were trying to put the company out of business, they did not succeed. And if they were trying to get the company to reverse its decision and provide contraceptive coverage, they did not succeed. If they were trying to harm Hobby Lobby economically, the boycott did succeed. Hobby Lobby revenue dropped considerably from $3.3 billion in 2013 to $2.7 billion in 2014. The effectiveness of the Hobby Lobby campaign was therefore mixed.

LGBT Rights Campaigns, 2004–2014

The Boycott Utah Campaign

The state of Utah was the target of a consumer activism campaign in 2008 after the passage of Proposition 8, a citizen initiative eliminating same-sex marriage in California. Organizers went after the Utah tourism industry to punish the Mormon Church for its role in getting Proposition 8 passed. Although the Mormon Church had been only one member of a multifaith coalition during the Proposition 8 campaign, it became a target because it had been the most effective member. Mormons had raised over $20 million to overturn same-sex marriage in California, and over 45 percent of out-of-state donations had come from the state of Utah.[38] The church also sent volunteers from Utah to California to canvas in favor of Proposition 8, an organizing tactic that proved crucial in days leading up to the election.

In response to the work by the Mormon Church to pass Proposition 8, John Aravosis, a Democratic strategist and LGBT blogger, called for skiers to boycott Utah ski destinations, and for actors and directors to pull out of the Sundance Film Festival (located in Utah). The goal of this boycott was to harm the tourist economy of Utah and send a message to the Mormon Church, whose members are concentrated in that state. This was a campaign that used market tactics to influence the political position of a religious entity rather than a market campaign proper.

Aravosis, a first-generation Greek American, was politicized at an early age when his uncle was beaten and imprisoned in the early 1970s by the Greek military junta. His uncle held a number of powerful political posts after Greece returned to a democracy, including ambassador to the United Nations. Aravosis had an appetite for politics growing up, and he earned a joint law and master's degree in foreign service from Georgetown before becoming a political consultant and blogger.

In addition to a boycott, Aravosis and other grassroots organizers used direct activism and social media shaming. Over five hundred mothers of LGBT children, some of them Mormons, held a candlelight vigil outside the Mormon Temple in Salt Lake City the night of the election,[39] and protesters gathered outside of Mormon temples nationwide in the weeks following the decision. Several Facebook pages popped up to support the Utah boycott, and the website MormonsStole-OurRights.com was established to challenge the tax exempt status of the church.

Proposition 8 was eventually ruled unconstitutional, and same-sex marriage was reinstated in California in 2013. The vague goal of the boycott of impacting Utah tourism was probably accomplished. For a decade, the state had enjoyed steady growth in the number of out-of-state tourists each year, but Utah experienced a significant dip in visitors from 2008 to 2009 (from 20.4 million to 19.5 million).[40] Tourism rates rebounded the following year and have continued to increase since then. There is no way to know for sure whether this anomalous drop of nearly one million tourists in Utah was due to the boycott, but we do know that it went against national travel trends that year. In 2009, nationwide rates of travel increased despite a national economic downturn.[41]

The Target Campaign

In 2011, Lady Gaga, pop icon and singer known for her gay anthem "Born This Way," dissolved an exclusive distribution partnership with the giant retailer

Target due to the financial support by the company of conservative political candidates who held antigay stances.[42] An investigative journalist revealed that the Target Political Action Committee had contributed nearly three-quarters of its lobbying budget to candidates who were anti–gay rights.[43] Lady Gaga fans led the boycott efforts, and social media was alight with tweets and Facebook posts using the hashtag #BoycottTarget.

Target responded to Lady Gaga's public shaming tactic with a statement admonishing her for challenging their commitment to "an inclusive workplace environment." The two parties met to negotiate, but Lady Gaga terminated her distribution deal when Target executives would not agree to stop donations to antigay organizations and politicians.[44] This was a market campaign proper because it revolved around the policy position and actions of a business entity.

This was not Lady Gaga's first foray into political activism. This chart-topping pop singer has been active around disasters (the 2010 earthquake in Haiti, the tsunami in Japan in 2011, and Hurricane Sandy in 2012), environmental issues (Artists against Fracking), HIV-AIDS, and campus sexual assault. In 2016, she appeared on the Academy Awards stage with fifty survivors of campus sexual assault for a moving rendition of her song "Till It Happens to You" from the documentary *The Hunting Ground,* an exposé documentary on the campus rape epidemic. In 2012, she launched the Born This Way Foundation to promote youth empowerment and mitigate bullying. She has lobbied in favor of same-sex marriage and against policies that discriminate against LGBT individuals. After several months of boycott and social media pressure, Target announced it would limit its political contributions to antigay organizations, meaning this campaign was effective. The company also established a committee to review its workplace environment concerning LGBT issues. The boycott did not exact measurable economic damage, but it tarnished the company image as gay-friendly. Fred Sainz from the HRC spoke to factors that ultimately made the boycott successful: "Target's biggest asset and vulnerability is they market so transparently to our community. If that retailer does not fulfill on what we believe to be their brand promise, there are consequences."[45]

The Chick-Fil-A Campaign

In June 2012, Daniel Cathy, chief of the fast food giant Chick-Fil-A, took a strong stance against same-sex marriage on a radio show. Cathy stated, "I think we are inviting God's judgment on our nation when we shake our fist at Him and say, 'We know better than you as to what constitutes a marriage.' I pray God's mercy on our generation that has such a prideful, arrogant attitude to think that we have the audacity to define what marriage is about."[46] These comments came after revelations that the company had contributed millions of dollars annually to organizations opposing same-sex marriage. Shane Windmeyer, the executive director of the LGBT rights organization Campus Pride, initiated a boycott of the fast food chain, and student activists led the charge.[47]

Campus Pride was cofounded by recent college graduates M. Chad Wilson, Sarah Holmes, and Windmeyer in 2001 in Charlotte, North Carolina, with the mission of making college campuses safer for LGBT students. A dozen campuses effectively lobbied and petitioned to close down their Chick-Fil-A franchises, including Davidson College and Duke University. Grassroots activists started at least ten petitions pressuring Chick-Fil-A, some calling for the company to stop donating to antigay organizations, others demanding an apology from Cathy. These petitions gathered anywhere from 13 signatures to over 5,000. One popular petition called for Chick-Fil-A to "End the Hypocrisy! Stop Serving Gay Chickens." The creator of this humorous petition, Steven Hoffman from Middleton, Ohio, cited academic sources confirming that some chickens engage in homosexual behavior and chided Chick-Fil-A for serving anything less than "100 percent heterosexual" chicken. The goal of this campaign was to alter the public stance and campaign contributions of a business entity, so it was a market campaign proper.

Politicians and other prominent leaders from across the nation joined the boycott. Boston Mayor Thomas Menino told reporters, "Chick-Fil-A doesn't belong in Boston. You can't have a business in the city of Boston that discriminates against a population."[48] He also wrote a public letter to Cathy condemning the CEO's statements on the radio show. The mayors of Chicago, New York, and San Francisco also publicly chastised Chick-Fil-A for the avowed antigay positions of the company. Corporate affiliate, the Jim Henson Company, dropped a toy-licensing arrangement with the company. HarperCollins became the target of a secondary boycott when activists delivered a petition with over 80,000 signatures asking the company to stop its Bernstein Bears collaboration with Chick-Fil-A. HarperCollins chose to continue its partnership with the fast food chain, citing its commitment to free speech.

Activists organized a National Same-Sex Kiss-In Day outside Chick-Fil-A locations on August 4, 2012 (figure 5.2).[49] Carly McGehee, a Dallas activist, came up with the idea and promoted it through a dedicated Facebook page. Thousands of people participated in the kiss-in at 1,600 Chick-Fil-A franchise locations.

Some of the Chick-Fil-A campaign actions were extra-legal. In Torrance, California, Manuel Castro, an artist, was arrested for spraying graffiti that read, "Tastes Like Hate," on the side of a Chick-Fil-A franchise. Activists pasted stickers

FIGURE 5.2   National Same-Sex Kiss-In Day event, 2012

and spray painted marriage equality slogans outside Chick-Fil-A franchises in Maryland and Missouri around the time of the national kiss-in.

The Chick-Fil-A campaign had mixed effectiveness. It achieved one of its stated goals of getting the company to stop funding extremist antigay rights organization. Within a year, Chick-Fil-A had redirected its charitable funds to the United Negro Scholarship Fund and Habitat for Humanity.[50] The campaign did not garner much public support, however. In August 2012, Rasmussen Reports found that 61 percent of Americans held a favorable view of Chick-Fil-A, while only 13 percent said they were boycotting the fast food chain.[51]

Furthermore, the Chick-Fil-A boycott generated a counterbuycott that sent the company revenues soaring. Chick-Fil-A revenue increased 12 percent in the year following the boycott as conservative activists mobilized to patronize the restaurant.[52] The counterbuycott was led by Mike Huckabee, former Arkansas governor and Fox News host, who promoted the buycott through his cable program and social media. Huckabee declared August 1, 2013, Chick-Fil-A Appreciation Day.[53] Other prominent Republican politicians, including Sarah Palin, encouraged people to participate in Chick-Fil-A Appreciation Day, and the company experienced record sales as customers lined up around the block to make a political statement with their pocketbooks. The conservative voices had more of a short-term economic effect than did the antigay activists, but the brand took a hit among fast food patrons that could have long-term effects. The favorability of the Chick-Fil-A brand eventually went from mid-60 percent down to under 40 percent among customers overall.[54] Near the end of the boycott, Windmeyer struck an unlikely friendship with Cathy, borne out of mutual respect and dialogue during the boycott.

Ender's Game Campaign

In April 2012, gay rights activists organized a boycott of the film Ender's Game because of the very public antigay stance of the author, Orson Scott Card.[55] Card is a member of the Mormon Church and a former board member of the National Organization for Marriage (NOM), a nonprofit that opposes same-sex marriage. During the California Proposition 8 debate in 2008, Card labeled homosexuality a "deviant behavior" and promised to overthrow any government that allowed same-sex marriage.[56] Geeks OUT, an activist organization that promotes the interests of the "queer geek community," initiated a boycott of Ender's Game when it was announced that Card's popular book would be made into a film.

Geeks OUT was founded by five friends in New York in 2013, after they had endured years of discrimination in geek communities based on their sexual identity. The mission of Geeks OUT is to encourage visibility and acceptance of queer geeks in the comic and gaming worlds. The cofounders, Jono Jarrett, Matthew Levine, Keith Marran, Josh Siegel, and Joey Stern, are self-described "gay fan boys" intent on creating safe spaces for LGBT individuals through events, an informational blog, and online forums. In 2015, Geeks OUT hosted the first gay comic convention, Flame Con, in New York.

For the Ender's Game boycott, Geeks OUT circulated a MoveOn.org petition that received over 12,000 signatures, urging a boycott of the film on opening weekend. This was a market campaign proper because it put pressure on a business entity directly. Within a week of the start of the boycott, Lionsgate, the company producing the film, distanced itself from Card's beliefs and pledged to host a pro-LGBT benefit for its premiere, but this did not quell consumer activism.[57]

When *Ender's Game* opened in theaters in November 2013, Geeks OUT also organized Skip *Ender's Game* parties in cities throughout the United States where boycotters could meet up. *Ender's Game* was the top-grossing film on opening weekend, and it went on to make $125 million worldwide.[58] Nevertheless, the film cost $110 million to make, and it did not live up to revenue expectations. *Variety* deemed *Ender's Game* the biggest box office bomb of 2013, and it is not possible to isolate the economic effects of the boycott because the film received mixed reviews.[59] The stated goal of the Geeks OUT campaign was to raise awareness of Card's antigay positions, and this goal was achieved through a blitz of media coverage about the boycott.[60]

The Dump Russian Vodka Campaign

Dan Savage, a gay rights activist, called for a boycott of Russian vodka in summer 2013 to protest the Russian crackdown on LGBT individuals.[61] This was a campaign that used market tactics to influence government policy, so it was not a market campaign proper. Russian President Vladimir Putin signed a series of "gay propaganda laws" prohibiting "the promotion of non-traditional sexual relationships."[62] These laws prohibit gay pride events, the adoption of children by gay parents, and any other actions that can be interpreted as promoting same-sex relationships. They had immediate consequences for some LGBT people in Russia, who were fired from their jobs and faced violence for public displays of homosexuality.[63] Savage called for the boycott in a blog post on his well-trafficked website: "To show our solidarity with Russian queers and their allies and to help to draw international attention to the persecution of gay men, lesbians, bisexuals, trans people and straight allies in Vladimir Putin's increasingly fascistic Russia: dump Russian vodka."[64] Savage singled out Stolichnaya (Stoli) and Russian Standard as the brands to boycott, and he coined the hashtag #DumpStoli. The activist organization Queer Nation spread the word about the boycott through a social media campaign. Bars catering to gay and lesbian clientele across the globe dropped these brands.[65] In New York, over two hundred bars joined the boycott,[66] and consumer activists dumped bottles of Russian vodka in the street.

Savage was raised as a Catholic in Chicago, where he studied history and theater at the University of Illinois. He is a theater director, an advice columnist, and a radio host who regularly gets into hot water for his controversial statements and actions. In 2003, after Senator Rick Santorum (R-PA) compared homosexuality to bestiality and incest, Santorum set up a website defining the term *Santorum* as "the frothy mixture of lube and fecal matter that is sometimes a byproduct of anal sex."[67] Savage is also known for starting the "It Gets Better" media project in 2010 following the suicide of fifteen-year-old Billy Lucas, who was bullied for his perceived sexuality.

Stoli immediately responded to Savage's boycott with a condemnation of the Russian record on LGBT rights, and it posted a rainbow on its page with a banner that read, "Stolichnaya Premium Vodka stands strong and proud with the global LGBT community against the actions and beliefs of the Russian government."[68] In contrast, Russian Standard did not publicly respond to the boycott action. Savage's stated goal for the boycott was to raise awareness of the new Russian antigay laws in time for the 2014 Olympics in Sochi. The boycott action generated ample media attention, and Savage announced that it was a "huge success" in raising awareness of the issue.[69] The boycott officially came to an end in February 2014 after Stoli pledged to support the rights of LGBT people in Russia and made major donations to the LA Gay & Lesbian Center and the Russian Freedom Fund.[70]

The Boycott Barilla Campaign

During a radio interview in 2013, Guido Barilla, the chairman of Barilla Pasta, offended gay rights groups across the globe when he stated, "I would never do an advert with a homosexual family."[71] He went on to say that customers who do not like his position could purchase other brands of pasta. Shortly after the interview, the company issued an apology tweet stating that Barilla had the "deepest respect" for all people. The Italian gay rights group Equality Italia launched a boycott in Italy, and the Gay and Lesbian Alliance Against Defamation (GLAAD) and the HRC launched one in the United States. Within hours, #BoycottBarilla was trending on Twitter. This was a market campaign proper because it sought to pressure Barilla into changing its public position on LGBT families.

GLAAD was founded in 1985 in New York by Vito Russo, a film scholar; Gregory Kolovakos, an artist; Darryl Yates Rist and Allen Barnett, writers; and Jewelle Gomez, poet and playwright, in response to sensational, misleading, and homophobic media coverage of the AIDS crisis. GLAAD has effectively shifted the way in which the news media discuss LGBT people and issues through dozens of campaigns in the past three decades.

For the Barilla boycott, Linda Ferraro, the mother of a GLAAD staffer, started a Change.org petition that gathered just under 10,000 signatures, and Beth Allen, a self-identified lesbian mother of two from Maryland, started a MoveOn.org petition that received over 140,000 signatures. Same-sex marriage had just become legal in Maryland, and Allen had recently wed her partner of twenty years. This was her first activism campaign, one that was driven by anger at Barilla's comments. "They made me very angry because he was so dismissive. Not just that he said that he wouldn't show a gay family in his advertising, but that if gay people don't like it, they can just not buy the pasta. That seemed like a challenge."[72] Allen led the efforts, and other grassroots activists joined in by creating Facebook and Twitter accounts to support the boycott. Within a matter of weeks, Harvard University students got Barilla pasta removed from the university cafeteria.

Barilla makes up 30 percent of the U.S. pasta and ready-made pasta sauce market, with $430 million in annual sales, so the public shaming campaign was a potential threat to both its reputation and sales.[73] The pasta maker saw its sales decline as much as 10 percent in the first few months of the boycott,[74] and its reputation plummeted in the LGBT and allied communities.

In response, the company issued several video apologies. When these did not quiet the criticism, the company expanded healthcare benefits for transgender employees, provided diversity training to its 8,000 employees with an LGBT focus, created a Diversity & Inclusion Board to advise the company, and contributed money to LGBT rights organizations.[75] The company also featured a lesbian family on a promotional website and pledged to show LGBT individuals in future ad campaigns. A GLAAD spokesperson met with Guido Barilla and reported that he had undergone an "evolution" in thinking about LGBT rights. Consumer activists used boycott and social media tools to effectively accomplish their goal of getting Barilla to change its stance on LGBT issues.

The *Duck Dynasty* Campaign

In 2013, Phil Robertson, the patriarch of the reality television show *Duck Dynasty*, made antigay remarks in an interview with *GQ* magazine, in which he said, "Start with homosexual behavior and just morph out from there. Bestiality, sleeping around with this woman and that woman and that woman and those men. . . . Don't be deceived. Neither the adulterers, the idolaters, the male prostitutes, the homosexual offenders, the greedy, the drunkards, the slanderers, the swindlers—they won't inherit the kingdom of God. Don't deceive yourself. It's not right."[76] These comments elicited media attention and criticism, and GLAAD called for *Duck Dynasty* producer A&E to "re-examine their ties to someone with such public disdain for LGBT people and families."[77] This was a market campaign proper because it targeted A&E to change its program line-up.

Beyond being the most watched reality television series of all time, *Duck Dynasty* was also a successful merchandise brand bringing in about $400 million a year in revenue. Walmart accounts for about 50 percent of *Duck Dynasty* merchandise sales, stocking everything from clothing to recreational vehicles and prayer devotionals.[78] The boycott threat was initially effective. The network lost a considerable number of its 12 million viewers after Robertson's interview went viral, and A&E responded with an apology and an indefinite suspension of Robertson. The channel also began airing public service announcements "promoting unity, tolerance and acceptance among all people, a message that supports our core values as a company, and the values found in *Duck Dynasty*."[79]

In response, religious and conservative groups, including Faith Driven Consumer, organized a counterboycott of A&E to protest Robertson's suspension. They created a Change.org petition calling for his reinstatement that received 118,000 signatures. Another petition on the site IStandWithPhil.com received 265,000 signatures. The counterboycott and profit motives got Robertson reinstated a few weeks after his suspension.

Conservative groups also staged a related boycott of the Cracker Barrel restaurant chain after it pulled its *Duck Dynasty* merchandise in the wake of Robertson's comments. Activists took to Twitter and other social media to express their outrage at Cracker Barrel for its decision, most framing their concern as issues of freedom of expression and support for biblical teachings. After one day of a social media boycott blitz against Cracker Barrel, the restaurant restocked the *Duck Dynasty* merchandise and issued an apology: "When we made the decision to remove and evaluate certain *Duck Dynasty* items, we offended many of our loyal customers. Our intent was to avoid offending, but that's just what we've done. You told us we made a mistake. And, you weren't shy about it. You wrote, you called and you took to social media to express your thoughts and feelings. You flat out told us we were wrong. We listened."[80]

The *Duck Dynasty* campaign involved a boycott as well as social media, as did the counterboycotts of A&E and Cracker Barrel. The initial boycott was not successful in removing Robertson from the show for more than a few weeks or in shutting down production of the popular *Duck Dynasty* program. In 2015, Robertson again stirred controversy with his statements during an Easter Sunday address after describing an imaginary scenario in which an atheist family is raped and murdered because they are atheists.[81] Atheist activists did not respond with consumer activism, perhaps because the previous boycott generated more activism on the other side.

Mozilla Boycott

In 2014, Brendan Eich, chief executive officer (CEO) and cofounder of Mozilla, resigned after two weeks of an intense boycott campaign by LGBT groups.[82] Mozilla, an online giant and parent company of the Firefox browser, faced immediate scrutiny when Eich was promoted to its top position. Eich had never spoken publicly about his views, but six years prior to his promotion, he had contributed $1,000 to support the California Proposition 8 campaign. Eich responded with a public apology about the "pain" his political views may have caused and vowed to uphold a culture of equality at Mozilla. This was a market campaign proper because it targeted a business entity to cause a change.

The boycott of Mozilla was initiated and sustained by the tech community. Hampton Catlin, the CEO of software development company Rarebit, threw the first boycott punch when he announced that his company would withdraw all their products from Firefox. Catlin wrote a blog post about how Proposition 8 had prevented him from marrying his husband, which stood in the way of his husband's naturalization as a U.S. citizenship.[83] Within hours of this post, Twitter was trending with the hashtag #BoycottFirefox, with people pledging to switch to Google Chrome, the main competitor of Firefox. Over 70,000 people signed a CREDO Action petition demanding Eich's removal as CEO, and OkCupid, an online dating site, joined the boycott by making it difficult to access their site using Firefox. OkCupid also sent a message to its Firefox users stating that "Mozilla's new CEO, Brendan Eich, is an opponent of equal rights for same-sex couples. We would therefore prefer that our users not use Mozilla software to access OkCupid." In addition, about a dozen Mozilla employees put their jobs at risk by calling for Eich's resignation via Twitter.

The Mozilla boycott was effective. Eich stepped down as CEO on April 3, 2014, eleven days after he was promoted. The company cited "boycotts, protests, and intense public scrutiny" as the primary factors in Eich's decision.[84] Eich's resignation was met with a counterboycott from conservatives, who decried the move as an infringement of free speech.[85] Charles Krauthammer, a conservative commentator, was the first to call for a counterboycott during an interview on Fox News.[86] The conservative news site TruthRevolt mimicked the OkCupid message to Firefox users, asking them to access the site using another browser considering "Mozilla's crackdown on political and religious positions held by millions of Americans."[87] Activists took to Twitter with the hashtag #Boycott-Mozilla (compared to #BoycottFirefox, used by the initial boycott) to demand that Eich be reinstated. This counterboycott did not generate nearly as much attention and participation as the Chick-Fil-A or *Duck Dynasty* counterboycotts, and Eich was not reinstated as CEO of Mozilla.

Campaign Effectiveness

I have examined thirteen campaigns for gender and LGBT rights in this chapter. Social media played a key role in the more recent campaigns started by individuals compared to nonprofits, and the media were used to mobilize decentralized citizen discontent. That they were initiated as grassroots campaigns also meant that these campaigns were sometimes disorganized, with overlapping petitions and divergent messages. Social media and boycott tactics drove much of the activism rather than clear goals and overarching strategy. Regardless of the decentralization of many of these campaigns, they were generally effective in bringing about their desired goal.

In terms of effectiveness, as shown in table 5.1, two campaigns are ongoing (Flush Rush and the Beverly Hills Hotel Boycott). Successful campaigns took between eleven days to one and half years to achieve their goal. Seven achieved their stated goal, for a success rate of 63.6 percent. Two campaigns attained mixed success. The Hobby Lobby campaign hurt the bottom line of the company, but it did not compel the company to start offering contraceptive coverage to its employees. The Chick-Fil-A campaign reached its modest goal of raising awareness about the anti-gay-rights spending by the company, but a counterboycott actually improved revenue for the fast food chain.

Two campaigns, the NFL and *Duck Dynasty* boycotts, did not achieve their goals. The NFL efforts did not bring about Rice's permanent expulsion from the league, commissioner Goodell's firing, or a better domestic violence policy. The *Duck Dynasty* campaign was initially successful in getting Robertson, the family patriarch, suspended from the show, but a counterboycott against A&E and

TABLE 5.1 Effectiveness of gender and LGBT rights campaigns

CAMPAIGN	EFFECTIVE?
Flush Rush	Ongoing
GoDaddy	Yes
Beverly Hills Hotel	Ongoing
NFL	No
Hobby Lobby	Mixed
Target	Yes
State of Utah	Yes
Chick-Fil-A	Mixed
Russian Vodka	Yes
Barilla Pasta	Yes
Ender's Game	Yes
Duck Dynasty	No
Mozilla	Yes
Effectiveness = 63.6%	

a secondary boycott against Cracker Barrel led to his swift reinstatement. Powerful conservative counterboycotts are new—a reaction to the increased use of market campaigns in the culture wars. I examine conservative consumer activism in chapter 6.

Democratic Implications

The campaigns for gender and LGBT rights in this chapter improved democratic inputs and outputs through increasing political participation and discussion, and advancing the will of the majority. These campaigns also improved the representation of minority interests and protection of minority rights. In addition, the campaigns improved corporate accountability by monitoring charitable giving and the attitudes and actions of company leaders. As shown in table 5.2, campaigns for gender justice and LGBT rights contributed to seven democratic measures on average.

Promotes Robust Citizen Participation

All thirteen campaigns in this chapter fortified citizen participation by providing an unconventional political outlet (the marketplace) to express concern about

TABLE 5.2 Democratic contribution of gender justice and LGBT rights campaigns

CAMPAIGN	DEMOCRATIC SCORE (1–10)
Flush Rush	8
GoDaddy	6
Beverly Hills Hotel	9
NFL	5
Hobby Lobby	8
Target	6
State of Utah	6
Chick-Fil-A	7
Russian Vodka	9
Barilla Pasta	7
Ender's Game	7
Duck Dynasty	7
Mozilla	7
Average = 7.1	

political issues. Citizen participation was particularly high for the Chick-Fil-A and *Duck Dynasty* campaigns, which generated interest from millions of people through the initial boycotts and counterboycotts. The Hobby Lobby campaign was also particularly good at mobilizing citizen participation. Over a quarter of a million people used consumer activism to target the company to protest its position on contraceptives in the first few months of the campaign.

Promotes Political Equality in Participation and Representation

The market campaigns for gender and LGBT rights did not improve equality in participation because women and LGBT people vote at higher rates than the general public,[88] but they did improve equality in representation. Even though these (overlapping) groups have higher rates of voter turnout, politicians are less responsive to the concerns of women and LGBT individuals, so all campaigns that forward their interests and rights improve equality of representation. In direct terms, the boycott of the state of Utah following the passage of California Proposition 8 improved political representation for LGBT individuals, whose voices had been overruled by the majority of Californians who had voted to overturn same-sex marriage in the state.

Promotes the Will of the Majority

Most of the campaigns reviewed in this chapter improved democratic inputs by promoting the will of the majority. Over 60 percent of Americans supported mandated healthcare insurance coverage of contraceptives at the time of the Flush Rush and Hobby Lobby campaigns, so these boycotts advanced the majority opinion.[89] It is safe to assume that a majority of Americans oppose capital punishment for homosexuality and state-sanctioned rape of wives older than thirteen, so the Beverly Hills Hotel boycott also represented majority interests. All the same-sex marriage campaigns after 2012 also reflected majority will because this became a majority position in November of that year, when 53 percent of Americans said the state should recognize gay marriage.[90] (Since that time, support for same-sex marriage has climbed to 60 percent, and in 2015, the Supreme Court ruled that it is legal in all fifty states.) The Utah and Target campaigns involving same-sex marriage occurred before this was a majority position in the United States, so they were minority interest campaigns. The GoDaddy campaign was a minority interest because the harms of female objectification are contested even among feminists.

Promotes Active Media

Most of the campaigns I discuss in this chapter promoted more active media by putting issues on the agenda that were not being covered by mainstream outlets, with the exception of the NFL, Hobby Lobby, and *Duck Dynasty* incidents, which immediately received mainstream media coverage. The remaining ten campaigns picked up steam on social media, which translated into mainstream media coverage. Four of the campaigns promoted active media by directly targeting media figures or entertainment media content (Flush Rush, GoDaddy, *Ender's Game*, and *Duck Dynasty*). These campaigns pushed back against sexism and anti-LGBT sentiment expressed by a popular radio talk show host, an Internet company, a notable book author, and a reality television star. Marketplace activism has raised the stakes in media accountability by holding media figures responsible for the political implications of their statements.

Improves Public Discussion on Policy Issues

All thirteen consumer activism campaigns improved public discussion on policy issues. Americans were mobilized to debate contraception coverage, sexist media portrayals, Sharia law, domestic violence, same-sex marriage, freedom of speech, and whether corporations should be held accountable for the views of their leaders. All these campaigns involved deep cleavages along moral lines, so debate was particularly intense. Consumer activism provided a complementary outlet for expressing political voice during ongoing legislative and legal debates about mandated contraception insurance coverage and same-sex marriage.

Promotes Political Equality in State Protection and Public Resources

A few campaigns advanced equality in state resources and protection, a key democratic output. The Hobby Lobby campaign to mandate employer insurance coverage of contraceptives improved democratic outputs by promoting equality in public resources. These efforts sought to make sure all female employees have the same access to coverage for family planning, regardless of where they are employed. Campaigns to legalize same-sex marriage also improved equality in public resources because marriage is tied to a number of public benefits, specifically, social security and Individual Retirement Accounts.[91] The Russian Vodka campaign sought to improve equality in state protection by bringing to light the reality that Russian law enforcement was standing by while LGBT people were being targeted with physical violence in public.

Promotes Corporate Political Accountability

All thirteen campaigns for gender and LGBT rights improved corporate account-ability to viewers, listeners, and the public more broadly. Many of the efforts forced companies to be more concerned about the views and action of their lead-ers and representatives, such as Rush Limbaugh, the sultan of Brunei, Ray Rice, Roger Goodell, Dan Cathy, Guido Barilla, Orson Scott Card, Phil Robertson, and Brendan Eich. Companies now think twice about promoting leaders with a controversial political record and aligning their brand with representatives that might harm the company image. Furthermore, CEOs and other corporate rep-resentatives who take positions on one side in culture wars will almost assuredly become a target of consumer activism. The Target and Chick-Fil-A campaigns increased corporate accountability for charitable donations made to organiza-tions and political leaders.

Promotes Government Accountability to Citizens

None of the market campaigns in this chapter had a direct effect on legislation or legal decisions in a way that promoted greater U.S. government accountability. Two of the market campaigns for LGBT or gender justice improved government accountability outside the United States: the boycott of Russian vodka to protest the treatment of Russian LGBT citizens and the Beverly Hills Hotel action to halt the enforcement of Sharia law in Brunei. Although the campaign against the state of Utah involved a state actor, activists were punishing the state for the actions of the Mormon Church, not the actions of Utah. Both of the campaigns to hold government accountable involved the use of U.S. consumer power to pressure foreign governments to alter their laws and practices.

Protects against the Encroachment of Minority Rights

All the gender and LGBT rights campaigns discussed in this chapter protected against encroachment on minority rights. Although women are not a numeric minority, they remain vastly underrepresented in political leadership posi-tions, which translates into their interests not being adequately represented in legislation.[92] LGBT individuals are a numeric minority. The Beverly Hills Hotel and Russian Vodka campaigns are distinct in that they forwarded the rights of oppressed minorities outside the United States.

Protects against Government Encroachment on Civil Liberties

Campaigns examined here advanced civil liberties. The Beverly Hills, Russian Vodka, and Hobby Lobby campaigns were attempts to protect against government encroachment on the rights of women and LGBT individuals. The aim of these campaigns was to protect citizens against government infringement in their lives, ensuring that they are entitled to family planning and to not be legally raped, beaten, or put to death based on their gender or sexual identity. These three campaigns pushed back against formal laws or court rulings legalizing government encroachment on these liberties.

In this chapter, I have analyzed thirteen national consumer activism campaigns involving gender and LGBT rights from 2004 to 2014. I have found that over 60 percent of these campaigns were effective and that two inspired powerful counterboycotts that curbed their effects. All the campaigns in this chapter used boycotting and social media tools, about half used direct action, and none called for shareholder actions or divestment. The market campaigns for these issues were often led by grassroots movements instead of by nonprofit organizations, so they were mostly decentralized.

These organized efforts improved the health of U.S. democracy by getting millions of Americans to act in ways that hold corporations accountable for their political actions. These campaigns also increased the salience of, and public discussions about, major policy issues such as family planning and same-sex marriage. Most of the campaigns I discuss in this chapter furthered the voice and will of majority opinion while simultaneously improving the protection of minority rights and the representation of minority interests. All the campaigns improved corporate accountability to citizens on policy issues that are regulated by government. Campaigns for gender and LGBT rights complemented existing electoral debates, legislation, and judicial decisions by mobilizing more citizens around hotly debated culture war policies.

"YES TO JESUS CHRIST, NO TO *JC*"
Campaigns for Conservative Causes

In this chapter, I approach the market campaigns of the past decade from a different angle. Instead of focusing on a policy domain or a set of related domains, I analyze twenty conservative campaigns from 2004 to 2014. This ideological lens highlights the relatively new and expanding use of market campaigns by conservative groups in the United States. Prior to the start of the culture wars (the increasing number of hotly contested policy issues that polarize the public, such as homosexuality and gun control) in the 1970s, the use of consumer activism by those on the ideological right was rare. The culture wars ignited with the Civil Rights Movement, the Women's Movement, and the Gay Rights Movement, all of which openly challenged existing power structures and traditional ways of living.

Until the 1970s, U.S. consumer activism was a mostly liberal affair, and liberals continue to use these political tools more frequently to respond to changing social norms regarding relationships, gender roles, and sexuality. Conservative efforts, unlike liberal consumer activism, which comes from a variety of grassroots and organizational sources, primarily are started by two organizations: the American Family Association (AFA) and its online campaign One Million Moms (OMM), and Focus on the Family (FOTF). Methodist Pastor Donald Wildmon founded the AFA in 1977 in Southhaven, Mississippi, and his son Tim Wildmon now runs the organization. The senior Wildmon left the ministry and moved his family to start the organization after watching television one night and discovering that there were no programs appropriate for his family with young children. The first action of the AFA was to boycott Sears for its sponsorship of *Three's*

Company, Charlie's Angels, and *All in the Family*. This campaign caused Sears to withdraw its sponsorship of the first two programs. In the past four decades, the AFA has organized over a dozen campaigns to protest companies that offer benefits for same-sex couples, waged a successful 1986 boycott to stop 7–11 from selling *Playboy* and *Penthouse*, and in 1993 protested the television program *NYPD Blue* for its sexual and violent content. Today, the AFA is running a nationwide boycott of Target for its policy that allows transgender individuals to use the bathroom of their choice. According to a video on the AFA website, its goal is to provide "practical ways to get involved in the culture war."[1] In 2010, the AFA formed OMM, an online extension of its consumer activism campaigns to combat the "immorality, violence, vulgarity and profanity the entertainment media is throwing at your children."[2] OMM has called for over a dozen boycotts since it was formed, some of which are examined in this chapter.

Focus on the Family (FOTF) is the second prominent conservative organization that regularly organizes and joins boycotts. Founded in 1977 by Dr. James Dobson, FOTF opposes premarital sex, same-sex marriage, abortion, and divorce. It promotes abstinence-only sex education and traditional gender roles. Dobson is an evangelical author, radio host, and psychologist who was born in Shreveport, Louisiana, the son of a Nazarene preacher who learned to pray before he learned to talk. Dobson gave his life to Jesus at the age of three.[3] He went on to earn a PhD from the University of Southern California (USC), and then worked at the USC Keck School of Medicine for over a decade. Dobson gained national recognition when he published the controversial book *Dare to Discipline* in 1970, which endorsed corporal punishment for children.[4] Dobson's profile grew when he interviewed serial killer Ted Bundy the day before his execution. During the interview, Bundy stated that his violent actions had been shaped by pornography.

By the 2000s, a number of conservative organizations had developed sophisticated mobilizing mechanisms to target companies that stood on the other side of culture war issues. As we have seen in chapter 5, conservative groups quickly established a counterboycott to reinstate Phil Robertson on the A&E reality show *Duck Dynasty*, and they gave Chic-Fil-A its most profitable day ever with a counterbuycott. Even though conservative consumer activism went mainstream two decades after liberal consumer activism, many organizations now have well-established mechanisms to reach conservative consumers.

Consumer activism remains a point of controversy for some conservatives for political and religious reasons. In terms of politics, conservatives are aligned with the Republican Party, a party with a pro-corporate sentiment that discourages the use of consumer activism. I experienced this value system firsthand for five years as a political commentator for Fox News, where hosts and guests often described boycott actions as "un-American" because they were framed as an anti-corporate impediment to the free market. Other conservatives eschew boycotts on religious grounds. Joe Carter, a Christian theologian, writes that boycotts are un-Christian because they are a form of "moral extortion": "By cutting off economic ties with a corporation or business, the boycotters are using coercion to force people to do something they would not willingly do on their own. While Christians may have legitimate reasons for not using a certain product or associating with a particular business, banding together to cut off commerce to an otherwise licit venture has no obvious biblical warrant."[5] Alan Noble, a Christian religious scholar, echoes the sentiment that conservative causes are better served with tactics that "actively demonstrate Christ's love" rather than bullying business entities through boycott pressure.[6] In short, boycott actions are too coercive to be biblical for some Christians.

Despite the controversy surrounding its use on the right, consumer activism is a popular political tool for conservatives, especially evangelicals concerned with changing moral standards and gun rights advocates who push back against threats to gun ownership. Twenty national conservative campaigns were conducted from 2004 to 2014. All but one of these campaigns used boycotting as a tool. Eleven used social media as a tool, a lower rate than the liberal campaigns examined in previous chapters. Social media is a more effective tool for campaigns with mainstream support, so it makes sense that this communication medium would be used less by conservative causes that target a subset of the population for support. Only three conservative campaigns used direct action. One of the common refrains of conservative campaign organizers is that direct action raises the potential for the campaign to backfire and draw more people in to see the questionable material they are boycotting. This concern, and the Christian principle of turning the other cheek to avoid confrontation, mediates against the use of frequent direct action. Only one of the campaigns in this chapter used divestment as a tactic.

Conservative consumer activism falls into four primary policy areas: campaigns opposing gay rights, efforts to promote traditional families and morality, campaigns against demeaning or misleading depictions of religion, and efforts to promote gun rights.

Campaigns against Gay Rights

Conservative consumer activists have been vocal opponents of same-sex marriage, LGBT employment antidiscrimination clauses, and the hiring of LGBT people in high-profile positions.

The Disney Campaign

From 1997 to 2005, the Southern Baptist Convention staged a national boycott of Disney theme parks, films, and its television network to protest the support by the company of LGBT people. They objected to Disney hosting of "Gay Days" at its theme parks, its provision of same-sex benefits, and the violent and sexualized content of some Disney media.[7] Activists were particularly troubled by the production by the Disney parent company of *Ellen*, a hit 1990s television show that portrayed the life of an openly gay woman. The Southern Baptist boycott criticized the policies of the company, but it did not demand specific outcomes. This was a market campaign proper because its goal was to change the political stance of a business entity (Disney).

Southern Baptists are the largest protestant denomination in the United States. Because of this, their 16 million members had the potential to affect the Disney bottom line, but mobilization was difficult because the boycott was not mandatory for individual Baptists or churches. For example, President Bill Clinton, a Southern Baptist, told reporters that he was not participating in the boycott, and Baptist pastors across the nation publicly stated that their churches were not part of the boycott. This campaign was not economically effective. In fact, in the first few months of the boycott, attendance at Disney theme parks rose 9 percent, and by the end of the year profits had risen 27 percent.[8] If anything, the boycott improved the Disney revenues. The Southern Baptists ended the boycott after eight years without achieving its goal when Michael Eisner, Disney CEO, stepped down in 2005.[9]

The Procter & Gamble Campaign

In 2004, FOTF and AFA started a boycott of the consumer goods company Procter & Gamble (P&G) after it opposed a statute restricting gay rights in Cincinnati, Ohio, the home of its corporate headquarters.[10] P&G had donated $10,000 to a campaign whose aim was to overturn the statute.[11] In response, Dobson (FOTF) told his 9 million listeners that when companies "become politically involved in an agenda opposed by a majority of Americans, they're alienating their customers."[12] FOTF and the AFA targeted the best-selling P&G brands for the boycott: Tide laundry detergent, Crest toothpaste, and Pampers diapers.[13] The campaign also circulated an online petition in support of the boycott that garnered 287,000 signatures.[14] Campaign organizers used social media and Christian media to get the message about the boycott out. This was a market campaign proper that targeted the political position and campaign contributions of a business entity.

The P&G boycott did not have an economic impact, but it did achieve its stated goal of raising public awareness.[15] The campaign was covered for months by national news outlets, including Fox News and the *New York Times*. Organizers ended the campaign in less than a year, and FOTF stated that P&G was "backing off its support for the homosexual agenda,"[16] but there is no evidence that the company changed its practices concerning LGBT issues. P&G has become more open about its support of LGBT individuals as homosexuality gained mainstream acceptance. In 2011, the company became an official sponsor of Cincinnati Pride, a festival celebrating LGBT people, and in 2014, the company officially came out in support of same-sex marriage.[17]

The McDonald's Campaign

In May 2008, global fast food leader McDonald's became a target of another AFA boycott when it sponsored an event for the National Gay and Lesbian Chamber of Commerce (NGLCC). The AFA called this boycott because McDonald's "refused to stay neutral in the cultural war over homosexuality."[18] The stated goal of the AFA action was to force the company to distance itself from the NGLCC and to remove the McDonald's logo from the NGLCC website. The AFA sent alerts to its 3 million members and wrote a piece about the McDonald's action in its monthly newsletter. It made use of online technology to get the word out, but the AFA did not use social media. This was a market campaign proper because it targeted the political position of a business entity.

The boycott did not have a measurable economic effect—McDonald's profits increased in the months following the boycott announcement—but it did achieve its goals. In October 2008, the AFA declared victory[19] after McDonald's publicly announced that it would not renew its membership in the gay rights organization and its logo was taken off the website of the nonprofit at the end of the year. The company also sent an email to all its franchise owners stating, "It is our policy to not be involved in political and social issues. McDonald's remains neutral on same sex marriage or any 'homosexual agenda.'"[20] A McDonald's spokesperson denied that these actions were a response to the boycott, but their timing and public nature suggest otherwise. This was a successful boycott campaign.

The Microsoft Campaign

In April 2005, Microsoft withdrew its support for a bill being considered in the Washington State legislature that would have banned discrimination against gays and lesbians.[21] Microsoft, a company that had a long history of supporting LGBT workplace protections and benefits, had initially supported the bill but withdrew its support after boycott pressure from a local megachurch. The boycott was initiated by Reverend Ken Hutcherson of the Antioch Bible Church, a multicultural evangelical congregation in the Seattle suburb of Kirkland.[22]

Hutcherson, also known as "The Hutch," was a retired NFL linebacker who would often call into his good friend Rush Limbaugh's show (he attended Limbaugh's fourth wedding in 2010). Hutcherson had been born to a poor single mother in Alabama during a time of aggressive racial segregation. He once told a reporter that he played football because he could "hurt white people legally."[23] In high school, he had a spiritual awakening and decided to pursue social justice through biblical teachings and work, which he did until his death from cancer in 2013. For the Microsoft action, Hutcherson threatened to organize a national boycott if the company did not change its position on the pending legislation and fire two Microsoft employees who had testified in support of the bill. Hutcherson also demanded that Microsoft issue a statement that LGBT antidiscrimination laws were unnecessary. Although the ultimate aim of the campaign was government policy, this was a market campaign proper because its immediate goal was to change the political stance of a business entity.

Hutcherson used mainstream media to gain attention for his cause. The boycott action caught the attention of national religious organizations that pledged their support, and Microsoft almost immediately withdrew its support for the bill. This boycott was only partially successful because Microsoft did not fire the two employees who had testified in favor of the bill nor did the company issue a statement about the matter. The bill did not muster enough votes to pass.

In 2015, Microsoft joined many other high-profile companies in its public support of the Supreme Court decision in favor of same-sex marriage. Because a majority of Americans are now in favor of LGBT rights and protections, this conservative boycott pressure that was somewhat effective in 2005 would be less effective today. These conservative campaigns against pro-LGBT corporations were late attempts to slow a turning tide of public opinion and laws.

The *Brokeback Mountain* Campaign

In 2005, Walmart faced a boycott from Christian conservatives to prevent the retail giant from selling DVDs of *Brokeback Mountain*. This film tells the story of a love affair between two gay cowboys. It opened to critical acclaim and won an Academy Award, making it a perfect high-profile target for a conservative campaign. The AFA initiated a secondary boycott of Walmart a week before the retailer stocked the film to protest the attempt by the company at "normalizing" homosexuality.[24] The AFA had previously expressed concern about the 2003

expansion of the Walmart antidiscrimination policy to include LGBT individuals. This was a market campaign proper, with the goal of pressuring Walmart to
change its practice of selling the film.

The AFA recruited FOTF, Faith2Action, and a host of other Christian organizations to join the campaign. Faith2Action was started by Janet Porter in 2011
to promote pro-life and pro-family issues. As stated on the Faith2Action website,
"Our goal isn't to just survive the cultural war, but to *win* it."[25] Porter's activism
started in high school when she was shown a picture of an aborted fetus. Since
that time, she has been a tenacious pro-life advocate who played an instrumental
role in the first ban on late-term abortions.

For the *Brokeback Mountain* campaign, Faith2Action, AFA, and FOTF used
online tactics to spread the word of the boycott including an online petition that
received nearly 100,000 signatures. Christian activists also strategically placed
a spate of negative film reviews in online Christian publications in an effort to
convince people to boycott the film.[26]

The secondary boycott was not effective in getting Walmart to halt sales of
Brokeback Mountain DVDs, nor was it economically effective. Overall, Walmart
revenues during the month of the boycott did not dip, and LGBT activists organized a buycott of the DVD, which boosted sales of the film. *Brokeback Mountain*
sold a record-breaking 1.4 million copies through retail stores the first day it went
on sale.[27] This market campaign did not achieve its goal.

The J. C. Penney Campaign

In February 2012, OMM organized a boycott of retailer J. C. Penney for hiring
Ellen DeGeneres, the lesbian talk show host, as its spokesperson.[28] The goal of
the campaign was to compel the retailer to fire DeGeneres and replace her with
a heterosexual spokesperson. J. C. Penney responded to the boycott action by
affirming its partnership with DeGeneres because "America believes in Ellen."
DeGeneres answered OMM directly on her daytime talk show: "My haters are
my motivators."[29] This was a market campaign proper because its goal was to get
a business entity to change its spokesperson for political reasons.

In an unexpected move, Bill O'Reilly a top-rated Fox News host, condemned
the OMM action as a "witch hunt": "The essential question is that a conservative
group in this country is asking a private company to fire an American citizen based
upon her lifestyle. I don't think that's correct."[30] O'Reilly's reaction to the boycott
received more press than OMM's initial call for the boycott, and the campaign
soon folded. It had no measurable economic effect on J. C. Penney, and it did not
achieve its goal of getting DeGeneres fired as the company spokesperson. The rift
on the right between OMM and O'Reilly is indicative of a divide in the Republican

Party along religious lines. Even though O'Reilly identifies as a Catholic, he was critical of the boycott that was embraced by the evangelical base behind OMM.

The Guinness Campaign

In 2014, conservative media tycoon Rupert Murdoch urged Irish people to boycott Guinness beer after the company pulled its sponsorship of the St. Patrick's Day parade in New York because parade officials would not allow LGBT groups to march.[31] Murdoch called for the boycott via Twitter. News of this consumer action was quickly picked up by mainstream news organizations because of Murdoch's prominent position as a leading Republican media owner. This was a market campaign proper, intended to affect the profits of a business entity because of a political position.

Murdoch was born in Australia and inherited his media empire and conservative leanings from his father. The younger Murdoch branched out into the U.K. and U.S. media and has built the world's second largest media conglomerate.

Murdoch's boycott lacked an organized campaign operation, but his status as the owner of Fox News and other major news outlets propelled interest in the boycott. The Catholic League asked its 230,000 members to join Murdoch in boycotting Guinness. It also contacted bars and restaurants throughout the South to ask them to stop selling the Irish beer.[32] The Catholic League circulated an online petition that gathered over 100,000 signatures, calling Guinness a "corporate bully" for withdrawing its support from the parade.[33]

In the first year of the boycott, Guinness saw a slight decline in sales, but it is difficult to determine whether this was a result of the boycott or part of a longer six-year decline in sales of all beer brands.[34] The fact that beer sales in the United Kingdom and other European countries have dropped more than in the United States, where the boycott is based, indicates that this decline has more to do with drinking trends than with the boycott itself. Moreover, the boycott campaign does not have a clearly defined goal or action it would like Guinness to take, so it is difficult to measure campaign success. This ongoing boycott has been effective in raising public awareness about the support by Guinness for LGBT rights with Americans who disagree with this position.

The Michael Sam Campaign

In May 2014, Jack Burkman, an influential evangelical lobbyist, announced a boycott of any NFL team that drafted Michael Sam, an openly gay player, to "rough [them] up financially."[35]

Burkman was born and raised in Pittsburgh and holds a law degree from Georgetown University. He had previously worked to ban gays from playing in the NFL, expressing his concern that "openly gay football players send a terrible message to our youth about morality."[36]

Burkman officially called for a boycott of the St. Louis Rams when they drafted Sam. Jeff Fisher, a Rams coach, responded that the team was proud to be a part of history in selecting Sam in the NFL draft. Burkman also initiated a boycott of Visa, the first company to hire Sam as an ad spokesperson.[37] "Visa and the Rams will learn that when you trample the Christian community and Christian values, there will be a terrible financial price to pay."[38] The ultimate goal of the boycott was to get Sam fired from his contracts with the NFL and Visa. This was a market campaign proper because it aimed to change the practices of business entities.

Burkman organized Christian groups in twenty-seven states, encouraging their members to divest from Visa and stop attending Rams games, stop purchasing Rams merchandise, and cease using Visa services. Burkman used mainstream media appeals rather than social media to gain support for his campaign. This boycott was not successful in achieving its goal or in having a financial impact. It had no noticeable financial effect on the Rams or on Visa, and Sam's jersey was the second best-selling rookie jersey in the NFL the year he was drafted.[39] When Sam signed with the Dallas Cowboys in September 2014, Burkman called for a protest outside the stadium.[40] The protest never materialized, and in 2015, Sam signed with the Canadian Football League, bringing an end to Burkman's unsuccessful boycott actions. Some journalists speculated that the entire campaign may have been a publicity stunt for Burkman to attract more clients.[41]

Campaigns for Morality and Motherhood

Conservative consumer activists have also waged morality campaigns against perceived threats to traditional gender roles, traditional motherhood, family planning, and indecency. In the introduction, I defined *consumer activism* as citizen actions directed toward business entities to explicitly influence the distribution of social goods or social values. The "culture war" campaigns in this section are inherently political because they are fundamentally a fight over which social values are accepted.

The *Kinsey* Campaign

In 2004, the conservative group Concerned Women of America (CWA) teamed up with FOTF to boycott the film *Kinsey* because they believed it "normalizes pedophilia."

CWA was formed in 1979 by Beverly LaHaye, the spouse of Timothy LaHaye, a popular televangelist. She started the organization after she watched Barbara

Walters interview prominent feminist Betty Friedan and concluded that feminists were a threat to traditional family arrangements. The LaHayes had met during college at Bob Jones University and have been married for more than sixty years.

CWA took issue with the positive portrayal by the movie of Alfred Kinsey, biologist and the father of the Sexual Revolution.[42] Kinsey's research in the 1940s and 1950s produced the field of sexology, challenging traditional understandings of sexuality. His work has long been criticized by social and religious conservatives because it spawned the Sexual Revolution of the 1960s and 1970s, seen by many religious conservatives as an affront to traditional, biblical family values. For example, Kinsey believed that adultery can improve marriage, no sexual acts are abnormal, homosexuality is common, and pornography is harmless. Conservatives hold Kinsey responsible for what they deem to be damage from the Sexual Revolution: high divorce rates, HIV/AIDS, and child sexual abuse.[43] CWA and FOTF are critical of Kinsey's work because he had interviewed a pedophile who was still actively violating children. Michael Craven from the National Coalition for the Protection of Children & Families told reporters that "Kinsey's impact on our culture has been nothing short of devastating and there has been little opportunity to challenge his ideas in the marketplace of ideas until now."[44] The *Kinsey* film allowed long-standing conservative critiques of Kinsey to come into public light. The goal of the *Kinsey* campaign was to stop the production of the film and, once the film opened, to get it rated NC-17 to harm its sales. This was a market campaign proper because its goal was to change the practices of a business entity.

A coalition of organizations used Christian media to spread word about the boycott with Dr. Laura Schlessinger, a radio personality, doing the heavy lifting. Schlessinger, known as Dr. Laura, is a Long Island native who grew up in a self-described dysfunctional home that shaped her later work dispensing family and relationship advice. Schlessinger earned a PhD in physiology from Columbia University, and after dispensing advice for years on the radio, obtained a certificate in marriage and family counseling from USC. She is known for her humor, her wit, and her conservative approach to relationships, for example, advising women to submit to their husbands.

The campaign to stop the production of *Kinsey* started as soon as Myriad Pictures announced in 2002 that the film was in production, two years before its release.[45] Activists urged Liam Neeson, the star, to pass on the project and demanded that the studios involved halt their production of the film. They organized a letter-writing campaign that convinced potential distributor MGM/United Artists to pass on the film.[46] Fox Searchlight picked up the film, which put some Republicans in a quandary because that company also owns the conservative channel Fox News.[47] Schlessinger and Dr. Judith Reisman, the author of a book that is critical of Kinsey, tried to purchase ads in *Variety* alleging Kinsey was a pedophile and a pervert, but their ads were rejected as obscene.[48] The campaign organized the distribution of leaflets at theaters after showings of *Kinsey*. Despite warnings that protesting outside theaters could increase public attention and ultimately benefit the film, the Traditional Values Coalition broke rank and organized vocal protests outside theaters across the nation on opening night.[49]

This market campaign caused the filmmakers to be highly cautious in their public delivery of the film. *Kinsey* opened in Washington, DC (instead of the usual venue, Los Angeles) and in New York with a select audience of reporters, researchers, and bloggers to ward against bad reviews from conservative critics. A later select screening of *Kinsey* in Los Angeles was shut down after fifteen minutes when it was discovered that Reisman was in the audience. Nevertheless, the *Kinsey* campaign was not successful at shutting down production, changing the rating of the film from R to NC-17, or affecting its box office success. The film opened to positive critical acclaim and received eleven awards and twenty-seven nominations, including an Academy Award for Best Supporting Actress for Laura Linney. It grossed a respectable $17 million worldwide.

The Motrin Campaign

In 2008, Motrin was targeted by "mommy bloggers" for an ad suggesting that wearing babies in a carrier is like fashion and that it is painful.[50] The ad in question was particularly troubling to Christian moms for depicting motherhood as painful—seen as yet another attack on traditional female roles. The ad used graphics, words, and a voiceover from a young mom saying, "Wearing your baby seems to be in fashion. I mean, in theory, it's a great idea. . . . Supposedly, it's a real bonding experience. They say that babies carried close to the body tend to cry less than others. But what about me? Do moms who wear their babies cry more than those who don't? I sure do. These things put a ton of strain on your back."[51]

A Los Angeles–based mommy blogger, Jessica Gottlieb, wrote a blog post that triggered a digital tsunami against Motrin-maker Johnson & Johnson. This was a market campaign proper because it directly targeted the practices of a business entity.

Gottlieb, a native Californian with an MA in education from Pepperdine University, writes about myriad parenting issues from a socially conservative perspective. She started her online career as an eBay entrepreneur and initially blogged anonymously on the site Pissed Off Housewife about life after losing a friend due to AIDS. She started her personal parenting blog in 2007, and it has become one of the most popular mom blogs with over 500,000 hits per month. Gottlieb used this considerable reach to launch a national consumer boycott of Motrin.

Hundreds of mommy bloggers shared Gottlieb's post or wrote similar posts about the ad.[52] Activists set up a Facebook page with the tagline "Babywearing isn't painful. Boycott Motrin for saying it is," which attracted over 3,000 members. Gottlieb also took to Twitter with the hashtag #MotrinMom to publicly shame the company, and it became a top Twitter trend within hours.

One day after the ad debuted, Johnson & Johnson pulled it from television and the company website and issued a statement of apology. This grassroots social media campaign was highly effective in achieving its goal of getting the company to remove the offending ad, a goal activists achieved in less than twenty-four hours.

The Komen Campaign

Starting in 2011, the Southern Baptist Convention and a coalition of pro-life groups started putting pressure on the Susan G. Komen for the Cure foundation to end its affiliation with Planned Parenthood using boycotts. Komen, the world's largest funder of breast cancer research, funded breast cancer screenings through the abortion provider Planned Parenthood. Catholic leaders from churches in Ohio and Missouri petitioned the Komen foundation to cease its partnership with Planned Parenthood, and the Southern Baptist Convention boycotted the purchase of pink Komen Bibles (that raised $1 each for cancer research).[53] This was a market campaign proper because it sought to alter the political behavior of a business entity, in this case, a nonprofit with over $400 million in assets.

By summer 2012, Liz Thompson, the Komen president, was spending half her time attending to conservative boycott pressure, and she wanted "out of the culture wars."[54] In an effort to appease conservative consumer activists, Komen decided to withdraw its Planned Parenthood funding. Instead of pulling Komen out of the culture wars, this move plunged the foundation into the heart of it.

Pro-choice activists called for a counterboycott of Komen for its decision to break with Planned Parenthood. Activists used Twitter and Facebook to express their concern over the Komen decision. The feminist blogosphere lit up with posts about the issue,[55] and celebrities as well as politicians chastised Komen, including Dana Delaney, an actor, and Senator Barbara Boxer (D-CA). Within a day, #BoycottKomen was a trending Twitter topic, and a Facebook post from Komen explaining its decision received over 5,000 comments, most of them negative. A content analysis of the online comments about Komen found that three-quarters of them were critical of Komen and 20 percent stated that the writer would no longer donate to the foundation.[56] This counterboycott had the side-effect of raising awareness about Planned Parenthood breast cancer screenings, and the number of new screening appointments soared in the week of the boycott announcement. The Komen decision backfired economically because Planned Parenthood raised $400,000 from 6,000 donors in the days following the decision.[57] Komen saw its income from contributions, entry fees for fundraising events, and sponsorship decline 22 percent in the year after the controversy.[58]

The initial boycott from pro-life forces was effective in getting Komen to stop funding Planned Parenthood, but it produced a counterboycott led by pro-choice activists that was much more effective. Within three days of its decision, the existence of Komen as an organization was threatened as nonprofit and corporate affiliates withdrew their support and tens of thousands of people signed petitions promising to boycott the foundation.[59] The Komen foundation responded to the counterboycott by reinstating its funding of Planned Parenthood less than seventy-two hours after making that decision, and within weeks, all the top leaders in the foundation had resigned. Participation in Komen events has been lower in the years since the controversy, and prolife organizations remain openly critical of Komen partnering with Planned Parenthood.[60]

The Urban Outfitters Campaign

Retailer Urban Outfitters was the target of a 2012 boycott by OMM for the racy content of its catalog.[61] The edgy catalogs of the company featured two young women kissing, block candles that spelled out *fuck*, an "It was fucking awesome" photo album, and scores of scantily clad models. OMM decried the catalogs as "tasteless and vulgar," and it asked Christians to avoid shopping at the store.[62] Organizers used Twitter and an online petition to support the boycott, which gathered 18,000 signatures. This was a market campaign proper because the goal was to compel a business entity to change its practices, in this case, to stop using ads that run counter to traditional family values.

OMM has run many campaigns against Urban Outfitters. In 2004, OMM successfully convinced Urban Outfitters to stop selling Jesus Dress Up!, a refrigerator magnet game with Jesus on the cross, who could be clad with interchangeable outfits (figure 6.1).[63] In 2008, the organization ran a successful regional action to convince Urban Outfitters not to sell "I Support Same-Sex Marriage" t-shirts in its California stores. In addition, that same year Richard Hayne, the Urban Outfitters CEO and founder, contributed over $13,000 to Rick Santorum, an antigay Republican presidential candidate so the company also faced a boycott from LGBT activists. This seeming contradiction demonstrates the difficulty of categorizing companies by political ideology because any company may hold ideologically inconsistent positions.

FIGURE 6.1   Sarah Silverman, comedian, displays her Jesus Dress Up! magnet set, 2009

The 2012 OMM boycott campaign against Urban Outfitters for its catalog content was not effective. It did not cause revenue to decline, nor did it elicit a response from the company. Urban Outfitters continues to publish catalogs with same-sex kisses, curse words, and hypersexualized material.

The Shame on Kraft Campaign

In June 2013, OMM launched a boycott against food company Kraft for its two-page Zesty Guy magazine ad, which depicts a naked man on a picnic blanket with the blanket barely covering his private parts (figure 6.2). According to the OMM press release about the boycott, "Christians will not be able to buy Kraft dressings or any of their products until they clean up their advertising." Kraft responded that the ad "is a playful and flirtatious way to reach our consumers. People have overwhelmingly said they're enjoying the campaign and having fun with it."[64] OMM launched an online petition that received over 12,000 signatures, and it used Facebook to spread the word about the boycott. This was a market campaign proper because it directly targeted the practices of a business entity.

This OMM campaign backfired because it boosted interest in the ad. Kraft commissioned another five photos from the ad agency showing Zesty Guy scantily clad in different locations.[65] The company also created a series of "Let's Get Zesty" television ads, some of which went viral, with over half a million views. The OMM boycott and social media campaign against the initial ad quieted within a matter of months as the organization turned to other issues to protest.

FIGURE 6.2 The Kraft "Let's Get Zesty" ad, 2013

The Shame on Kmart Campaign

During the 2013 Christmas shopping season, Kmart put out an ad featuring models wearing Joe Boxer underwear that went viral. The men in the ad performed pelvic thrusts in a sexualized way to the tune of "Jingle Bells." At one point in the video, the men squat down and shake their hips in a way that suggests their testicles are creating the bell sounds of the song. OMM responded with a social media campaign that intended to shame Kmart into pulling the ad, deeming it "inappropriate" and "filth."[66] OMM created a Shame on Kmart campaign on Twitter and Facebook that asked consumers to express their concerns directly to Kmart. This was a market campaign proper because its organizers wanted to change the marketing practices of a business entity that they felt threatened traditional family values.

Kmart responded with an apology for offending "some" people, but the company refused to remove the video. It had received over 850,000 hits by the end of the holiday season. This social media shaming campaign was not effective in achieving its goal of getting the commercial pulled from the airwaves or the Internet.

The CookieCott Campaign

In 2014, the Texas advocacy organization Pro-Life Waco (PLW) initiated a national boycott of Girl Scout cookies after the Girl Scouts' Twitter account retweeted a link to a discussion of candidates for the *Huffington Post* Women of the Year award.[67] The discussion included Wendy Davis, Texas state senator and a pro-choice activist, and although the tweet in question did not mention Davis, John Pisciotta, the boycott organizer, argued that it represented "praise for the whole group," including Davis.[68]

PLW was formed in 2007 by John Piscotti, a retired Baylor University economics professor who has been dedicated to the pro-life cause all his adult life. Conservative groups have long been concerned that the curriculum of the Girl Scouts included pro-choice advocates (e.g., Betty Friedan and Gloria Steinem) and that the organization had connections to Planned Parenthood at the local level.[69] The Girl Scouts does not take a position on abortion or family planning more broadly,[70] but conservative concerns about the organization go beyond abortion. For decades, Republican talk show hosts have criticized the Girl Scouts as a "wicked organization" that promotes a version of womanhood that "is antithetical to a biblical vision for womanhood."[71] As a child, I heard similar refrains from my evangelical pastor, and my parents forbade me to join the Girl Scouts or purchase cookies from the organization because it promoted a notion of womanhood that went against the Bible. In 1995, conservatives started the American

Heritage Girls to offer a more traditional alternative to the Girl Scouts. This group offers a Respect Life badge that a girl can earn by being active in the pro-life movement.[72]

PLW was joined in its boycott by the Human Rights Institute and Catholic Family, and together they formed the CookieCott campaign. It quickly made national headlines with the early help of the conservative news outlet Breitbart. com, which broke the story. Within a week, CookieCott had 35,000 Google search hits, and most mainstream news organizations had written an original piece about the action.[73] Organizers put up the website CookieCott.com, with corresponding Facebook and Twitter accounts. They hosted a twitterfest during which they encouraged activists to tweet their support for #Cookiecott. This was a market campaign proper because its goal was to change the perceived political affiliations of a business entity, in this case a nonprofit with just under $200 million in assets.

CookieCott is an ongoing campaign to put the Girl Scouts out of business because 80 percent of the funding of the organization comes from cookie sales. The boycott has successfully raised awareness of the feminist content of the Girl Scouts, and it has perhaps contributed to a long-term decline in Girl Scout membership that started in the early 2000s. The organization has seen a 27 percent drop in membership since its peak in 2003, including a 6 percent drop after the start of CookieCott.[74] Youth-serving organizations across the board have seen similar declines in membership due to parents having less disposable income and time to take their children to activities, so the effects of the boycott are not clear. The sale of Girl Scout cookies has also seen a steady decline as a result of decreasing troop numbers and fewer door-to-door visits.[75] Given this context, it is difficult to discern whether the boycott has had an economic effect on the Girl Scouts, although it probably has. Membership in the conservative competitor, American Heritage Girls, shot up by about 5,000 in the months following CookieCott.[76]

Organizers relaunched CookieCott 2015 after the Girl Scouts honored Representative Barbara Lee (D-CA) during Black History Month (the person credited with coining the phrase "war on women" and a pro-choice politician).[77] This ongoing campaign has had mixed effects to date, but it has not yet achieved its goal of closing down the Girl Scouts for good.

Campaigns Involving Depictions of Religion

Two market campaigns initiated by conservatives challenge demeaning or misleading representations of biblical figures and events.

The Da Vinci Code Campaign

The Vatican called for a boycott of the film *The Da Vinci Code* two weeks before it opened in May 2006.[78] The film, based on a best-selling book by Dan Brown, contained what Catholic leadership deemed "slanderous" offenses against Christianity. The Vatican was especially critical of what it saw as a double standard that allowed Christianity to be mocked but prohibited similar mocking of Islam or Judaism because it would provoke a global outcry. For example, the book and the film alleges that Jesus married the biblical figure Mary Magdalene and bore children and that the Catholic group Opus Dei engaged in violence to cover up this history. Although the boycott was initiated by the Vatican in Rome, Catholic leaders in the United States orchestrated a national boycott campaign from the pulpit. Protesters gathered outside theaters showing the film on its opening day in dozens of U.S. cities.[79] This was a market campaign proper that sought to punish the filmmakers and distributors for political reasons, in this case, for defaming the values of Christianity.

Barbara Nicolosi, a grassroots activist and the most prominent voice in this campaign, encouraged Christians to "othercott" by attending the Disney film *Over the Hedge* on the opening night of *The Da Vinci Code* to bump it from a top revenue spot. Nicolosi is a screenwriter who founded the first program to train Christian screenwriters. She was born in New Brunswick, New Jersey, and earned an MA in television and film from Northwestern University. Nicolosi was a consultant on *Saving Grace,* a Christian television series, and *The Passion of the Christ*, a Christian film.

The goal of the campaign was to send a message to the filmmakers by lowering the box office returns, but even though the film was critically panned for reasons unrelated to the boycott, the film grossed $217 million in the United States alone.[80] At the time, the film enjoyed the second biggest opening, so the boycott had no measurable economic effect. Some church leaders speculated that the boycott may have had the reverse effect of piquing viewer interest and increasing revenues, but this did not stop the Vatican from calling for a boycott of *Angels and Demons*, the sequel to *The Da Vinci Code*.[81] This second boycott did not muster enough support for inclusion in this study.

The *JC* Campaign

When Comedy Central started development of the animated show *JC* in 2010, the network faced a boycott from a powerful coalition called Citizens Against Religious Bigotry (CARB). CARB is composed of over twenty prominent Christian and Jewish organizations, including the Family Research Council and the Parents Television Council. *JC* was a show about Jesus making it as a regular guy in New York City, trying to escape his position and his uncaring father.[82] The coalition was concerned that this program would follow in the footsteps of other Comedy Central depictions of Jesus and God, such as *South Park,* which it claimed "promotes religious bigotry and discrimination."[83] CARB also claimed that Comedy Central had a double standard for Christianity and Islam because the company refused to censor offensive portrayals of Christian figures but had censored a *South Park* depiction that mocked the Prophet Muhammad just a few months earlier. (Comedy Central was responding to online threats from the Islamic group Revolution Muslim.) This was a market campaign proper with the goal of convincing Comedy Central to change its content for political reasons— to not mock Christian values.

The goal of the CARB campaign was to prevent *JC* from getting on the air. The strategy was to use a secondary boycott threat against potential sponsors if they bought ad time on the show. L. Brent Bozell, a CARB representative, asked, "Why should [advertisers] be supporting a business that makes a habit of attacking Christianity and yet as a formal policy to censor anything considered offensive to followers of Islam? This double standard is pure bigotry, one from which advertisers should quickly shy away."[84] The coalition contacted three hundred potential advertisers, urging them to avoid sponsoring *JC.*[85] CARB also created an online petition against the show, which received over 50,000 signatures, and the "Yes to Jesus Christ, No to *JC*" Facebook page. Two months after it started the boycott, CARB announced that all the sponsors they had contacted had agreed not to purchase ad time on *JC.*[86] Comedy Central did not respond to the boycott, but *JC* never aired on the channel and CARB took credit for an effective boycott action.

Campaigns for Gun Rights

Three national conservative campaigns from 2004 to 2014 advanced gun rights. These campaigns diverge from campaigns opposing gay rights, promoting biblical ideas of morality, and contesting demeaning depictions of Christianity in that the right to own and carry guns is not based on religious arguments. Nevertheless, they are all conservative causes, and both conservative Christians and gun rights advocates identify overwhelmingly with the Republican Party.

The ConocoPhillips Campaign

In 2005, the National Rifle Association (NRA), an influential lobbying group for gun owners and makers, called on its 4 million members to boycott Conoco-Phillips after the oil giant filed a federal lawsuit to block a law in Oklahoma allowing employees to keep guns in their vehicles parked in the company lot.[87] This law had been passed after a series of workplace shootings that received national media attention. Several other companies in the state also attempted to block this law, but the NRA singled out ConocoPhillips as a high-profile company with locations throughout the United States. This was a market campaign proper because the aim of the organizers was to change the political position of a business.

Wayne LaPierre, an NRA leader, issued a press release about the boycott stating, "If you are a corporation that is anti-gun, anti-gun owner or anti-Second Amendment, we will spare no effort or expense to work against you to protect the rights of your law-abiding employees."[88] LaPierre asked NRA members to boycott all Conoco, Phillips 66, and Union 76 stations, and he urged gas station owners to put pressure on the parent company to drop the federal lawsuit.[89] The NRA spread the word about its boycott through online gun-owner sites and billboards reading, "ConocoPhillips Is No Friend of the Second Amendment," strategically placed in areas of the country with a high concentration of gun owners.[90] The campaign also used direct action to further its cause. A month after the start of the boycott, the NRA hosted a rally in Oklahoma to protest ConocoPhillips.

The NRA boycott pressure compelled several companies to drop out of the lawsuit,[91] but the campaign did not accomplish its goal of getting Conoco-Phillips to drop out. A federal district court overturned the law in favor of ConocoPhillips the following year, but in 2009, the Tenth U.S. Circuit Court of Appeals upheld the Oklahoma state law in favor of the NRA (overturning the ruling of the lower court),[92] and more than thirty other states have passed similar laws since the boycott. Nevertheless, the NRA was not able to get ConocoPhillips to change its position regarding the law, so this was an ineffective marketplace campaign.

The Cooper Firearms Campaign

Dan Cooper, the founder and CEO of Cooper Firearms of Montana, resigned on October 17, 2008, three days after grassroots activists targeted the company for a boycott because Cooper had contributed $3,300 to Barack Obama's presidential campaign.[93] This was a market campaign proper because activists wanted to change the political position of a business entity.

Cooper initially took to social media, defending his decision to support the Democratic candidate because of Obama's message about "the retooling of America, which involves the building of middle-class jobs and helping American small business be competitive with those overseas."[94] This explanation was not adequate for many gun rights activists, who took aim at Cooper Firearms for supporting a presidential candidate who was not pro-gun. An activist using the name "Peter" posted an Open Letter to Dan Cooper on the website Firearms and Freedom.[95] This letter was widely circulated, and grassroots activists called for a boycott of the gun maker to compel the company to fire Cooper. They used social media to spread the word and also initiated a letter-writing campaign. The company received over 1,000 messages in one week. This campaign was effective in that it gained a swift apology from the company and the resignation of its founder.

The Groupon Campaign

In early 2013, Groupon, an online marketplace company, decided to stop selling any gun-related products or services in response to the mass shooting at Sandy Hook, an elementary school in Connecticut, that left twenty children and seven adults dead, including the shooter.[96] Groupon issued a statement that it was "bowing to consumer pressure," but the company quickly faced intense criticism from gun rights consumers, who started a boycott.[97]

Michael Cargill, the owner of Central Texas Gun Works, initiated the boycott, but within days, it went viral through blogs, an online petition, and other forms of social media. Cargill, a self-described gay black Republican, owns the first gun shop in the nation to sell guns using bitcoins (a form of online currency), which made him the first online gun retailer. He grew up in a liberal family that shunned firearms but purchased his first gun after his seventy-year-old grandmother was robbed and raped while leaving a library.[98] Cargill spent twelve years in the army, where he became a gun specialist. He switched his party allegiance to Republican in 2014 because the Democrats "make people feel guilty about protecting themselves."[99]

Cargill demanded that Groupon reverse its decision or face economic consequences from gun owners across the United States. He used Facebook, Twitter, and LinkedIn to spread the news, and the campaign soon had an online life of its own. This was a market campaign proper because the goal was to get Groupon to reverse a decision it had made that reflected a specific political stance.

Cargill also appeared on a Fox Business Show a few weeks after the boycott started to announce that the boycott had "hurt [Groupon] really bad."[100] But the boycott did not have an overall economic effect on the company; Groupon issued a second-quarter earnings statement showing that this had been its "strongest quarter ever in North America."[101] Despite this, less than six months after the boycott started, Groupon reversed its decision and again started offering gun and gun-related services.[102] The company did not attribute this change to the boycott action, but the timing makes it clear that this boycott action was effective in getting Groupon to reverse its decision.

Campaign Effectiveness

Of the twenty 2004–2014 conservative consumer activism campaigns I have examined in the chapter, two are ongoing (Rupert Murdoch's boycott of Guinness beer and CookieCott against the Girl Scouts). Of the remaining eighteen, only six campaigns were effective, and two had mixed success (the Komen and Microsoft campaigns); the remaining campaigns did not achieve their goals. Two out of the three campaigns to promote gun rights were effective, which speaks to the power of pro-gun groups to mobilize their membership (Table 6.1).

The success rate for conservative campaigns is considerably lower than the success rate for liberal campaigns for progressive causes such as civil rights, environmental protection and animal rights, and gender and LGBT rights. This is probably due to the fact that conservative consumer activism is mostly a reaction to changes in society, such as the emerging support for same-sex marriage, the shift toward more sexualized content in media, and the normalization of irreverent

TABLE 6.1   Effectiveness of conservative campaigns

CAMPAIGN	EFFECTIVE?
Disney	No
Procter & Gamble	Yes
McDonald's	Yes
Microsoft	Mixed
Brokeback Mountain	No
J. C. Penney	No
Guinness	Ongoing
Michael Sam	No
Kinsey	No
Motrin	Yes
Komen	Mixed
Urban Outfitters	No
Shame on Kraft	No
Shame on Kmart	No
CookieCott	Ongoing
The Da Vince Code	No
JC	Yes
ConocoPhillips	No
Cooper Firearms	Yes
Groupon	Yes
Effectiveness = 33.3%	

media content. Conservatives are using consumer activism to push against a tide of changing cultural values, a more difficult task than being carried by this tide.

Democratic Implications

Many of the campaigns I have discussed in this chapter improved democratic inputs by increasing the overall rates of political participation and discussion of policy issues, as well as advancing the will of the majority through market channels. They all improved corporate accountability to consumers by pressuring the companies to at least think twice about issuing content that offends some political sensibilities, and one campaign made government more accountable to the will of the majority. Conservative campaigns opposing LGBT rights and protections actually reduced democracy by encroaching on minority political rights.

As shown in table 6.2, the conservative market campaigns improved democracy an average of 4.35 measures out of 10.

TABLE 6.2 Democratic contribution of conservative campaigns

CAMPAIGN	DEMOCRATIC SCORE (1–10)
Disney	5
Procter & Gamble	5
McDonald's	5
Microsoft	6
Brokeback Mountain	5
J. C. Penney	3
Guinness	4
Michael Sam	3
Kinsey	4
Motrin	4
Komen	4
Urban Outfitters	4
Shame on Kraft	4
Shame on Kmart	4
CookieCott	4
The Da Vince Code	4
JC	4
ConocoPhillips	5
Cooper Firearms	5
Groupon	5
Average = 4.35	

Promotes Robust Citizen Participation

All twenty conservative campaigns improved democratic health through higher overall rates of political participation. Combined, these campaigns offered a political voice to over 2 million Americans through market channels. For campaigns involving culture war issues, this voice is a particularly important counterweight to changing culture norms that have significant political importance, such as gender roles and sexuality. Many of these conservative actions were reactions to offensive media content, an area where formal political lobbying has lost its effectiveness with market deregulation and the oligopolistic nature of the media industry (in which only a few major companies own most of the content).[103] In other words, as conservatives lost the battle against hypersexualized, hyperviolent, lewd, and anti-Christian content in the electoral arena, they turned to consumer activism to advance their concerns.

The three gun rights campaigns examined here also used market channels to express displeasure at corporate decisions that were not within the purview of formal political institutions. There are no laws against ConocoPhillips filing a federal suit to stop a law, Dan Cooper contributing to a Democratic political candidate, or Groupon deciding not to offer guns and gun services, so activists could not have used formal political channels to respond. Instead, they used consumer dollars to punish these companies for actions that were perfectly legal but offensive to gun rights advocates.

Promotes Political Equality in Participation and Representation

The campaigns reviewed in this chapter were mostly morality driven and did not improve racial, gender, or economic equality in participation or representation. Nearly 70 percent of Americans identify with some Christian faith, and this group is economically diverse, gender equal, and two-thirds white.[104] The gun rights campaigns also did not advance equality of participation or representation because most gun owners are majority white and male with the means to purchase expensive items.[105] Christians and gun rights activists are not underrepresented groups, and in fact, they have ample Republican political representation in state legislatures, both houses of Congress, and the White House.

Promotes the Will of the Majority

In terms of improving democracy by furthering the will of the majority, all the campaigns opposing LGBT rights before November 2012 supported the majority opinion,[106] including the Disney, Procter & Gamble, McDonald's, Microsoft, and

Brokeback Mountain actions. It is telling that the antigay campaigns launched in 2012 and afterward were not successful because they fell during a time of rapid public opinion change, when antigay advocates were swimming against the tide. The J. C. Penney campaign even elicited opposition from prominent conservatives, something that would have been unlikely just half a decade earlier. The three gun rights campaigns also advanced the will of the majority because according to polls 73 percent of Americans support gun ownership and oppose restrictions beyond background checks.[107]

Promotes Active Media

Most of the campaigns I have discussed in this chapter promoted more active media by putting issues on the agenda that were not being covered by mainstream outlets. Conservative campaigns are the primary way that the public learns about the pro-LGBT stances of businesses such as Disney, Procter & Gamble, McDonald's, Microsoft, and Guinness. The conservative market campaigns compelled the mainstream media to report on politicized business activities that otherwise might have gone unnoticed by the public. The conservative market campaigns also put three gun-ownership topics on the media agenda.

The financial relationship between Komen and Planned Parenthood was made public by the Komen conservative campaign and subsequent mainstream media coverage, and the same can be said for public awareness around the feminist leanings of the Girl Scouts. The market campaigns targeting Urban Outfitters, Kraft, Kmart, and *Kinsey* also improved media coverage of hypersexualization in popular culture. Hypersexualization in entertainment and advertising media has become the norm in U.S. society, a norm that is rarely challenged in press coverage. *The Da Vinci Code* and *JC* campaigns put the topic of religious representation on the agenda that otherwise would not have received mainstream media attention.

Of the twenty conservative market campaigns, twelve also advanced more active media by creating alternative coverage through social media. The Motrin campaign was initiated in online blogs, and the Guinness boycott started on Twitter. All three gun rights actions made extensive use of social media and online gun forums to increase awareness of the concerns.

Improves Public Discussion on Policy Issues

All the conservative campaigns reviewed in this chapter improved public discussion on policy issues. Americans debated LGBT protections and rights, whether the Sexual Revolution was good for the country, abortion, hypersexualization and violence in media content, traditional gender roles, representations of religion in media, and gun rights. These campaigns triggered passionate debates in the social and mainstream media around a plethora of culture war issues.

Promotes Political Equality in State Protection and Public Resources

The NRA sought to give its members more voice in formal political channels by boycotting ConocoPhillips, an energy company that had filed a lawsuit opposing NRA interests. In doing so, it promoted political equality in state protection by allowing citizens to arm themselves on the worksite as they see fit. The other campaign that involved the state was the efforts against Microsoft to reverse its position on a LGBT bill before the Washington State legislature.[108] The goal of the Microsoft action was to diminish state protection of an underrepresented group (LGBT individuals), not to improve it.

Promotes Corporate Political Accountability

Virtually all the market campaigns reviewed in this chapter promoted greater corporate political accountability to consumers for decisions with political significance. All the campaigns opposing LGBT rights made the targeted corporation more aware of the range of consumer opinions on this issue, and in some instances, such as the McDonald's and Microsoft campaigns, companies decided to remain neutral in the culture wars. The three actions targeting media (*Kinsey*, *The Da Vinci Code*, and *JC*) sent the message that Hollywood will draw the ire of activists for content that offends Christians, with the *JC* campaign cutting the legs out from under the production of the show through its sponsors. The Motrin boycott was a textbook lesson in corporate accountability and grassroots activism when an ad is deemed offensive by its target market for reasons of morality or tradition. The Urban Outfitters, Shame on Kraft, and Shame on Kmart campaigns tried to improve corporate accountability but actually drew attention to offending content through the publicity about the boycott. All three gun rights campaigns improved corporate accountability for gun policy stances and decisions.

Promotes Government Accountability to Citizens

The Microsoft and NRA campaigns were the only efforts involving a governmental entity. The Microsoft campaign effectively convinced the company to reverse its position on a controversial LGBT bill, a bill that did not reflect majority public opinion at the time and failed by just a few votes. The Microsoft campaign improved democracy by making the legislature more accountable to the will of the people through a secondary political action against Microsoft, but it also diminished democracy by suppressing the rights and protections of an under-represented group. The NRA campaign pushed a position that was eventually upheld in the courts, but it is difficult to say whether the boycott played a role in this judicial decision.

Protects against the Encroachment of Minority Rights

None of the conservative campaigns I have examined in this chapter protected against encroachment on minority rights. In fact, the eight campaigns opposing LGBT rights were attempts to limit and infringe on the rights of a minority group. Overall, these eight campaigns improved participation rates and public policy discussion, and some even represented the majority will while simultaneously reducing democratic outputs by curbing the rights of minorities.

Protects against Government Encroachment on Civil Liberties

None of the market campaigns in this chapter sought to protect citizens or groups from government encroachment on their civil liberties. Some of the conservative campaigns pose a democratic concern in that that they sought to limit the rights of others. In *The Democratic Virtues of the Christian Right*,[109] Jon Shields reports that the Christian right is frequently accused of threatening democratic values by journalists and academics by blurring the line between church and state, and prizing ideology over reason. Shields analyzes survey data, media, and interviews with three dozen Christian right organizations in six major cities; he concludes that these groups are reinvigorating U.S. politics. Rather than the Christian right being a threat to democratic principles, he finds that it is fulfilling the ideals of the New Left by getting previously alienated people involved in politics around the major moral questions of the day. Shields is cautious about the prejudices that are enflamed by the religious right, but he finds that, on net, they improve democracy through higher rates of political debate and participation. His positive findings about the religious right are generally upheld by my analysis in this chapter; nevertheless, overt efforts to curtail the rights of certain groups (e.g., LGBT individuals in terms of employment rights and women in terms of reproductive rights) do pose a threat to democracy. Conservative consumer activism is distinct from liberal activism in that it contributes to some democratic principles but depletes others.

Conservatives waged twenty campaigns that reached a national audience from 2004 to 2014. They used fewer tools in the consumer activism toolbox than did liberal campaigns. Almost all used boycotts, but only half used social media because they conduct more targeted mobilizations rather than reaching for a wide audience. The conservative campaigns also used direct action far less than did liberal campaigns to avoid increasing attention to offending material. Divestment was used in only one conservative campaign.

The conservative market campaigns for gun rights were as effective as the liberal campaigns for civil rights, environmental protection and animal rights, and gender and LGBT rights analyzed in previous chapters; however, conservative actions around moral issues were far less effective. Overall, the 2004–2014 conservative campaigns were half as effective as liberal campaigns occurring during this time because the goal of conservative consumer activism is mostly to maintain traditional values in a world where values, beliefs, and practices are constantly changing.

Even though the conservative campaigns were less effective in terms of achieving their stated goals, they strengthened democracy by increasing the overall rates of political participation. Campaigns driven by moral concerns offered conservatives an outlet for political expression and power in the media during a time when deregulation and consolidation have contributed to offensive content. In a similar fashion, the gun rights campaigns provided an outlet for dissent against companies engaging in perfectly legal acts that went against activists' political beliefs. The campaigns examined in this chapter also improved democracy by expanding overall rates of and spaces for public discussions of major culture war policy issues. About half the campaigns furthered the will of the people because they reflected the majority public opinion at the time. All the campaigns analyzed here improved corporate accountability, and one campaign made government more accountable to the will of the majority.

On net, the conservative use of consumer activism improved the health of democracy, but campaigns opposing LGBT concerns reduced democracy by curbing the rights and protections of this minority group. Although it is rare that consumer activism is used in this way, and most of the actions in this chapter did not suppress minority rights, the potential exists and should be highlighted. Not all consumer activism strengthens democracy.

Conservatives are losing the culture wars[110] as Americans become more permissive of family arrangements, family planning, and sexual practices that were once considered alternative lifestyles. As public opinion shifts and the laws shift with it, I anticipate that conservatives will use consumer activism at an even higher rate to push against this cultural tide. The early months of Donald Trump's presidency demonstrate that consumer activism has become a regular staple of conservative politics in the United States.

WHO RULES?

Corporate Power and Models of Democracy

Citizens and scholars have sounded the alarm for over a century about the threat that business influence poses to democracy. David Vogel writes that Americans grew concerned about corporate power in politics after the Civil War, when "industrial capitalism created potential tension between the nation's central economic institutions and its democratic heritage."[1] Prior to that time, business power was local, business entities were required to serve the public good and refrain from influencing elections or public policy, and the states had the power to revoke a corporate charter at any time. In 1819, the Supreme Court tried to rescind the ability of the states to revoke corporate charters by ruling in *Dartmouth v. Woodward* that New Hampshire did not have the power to revoke a charter granted by King George III to Dartmouth College. In response, states across the nation passed a rash of laws strengthening their hold over corporate charters, and in 1855, the Supreme Court confirmed state power over "artificial bodies" in *Dodge v. Woolsey*. Nevertheless, corporate leaders continued their fight for control of resources, labor rights, and political sovereignty, and the industrial age provided the perfect opening to advance their interests. With the new wage-labor economy that was replacing farming, citizens faced the possibility of unemployment for the first time. Corporate leaders exploited this fear, persecuted labor organizers, and purchased newspapers to frame business leaders as heroes and shape public opinion in their favor. They also circumvented the corporate charter laws and exerted direct influence on state legislators to relax their oversight.

The states ultimately lost control of corporate oversight through a series of court rulings in favor of corporate rights and property protection, and in 1886, the Supreme Court put the last nail in the coffin with *Santa Clara County v. Southern Pacific Railroad,* which established "corporate personhood." According to Thomas Hartmann, a political analyst, the court did not actually rule on classifying corporations as "natural persons," but a court clerk interpreted this as the will of the court and it has been used as precedent since then.[2] The *Santa Clara* case extended the 14th Amendment, which had been established to grant rights to recently freed slaves, to apply to "corporate persons." Business entities quickly used this ruling to increase their power over laborers, labor organizers, and politicians. As business power in politics and policymaking grew, critiques of the corporate threat to democracy reached a fever pitch with the Populist (1870s–1890s) and Progressive (1890–1920) movements.

Corporate personhood created a unique type of "person"—one with great economic, political, and social influence. Corporations operate on the principle of serving, first and foremost, their shareholders' best interests, and this profit motive often comes into conflict with the interests of employees, consumers, other stakeholders, and the environment. Joel Bakan, a law professor, makes the nuanced case that the mandate of putting profit above all other considerations sets up the corporation as a sociopathic entity that pursues its economic self-interests, often with indifference for others.[3] Naomi Klein, a documentarian and author, makes a similar argument in *The Shock Doctrine,* in which she describes global corporations taking advantage of disaster-shocked countries and people to turn usurious profits and wrest control of natural resources from the locals.[4] It is important to note that the corporate profit imperative is a well-accepted practice, but it is not codified into law. According to Lynn Stout, a law professor, CEOs actively framed the profit motive as a legal obligation in the 1970s, and the public and politicians believed this myth.[5] This means that, despite corporate personhood, publicly traded business entities can legally consider interests other than profits if compelled to by outside pressures, such as consumer activism.

In this chapter, I analyze consumer activism within broader questions of corporate power and democracy. I pose and answer a series of related questions: Do business entities hold a privileged position in U.S. politics that threatens democracy? How does marketplace activism fit within existing models of democracy? How does this type of activism differ from traditional political activism in the context of democratic principles? I begin with a look at business influence in politics and turn to a discussion of the main models of democracy in political theory, emphasizing whether consumer activism improves democracy under each model. I conclude with an examination of how consumer activism compares to traditional activism when it comes to democratic principles.

The Political Influence of Business

Do business entities hold a privileged position in U.S. politics? Academics disagree on this question. Pluralist theorists believe that businesses are interest groups, and like other interest groups, they compete in the political marketplace. Proponents of elitist theory conclude that businesses enjoy advantages over citizens when it comes to elections and policymaking and that their influence disrupts the interest-group politics that James Madison envisioned would provide a check against single interests dominating the political process. According to David Vogel, pluralists dominated the academic debate from the 1940s through the late 1960s, but in the 1970s, two prominent scholars—Robert Dahl and Charles Lindblom—reversed their pluralist position and concluded that business leaders have a particularly powerful role in U.S. politics because of their unique role in providing for the public welfare. In his influential 1977 book *Politics and Markets*, Lindblom concludes, "the large private corporation fits oddly into democratic theory and vision. Indeed, it does not fit."[6] Vogel later complicated the pluralist-elitist debate with his analysis that corporate political power fluctuates depending on global economic conditions (e.g., businesses wield more political influence during economic downturns) and shifts in the political system (e.g., new relaxations of campaign financing laws increase the political power of businesses, but new networked social movements increase the political influence of citizens). I side with the elitist position in this debate, based on compelling evidence that corporations have the upper hand in policy influence, electoral influence, and hidden influence.

Policy Influence

According to David Rothkopf, a political scientist, corporations have eclipsed government on a global scale in terms of revenue, employment, and global physical presence,[7] and their reach into politics has long grown to protect this privileged position. The goal of interest groups is to influence policy outcomes, and U.S. businesses have a compelling interest in policy outcomes, given that their profits are routinely affected by regulation.[8] William Greider, an author who investigates corporate political influence, provides evidence that corporate power in politics has grown tremendously in recent decades as the traditional linkages between citizens and government (political parties, interest groups, and media) have atrophied and corporate interests have eagerly filled the vacuum.[9] Corporate presence and influence in Washington politics, and all fifty state capitals, makes sense given that corporations have an overriding profit motive and thus a deep interest in politics that influences their bottom line. Furthermore, businesses have the resources to influence politics in ways that most citizens cannot. Given that corporations are regulated, it would be unreasonable for them *not* to pursue influence in politics.

Corporations are political power brokers that wield great influence in policy decisions and implementation, and this often comes at the expense of citizen interests.[10] In the past four decades, business lobbying has transformed from a small, somewhat disorganized, reactive industry into a powerful proactive force in U.S. politics. Business interests spend $2.6 billion per year lobbying, more than the amount it takes to run the House and Senate. For every $1 spent by citizen interest groups, corporations spend $34.[11] Lobbyists wield influence through drafting legislation, providing expensive research and public opinion data (that helps political leaders frame the debate in a way that is conducive to corporate interests), providing the revolving door between industry and politics, capturing congressional committees by creating close alliances between them and industry officials, creating Astroturf support groups, and making campaign contributions.[12] Corporate influence via elections has grown with the ascension of dark money, funds used in elections that are (legally) not disclosed to voters.

Frank Baumgartner and Brian Jones, political scientists, document how corporate interest groups influence the policy process at every stage: setting the policy agenda, defining policy options, and influencing the passage of policy and its implementation.[13] An extensive literature has found no consistent effect of corporate political action committee contributions on roll-call votes, but the policy influence of these groups is often substantial in other ways.[14] For example, campaign contributions rarely change votes, but they do inspire legislators to become more active in passing bills they are already inclined to support.[15] Also, corporate resources spent to gain specific earmarks are effective, and intuitively, lobbying is more effective when it garners little opposition from public interest groups.[16] According to Baumgartner et al., business interest groups are more effective at stopping than at enacting policies; moreover, corporate interests dominate policy implementation hearings throughout the federal bureaucracy.[17]

Not all scholars agree that business interests trump citizen interests in the policy process. Matt Grossmann, a political scientist, finds that citizen interest groups have more policy influence than business groups. He examines interest-group influence across fourteen policy domains involving 790 policy enactments from 1945 to 2004 and finds that the most common and effective tools of influence are lobbying and providing research to policymakers.[18] The ability of interest groups to mobilize members and resource advantages does not increase its success. Grossmann and Jeffrey Berry observe that liberal interest groups considerably outnumber conservative groups, and even though business groups outnumber public advocacy groups by a significant margin, they find that advocacy groups have more overall policy influence than business groups.[19]

Other scholars present empirical evidence that business groups have more power in the policy process than citizens, as evidenced by policy decisions concerning natural resources, technological development, product development, as well as the cozy working relations between regulators and the regulated. The analysis of Belén Balanyá et al. shows that corporations have successfully deregulated and privatized every major public policy domain.[20] In addition, a 2014 empirical study by Martin Gilens and Benjamin I. Page of who rules in the United States finds that economic elites and corporate lobbyists have "substantial independent impact" on policy, while citizens and citizen interest groups "have little or no independent influence."[21] More specifically, they compare the relative influence of everyday citizens, economic elites, citizen interest groups, and business-oriented interest groups using a data set of 1,779 policy issues. Gilens and Page conclude that economic elites and business interest groups have the most impact on government policy and that everyday citizens and the interest groups that represent their interests have little measureable influence. Their findings support the elite theory of business influence in politics. When it comes to questions of democracy, the Gilens and Page study is superior to the Grossmann study because it measures the influence of ordinary citizens as opposed to comparing influence across types of interest group. Given this, I conclude that the elite theory of business influence best describes the role of the corporation in U.S. politics.

Electoral Influence

Business entities also exert power in politics through the electoral process. Candidates rely on contributions from industry and corporate groups, as well as business leaders, to gain their seats of power. Once elected, they are beholden to the interests that made that possible. Larry Bartels, a political scientist, finds that members of Congress largely ignore the interests of their low-income constituents but are responsive to the preferences and priorities of their wealthiest constituents.[22] Corporate spending on candidates and lobbying is a wise investment that usually pays off. According to the Institute for Policy Studies, corporations make up fifty-one of the one hundred largest economies in the world, and 53 percent of the major U.S. companies did not pay the standard 35 percent federal tax rate during the years examined.[23] Furthermore, due to hefty tax rebates, Texaco, PepsiCo, Enron, WorldCom, Chevron, and General Motors paid zero in federal income tax in some years. These statistics illustrate that corporations have become political entities in their own right due to their sheer economic power in the global market. They also illustrate the wisdom of corporations' investing in candidates.

Moreover, recent court decisions have essentially allowed corporations and business leaders to contribute an unlimited amount of money to political candidates. In the 1976 *Buckley v. Valeo* decision, the Supreme Court ruled that individual campaign contributions constituted a form of free speech. In 2010, the Court extended this logic to corporations (deemed "people") in *Citizens United v. FEC*. This decision made it infinitely easier for corporations (including foreign companies) and labor unions to spend unlimited sums of money to sway elections. Prior to the *Citizens United* decision, corporations were already spending generously on elections through issue advocacy organizations that did not directly advocate for the defeat or election of a candidate (also known as 527s). *Citizens United* created a new type of political organization, known as a super political action committee (Super PAC), that can raise and spend unlimited funds to elect or defeat candidates. Super PACs raised nearly $700 million in the 2012 election cycle and $1.2 billion in the 2016 election.[24] The only downside to Super PACs for corporations was that the donor names were public, but *Citizens United* fixed that problem as well. The Supreme Court ruled that 501c(4)s, organizations with a social welfare purpose, could spend money in politics without disclosing the donor names. Nondisclosed spending, also known as dark money, went from $5.2 million in 2006 to over $300 million in the 2012 presidential election and ten times that amount in the 2016 election.[25] Corporations had already gained substantial influence in politics prior to *Citizens United*, but this ruling gave them the keys to the political castle.

Corporate political influence contributes to what Mark Warren, a political theorist, calls a "democratic deficit" in the United States, meaning that, although the United States is classified as a democracy, at least one foundational democratic component is under threat.[26] The United States is in democratic deficit because overbearing corporate influence in the electoral and policy processes erodes the pillars of democracy. Popular sovereignty is diminished when elected leaders are beholden to corporate interests at the expense of citizen interests. Political liberty shrinks when corporations can establish policies that incarcerate Americans for profit. Political equality disappears when the "one person, one vote" principle does not apply to political elites and corporations.

Hidden Influence

In addition to overt influence on policies and elections, corporate interests also have hidden political influence through covert lobbying efforts and their power to shape public opinion. As an example of hidden lobbying, the American Legislative Exchange Council (ALEC) is a nonprofit organization that has circumvented Internal Revenue Service (IRS) limitations on political activities. Founded by three prominent conservatives in 1973, ALEC describes itself as a "nonpartisan membership association for conservative state lawmakers who share a common belief in limited government, free markets, federalism, and individual liberty."[27] ALEC influences public policy through forums that bring legislators and corporate leaders together to create model legislation ready to be introduced in state legislatures. ALEC boasts a membership of nearly 2,000 legislators across the country—nearly one-third of state legislators—and its legislation has a 20 percent passage rate.[28] Even though nonprofit organizations are restricted from engaging in political activities, the unorthodox method of "educating" legislators used by ALEC has allowed the organization to get around this law. ALEC has worked behind the scenes to pass the "show me your papers" law in Arizona (SB 1070) as well as "stand your ground" gun laws, pro-fracking laws, and voter ID laws in multiple states.

But the biggest hidden influence of this organization has been its contribution to the expansion of the private prison system. ALEC represents over 125 companies that finance prison construction, build prisons, operate prisons, furnish prison services (e.g., telephones and clothing), provide tertiary services (e.g., ankle bracelets and in-car breathalyzers), and use prison labor. It is the largest prison lobby in the United States, and its influence is mostly hidden. In 2011, a whistleblower leaked a cache of eight hundred model ALEC bills, and one out of every five bills involved the prison industry. According to Rebecca Cooper et al., ALEC has expanded the prison population by creating new crimes, expanding the definitions of existing crimes, enhancing the enforcement of existing crimes, amending the trial process in ways that increase the likelihood of incarceration, and lengthening prison sentences.[29] ALEC has used model legislation to expand use of private prisons, goods, and services (22.3 percent of the model prison bills), promote greater use of prison labor (2.1 percent), and increase the size of the prison population (84.3 percent). The United States has the highest incarceration rate of any industrialized nation, accounting for 25 percent of the global prison population, and because of the prison lobby, incarceration rates have climbed significantly in the past decade, even with declining rates of crime.[30] Many factors have contributed to this expansion, but hidden corporate influence is certainly a contributing factor. ALEC has worked to put more bodies behind bars for longer periods of time to boost corporate profits.

Another way business interests exert political power is by shaping public opinion. Corporations have greater influence in the lives of everyday Americans than ever before through cradle-to-grave marketing, and they have a greater influence in politics than any time since the Gilded Age.[31] In *The Age of Acquiescence,*

Steve Fraser, a labor historian, asks why everyday Americans responded with fury at inequality in the country during the Gilded Age, but few are actively working to address the seismic wealth inequality today, when about 1 percent of the population holds more wealth than the bottom 95 percent combined. (The passionate Occupy Wall Street efforts and support for Bernie Sanders in the 2016 presidential election were motivated by wealth inequality concerns, but neither movement was mainstream.) Fraser finds that most people are unable to imagine alternative economic systems because corporate capitalism has been deemed normal and good, and that key fables such as "the rebel billionaire" trope and "contract work as a form of liberation" cool the coals of resistance. Corporate and capitalist myth making is part of the hidden influence of business entities. Corporations have more access to the minds of everyday people through communication technologies and ubiquitous entertainment media, which means they have more power to shape the hearts and minds of Americans than ever before in the history of our polity.

According to Greider, corporations are able to keep issues of fundamental importance to the public good off the agenda because most citizens do not have the resources and time they need to identify their interests, let alone sufficiently advocate for them.[32] For example, the climate change denial industry, which has managed to delay major political action on this issue since the 1970s, is funded by dark money moving through 140 foundations that spend tens of millions of dollars on a misinformation campaign each year.[33] In a similar vein, Lindblom finds that corporations play such a major role in the economy that the public tends to view corporate interests as the national interest.[34] For example, U.S. military spending that lines the pockets of private companies accounts for 37 percent of total global military spending,[35] driven by the seemingly national interest of being the strongest military power in the world. President Dwight D. Eisenhower spoke of the confusion of national interests with corporate interests when he warned the country about the military-industrial complex in his 1961 presidential farewell address and concluded that "only an alert and knowledgeable citizenry can compel the proper meshing of the huge industrial and military machinery of defense with our peaceful methods and goals so that security and liberty may prosper together."[36] Eisenhower did not consider how influential business interests are in shaping citizen interests in ways that limit democratic choice.

John Gaventa, a political scientist, finds that a "culture of silence" is promulgated by the powerful and precludes development of "consciousness"— "self-determined action or reflection upon their actions"—that is necessary for true democratic participation.[37] In this environment, citizens become unable to identify their own interests and, instead, espouse the values and language of the dominant elite. In this culture of silence, the interests of elites dominate the political scene, and citizens are denied the possibility of exploring, identifying, and pursuing their own interests. "Since citizens have been socialized into compliance, so to speak, they accept the definitions of political reality as offered by dominant groups, classes, or government institutions."[38]

Gaventa presents a nuanced model to explain why corporate interests are able to access and maintain political power. First, they get a seat at the table through campaign contributions and electing fellow like-minded business people. Second, they set the rules of the game to benefit their interests through tax law and regulations. Last, they convince citizens that their interests align with corporate interests. Gaventa finds that the supplanting of true citizen interests with corporate interests prior to citizens entering into the political arena is more damaging to democracy than even the issue of group inequalities in representation. Under this theory, even if these inequalities were extinguished, citizen interests would still be misrepresented because their espoused interests are, in reality, the interests of elites and business.

Models of Democracy

Political theorists have debated the ideals of democracy for centuries. Current normative models emphasize citizen participation (participatory democracy), deliberation (deliberative democracy), and the democratization of economic institutions (economic democracy). How does consumer activism affect each model of democracy?

Participatory Democracy

The participatory democracy model was popularized in the 1960s as a critical response to representative democracy, wherein citizens entrust elected leaders to act in accordance with their wishes. Under this model, democracy is healthy only when its citizen participation rates are high. The basic components of participatory democracy are (1) citizen exercise of direct responsibility in political decision making and (2) self-governance fostered through active, empowering citizen participation. Carol Pateman and Crawford B. MacPherson wrote early texts in the 1970s on the principles and importance of participatory democracy, and Jane Mansbridge and Benjamin Barber developed the contours of the model.[39]

Mansbridge proposes a model of participatory democracy in which citizens work together to find consensus through rational dialogue.[40] She is critical of the prevailing model of adversarial democracy, in which citizens see interests in constant conflict through elections, with winners and losers, because it socializes the public to believe that a common or public interest is elusive. Consequently, citizens have settled for representative democracy, in which elected leaders have the task of protecting liberty and equality in a system in which politics is considered fair as long as elections are competitive. Instead of this, Mansbridge advocates a version of democracy in which people who disagree can reason together until they find a common workable answer, driven by the shared goals of equal respect and personal growth. According to Mansbridge, this is feasible only in small-group settings. Her idea is that the process of reaching common ground, ideally through face-to-face interactions, will strengthen the notions of citizenship and community. As we have seen, some forms of marketplace activism entail in-person collaboration, but most contemporary campaigns mobilize consumer activists online and do not meet Mansbridge's criteria for participatory democracy.

In a similar but somewhat divergent vein, Barber proposes "strong democracy," a democratic model with "responsible, competent citizens" who engage in active "self-governance."[41] Strong democracy promotes robust democratic citizenship over formal institutional mechanisms. Participatory democracy involves public talk, decision making, and action, all in quick succession. In an effort to be practical about the limits of citizens' ability and desire to participate in politics, Barber proposes a system in which "all the people govern themselves in at least some public matters at least some of the time."[42] This, according to Barber, is the remedy for the ills of representative democracy, which produces apathy and passivity in citizens by focusing on the rights of the individual at the expense of the common good. Citizen apathy limits the representativeness of policy decisions, but participatory democracy enlightens and empowers citizens by involving them in the political decision-making process. Unlike Mansbridge's model, which requires small group gatherings, Barber advocates sustained participation through town hall meetings, regional assemblies, and national gatherings. Consumer activism is a better fit of Barber's conception of participatory democracy than Mansbridge's because it produces a form of strong democracy by involving citizens in self-governance.

The contemporary debate about participatory democracy has shifted to ideas about radical democracy. Jason Vick considers radical democracy to be an updated form of participatory democracy, drawing on the basic tenets of participatory democracy outlined in Pateman's path-breaking work: "A strong emphasis on citizen participation, an egalitarian sensibility, an expansive notion of the political, a concern for individual development, and a critique of existing democratic practices and capitalist economic practices."[43] Participatory democratic theorists are concerned with citizen participation, while radical democratic theorists are concerned with the conditions of democracy that create participatory inequalities. Radical democratic theorists, including Jacques Rancière and Sheldon Wolin, follow in Pateman's footsteps with their analysis of social organizations, including the family and the workplace, that create participatory inequalities. Consumer activism fits well with these developments in participatory democracy because it expands conceptions of the political and is implicitly critical of the role of business interests in politics, an organization that contributes to participatory inequality.

Radical participatory democracy models have mostly been eclipsed in scholarship by deliberative democracy (see next section). Jeffrey Hilmer makes the case for a revived emphasis on participatory democracy because work on deliberative democracy has narrowed the scholarly focus to the process of deliberation and taken the focus away from the various locations of participation (e.g., the public sphere, the household, and the workplace).[44] Participatory democracy considers both the modes and locations of participation, and as such, it is a more useful measure of democratic health. My analysis here responds to this call to revive the focus on participatory democracy, which encompasses the analysis of both the form (political boycotting and buycotting, political investing, social media shaming, and direct actions) and location (marketplace) of political participation.

Marketplace activism improves democracy under the basic participatory model because it boosts citizen participation during a time when traditional types of political participation are declining, and it entails citizens' advocating for their interests rather than political representatives. Pateman emphasizes the need for all democratic systems to be democratized in the participatory model, including the economic sphere and the workplace, and consumer activism answers that call. It is a form of self-governance in the economic realm, and as such, a critical component of a strong democracy. Self-governance is citizens banding together to boycott sweatshops; it improves working conditions while simultaneously providing citizens with a political voice. When millions of Americans avoid products that have been tested on animals, corporations respond to this self-governance, resulting in de facto public policy. When eight prominent high-tech companies pledge to boycott products from old-growth forests in response to consumer pressure, this constitutes self-governance. When the town of Arcata, California, passes a resolution allowing citizens to hold corporations accountable for their social and political practices, and more than half of the citizens of the town are involved in determining guidelines for corporate conduct, this is self-governance.

Consumer activism does not fit every requirement of participatory democracy; in fact, it is closer to models of adversarial democracy, in that campaigns are competitive (with the targeted corporation), not consensus seeking. Nevertheless, consumer marketplace activism does foster citizenship and community through easy grassroots activism. It is a quicker and more direct way to express an interest than the lengthy process of lobbying for legislative outcomes or the indirect act of periodically voting for a candidate. Citizens are also more likely to see an effective outcome for their efforts given the high rates of success of consumer activism campaigns. Citizens are more politically efficacious in economic, rather than political, institutions because of the profit imperative, which empowers many to advocate for their interests in the marketplace, as discussed in chapter 2. Consumer activism also fosters community through what Benedict Anderson calls imagined communities that come together around shared interests and actions, mostly via online forums.[45] In addition to contributing to the overall tally of citizen action, on which participatory democracy relies, consumer activism also suggests alternative paths for a more active, empowered, self-governing citizenry.

Deliberative Democracy

Theories of deliberative democracy developed in the 1980s from constitutional and social theory scholars who were critical of the participatory models of the 1960s and 1970s. Joseph Bessette, a political scientist, coined the term *deliberative democracy* in 1980 to describe a form of government that revolves around citizen deliberation for decision making.[46] Participatory democracy requires citizens' input on decisions that affect their lives, whereas deliberative democracy requires deliberation and debate prior to reaching policy decisions. It entails pondering the pros and cons of common problems and citizens being open to shifting their positions based on new information and dialogue with others.

Bessette writes that the framers of the Constitution endorsed a form of deliberative democracy that lies somewhere between direct democracy and a system in which representatives make decisions as trustees, disconnected from real-time popular sentiments.[47] Consumer activism furthers deliberative democracy in some ways but not in others. Cass Sunstein, a legal scholar, argues that the Constitution includes an alternative vision of democracy that is not limited to interest-group competition but, instead, seeks to cultivate an individual's preferences through self-rule and face-to-face citizen exchange.[48] Bessette and Sunstein both refute the notion that pluralism is merely an aggregation of private interests and that the common good is the aggregation of individual preferences. Rather, they find that the common good can be achieved only through a reflective public deliberation process that transforms the preferences of at least some participants. The empirical work of Jim Fishkin, a political scientist, in his deliberative poll experiment enacts the principles of deliberative democracy by bringing people together to deliberate policy issues in an enlightened and reasonable way.

He finds that opinions are often transformed through deliberation and that ordinary people derive personal benefit from the deliberative process.[49]

Jon Elster, Bernard Manin, and Joshua Cohen more recently have defined the contours of deliberative democracy. Elster challenges the assumptions about rational choice underlying much of the early work on deliberative democracy, which assumes that citizens are self-interested, rational actors.[50] Elster, echoing Gaventa, notes that an individuals' choices are often constrained by influential forces, which can shape policy options in ways that make some seem unavailable; therefore, aggregate preferences may not map onto the public good. Manin proposes that democratic legitimacy derives from the process by which individual will is formed, that is, deliberation itself.[51] Decisions may not represent the will of all, but they are legitimate if everyone has a right to participate in the deliberative process. Cohen emphasizes the ways in which material inequalities among citizens lead to inequities in their ability to deliberate.[52]

Iris Marion Young was an early critic of deliberative democracy because of its privileging of rational dialogue at the expense of experiential testimony, a bias that marginalizes the voices of women and minorities. She proposes a deliberative model of democracy that widens the net of who participates in political decision making through the principles of inclusion, equality, reasonableness, and publicity.[53] The inclusion principle dictates that a political decision is only legitimate if everyone who is affected by the decision takes part in the decision-making process. The second principle, equality, means that citizens have equal voice and power in the deliberative process. The reasonableness principle entails that people enter into the deliberation with the goal of finding a common outcome, one based on reason, and that there are reasonable, predetermined rules to facilitate such an outcome. Publicity, the last component of Young's model of deliberative democracy, entails that the deliberation be transparent, with language and reasoning that are easily accessible to all citizens. In a perfect world, these ideal principles would be enacted in orderly face-to-face deliberations with fellow citizens. Young acknowledges that this brand of democracy is difficult to enact because "most people would rather watch television, read poetry, or make love" than discuss politics.[54] Consumer campaigns have the potential to bring citizens together to deliberate on a policy topic, but most contemporary market campaigns are conducted online, which does not meet Young's criteria.

Consumer activism does little to move the needle on deliberative democracy. As evidenced in many of the case studies in the previous chapters, marketplace activism often involves the deliberation of political issues in social media and other online forums, but it rarely involves everyone who is affected by the political decision at hand. Furthermore, it does not involve reasonable or face-to-face deliberation, and it tends to reflect extreme political positions rather than reasonable debate. Activism in the marketplace is reactive and sometimes rash rather than deliberative. It reinforces the notion of "us versus them" that is indicative of contemporary ideological polarization and the culture wars. In this sense, consumer activism is antithetical to the process and personal benefits of deliberative democracy.

Nevertheless, marketplace activism improves general deliberation by putting issues on the public agenda that otherwise would not be known or discussed. The sixty-one campaigns that I have analyzed in this book improved the public discussion of policy issues, which contributes to deliberative democracy as it is more broadly conceived.[55] Mansbridge and colleagues propose that deliberative democracy on a large scale incorporates citizen discussion into formal state processes, such as testimony at public hearings, in addition to talking in everyday settings.[56] Therefore, citizen dialogue would take place in social movements, at the workplace, in households, and online. Democratic legitimacy is still contingent on the quality of the deliberation, but it is fair to say that some deliberation is better than none. Marketplace activism contributes to democracy using the large-scale deliberative yardstick, by enabling the discussion of policy issues that otherwise might go unnoticed by citizens.

Marketplace activism also addresses the inequalities that Young, Cohen, and Elster see as a threat to democracy. Consumer activism has a long history of use by citizens who are formally or informally disenfranchised from politics and policy decision making. Marginalized citizens can appropriate collective political power in the marketplace when their voices are not heard in the halls of Congress or the White House. As described in chapter 1, consumer activism has been used by colonists, African Americans, women, and other marginalized groups to advocate for interests for which they could gain no formal political traction. In this sense, for marginalized people, economic institutions can be more democratic than political institutions.

Consumer activism has often been used by privileged people to advocate for the interests of vulnerable citizens: enslaved peoples, impoverished workers in less-developed countries, and undocumented migrant workers in the United States. Of course, privileged people advocating for the interests of those with less power in the political process is not a substitute for including all citizens in political decision making, whether participatory or deliberative, because citizens are best able to articulate their own interests. (And the practice of citizens exercising their privilege on behalf of vulnerable citizens may also uphold the prevailing system of privilege by reinforcing elite power.) The marketplace is a relatively unique avenue for citizens of privilege to directly promote the interests of vulnerable or marginalized citizens. This can occur in political institutions, for example, when wealthy citizens vote for liberal candidates who seek to redistribute their wealth; however, this action is not as targeted as consumer activism. Activism in the marketplace is typically laser focused on the interests of a specific group of people in a way that voting for a candidate or enacting legislation is not. This direct advocacy enables a strategic use of privilege that is unique to consumer activism and improves the inequalities that threaten democracy.

Economic Democracy

Economic democracy theorists conclude that the United States cannot be considered a legitimate democracy until its economic institutions are democratized. In the corporate sphere, democracy is imperiled by corporate influence in politics, inequalities created by corporate capitalism, and the lack of citizens' right to self-governance in the workplace.

The ascension of corporate power in politics in the past two decades has generated some intense critiques of the role of business from political theorists. Neo-Marxists worry that capitalism has led to corporate power in society eclipsing government power. David Ciepley, a political theorist, points out that the current state of politics, wherein corporations have inordinate policy influence, is not the first time this has happened. The world's first publicly traded company, the East India Company (established in 1600), generated more revenue than Britain and during its peak "ruled" one-fifth of the world's population.[57] Early liberal political thinkers tried to prevent a second era of corporate monopolies through regulation that classified corporations as private contractual entities, a designation that enabled them to gain great power during industrialization.[58] Prior to the twentieth century, U.S. corporations were exclusively contracted to serve the public good (e.g., building public roads) and had to seek regular renewals of their charter to ensure they were fulfilling this obligation. With industrialization came the designation of corporations as private, allowing them to shift away from serving the public good to serving the profit interests of shareholders. Corporations no longer have a legal obligation to serve the public good, but society continues to treat them as though they are prepolitical, despite their inherently political nature and role.[59]

Ciepley proposes that corporations be governed by distinct norms and rules because they are distinct entities that are both public and private.[60] He notes that corporate personhood is derived from court rulings and laws, and as such, corporations exist because the government allows them to exist, which makes them inherently political organizations. Ciepley further observes that corporations are like governments in terms of their power to influence society and that, although their ability to govern and be considered people is derived from the government, they are also private entities. He challenges the prevailing liberal contractual approach to corporations, arguing that they transcend all the dichotomies that underlie a liberal treatment: government versus market, public versus private, privilege versus equality, and status versus contract. Because of this, corporations do not fit with a liberal approach because the contractual approach gives businesses rights they should not have, provides incentives for irresponsibility, and limits their public benefit.

Political theorists have articulated a second line of reasoning for democratizing economic institutions. In *A Preface to Economic Democracy*, Dahl writes that many of the Framers were concerned that the new democracy they were forming under the Constitution would pose a threat to economic liberty: that political liberty, political equality, and majority rule might impede property owners from using their property as they like.[61] What the Framers did not envision was the threat that economic liberty posed to political equality: that corporate capitalism would produce class and social inequalities that weaken the ability for citizens to engage in democracy in a roughly equal fashion. Dahl concludes that the only way to mitigate this democratic threat is through economic democracy, in which corporations adopt the practices of democracy, namely, employee participation, equal voting rights, and control over aspects of production that can be subject to collective decision making. Dahl envisions collective private enterprises with some government regulation that would remedy political inequality in broader society.

Dahl proposes an alternative economic system because capitalism is an inherent threat to democracy by creating stark inequalities when it is operating lawfully and as intended. The call for alternatives has intensified in the past decade as economic classes have become historically unequal. According to the Pew Research Center, the gap between the rich and everyone else reached record high levels in 2014.[62] The wealth of upper-income Americans is now seven times the wealth of middle-class Americans, and nearly seventy times that of low-income Americans. Erik Olin Wright, a sociologist, builds on Dahl's theory in his book *Envisioning Real Utopias*.[63] He agrees that corporate capitalism inherently creates income and wealth inequalities that diminish social justice and democracy through workplace dictatorships and by allowing private wealth to determine access to political power. He writes:

> The argument here is that the central mechanisms and processes that make capitalism a distinctive way of organizing economic activity inherently create obstacles to universalizing the conditions for human flourishing and deepening democracy. This does not imply that all social injustices are attributable to capitalism, nor does it imply that the complete elimination of capitalism is a necessary condition for advances

in social and political justice. But it does imply that the struggle for human emancipation requires a struggle against capitalism, not simply a struggle within capitalism.[64]

Wright points out that economic systems are always a hybrid of capitalism (corporate rule), statism (government rule), and socialism (collective citizen rule). He advocates that economic institutions be reengineered to reduce the power of capital and increase social power, that is, power derived from collective action and voluntary citizen cooperation. For democracy to thrive under Wright's model, social power should trump both corporate and state power, meaning political and economic institutions should be run through collective decision making.

Workplace democracy theory has its roots in classic Marxist theory, which finds that class conflict is inherent to capitalism because of the contradiction between the mechanized and alienating work of the masses and the profits appropriated by a small number of people who own the means of production.[65] Classic Marxists believe that this conflict will theoretically inspire a revolution to replace capitalism with socialism (shared community ownership of the means of production) and, eventually, communism (public ownership of the means of production with compensation based on ability and need).

In *After Occupy: Economic Democracy for the 21st Century*, Tom Malleson also makes the case for extending the principles of political democracy to economic institutions.[66] He criticizes several democratic camps, including classic liberalism for its myopic focus on the political realm with little focus on the economic realm, classic Marxism for its emphasis on state ownership (which does not sufficiently include collective decision making), and anarchism for its lack of feasibility due to the cost of true equality in collective decisions. Malleson is critical of utopian theories that rely on unlikely revolutions and, instead, proposes more practical solutions to the antidemocratic nature of the U.S. economic system, which he calls "radical realism." He calls for a democratization of the workplace, the market, and the financial sector and proposes that most workers should have the right to convert their workplace into a co-op run using collective decision making. For the financial sector, Malleson sees the impracticality of collective decisions and proposes instead that those making investment decisions be held accountable by the people those decisions affect. He advocates the adoption of investment accountability mechanisms and the creation of public community banks. Similar to Wright, Malleson is arguing for increased market socialism rather than state socialism. He provides examples of democratic alternatives currently in existence, such as worker cooperatives in Italy, participatory budgeting in Brazil, investment controls in Malaysia, and public banks in India.

Consumer activism improves economic democracy on many counts. It democratizes economic entities by permitting citizens to hold them directly accountable for their de facto policy decisions (e.g., making the decision to offer benefits to same-sex partners) as well as their influence in politics proper (e.g., making campaign contributions to a candidate who opposes LGBT rights). Consumer activism also reveals the simultaneous private and public nature of the corporation in a way that shifts public imagination. As shown in contemporary consumer campaigns, this brand of activism informs the public that corporations take political positions on LGBT rights, abortion, female sexual objectification, feminism, gun regulations, animal rights, environmental regulations, and a host of other policies. It brings to light the fact that business entities engage with, and influence, public policy, thus publicizing the private sphere in line with Ciepley and other theorists who conclude that business entities are both private and public.

Consumer activism is also a unique tool for addressing the inequalities inherent in corporate capitalism, identified by Dahl and Wright. Consumer activism has a long history of use by marginalized and disenfranchised groups, and it is employed to rectify economic, social, and political inequalities created and perpetuated by corporate capitalism. While workplace democracy theoretically empowers employees to participate in policy decisions, consumer activism realistically empowers consumer citizens to weigh in on corporate policies. Sometimes these policies affect the lives of workers in corporations, such as improved working conditions in the Mt. Olive Pickle Company, Taco Bell, Apple Foxconn, and Bangladesh factory campaigns, but most campaigns involve private citizens holding economic entities accountable for actions that extend beyond their corporate walls. If the goal is to make the workplace more democratic, consumer activism is yet another way to work toward that goal.

Traditional versus Consumer Activism

Malleson and I are in agreement that the market "should be neither loved nor loathed" but should, instead, be acknowledged for its democratic potential.[67] Consumer activism exposes this democratic potential in ways such as challenging the prevailing notion that democratic potential lies exclusively with citizen engagement in government, whether participatory or deliberative, or that employees are the sole or primary democratic actors when it comes to economic democracy. Indeed, higher rates of marketplace activism strengthen democracy by expanding who is involved in the political process and improving representation and policy outcomes through heightened public debate. Consumer activism also advances democracy through better government and corporate political accountability, as well as attention to minority concerns. The marketplace is an undertheorized site for citizen engagement. Consumer activism improves participatory and economic democracy, and its reliance on social media complicates notions of deliberative democracy. Consumer activism demonstrates that democratic principles can thrive even in a consumer society with a politically apathetic citizenry.

But consumer activism differs from traditional forms of political participation in notable ways. Compared to traditional activism, consumer activism is easy, reactive, erodes traditional popular sovereignty, and arguably diminishes civic identity.

Slacktivism

Many forms of consumer activism are easier to perform, less time consuming, and less resource intensive than traditional forms of political participation (e.g., voting, volunteering for a campaign, lobbying against a bill, and writing a check to a political party). Boycotting, buycotting, and socially conscious investing use simple direct resources that were already slated for use elsewhere, and the only time required is the time it takes to research a company or product. Online activism is especially easy to perform because it requires no resource expenditure other than a few minutes to read up on a campaign and sign a petition. Direct consumer activism can be more time intensive, which is probably why far fewer people engage in this type of consumer activism. Compared to activism that targets political institutions, activism in the marketplace is more accessible because it involves everyday aspects of our lives, such as shopping.

Online activism—labeled slacktivism—a staple of contemporary consumer activism, has been criticized for having a low barrier to entry and no requirement of collective activity. The three primary criticisms of slacktivism are that it does little to further a cause, it is a shallow way to engage an issue, and it may lower rates of in-person activism because it is used as a stand-in for meaningful activism.[68] In this book, I have already debunked the first criticism: that online activism is not effective. The effectiveness rates for consumer campaign range from 33 percent for conservative campaigns to 83 percent for campaigns involving racial and economic justice, and social media use in a campaign increases its effectiveness. Furthermore, the marketplace is sometimes the only outlet certain groups have to press their cause when they have been marginalized from political institutions. Most individual political actions are ineffective in and of themselves, whether aimed at political or economic institutions. Contrary to the cliché we tell our students, one vote almost never makes a difference in elections, and even substantial contributions to a political cause or candidate are not sufficient to get the measure passed or the candidate elected. It is the collective nature of these actions, the sum total, that makes them effective (or not). Who is to say that taking the time to sign a petition is any more or less effective than going to a voting booth and casting a vote, or constructing a sign and joining a protest? Like electoral and protest activism, consumer activism derives its power from collectivism, mobilizing enough people to bring about attention and a desired outcome. It is curious that online activism is held to standards in political science that are not applied to other forms of participation.

The few studies that exist on online activism do not support any of its three primary criticisms. When it comes to rates of participation, as noted in chapter 2, for the vast majority of participants use consumer activism as a supplement to, rather than a replacement of, traditional forms of participation. A 2011 study by the Georgetown University Center for Social Impact Communication finds that citizens who promote social causes online participate in twice as many other political activities around a cause than do others.[69] Furthermore, citizens who engage in online activism are equally as likely to donate to causes, twice as likely to volunteer their time for a cause, four times more likely to contact a political leader, and five times more likely to encourage friends and family to promote a political cause. In other words, slacktivism is a myth. As Sharn Ahmed from the Uncultured Project puts it, online activism is a "gateway drug" that pulls citizens deeper into a cause.[70]

Yu-Hao Lee and Gary Hsieh tease out the cause and effect relationship between online and traditional activism and confirm that engagement in online activism increases traditional activism. Using an experimental setting, they find that participants who signed an online petition were significantly more likely to donate money to a related cause.[71] Also, subjects who did not sign the online petition donated more money to an unrelated cause, which suggests there is a balancing moral effect for not signing the petition. In other words, even the low-cost online activity of signing a petition has positive effects on subsequent civic actions.

Online activism should cause scholars to reassess how they define and measure collective action to fully capture the effects of social media activism. Pablo Barberá and his colleagues analyzed Twitter activity during the peak of the Occupy Wall Street and Arab Spring movements.[72] They found that Twitter users who were not actively partaking in live protests did not Tweet about the issue as much; nevertheless, their sheer numbers caused the message of the movement to reach an audience many times the size of the audience reached by activists who were on the ground. The researchers conclude that peripheral activists, or slacktivists, played a crucial role in catapulting both movements into the public consciousness.

I see two noteworthy aspects here when it comes to collective action. First, both core and peripheral activists see themselves as part of the movement, even though they are playing very distinct (but important) roles. Before social media, the movement would have included only core activists who were protesting in person. Today, people across the globe can get involved from their laptops and smartphones, making a financial contribution or tweeting support during their lunch hour or reposting moving stories from activists on the other side of the world. I propose that the seemingly individual nature of online activism actually expands the collective nature of social movement activism by bringing peripheral players into the cause and that these peripheral players are, in turn, crucial to its success.

Second, online activism challenges traditional ideas of collective action by empowering peripheral activists. It allows people who are concerned about an issue to get involved when they otherwise might not have the time or resources to travel and be part of the core protest group. For example, my activist students who could not take time away from school and relocate to Zuccotti Park in New York or who did not have the time or resources to camp in downtown Los Angeles were able to be highly active in the Occupy movement from their dorm room. Further research is needed on the extent to which online activism can empower people by offering opportunities for radical activism that were previously available only to citizens with the means and time to be core activists in movements.

Critiques of online activism tend to treat this type of participation as a monolith, when in reality these activities vary widely. An extreme example of very intensive online activism is my work as an early architect of the Campus Anti-Rape Movement (CARM). From my kitchen table, I set up multiple websites, Facebook pages, Twitter accounts, and other online forums for activist organizations that now reach tens of thousands of citizens on a regular basis. Early on, I facilitated online forums for survivor activists to connect with one another and share strategies for organizing and Title IX templates for federal complaints for them to file against their educational institutions. A network of activists working on laptops across the nation put campus sexual violence on the White House agenda for the first time ever when President Obama told survivors "I've got your back" in a January 2014 public address and launched the "It's on Us" campaign to hold schools accountable.[73]

Slactivist online organizing made campus rape a national issue. Clifford Kirkpatrick and Eugene Kanin, sociologists, first identified the problem of campus sexual violence in 1957,[74] and activists first blew the whistle in the mid-1980s when Mary Koss, a psychologist, verified that one out of every four female students face being raped on campus, mostly perpetrated by people they know.[75]

Activists have been trying to get campus administrators to take this issue seriously for over thirty years, and in 2013, social media has shattered the silence around issues of sexual assault and rape on campus. Until that time, campus activists were working on programs and policies on their individual campuses, in relative isolation. Many assumed that their experience of institutional betrayal was unique, but through social media sharing, they learned that virtually every campus mishandles reports of sexual assault and rape. Emerging technologies allow activists to now share stories of violence and institutional betrayal, ideas for public shaming campaigns, federal complaint templates, and the nuts and bolts strategies for organizing. Today, campus activists stay connected in real time via Facebook, Twitter, Tumblr, Google+, Skype, and Snapchat. Like the new CARM, the #BlackLivesMatter movement is also a testament to the power of "slacktivism" to put policy issues on the agenda and gain policy concessions.

In terms of consumer activism and the type of civic engagement it produces, I propose that citizens may also be more inclined to engage in consumer activism because it is typically more direct, effective, and leads to quicker outcomes. Economic institutions have marketplace incentives compelling them to respond more quickly and affirmatively to activists than political institutions. Electoral and policy processes are intentionally drawn out, and citizens who campaign for their desired candidate or lobby for a policy outcome may wait years to see results. Consumer activism is a more direct form of political participation, one that offers quicker gratification, which encourages future consumer activism. The relative ease and effectiveness of activism in the marketplace undoubtedly explains its frequent use. Because the goal of corporations is to make money, consumer activism is a uniquely powerful tool in the fight to regain a democratic government that is responsive to the people. In fact, given the tight relationship between corporations and political leaders, it may be the only tool capable of ultimately bringing about change. Although it is underutilized in the larger fight against encroaching corporate power, consumer activism has had measurable positive effects on the democratic process and outcomes.

Reactive

Consumer activism is almost always a reaction to a business practice or decision. It holds little resemblance to the orderly, regular act of casting a vote. As such, it is typically focused on a single issue about which activists feel very passionate. Consumer activism is messy compared to traditional electoral activism. There are more frequent opportunities for citizens to engage in consumer activism than in electoral or policy participation, and at any time, citizens can engage in multiple marketplace campaigns that fit their interests and ideological leanings.

As a reaction to business decisions, consumer activism is limited in its systemic critiques of capitalism, patriarchy, white supremacy, or other foundational systems of power. It is especially limited in challenging capitalism because it employs a capitalist method of "voting" with one's dollars. Audre Lorde argues that "the master's tools will never dismantle the master's house"; that is, working within the dominant system, using its rules and tools, will ultimately fail to dismantle that system.[76] In other words, consumer activism uses the profit imperative to compel business entities to change their practices, which fundamentally reinforces the profit imperative, which limits economic democracy.

The episodic nature of consumer activism limits its effectiveness as a check on corporate power. Business influence in politics is substantial, as evidenced by corporate success in electing political leaders and in shaping legislation and public opinion. Jeffrey Berry and Andrew McFarland believe that countervailing citizen interests are able to effectively keep corporate power in check.[77] Candice Hollenbeck and George Zinkhan find that the consumer voice has been emboldened in recent years by new social media,[78] a finding that is substantiated in my case study analysis of contemporary consumer activism. Nevertheless, consumer activism is not enough to effectively curb corporate power in politics because it is mostly directed at specific companies or products rather than addressing the underlying systemic issues with business practices and power. By definition, successful consumer activism campaigns have clear goals that involve a specific corporate practice, which means corporations are held accountable only for that particular issue. For example, the 2010 campaign to hold BP accountable for the massive oil spill in the Gulf Coast achieved that goal, but it did nothing to address the $5.6 million BP spent on lobbying in the United States in 2014, the fact that thirty-one out of forty-three BP lobbyists had previously served in government jobs related to the industry (the revolving door), or the efforts by the company to drill in ecologically vulnerable areas.[79] Consumer activism holds the potential to be an effective countervailing force to overbearing corporate power, as demonstrated by Occupy Wall Street, which shifted public debate and attention around the financial crisis, but few campaigns address corporate power directly.

Another reason that consumer activism is limited in its ability to check overbearing corporate power is the ease at which corporations can co-opt consumer campaigns and rhetoric. The premise of cause marketing is to commodify a cause and sell it to consumers with the intention of making a buck. For example, businesses have adopted the language of environmentalism with "green" practices, products, and brands, but in actuality, few are faithfully pursuing an environmental agenda. Instead, they strategically employ symbolic change and "greenwash," selectively disclosing positive information about their practices to create an artificially positive image.[80] In the past decade, corporate claims of eco-friendly performance have increased rapidly to appeal to customers and eco-conscious investors, but the incidence of misleading environmental information has also increased. According to Thomas Lyon and A. Wren Montgomery, business scholars, greenwashing comes in the forms of hiding practices that are not eco-friendly, establishing dubious "green" labeling schemes, funding ineffective programs, and providing overtly misleading labels or marketing text.[81] Consumer activists have responded with new corporate ratings that get beyond the greenwashing,[82] but this is the dance: corporate leaders make decisions to maximize profits and these conflict with the interests of some stakeholders, those stakeholders use consumer and other forms of activism to hold the corporate leaders accountable, the corporation claims to have made a change, and the activists discover that the change is more symbolic than real and they push back with further activism. This dance is exhausting for both sides, but the corporations have fancier shoes and moves, and they always take the lead.

Despite limitations with regard to bringing about systemic change, consumer activism is able to challenge capitalism and other systems of power at the margins by broadening notions of what is profitable. For example, because of the potential public reaction companies now think twice about sexist advertising and poor workplace conditions; consumer activists have put them on their guard. On rare occasions, consumer activists have fundamentally altered the way businesses conducted themselves on a systemic level, for example, the way slaughter houses kill cows.

But systemic change via consumer activism comes at a cost because it quantifies and commodifies social justice in a neoliberal way (i.e., all aspects of life become configured in economic terms). The rapid growth in cause marketing, in which businesses use social justice to advance their profits, is evidence of neoliberal commodification. Companies are listening to the social and political concerns of potential consumers, branding those concerns, and selling them back to them for profit in a way that sometimes entails systemic change (as long as it is profitable). Economic accountability through consumer activism is a stronger form of accountability than the intermittent elections for public officials, but it shifts the imperative for change from justice to profit.

Erodes Popular Sovereignty

Consumer activism also poses a fundamental challenge to the political system by eroding popular sovereignty. If democratic governments derive their legitimacy and power from the consent of the people, what does it mean for government legitimacy that, when fewer citizens are engaging the political sphere, more citizens are engaging the economic sphere for political reasons? As shown in chapter 2, most people who participate in consumer activism also engage traditional activism, but this diversification of political tools threatens the position of government as the preeminent political body. Direct challenges to corporations for political purposes both reflect and reinforce the declining legitimacy of the state. Consumer activism puts the state on notice that it is failing to sufficiently represent the interests of its citizens. The percentage of Americans who "trust the government in Washington" "almost never" or only "some of the time" went from 30 percent in 1966 to 75 percent in 1992, and then up to 81 percent by 2012.[83] Trust in the federal government rebounded after the terrorist attacks on the Pentagon and the World Trade Center on September 11, 2001, but it has since fallen to lower than pre-9/11 levels.[84] Citizens have less faith in government institutions because they have become more critical of authority, are more aware of corporate influence in elections, have witnessed the immense power of corporations to shape their daily lives, and are less trusting of government to represent the public interest.[85] Political theorists have long noted that the legitimacy of the government ultimately rests with the citizens, so a decline in conventional participation signals an erosion of government legitimacy that consumer activism cannot possibly replace and may even exacerbate.

David Vogel notes that Americans see corporations as the primary locus of power in society and that citizen challenges to corporate power are a reflection of the declining legitimacy of the state in society.[86] It is telling that political efficacy has steadily declined since the 1970s, while consumer efficacy has steadily increased.[87] In other words, citizens are less likely to believe that their political voice is being listened to by government officials but more likely to believe that their consumer voice is being heard. As the locations and modes of political power have evolved, so have the forms of political participation and possibilities for self-governance that target corporations. Citizens are aware that business power has grown at the expense of political institutions, and they are responding to this by their altering modes of participation in a way that provides an alternative expression of popular sovereignty. Consumer activism exposes the political nature of economic institutions and furthers economic democracy by holding these institutions politically accountable, but it does so at the expense of state legitimacy.

Erodes Civic Identity

Consumer activism may contribute to a decline in civic identity. As laid out in chapter 1, citizenship has always had a uniquely consumer bent in the United States; as discussed in chapter 2, consumer citizenship has replaced producer citizenship after World War II. The new citizen consumer views relationships through the lens of exchange, and they view themselves as consumers in their relationships with societal institutions. In *Undoing the Demos*, Wendy Brown, a political theorist, writes that the configuration by neoliberalism of "all aspects of existence in economic terms" erodes political agency because citizens view themselves as economic actors, not political actors.[88] According to Wendy Brown, this hollowing out of citizenship poses a fundamental threat to the democratic principles of political equality, liberty, and popular sovereignty. Under neoliberalism, equality is recast as the equal right to compete rather than equal participation in shared rule. Liberty is reduced to unimpeded market freedom rather than existential freedom or political participation. Popular sovereignty becomes incoherent as individual activities in the marketplace eclipse shared participation and deliberation. Neoliberalism has reimagined public institutions and services as private goods for individual consumption in ways that have profoundly remade the social and political world into marketplaces. Mark Brown, a political theorist, concludes that consumer action cannot substitute for more collective forms of political action because it "risks obscuring the need for more fundamental political change."[89] Wendy Brown finds that democracy requires citizens to recognize that freedom rests in self-rule, not simply market conduct aimed at enhancing individual value. "When this dimension of being human is extinguished, it takes with it the necessary energies, practices, and cultures of democracy, as well as its very intelligibility."[90]

Consumer activism both confirms Wendy Brown's fears and challenges her conclusions regarding neoliberalism. Consumer citizenship has eclipsed producer citizenship in the United States, and marketplace activism reinforces the notion of citizens as economic actors. But consumer activism also invigorates civic citizenship by publicizing the private and thus politicizing economic activities. Although neoliberalism reduces everything to an economic exchange, consumer activism redefines economic exchanges as political. Activism in the marketplace encourages consumer citizens to envision patently economic exchanges as political and to pursue political outcomes through boycotts, socially conscious investing, online activism, and direct activism. It constitutes self-governance in the economic sphere that bolsters citizens as political actors.

I began this chapter with the history of how corporations gained a foothold in U.S. culture and politics through political pressure and court rulings. I then turned to three related questions to gauge whether business holds a privileged place in politics, how consumer activism fits within existing models of democracy, and how consumer activism differs from traditional types of participation when it comes to strengthening democratic principles. I conclude that business holds a uniquely powerful position in U.S. politics compared to citizens, as evidenced by its substantial policy influence, electoral influence, and hidden influence in the form of covert lobbying and shaping public opinion. I also find that, in the face of overbearing corporate influence, consumer activism strengthens participatory democracy by increasing the rates of citizen participation and fostering self-governance. Consumer activism also improves economic democracy by democratizing the corporate sphere through citizen activism. It is an alternative way to politicize economic institutions to hold them accountable. Although activism in the marketplace does not fit neatly within the deliberative model of democracy, it complicates the ideas of deliberation because social media has opened unique spaces for public dialogue and action. Compared to traditional forms of participation, I find that consumer activism is easier to engage in and has a higher frequency but that its reactive nature limits its ability to levy systemic critiques or bring about systemic change. Furthermore, by engaging economic rather than political institutions, consumer activism erodes the popular sovereignty that grants government legitimacy. It also erodes civic identity by recasting citizens as economic rather than political actors. From the perspectives of political theory and human theory, consumer activism both contributes to and deteriorates democratic principles.

THROWING STONES AT GOLIATH

There is no doubt that consumer activism (citizen actions directed toward business entities to explicitly influence the distribution of social goods or social values) strengthens democracy on many counts. More Americans are using it during a time when democracy is threatened by declining electoral engagement[1] and overbearing corporate influence in politics. A related question is whether marketplace activism is an effective countervailing check on business influence. Consumer activism has rewritten the rules of political participation and has the potential to be an effective countervailing force, but I conclude that this potential has yet to be realized. When it comes to keeping corporate power in check, political activism in the marketplace is akin to David throwing stones at Goliath. While consumers have the power to land a fatal blow, this power has yet to be realized.

Business continues to enjoy a privileged place in politics through the policy process, elections, hidden lobbying efforts, and the power to frame citizen inter-ests. Corporations have filled the vacuum left by the atrophying of the traditional conduits between citizens and government (e.g., political parties, the media, and citizen interest groups).[2] In the last half century, we have essentially created a new form of government in which business interests dominate policy decisions and most aspects of American lives—what Lizabeth Cohen, a historian, labels a "consumer republic."[3] Corporations have as much power in the political process today as they did during the Gilded Age, but the difference is that only a minority of Americans seem concerned about this.[4]

Fortunately, although Americans have been withdrawing from formal politics since 1960, they are more likely than ever to hold corporations politically accountable using consumer activism. This unique U.S. political tradition is tightly bound with personal identity, national identity, and conceptions of political freedom. The American Revolution was helped along by colonists' shared identity, which developed through shared consumer behavior,[5] and since that time, this tool has been used to promote the interests of the disenfranchised and powerless in ways that have mostly strengthened democracy. Activists have used boycotts, shareholder actions, direct actions, and shaming through social media to push a mostly liberal political platform; however, in recent decades conservatives have started using consumer activism with regularity as well. Consumer activism has been used to push for more transparent governance, the abolition of slavery, gender equality, better treatment of animals, racial equality, LGBT rights, fair wages for immigrant workers, global economic justice, and environmental protection. On rare occasions, consumer activists have tried to curtail the rights of minority groups (e.g., Chinese immigrants and LGBT individuals), but on the whole, it has improved democratic inputs and outputs throughout U.S. history.

I have examined eight eras of consumer activism in this book, all of which strengthened democratic inputs by improving the rates of political participation and public deliberation on policy issues. At various points, consumer activism has also advanced political equality by amplifying the voices of the less powerful and disenfranchised: women before they got the vote, black Americans during slavery and Jim Crow laws, immigrant workers, and laborers in other countries affected by U.S. corporate and political practices. Marketplace activism has been an especially important political tool for women and people of color, who have historically used market channels when they lacked formal political power. The past two decades have also seen transnational consumer activism in which Americans have targeted global companies to improve the lives of people in other countries. The Chinese exclusion efforts of the nineteenth century and the contemporary campaigns against LGBT rights are exceptions to the typically pro-democratic use of consumer activism; the aim of both was to curtail the rights of minority groups.

The majority has also used consumer activism when it was unable to get traction on issues through governmental channels. For example, governmental bodies initially ignored Revolutionary activists (1760s), Progressive reformers (1890s), and Global Justice Movement activists (1990s) because they were protesting the actions of the very entities they sought to reform. Consumer activism over time has also strengthened democratic outputs by promoting political equality in state protection and public resources for immigrants, black Americans, and other minority political interests. Consumer activism has improved corporate political accountability and government accountability, as evidenced by the passage of new laws and better enforcement of existing laws involving political representation; consumer protection; and the rights of African Americans, women, and LGBT individuals.

The current era of consumer activism is unlike any we have seen in the past. New communication technologies have altered the balance of power between citizens and corporations because everyday people can now press their political claims through blogs, Facebook, Twitter, and other social network platforms. High relative levels of consumer activism are part of a larger shift in political participation toward individualized civic activities at the expense of collective political action, and scholars must include consumer activism in their measures of participation if they want to capture the full picture of contemporary political activity. About 18 percent (one out of five) Americans boycott and 23 percent buycott annually in the current social media era.[6] Young Americans are far more likely than older Americans to engage in consumer activism, with half boycotting at least once a year. People under thirty are more likely to engage in consumer activism than raise money for charity, volunteer for an organization, or contact a public official. Consumer activism mostly supplements rather than supplants electoral participation because consumer activists are significantly more likely to vote and protest than are other Americans.[7] For 15 percent of young Americans, consumer activism is their sole political tool.

The contemporary era of consumer activism rewrites the decline in participation narrative. Although engagement in electoral politics has been dropping since 1960, individualized actions, including consumer activism, have been on the rise. The rates of political boycotts and buycotts have dramatically increased in recent decades in both industrialized and less-industrialized countries,[8] but the rates have especially increased in the last decade with the advent of social media. Consumer activism through social media is "putting the roots back in grassroots"[9] by politically engaging citizens through the marketplace in ways that strengthen political equality, political liberty, and popular sovereignty.[10]

In this chapter, I focus on the democratic implications of the current era of consumer activism, bringing together the qualitative analysis from previous chapters and my analysis of the democratic benefits and drawbacks of activism in different policy domains. I then explore the recent trends in corporate power and analyze whether consumer activism can be an adequate countervailing force.

The Social Media Era of Consumer Activism

Unlike previous eras of consumer activism, the contemporary era is not anchored to a larger social movement; instead, it is tethered to many movements and causes. With the help of social media, consumer activism has truly become a tool of the masses. The frenzy of consumer activism on both sides of the political aisle in the early part of Donald Trump's presidency demonstrates that millions of Americans see corporations as institutions that must be held politically accountable.

My first major finding is that social media have changed the face of consumer activism. Anyone can start a petition to shame or boycott a company for political reasons, upload an undercover video to expose corporate abuses, or simply click a few buttons on his or her smartphone to join the latest campaign to hold a business or industry accountable. I analyzed sixty-one national market campaigns from 2004 to 2014, involving civil rights, economic campaigns, environmental protection, animal rights, gender equality, LGBT rights, gun rights, abortion, and representations of religion. In my analysis, I included only campaigns that were national in both scope and media attention, so my sample has a built-in bias, in that these campaigns had already achieved some success in drawing public attention.

My second major finding is that, although anyone can start a consumer activism campaign in the social media age, almost all the campaigns that rose to national prominence were initiated by an established nonprofit or coalition, aided by an army of online activists. Some were started by everyday people who decided to launch a campaign that ultimately went viral, including the Great American Boycott to raise awareness of U.S. reliance on immigrant workers, the Boycott Arizona campaign to raise awareness of its new "show me your papers" law, #BlackLivesMatter to put police racism on the public agenda, the BP campaign to get the company to quickly restore the Gulf Coast and compensate losses, and the Cooper Firearms campaign to remove the CEO for supporting President Obama. Compared to grassroots campaigns, efforts initiated by nonprofits tend to be better organized with a clearer goal and to be more effective. That said, the potential for everyday Americans to launch a national political campaign is new and powerful. Ordinary Americans with a grievance, a laptop, and some social media skills have the potential to shape the national policy agenda in ways that previously were impossible.

My third finding of note is that, although consumer activism has mostly been a liberal tool, conservative campaigns are commonplace today, especially under the Trump presidency. Conservative marketplace activism historically happened on rare occasions (counterboycotts during the Free Produce Movement, Chinese exclusion efforts, Southern economic nationalism leading up to the Civil War, and counterboycotts during the Civil Rights Movement), but it went mainstream with the culture wars that ignited in the 1970s. For example, liberal boycotts to protest antigay comments by Phil Robertson from *Duck Dynasty* and by the CEO of Chick-Fil-A resulted in much more powerful counterboycotts and counterbuycotts by conservatives. Similarly, conservative consumers came out in force to support Hobby Lobby after a boycott was started by liberals concerned about the company's opposition to employee healthcare coverage of contraceptives. Liberal campaigns still constitute the vast majority of consumer activism at the individual and campaign levels, but conservatives are using this activism more often than in the past.

Marketplace Activism Tools

The current era is the first to use all four types of consumer activism: political purchasing, shareholder actions, social media, and direct action. Boycotting remains the most popular organizing tool by far, with 97.1 percent of campaigns using it.

My fourth major finding is that a vast majority (78.6 percent) of the campaigns also used social media shaming, a tool that has been available only in the past decade. About half (50.8 percent) of the campaigns used direct action, but only 4.9 percent engaged in shareholder actions. Virtually all the liberal campaigns I analyze used social media, including every campaign that took place from 2010 on. In contrast, only 57.8 percent of conservative campaigns used social media. Almost every conservative campaign was started by an established nonprofit with resources, so it is not clear why significantly fewer conservative campaigns used this powerful tool. Perhaps the activists were targeting a select group (e.g., evangelicals) instead of trying to mobilize the wider public. Social media shaming is especially important for the success of marketplace campaigns because campaigns that have the potential to inflict reputational damage have been more effective than those that only threatened the bottom line of a company.[11] From a business perspective, the volatile, viral nature of social media means reputational damage could be substantial and have long-term effects that are hard to predict and control.

Effectiveness of Marketplace Actions

Previous studies have found that consumer activism is generally effective. Major boycotts cause stock values to significantly decline in the months following the action,[12] and many boycotts affect the reputation of companies for years in ways that are difficult to quantify. In the 1990s, about one out of every four major national boycotts achieved its desired goal.[13]

And my fifth major finding is that campaigns are even more effective today. Of the forty-eight campaigns that have come to a close in my data set, 58.3 percent achieved their stated goal, 6.2 percent achieved some of their goals, and 35.4 percent were not successful. That is, nearly two-thirds of the high-profile consumer activism efforts achieved some or all of their campaign goals.

I speculate that this increase in effectiveness is due to the greater reputational threat posed by the public nature of social media shaming. Consumer activists can inflict more reputational damage on a company, more rapidly, using Facebook, Twitter, and other online communications. Another possible reason that market campaigns are more effective today than in the past is that corporations have altered their structures to better respond to campaigns. That is, in the past two decades companies have created permanent social media and crisis management teams, and they have increased their cause marketing expenditures twentyfold.

Successful campaigns took an average of one year and five months to accomplish their goals, and activists called off unsuccessful campaigns after an average of one year and two months. Ongoing campaigns have been active an average of six years, which suggests that many will ultimately fail to achieve their goals because they have yet to succeed after such a lengthy period. My qualitative analysis of market campaigns in the past decade confirms Brayden King's findings that campaigns are more effective when they are organized by established groups, have a clear goal, target high-profile businesses, require little in the way of costs to participants, involve direct action, and are able to draw media attention and celebrity involvement.[14]

My sixth major finding is that campaigns that used social media were more effective than those that did not (67.6 compared to 46.1 percent). In addition, campaigns that used direct action were more likely to be successful than those that did not (68.1 compared to 50.0 percent). There was not enough variation in the use of boycotts (high) or shareholder actions (low) to analyze whether they affected campaign success.

My seventh major finding is that conservative campaigns were significantly less effective than liberal campaigns. Only one out of three (33.3 percent) conservative efforts were effective, compared to three out of four (76.6 percent) liberal campaigns. This gap is most likely partially due to the greater use of social media by liberal campaigns, but it is also likely to be the result of conservative campaigns being a reaction to changes in society: rising support for same-sex marriage and LGBT rights more broadly, the shift toward more sexualized content in the media, and the normalization of crass irreverent media content. Conservatives used consumer activism to hold back a tide of changing cultural values, a more difficult task than leading the tide of change.

Democratic Implications

The United States is currently experiencing a democratic deficit because of the foothold corporations have acquired in politics. Corporate interests trump citizen in the policy process and elections. Consumer activism is a method of checking corporations in a way that is direct and speaks the language of business interests: profits. Consumer activism generally strengthens U.S. democracy according to my systematic analysis of democratic outcomes. The high-profile marketplace campaigns of the last decade strengthened democracy by energizing and mobilizing citizens around a multitude of political issues. All the sixty-one campaigns improved at least one measure of democracy, and most advanced multiple measures of democratic inputs and outputs.

The campaigns for racial and economic justice in the last decade had measurable public policy effects. They improved wages and working conditions for immigrants, migrant workers, and laborers in other countries; they reduced racial profiling by police and retailers; and they protested offensive images and stereotypes of people of color. These campaigns strengthened democracy by expanding the overall rates of political participation for people excluded from formal political channels (e.g., undocumented immigrants and laborers in other countries) or who experienced government indifference to their position (e.g., Arizona legislators passing SB 1070). Consumer activism also improved deliberations on political issues by putting them immediately on the policy agenda instead of waiting for political leaders to do so. For example, activists addressed racial profiling by retailers (e.g., Barneys and Macy's), which caused a new de facto policy change to be enacted by retailers without a legislative bill or political decision. All the campaigns for racial and economic justice promoted political equality in representation and state protection by putting forward the concerns of groups that lack political power and protecting the civil rights and liberties of racial minorities.

The campaigns for racial and economic justice also improved government and corporate political accountability by pushing against policies that are seen as discriminatory (racial profiling using SB 1070 in Arizona), establishing new government policies (the removal of the Confederate flag in South Carolina and new labor codes for factories in Bangladesh), obtaining better enforcement of existing laws (racial discrimination in the Barneys, Macy's, #BlackLives-Matter, and McDonald's campaigns), and establishing new nongovernmental practices (better wages and working conditions at Apple Foxconn, Russell Athletics, Mt. Olive Pickle Company, and Taco Bell). These campaigns demonstrate that consumer activism continues to be a weapon of the weak, made more powerful in recent years with the use of smartphones and social media. The past decade is also unusual in that economically privileged Americans of all races were more likely to use their power in the marketplace to improve working conditions for vulnerable people of color in the United States and other countries (e.g., Apple workers in China and factory workers in Bangladesh and Honduras). Global consumer activism has been more frequent in the current era because of economic globalization and the online networking of social movements.

Campaigns for environmental protection and animal rights in the past decade improved democracy by bringing more people into the political process on policy issues often overlooked by the government. The Animal Rights Movement has been at the forefront of driving the scant policies in place to protect animals, and consumer activism is the new popular tool to put issues on the policy agenda. For example, political leaders did not consider legislation against the containment of orcas until the *Blackfish* documentary and campaign started targeting SeaWorld; similarly, Artists against Fracking and other activists put this policy issue on the legislative agenda. The environmental and animal rights campaigns raised awareness of natural resource depletion, pollution, and animal mistreatment and produced public deliberations on these issues. *The Cove* and the Canadian Seafood boycott got Americans talking about the treatment of animals in other countries. The Exxon/Mobil and BP efforts increased public awareness and debate about the effects of U.S. dependence on oil. All these campaigns improved corporate political accountability, but more than half exercised political power over corporate practices in other countries. For example, the Stop Staples, Kleercut, and Nestlé Palm Oil campaigns held these corporations accountable for cutting old-growth forests in countries outside the United States after the practice had been restricted in the United States by President Bill Clinton. In these cases, activists established new de facto industry policies for practices not regulated by the U.S. government. Domestically, the DiGiorno campaign established new animal treatment policies in the United States, as did the Kentucky Fried Cruelty campaign in Canada. Documentary films and viral videos were important catalysts for environmental and animal rights campaigns in the past decade.

Campaigns for gender equality and LGBT rights improved democratic inputs and outputs through increasing participation and public deliberation. These organized efforts improved the health of U.S. democracy by getting millions of Americans to act in ways that held corporations accountable for their political actions. These campaigns also increased the salience and public deliberation of major policy issues, such as family planning, same-sex marriage, domestic violence, Sharia law, and Russian antigay laws. Consumer activists took to the streets to protest outside the Beverly Hills Hotel, NFL games, and Hobby Lobby. They staged a kiss-in at Chick-Fil-A and poured vodka out on city streets to show their objection to antigay comments from corporate leaders. Millions of Americans participated in boycotts, counterboycotts, and other consumer actions around issues of gender equality and LGBT rights. The gender equality and LGBT rights campaigns also improved democratic outputs by increasing corporate accountability of political donations (e.g., Target, Chick-Fil-A, and Mozilla) and the public statements made by CEOs. These campaigns complemented existing electoral debates, legislation, and judicial decisions by mobilizing more citizens around hotly debated culture war policies.

Conservative marketplace campaigns improved democratic inputs by increasing the overall rates of political participation and discussion of policy issues. Conservative activists used consumer dollars to vote against the shifting tide of public opinion and policies in favor of LGBT rights. These campaigns strengthened democratic outputs by holding corporations accountable to consumers by pressuring them to think twice about religious and racy content that might offend a sizable number of Americans. Most of the campaigns against LGBT rights and sexual content in advertising were not successful, and some even drew positive attention to the issue; for example, the Shame on Kraft campaign that made some racy ads wildly popular. Nevertheless, a few of the culture war campaigns were successful, for example, the efforts to stop the Comedy Central production of JC. Gun rights campaigns had significantly greater success than other conservative campaigns.

On net, conservative use of consumer activism improved the health of democracy, but campaigns opposing LGBT rights reduced democracy by curbing the rights and protections of this minority group. Historically, similar instances have been the Chinese exclusion efforts by unions and racists in the mid-1800s and counterbuycotts to support white businesses targeted by civil rights activists. It has been rare for consumer activism to be used in this way, and it is important to point out that most conservative campaigns do not impinge on minority rights. Nevertheless, consumer activism can be used in ways that limit democracy by restricting minority rights while simultaneously expanding democracy by getting more people to participate and discuss policy issues.

When it comes to normative theories, consumer activism improves participatory democracy by increasing rates of citizen participation and fostering self-governance. It improves deliberative democracy by fostering public discussions of policy topics that otherwise might be overlooked. Consumer activism also improves economic democracy by democratizing the corporate sphere and holding business entities accountable for political decisions that affect the lives of their employees, customers, and other stakeholders. I also find that, although consumer activism increases public deliberations of policy issues in online forums, it does not meet the standard of thoughtful, face-to-face dialogue required for deliberative democracy. It does, however, enable greater public discussion more broadly.

Consumer activism has different democratic implications than traditional forms of participation that engage political institutions. Activism in the marketplace is typically easier to engage in, especially if the activism is online.

The ease of engagement leads to more frequent engagement in marketplace activism than does electoral participation. Nevertheless, consumer activism has some democratic drawbacks compared to traditional activism. Marketplace activism is highly episodic in nature, which makes it a limited tool for bringing about systemic change. Additionally, the new vogue of consumer activism is a by-product of consumer citizenship that has become hegemonic in the public consciousness since the 1970s, and it reinforces this form of citizenship through a neoliberal reincarnation of citizens from political actors into economic actors.

The fact that marketplace activism is now routinely practiced by a sizable number of Americans is both an indication of and a contributing factor to the erosion of popular sovereignty. Direct challenges to corporations for political purposes are a reflection of the declining legitimacy of the state. Savvy citizens are aware that corporate political power has grown at the expense of formal political institutions, and they are responding to this by altering their modes of political participation. The privileged position of business in politics has been cosigned by the political institutions from which corporations derive their very existence, a relationship that is driven by perverse incentives that encourage political leaders to respond to business interests over citizen interests. Consumer activism is a logical response to this power arrangement, one that deserves more focus and study.

Consumer activism has a unique history in the United States, one that is deeply embedded in ideas of citizenship and freedom. From the Boston Tea Party to the campaign urging Groupon to resume its sale of firearms, Americans have linked consumption, or its withdrawal, with politics. This form of political participation has surged in the last decade, enabled by social media and the access they provide to activism. Business entities now function in a highly politicized environment in which their practices in other countries and the errant words of their CEO could lead them to be confronted by critiques from tens of thousands of citizens in public forums.

This publicizing of the private sector is a boon for democracy as measured by robust citizen participation, greater equality in representation that leads to more equitable policy outcomes, decisions that reflect the will of the majority, active media, public discussion of issues, greater governmental and corporate accountability to citizens, and the protection of minority rights and civil liberties. Consumer activism also reinforces the democratic fabric of our society by furnishing citizens with an outlet for effective self-governance, targeting economic institutions that have a profound effect on our everyday lives. To date, consumer activism has not been an effective countervailing check on corporate power in politics, a power that accelerated with the *Citizens United* decision to allow an unlimited amount of money in elections. Nonetheless, high rates of consumer activism are a sign of revitalized civic engagement in the United States that comes at a time when our political institutions are suffering a democratic deficit from overbearing corporate influence.

Notes

INTRODUCTION

1. "Kalle Lasn: Biography," Activist Facts, https://www.activistfacts.com/person/3438-kalle-lasn/ (accessed July 24, 2015).

2. Ruth Milkman, Stephanie Luce, and Penny Lewis, "Changing the Subject: A Bottom-Up Account of Occupy Wall Street in New York City," Russell Sage Foundation, 2013, http://sps.cuny.edu/filestore/1/5/7/1_a05051d2117901d/1571_92f562221b8041e.pdf (accessed March 2014).

3. Matthew Cooper, "Poll: Most Americans Support Occupy Wall Street," *Atlantic*, October 19, 2011, http://www.theatlantic.com/politics/archive/2011/10/poll-most-americans-support-occupy-wall-street/246963/.

4. Jackie Smith, "Globalizing Resistance: The Battle of Seattle and the Future of Social Movements," *Mobilization* 6, no. 1 (2001): 1–20.

5. Simone Wilson, "City Council Unanimously Passes Occupy L.A. Resolution—Protesters Struggle to Distance Themselves from Democrats, Union," *LA Weekly*, October 12, 2011, http://blogs.laweekly.com/informer/2011/10/city_council_passes_occupy_la_reso lution_democrats_unions.php?page=2; Derek Thompson, "Occupy the World: The '99 Percent' Movement Goes Global," *Atlantic*, October 15, 2011, http://www.theatlantic.com/business/archive/2011/10/occupy-the-world-the-99-percent-mment-goes-global/24 6757/.

6. CNN Wire Staff, "New York Court Upholds Eviction of 'Occupy' Protesters," November 15, 2011, http://articles.cnn.com/2011-11-15/us/us_new-york-occupy-evic tion_1_protesters-demonstrators-tents?_s=PM:US; Caroline Fairchild and Jillian Berman, "How 7 Occupy Wall Street Issues Stack Up 2 Years Later," Huffington Post, September 17, 2013, http://www.huffingtonpost.com/2013/09/17/occupy-wall-street-issues_n_3937483.html.

7. Stuart Pfeifer and Scott Reckard, "One Facebook Post Becomes National Movement to Abandon Big Banks," *Los Angeles Times*, November 4, 2011, http://articles.latimes.com/2011/nov/04/business/la-fi-bank-transfer-20111105.

8. Harrington Investments, "Occupy Wall Street: Unfinished Business," 2015, http://harringtoninvestments.com/socially-responsible-investing/occupy-wall-street/.

9. Alan Pyke, "Here's How Occupy Wall Street Freed Americans from Millions in Debt," *Think Progress*, November 13, 2013, http://thinkprogress.org/economy/2013/11/13/2934631/occupy-rolling-jubilee-debt/; George Lakey, "Confronting the 1 Percent Directly," OccupyWallStreet.net., 2012, http://occupywallstreet.net/story/confronting-1-percent-directly.

10. Mark Warren, "What Is Political?" *Journal of Theoretical Politics* 11, no. 2 (1999): 207–31.

11. David Easton, *A Framework for Political Analysis* (Englewood Cliffs, NJ: Prentice Hall, 1965), 50; Harold Lasswell, *Politics: Who Gets What, When, How* (New York: Meridian Books, 1936).

12. Max Weber, *Wirtschaft und Gesellschaft*, 2 vols. (Tubingen: J.C.B. Mohr, 1925); Robert Dahl, "The Concept of Power," *Behavioral Science* 2, no. 3 (1957): 201–15, 206; Lasswell, *Politics*.

13. Dahl, "Concept of Power," 202.

14. Sidney Verba and Norman Nie, *Participation in America: Political Democracy and Social Equality* (New York: Harper and Row, 1972), 2.

15. Ibid., 2.

16. Sidney Verba, Kay Lehman Schlozman, and Harry E. Brady, *Voice and Equality: Civic Voluntarism in American Politics* (Cambridge, MA: Harvard University Press, 1996), 38.

17. See Steven J. Rosenstone and John Mark Hansen, *Mobilization, Participation, and Democracy in America* (New York: Macmillan, 1993), 3.

18. N. Craig Smith, *Morality and the Market: Consumer Pressure for Corporate Accountability* (New York: Routledge, 1990).

19. Dietlind Stolle, Marc Hooghe, and Michele Micheletti, "Politics in the Supermarket: Political Consumerism as a Form of Political Participation," *International Political Science Review* 26, no. 3 (2005): 245–69, 246.

20. Michele Micheletti and Dietlind Stolle, "Political Consumerism," in *Youth Activism: An International Encyclopedia*, 2 vols., ed. Lonnie R. Sherrod, Constance A. Flanagan, Ron Kassimir, and Amy K Syvertsen (Westport, CT: Greenwood Publishing. 2006), 238.

21. A more accurate term than *consumer activism* for the actions I analyze in this book is *marketplace activism*, but *consumer activism* is the standard term used in the fields that study this topic. In this book, I use the two terms interchangeably.

22. Lawrence B. Glickman, *Buying Power: A History of Consumer Activism in America* (University of Chicago Press: Chicago, 2009), 26.

23. Ibid., 27.

24. Monroe Friedman, *Consumer Boycotts: Effecting Change through the Marketplace and the Media* (New York: Routledge, 1999).

25. Francis E. Peters, *The Monotheists: Jews, Christians, and Muslims in Conflict and Competition*, vol. 1, *The Peoples of God* (Princeton: Princeton University Press 2005).

26. Glickman, *Buying Power,* 115.

27. "Nestlé: The World's Biggest Boycott," *Ethical Matters*, 2001, http://www.getethical.com/matter/boycotts.Nestlé.html (accessed December 20, 2011).

28. Smith, *Morality and the Market.*

29. Ibid.; Moussa Awounda, "Breastfeeding on the World Agenda," *Health Tribune*, October 21, 1998, http://www.tribuneindia.com/98Oct21/health.htm. Senator Kennedy did not comply with activist requests that he sponsor legislation to halt irresponsible corporate practices overseas.

30. Smith, *Morality and the Market,* 240.

31. Ibid.

32. David Vogel, "Dimensions of Political Consumerism: An Historical Perspective," paper prepared for the International Seminar on Political Consumerism, Stockholm, Sweden, May 31–June 3, 2011.

33. Matthais Schmelzer, "Marketing Morals, Moralizing Markets: Assessing the Effectiveness of Fair Trade as a Boycott," *Management and Organizational History* 5, no. 2 (2010): 221–50.

34. Laura T. Raynolds, "Mainstreaming Fair Trade Coffee: From Partnership to Traceability," *World Development* 37, no. 6 (2009): 1083–93.

35. "Fair Trade USA, 2011," *Almanac*, 2011, http://fairtradeusa.org/sites/default/files/Almanac%202011.pdf.

36. Ibid.

37. Amy Gahran, "Survey Says Most U.S. Cell Phone Owners Have Smart Phones; So What?" CNN, March 2, 2012, http://www.cnn.com/2012/03/02/tech/mobile/smartphones-majority-pew-gahran/index.html.

38. Quoted in Margot Roosevelt, "How Green Is Your Money?" *Time Magazine*, October 16, 2000, 79.

39. "2001 Report on Socially Responsible Investing Trends in the United States," *Social Investment Forum Foundation*, 2001, http://ussif.org/pdf/research/Trends/2001%20Trends%20Report.pdf.

40. "Proxy Power: Shareholder Successes on Climate, Energy, and Sustainability," Ceres, February 2010, http://www.ceres.org (accessed March 2, 2011).

41. "2001 Report on Socially Responsible Investing."

42. Borkowsi, "Responsible Wealth."

43. Damien Carrington, "Fossil Fuel Lobby Goes on the Attack against Divestment Movement," *Guardian*, February 11, 2015, http://www.theguardian.com/environment/damian-carrington-blog/2015/feb/11/fossil-fuel-lobby-goes-on-the-attack-against-divestment-movement.

44. See Chris Morran, "Abercrombie Realizes 7-Year-Old Girls Don't Need Push-Up Bikini Tops," Consumerist, March 29, 2011, https://consumerist.com/2011/03/29/abercrombie-realizes-7-year-old-girls-dont-need-push-up-bikini-tops/ (accessed February 17, 2017).

45. See Frederic Lardinois, "Change.org Hits 10 Million Members, Now the Fastest Growing Social Action Platform on the Web," TechCrunch.org, April 5, 2012, http://techcrunch.com/2012/04/05/change-org-hits-10-million-members-now-the-fastest-growing-social-action-platform-on-the-web/.

46. Friedman, *Consumer Boycotts*.

47. Naomi Klein, *No Logo*, 10th anniversary ed. (New York: Picador, 2009).

48. Tim Sullivan, "Nike Releases List of College Apparel Factories," *Hoya*, Georgetown University, October 11, 1999.

49. "The Shame of Sweatshops," *Consumer Reports*, August 18–20, 1999, 18.

50. Sullivan, "Nike Releases List."

51. Steve Greenhouse, "Anti-Sweatshop Movement Is Achieving Gains Overseas," *New York Times*, January 26. 2001; Jay R. Mandle, "The Student Anti-Sweatshop Movement: Limits and Potential," *Annals of the American Academy of Political and Social Science* 570 (2000): 92–103; Altha J. Cravey, "Students and the Anti-Sweatshop Movement," *Antipode* 36, no. 2 (2004): 203–8.

52. Steven Greenhouse, "Labor Fight Ends in Win for Students," *New York Times*, November 17, 2009.

53. "Shame of Sweatshops," 19.

54. "Kathie Lee, Look Out," *Washington Post*, February 15, 2011, A21; Robert Pollin, Justine Burns, and James Heintz, "Global Apparel Production and Sweatshop Labor: Can Raising Retail Prices Finance Living Wages?" Political Economic Research Institute, University of Massachusetts, Amherst, 2002, http://scholarworks.umass.edu/cgi/viewcontent.cgi?article=1012&context=peri_workingpapers.

55. Glen Martin, "Tree Sitter Recounts Life in the Clouds/Julia Butterfly Hill Is Tearful and Triumphant," *San Francisco Chronicle*, December 20, 1999, http://www.sfgate.com/news/article/Tree-Sitter-Recounts-Life-In-the-Clouds-Julia-2889260.php.

56. Stefan H. Leader and Peter Probst, "The Earth Liberation Front and Environmental Terrorism," *Terrorism and Political Violence* 15, no. 4 (2003): 37–58.

57. Ibid.

58. Christopher J. Covill, "Greenpeace, Earth First! and the Earth Liberation Front: The Progression of the Radical Environmental Movement in America," University of Rhode Island Senior Honors Projects, Paper no. 93, 2008, http://digitalcommons.uri.edu/srhonorsprog/93.

59. Michael Loadenthal, "The Earth Liberation Front: A Social Movement Analysis," *Radical Criminology*, no. 2 (2013): 15–46.

60. "Operation Backfire: Help Find Four Eco-Terrorists," Federal Bureau of Investigation, November 19, 2008, http://www.fbi.gov/news/stories/2008/november/backfire_11908.

61. Lance Bennett and Robert M. Entman, *Mediated Politics: Communication in the Future of Democracy* (New York: Cambridge University Press, 2001); Scott Keeter, Cliff Zukin, Molly Andolina, and Krista Jenkins, *The Civic and Political Health of a Nation: A Generational Portrait* (College Park, MD: Center for Information and Research on Civic Learning and Engagement, 2002), http://www.ehrenamtsbibliothek.de/literatur/pdf_1066.pdf.

62. "Issues 2001: Trends and People to Watch in the Year Ahead," *Newsweek*, December 15, 2000.

63. Pippa Norris, "Democratic Phoenix: Reinventing Political Activism" (New York: Cambridge University Press, 2002); Jorgen Goul Andersen and Mette Tobiasen, "Who Are These Political Consumers Anyway? Survey Evidence from Denmark," in *Politics, Products, and Markets: Exploring Political Consumerism Past and Present*, ed. Michele Micheletti, Andreas Follesdal, and Dietlind Stolle, 203–22 (New Brunswick, NJ: Transaction Press, 2003).

64. Norris, "Democratic Phoenix."

65. Bennett and Entman, *Mediated Politics*; Keeter et al., *Civic and Political Health*.

66. My analysis using Nexis to search for the term *consumer* in the story headline or the lead. The number of *New York Times* articles over this ten-year period ranged from 885 to 1,487, and the number of *Washington Post* articles ranged from 537 to 949.

67. "Voting with Their Wallets: New Research Finds Younger Americans, Liberals and West Coast Consumers Most Likely to Report Boycotting and 'Buycotting' Based on Values," PR Newswire, April 19, 2010, http://www.prnewswire.com/news-releases/voting-with-their-wallets-new-research-finds-younger-americans-liberals-and-west-coast-consumers-most-likely-to-report-boycotting-and-buycotting-based-on-values-91533949.html.

68. Rob Harrison, "Secondary Effects of Consumer Boycotts: A Collaborative Project," Ethical Consumer Research Association, 1998, http://www.i-way.co.uk (accessed June 14, 2001).

69. "Boycott: An Effective Change Strategy," Co-op America, Green Pages Online, 2001, http://www.coopamerica.org (accessed February 13, 2003).

70. Laza Kekic, "The Economist Intelligence Unit's Index of Democracy," *The World in 2007* (London: The Economist, 2007), http://www.economist.com/media/pdf/DEMOCRACY_INDEX_2007_v3.pdf.

71. Paul Cartledge, "The Democratic Experiment," BBC History, 2011, http://www.bbc.co.uk/history/ancient/greeks/greekdemocracy_01.shtml.

72. Michael Coppedge and John Gerring, with David Altman, Michael Bernhard, Steven Fish, Allen Hicken, Matthew Kroenig, Staffan I. Lindberg, Kelly McMann, Pamela Paxton, Holli A. Semetko, Svend-Erik Skaaning, Jeffrey Staton, and Jan Teorell, "Conceptualizing and Measuring Democracy: A New Approach," *Perspectives on Politics* 9, no. 2 (2011): 247–67.

73. Veeramalla Anjaiah, "Scholars Try to Find a Universal Definition of Democracy," *Jakarta Post*, June 7, 1004, http://www.thejakartapost.com/news/2004/06/07/scholars-try-find-universal-definition-democracy.html.

74. David F. J. Campbell, *The Basic Concept for the Democracy Ranking of the Quality of Democracy* (Vienna: Democracy Ranking, 2008).

75. Coppedge et al., "Conceptualizing and Measuring Democracy."

76. Joseph Schumpeter, *Capitalism, Socialism and Democracy* (New York: Harper & Brothers, 1947).

77. Jeremy Waldron, "A Rights-Based Critique of Constitutional Rights," *Oxford Journal of Legal Studies* 13, no. 1 (1993): 18–51.

78. Jeremy Waldron, *Law and Disagreement* (Cambridge, UK: Oxford University Press, 1999), 283.

79. Henry Shue, *Basic Rights* (Princeton: Princeton University Press, 1980).

80. Stanley Deetz, *Democracy in an Age of Corporate Colonization: Developments in Communication and the Politics of Everyday Life* (New York: SUNY Press, 1992).

81. See "Usage and Population Statistics," Internet World Stats, 1992, http://www.internetworldstats.com/ (accessed October 14, 2011).

82. "How Smart Phones Are Changing Consumers' Daily Routines across the Globe," Nielsen, 2014, http://www.nielsen.com/us/en/newswire/2014/how-smartphones-are-changing-consumers-daily-routines-around-the-globe.html.

83. Joanna Stern, "Cell Phone Users Check Phones 150x/Day and Other Fun Internet Facts," ABCNews.org, May 29, 2013, http://abcnews.go.com/blogs/technology/2013/05/cellphone-users-check-phones-150xday-and-other-internet-fun-facts/.

84. Jean Kilbourne, "Beauty . . . and the Beast of Advertising," Center for Media Literacy, 2010, http://www.medialit.org/reading-room/beautyand-beast-advertising; Louise Story, "Anywhere the Eye Can See, It's Likely to See an Ad," *New York Times*, January 15, 2007, http://www.nytimes.com/2007/01/15/business/media/15everywhere.html.

85. Belén Balanyá, Ann Doherty, Olivier Hoedeman, Adam Ma'anit, and Erik Wesselius, *Europe, Inc.: Regional & Global Restructuring and the Rise of Corporate Power* (London: Pluto Press, 2003); Daniel L. Levy and Daniel Egan, "Capital Contests: National and Transnational Channels of Corporate Influence on the Climate Change Negotiations," *Politics and Society* 26, no. 3 (1998): 337–61.

86. Martin Gilens and Benjamin I. Page, "Testing Theories of American Politics: Elites, Interests Groups, and Average Citizens," *Perspective on Politics* 12, no. 3 (2014): 564–81, 565.

87. William Domhoff, *Who Rules America?: The Triumph of the Corporate Rich*, 7th ed. (New York: MacGraw-Hill, 2013).

88. Balanyá et al., *Europe, Inc.*

89. Mark Warren, "Citizen Participation and Democratic Deficits: Considerations from the Perspective of Democratic Theory," in *Activating the Citizen*, ed. Joan DeBardeleben and Jon Pammett, 17–40 (New York: Palgave Macmillan, 2009); Charles E. Lindblom, *The Market System: What It Is, How It Works, and What to Make of It* (New Haven: Yale University Press, 2002).

90. David Vogel, *Kindred Strangers: The Uneasy Relationship between Politics and Business in America* (Princeton: Princeton University Press, 1996).

91. Robert Dahl, *Polyarchy: Participation and Opposition* (New Haven: Yale University Press, 1972).

92. Hanna F. Pitkin, "Representation and Democracy: Uneasy Alliance," *Scandinavian Political Studies* 27 (2004): 335–42.

93. Mark Warren, "What Can Democratic Participation Mean Today?" *Political Theory* 30, no. 5 (2002): 677–701, 679.

94. Ron Inglehart, "Postmodernism Erodes Respect for Authority, but Increases Support for Democracy," *Critical Citizens: Global Support for Democratic Governance*, ed. Pippa Norris, 236–56 (Oxford: Oxford University Press, 1999); Dennis Thompson, *Ethics in Congress: From Individual to Institutional Corruption* (Washington, DC: Brookings Institution, 1995); David Vogel, *Lobbying the Corporation: Citizen Challenges to Business Authority* (New York: Basic Books, 1978), esp. 9.

95. Russell Dalton, "Political Support in Advanced Industrial Democracies," in *Critical Citizens: Global Support for Democratic Governance*, ed. Pippa Norris, 57–77 (Oxford: Oxford University Press, 1999); Nadia Urbinati and Mark Warren, "The Concept of Representation in Contemporary Democratic Theory," *Annual Review of Political Science* 11 (2008): 387–412, esp. 389.

96. See Pippa Norris, "Introduction: The Growth of Critical Citizens?" in *Critical Citizens: Global Support for Democratic Governance*, ed. Pippa Norris, 1–29 (Oxford: Oxford University Press, 1999).

97. Urbinati and Warren, "Concept of Representation," 389.

98. Warren, "What Can Democratic Participation Mean Today?" 678.

99. Some consumer activism may appear to bend the rule of law, but civil disobedience in the face of injustice is often a last resort for people and groups experiencing mistreatment at the hands of government and criminals. For example, activists in the Black Lives Matter movement routinely bend the law by obstructing streets with protests, shutting down major highways, and chaining themselves to subways to protest police brutality. Like the early colonists who violated a litany of laws to protest British imperialism, contemporary activists sometimes gain the greatest political leverage through extra-legal means. Democracy and a state of lawlessness are certainly not compatible, but violations of the law can sometimes strengthen democracy if they ultimately improve some other measure of democracy, such as government accountability. I explore this idea further with an examination of extra-legal marketplace actions in the next chapter.

100. My ten-point rubric does not include an assessment of a written constitution or an independent judiciary because I am examining marketplace activism in the U.S. context and our system of government already has achieved both of these elements of democracy.

101. Loree Bykerk, "Business Power in Washington: The Insurance Exception," *Policy Studies Review*, no. 11 (1992): 677.

102. Samuel Barnes and Max Kaase, *Political Action: Mass Participation in Five Western Democracies* (Beverly Hills: Sage, 1979).

103. Keeter et al., *Civic and Political Health*.

104. Glickman, *Buying Power*, 22.

105. I was contacted by these researchers after consumer activism came up numerous times in the focus groups because I had written my dissertation on the subject. Keeter et al. were interested in the best methods for measuring boycotting and buycotting, a topic that had received scant attention in previous surveys of civic engagement.

106. Scott Keeter, Cliff Zukin, Molly Andolina, and Krista Jenkins, "Improving the Measurement of Political Participation," paper prepared for the Annual Meeting of the Midwest Political Science Association, Chicago, April 25–28, 2002, 2.

107. This example is actually more complicated because the colonial boycott efforts were led by merchants, who mobilized citizens. Thus, consumer activism was a both weapon of the weak and a weapon of the well-heeled, used to protect their financial interests.

108. Smith, *Morality and the Market*, 240; Vogel, *Lobbying the Corporation*; Robert Dahl, "Governing the Giant Corporation," *Corporate Power in America: Ralph Nader's Conference on Corporate Accountability*, ed. Ralph Nader and Mark Greed, 1–24 (New York:, Grossman, 1973); Scott Bowman, *The Modern Corporation and American Political Thought: Law, Power, and Ideology* (University Park, PA: Pennsylvania State University Press, 1996).

109. Robert Byrd, "Democracy's Third Estate: The Consumer," *Political Science Quarterly* 51, no. 4 (1937): 481–515; Jeffrey Lustig, *The Origins of Modern American Political Theory, 1890–1920* (Berkeley: University of California Press, 1982); Robert Dahl, *After the Revolution* (New Haven: Yale University Press, 1982); Bowman, *Modern Corporation*, xi.

110. Verba, Lehman Schlozman, and Brady, *Voice and Equality*; Robert Putnam, "Tuning In, Tuning Out: The Strange Disappearance of Social Capital in America," *PS: Political Science and Politics* 28, no. 4 (1995): 664–83.

111. Lawrence Glickman, "'Buy for the Sake of the Slave': Abolitionism and the Origins of American Consumer Activism," *American Quarterly* 56, no. 4 (2004): 889–912, 906.

112. Four cases did not fit into the categories and were not included in the analysis: (1) the 2008 boycott of the film *Tropic Thunder* for its portrayal of people with disabilities, (2) the 2009 boycott of Whole Foods for its CEO's position on the Affordable Care Act, (3) the 2010 boycott of new airport screeners, and (4) the 2010 boycott of Amazon for selling a book on how to engage in pedophilia.

1. A CONSUMER REVOLUTION?

1. Lawrence B. Glickman, *Buying Power: A History of Consumer Activism in America* (University of Chicago Press: Chicago, 2009), 297. *Consumerism* is defined as activities that promote the interest of consumers. The Consumer Movement is a series of organized actions that represent consumer interests. Historians locate the first era of the Consumer Movement during the Progressive Era, the second era during the New Deal, and the third era during the 1960s and 1970s.

2. For family studies, the most comprehensive book to date on consumer activism during the Progressive, New Deal, and Great Society eras in U.S. politics is Robert Mayer's *The Consumer Movement: Guardians of the Marketplace* (Boston: Twayne Publishers, 1989). For history, lucid goldmines of information about consumer society from the Progressive era forward can be found in Lawrence B. Glickman, ed., *Consumer Society in American History: A Reader* (Cornell University Press, Ithaca, 1999); Gary Cross, *An All-Consuming Century: Why Commercialism Won in Modern America* (New York: Columbia University Press, 2000); Lizabeth Cohen, *A Consume's' Republic: The Politics of Mass Consumption in Postwar America* (New York: Vintage Books, 2003). The best account of contemporary consumer activism is Monroe Friedman, *Consumer Boycotts: Effecting Change through the Marketplace and the Media* (New York: Routledge, 1999).

3. See Glickman, *Buying Power.*

4. Francis Fox Piven, *Challenging Authority: How Ordinary People Change America* (Boulder: Rowman & Littlefield, 1995); Francis Fox Piven and Richard A. Cloward, *Poor People's Movements: Why They Succeed, How They Fail.* (New York: Pantheon Books, 1977); Brayden G. King and Sarah A. Soule, "Social Movements as Extra-Institutional Entrepreneurs: The Effect of Protest on Stock Price Returns," *Administrative Science Quarterly* 52 (2007): 413–42.

5. Glickman, *Buying Power;* Timothy H. Breen, "Narrative of Commercial Life: Consumption, Ideology, and Community on the Eve of the American Revolution," in Glickman, *Consumer Society in American History,* 100–129.

6. Glickman, *Buying Power,* 1.

7. Chris Sunami, "The Fight for Reality: Seven Worldviews in Modern America," 2004, online post (accessed July 9, 2005).

8. John Locke, *Two Treatises on Government* (London: Printed for R. Butler, 1821).

9. Cohen, *Consumer's Republic,* 18.

10. Breen, "Narrative of Commercial Life."

11. Ibid.

12. James Axtell, "The First Consumer Revolution," in Glickman, *Consumer Society in American History,* 85.

13. Ibid., 86.

14. Breen, "Narrative of Commercial Life," 103.

15. Ibid., 160.

16. Ibid., 112.

17. Ibid., 111.

18. Glickman, *Consumer Society in American History*, 2.

19. Timothy H. Breen, *The Marketplace of Revolution: How Consumer Politics Shaped American Independence* (New York: Oxford University Press, 2005).

20. Ibid.

21. "The Boycott in New Hands," *Denver Evening Post*, August 21, 1899, 4, as quoted in Glickman, *Buying* Power, 26. James Scott examines boycotts and other economic tactics as subtle, individual forms of political resistance in *Weapons of the Weak: Everyday Forms of Peasant Resistance* (New Haven: Yale University Press, 1985).

22. For extended analysis of this argument, see Joan Hoff Wilson, "The Illusion of Change: Women and the American Revolution," in *The American Revolution: Explorations in the History of American Radicalism*, ed. Alfred F. Young, 385–431 (Dekalb: Northern Illinois University Press, 1976). See also Roger M. Smith, "The 'American Creed' and American Identity: The Limits of Liberal Citizenship in the United States," *Western Political Quarterly* 41, no. 2 (1988): 225–51.

23. Michael Schellhammer debunks the myth that only one-third of colonists supported independence from Britain in, "John Adams's Rule of Thirds, *Journal of the American Revolution* [online], February 11, 2013, https://allthingsliberty.com/2013/02/john-adamss-rule-of-thirds/. According to Schellhammer, only about 20 percent of the colonists were loyalists to the Crown during the American Revolution, which means the vast majority supported independence.

24. Lawrence Glickman, "'Buy for the Sake of the Slave': Abolitionism and the Origins of American Consumer Activism," *American Quarterly* 56, no. 4 (2004): 889–912.

25. Ibid., 890.

26. Ibid.

27. Ibid., 73.

28. Ibid., 890.

29. For an examination of how consumers engage in conspicuous socially conscious consumption, see Vladas Griskevicius, Joshua M. Tybur, and Bram Van den Bergh, "Going Green to Be Seen: Status, Reputation, and Conspicuous Conservation," *Journal of Personality and Social Psychology* 98, no. 3 (2010): 392–404.

30. James Fallows, "What Is an Economy For?" in Glickman, *Consumer Society in American History*, 57–77, 61.

31. Jean Pfaelzer, *The Forgotten War against Chinese Americans* (Berkeley: University of California Press, 2008).

32. *Coolies* is an ethnic slur for Chinese contract laborers.

33. Glickman, *Buying Power*, 125.

34. Pfaelzer, *Forgotten War against Chinese Americans*.

35. Ibid.

36. Ibid.

37. Glickman, *Buying Power*, 341.

38. Glickman uses this language ibid., 139.

39. James Bradley, *The Imperial Cruise: A Secret History of Empire and War* (New York: Little, Brown, 2009).

40. Delber L. McKee, "The Chinese Boycott of 1905–1906 Reconsidered: The Role of Chinese Americans," *Pacific Historical Review* 55, no. 2 (1986): 165–91.

41. The Chinese boycott of U.S. goods does not fit the parameters of this book because the action took place in another country; my analysis of democratic implications applies only to workers in the U.S. boycotting Chinese businesses and laborers.

42. Cohen, *Consumer's Republic*, 21.

43. Glickman, *Buying Power.*

44. Glickman, "Introduction," 3.

45. Michael J. Sandel, *Democracy's Discontent* (Cambridge, MA: Harvard University Press, 1996).

46. Mayer, *Consumer Movement,* 31.

47. Andrew Heinze, "From Scarcity to Abundance: The Immigrant as Consumer," in Glickman, *Consumer Society in American History,* 190.

48. Ibid., 197.

49. Glickman, *Buying Power.*

50. Ibid., 163.

51. Blair L. M. Kelley, *Right to Ride: Streetcar Boycotts and African American Citizenship in the Era of Plessy v. Ferguson* (Chapel Hill: University of North Carolina Press, 2010).

52. Helen Sorenson, *The Consumer Movement: What It Is and What It Means* (New York: Harper & Brothers, 1941).

53. Dana Frank, *Purchasing Power: Consumer Organizing, Gender, and the Seattle Labor Movement, 1919–1929* (New York: Cambridge University Press, 1994).

54. Sorenson, *Consumer Movement.*

55. Kathryn Kish Sklar, *Florence Kelley and the Nation's Work: The Rise of Women's Political Culture, 1830–1900* (New Haven: Yale University Press, 1995).

56. Ibid.

57. Glickman, *Buying Power,* 191.

58. Helen Sorenson, *Consumer Movement*; Cohen, *Consumer's Republic,* 18; Cheryl Greenberg, *Or Does It Explode?: Black Harlem in the Great Depression* (Oxford: Oxford University Press, 1997).

59. Cohen, *Consumer's Republic,* 57.

60. Glickman, *Buying Power,* 192.

61. Jean-Christophe Agnew, "Coming Up for Air: Consumer Culture in Historical Perspective," in Glickman, *Consumer Society in American History,* 389.

62. Kathleen G. Donohue, *Freedom from Want: American Liberalism and the Idea of the Consumer* (Baltimore: Johns Hopkins University Press, 2005).

63. Cohen, *Consumer's Republic,* 56.

64. Ibid., 55–56.

65. Ibid., 52.

66. Greenberg, *Or Does It Explode?*

67. Cohen, *Consumer's Republic,* 48.

68. Ibid., 3.

69. For a full analysis of the use of consumer tools during the Civil Rights Movement, see Cohen, *Consumer's Republic.*

70. Aldon Morris, *The Origins of the Civil Rights Movement* (New York: Free Press, 1984), 48–49.

71. Ted Ownby, *American Dreams in Mississippi: Consumer, Poverty and Culture* (Chapel Hill: University of North Carolina Press, 1999).

72. Friedman, *Consumer Boycotts.*

73. Ownby, *American Dreams in Mississippi,* 152.

74. Ibid., 153.

75. "Greensboro Lunch Counter Sit-In," Library of Congress, 2014, http://www.loc.gov/exhibits/odyssey/educate/lunch.html (accessed June 13, 2016).

76. Martin Luther King Jr., *Letter from Birmingham City Jail,* The Estate of Martin Luther King Jr., April 16, 1963, http://kingencyclopedia.stanford.edu/kingweb/popular_requests/frequentdocs/birmingham.pdf (accessed March 18, 2005).

77. James Peck, *Freedom Ride* (New York, Simon & Schuster, 1962).

78. See Raymond Arsenault, *Freedom Riders: 1961 and the Struggle for Racial Justice* (New York: Oxford University Press, 2006).

79. Morris, *Origins of the Civil Rights Movement.*

80. As quoted in Cohen, *Consumers' Republic*, 377.

81. Quoted ibid., 345.

82. See Dave Lieber, "Watchdog: JFK Launched the U.S. Consumer-Rights Movement," *Dallas News*, November 21, 2013, http://www.dallasnews.com/investigations/watchdog/20131121-watchdog-jfk-launched-the-u.s.-consumer-rights-movement.ece.

83. Kathleen Brown Ittig, "The Consumer Movement in the United States," *Bridgewater Review* 2, no. 1 (1983): 7–11.

84. Ibid.

85. Cohen, *Consumers' Republic*, 364.

86. Ittig, "Consumer Movement."

87. Linda Lear, *Rachel Carson: Witness for Nature* (New York: Houghton Mifflin Harcourt, 2009).

88. Ittig, "Consumer Movement."

89. Lou Harris, "Consumerism Efforts of Ralph Nader Draw Increased Support," Harris Survey, December 18, 1972, http://media.theharrispoll.com/documents/Harris-Interactive-Poll-Research-CONSUMERISM-EFFORTS-OF-RALPH-NADER-DRAW-INCREASED-SUPPORT-1972-12.pdf (accessed February 17, 2017).

90. Cohen, *Consumers' Republic*, 367.

91. Ibid., 369–70.

92. Friedman, *Consumer Boycotts.*

93. Joan Landes, *Feminism, the Public and the Private* (New York: Oxford University Press, 1998).

94. Betty Freidan, *The Feminine Mystique* (New York: Dell, 1963), 197. Freidan was criticized for failing to consider the interests of poorer women and women of color.

95. As quoted in N. Craig Smith, *Morality and the Market: Consumer Pressure for Corporate Accountability* (New York: Routledge, 1990), 5.

96. Ittig, "Consumer Movement."

97. Glickman, *Buying Power*, 293.

98. Mayer, *Consumer Movement,* viii; Friedman, *Consumer Boycotts.*

99. Mayer, *Consumer Movement*; Cohen, *Consumers' Republic*; Friedman, *Consumer Boycotts.*

100. Christine E. Selig, "Transforming Our World: U.S. Grassroots Organizations and the Global Justice Movement," Grassroots Global Justice Publications, 2010, http://ggjalliance.org/system/files/TransformingOurWorld_Final_hiRes.pdf.

101. Jeffrey M. Ayres, "Framing Collective Action against Neoliberalism: The Case of the Anti-Globalization Movement," *Journal of World Systems Research* 10 no. 1 (2004), 12–13.

102. *Charter of Principles*, World Social Forum, November 13, 2007, http://www.colorado.edu/AmStudies/lewis/ecology/wsfcharter.pdf (accessed February 17, 2017), 2.

103. Jackie Smith, "The World Social Forum and Challenges of Global Democracy," *Global Networks* 4, no. 4 (2004): 413–21.

104. Shea Howell, "Change Gonna Come," *Michigan Citizen*, July 4, 2010, http://www.boggscenter.org/fi-shea_07-10-2010_change_gonna_come.html.

105. Jackie Smith, "Globalizing Resistance: The Battle of Seattle and the Future of Social Movements," *Mobilization* 6, no. 1 (2001): 1–20.

106. William Finnegan, "After Seattle: Anarchists Get Organized," *New Yorker*, April 17, 2000, 49.

107. John Vidal, "UK: The Role of Email Activism: Anatomy of a Very Nineties Revolution," *Corporate Watch*, January 1999, 1.

108. Ibid., 2.

109. Agnieszka Paczynska, "Turtles, Puppets, and Pink Ladies: The Global Justice Movement in a Post-9/11 World," Working Paper in Global Studies no. 1, Institute for Conflict Analysis and Resolution, George Mason University, 2008.

110. Michael Boyer, "Where Have All the Anti-Globalization Activists Gone?" *Foreign Policy* blog, June 7, 2007, http://blog.foreignpolicy.com/mboyer.

111. This is based on a list of organized protests from the Wikipedia entry for the "Global Justice Movement," https://en.wikipedia.org/wiki/Global_justice_movement (accessed January 30, 2013).

112. Robert Edwin Kelly, A Lot More than the NGOs Seem to Think: The Impact of Non-Governmental Organizations on Bretton Woods Institutions, PhD diss., Ohio State University, 2005.

113. Paczynska, "Turtles, Puppets, and Pink Ladies."

114. Gary Coyne, Juliann Allison, Ellen Reese, Katja Guenther, Ian Breckenridge-Jackson, Edwin Elias, Ali Lairy, James Love, Anthony Roberts, Natasha Rodojcic, Miryam Ruvalcaba, Elizabeth Schwarz, and Christopher Chase-Dunn, "2010 U.S. Social Forum Survey of Attendees: Preliminary Report," Institute for Research on World-Systems, October 4, 2010, http://irows.ucr.edu/papers/irows64/irows64.htm (accessed January 3, 2011).

115. Breen, *Marketplace of Revolution.*

116. Victoria De Grazia, *The Sex of Things: Gender and Consumption in Historical Practice* (Berkeley: University of California Press, 1996); Smith, *Morality and the Market.*

117. De Grazia, *The Sex of Things*

118. Bridget Brennan, "Top 10 Things Everyone Should Know About Women Consumers," *Forbes*, January 21, 2015, http://www.forbes.com/sites/bridgetbrennan/2015/01/21/top-10-things-everyone-should-know-about-women-consumers/#3b6d725b2897 (accessed on February 17, 2017).

119. Friedman, *Consumer Boycotts*, 7.

120. David Vogel, *Lobbying the Corporation: Citizen Challenges to Business Authority* (New York: Basic Books, 1978); Friedman, *Consumer Boycotts*; Smith, *Morality and the Market*; Ownby, *American Dreams in Mississippi*; Morris, *Origins of the Civil Rights Movement.*

121. Friedman, *Consumer Boycotts*, 91.

122. Ibid., 3.

2. "WE ARE THE 99%"

1. Hui-Young Yu and James Nash, "Trump, Now Awash in Controversy, Readies Scion as New Brand," *Bloomberg*, October 26, 2016, https://www.bloomberg.com/news/articles/2016-10-24/trump-name-now-awash-in-controversy-readies-scion-as-new-brand.

2. Sarah Halzak, "Grab Your Wallet: The Woman Who Began Boycott of Products in US Retailers," *Independent*, February 14, 2016, http://www.independent.co.uk/news/world/americas/grab-your-wallet-trump-boycott-products-us-retailers-shannon-coulter-nordstrom-donald-jr-ivanka-eric-a7579776.html.

3. Jamie Peck, "The Resistance: 1, Ivanka Trump: 0," *Guardian*, February 9, 2017, https://www.theguardian.com/commentisfree/2017/feb/09/ivanka-trump-nordstrom-boycott-resistance.

4. Quoted in James Surowiecki, "The Trump-Era Corporate Boycott," *New Yorker*, January 9, 2017, http://www.newyorker.com/magazine/2017/01/09/the-trump-era-corpo rate-boycott.

5. Katie Mettler, "We Live in Crazy Times: Neo-Nazis Have Declared New Balance the 'Official Shoes of White People,'" *Washington Post*, November 15, 2016, https://www.washingtonpost.com/news/morning-mix/wp/2016/11/15/the-crazy-reason-neo-nazis-have-declared-new-balance-the-official-shoes-of-white-people/?utm_term=.74230 50e8094.

6. Zack Ford, "Trump Supporters Launch Boycotts of Pepsi, Oreos, and Netflix," *Think Progress*, November 16, 2016, https://thinkprogress.org/trump-pepsi-grubhub-boycotts-ca81001849e1#.yqfyd826p.

7. Quoted ibid.

8. Karl Utermohlen, "GrubHub Inc. Stock Falls after CEO's Anti-Trump Email to Employees," *Investor Politics*, November 11, 2016, http://investorplace.com/investorpoli tics/grubhub-inc-grub-stock/#.WKZ2gvkrLIU.

9. Quoted ibid.

10. Tina Casey, "Do Boycotts Work? Why Kellogg Could Get The Last Laugh over Breitbart News," *Triple Pundit*, Tuesday, February 14, 2017, http://www.triplepundit.com/2017/02/do-boycotts-work-kellogg-breitbart-news/.

11. Maya Kosoff, "How the #DeleteUber Campaign Revealed Uber's Fatal Flaw," *Vanity Fair*, February 16, 2017, http://www.vanityfair.com/news/2017/02/how-the-delete uber-campaign-revealed-ubers-fatal-flaw.

12. Mary Mazzoni, "3P Weekend: Are Boycotts the New Normal?," TriplePundit, February 10, 2017, http://www.triplepundit.com/2017/02/trump-boycotts-new-normal/.

13. Ibid.

14. Robert Mayer, *The Consumer Movement: Guardians of the Marketplace* (Boston: Twayne Publishers, 1989), viii; Lance Bennett and Robert M. Entman, eds., *Mediated Politics: Communication in the Future of Democracy* (New York: Cambridge University Press, 2001).

15. Juliet B. Schor, *Born to Buy: The Commercialized Child and the New Consumer Culture* (New York: Schribner, 2004), 1; Gary Cross, *An All-Consuming Century: Why Commercialism Won in Modern America* (New York: Columbia University Press, 2000), quotation on 5.

16. Lawrence B. Glickman, "Introduction: Born to Shop: Consumer History and American History," in *Consumer Society in American History: A Reader,* ed. Lawrence B. Glickman (Ithaca: Cornell University Press, 1999), 1.

17. John Kenneth Galbraith, *The Affluent Society* (New York: Mariner Books, 1985).

18. Jackson Lears, *Fables of Abundance* (New York: Basic Books, 1994).

19. Mayer, *Consumer Movement*, 31.

20. Michael J. Sandel, *Democracy's Discontent* (Cambridge, MA: Harvard University Press, 1996), 225.

21. Cross, *All-Consuming Century.*

22. Ibid., 2.

23. Lance Bennett and Robert M. Entman, "Mediated Politics: An Introduction," in Bennett and Entman, *Mediated Politics*, 2.

24. Harry C. Boyte, *The Backyard Revolution: Understanding the New Citizen Move-ment* (Philadelphia: Temple University Press, 1981); Sandel, *Democracy's Discontent;* Cross, *All-Consuming Century.*

25. Sandel, *Democracy's Discontent.*

26. Cohen's argument is laid out succinctly in Cross, *All-Consuming Century*, 2.

27. A small percentage of the population is actively anti-consumerist, as reflected in these individuals' minimal purchasing habits. The percentage of the population that participates in this lifestyle is too small to register on the Richter scale of national purchasing habits.

28. Schor, *Born to Buy.*

29. Central Intelligence Agency, "The Kitchen Debate—Transcript," July 24, 1959, https://www.cia.gov/library/readingroom/docs/1959-07-24.pdf (accessed February 18, 2017).

30. Lizabeth Cohen, *A Consumer's Republic: The Politics of Mass Consumption in Postwar America* (New York: Schribner, 2004).

31. Quoted ibid., 126.

32. American Experience, "Crisis of Confidence," Public Broadcasting Service, July 15, 1979, http://www.pbs.org/wgbh/americanexperience/features/primary-resources/carter-crisis/ (accessed on February 18, 2017), internet page 2. Note that the word *malaise* was never actually used in this speech and that the speech was initially looked upon favorably by the general public. Negative elite framing of the speech caused public support to decline.

33. Quoted ibid., 389.

34. Roger Simmermaker, *How Americans Can Buy American: The Power of Consumer Patriotism,* 2nd ed. (Orlando: Rivercross Publishing, 2005), 2.

35. Larry Chavez and Phillip Leslie, "Consumer Boycotts: The Impact of the Iraq War on French Wine Sales in the U.S.," *Quantitative Marketing and Economics* 7, no. 1 (2009): 37–67.

36. Bruce Horowitz, "Boycott Grinds On against French Food, Wine, Travel," *USA Today,* May 1, 2003, http://www.usatoday.com/travel/news/2003/2003-05-01-france.htm.

37. Ronald Inglehart, *Modernization and Postmodernization: Cultural, Economic, and Political Change in 43 Societies* (Princeton: Princeton University Press, 1997).

38. Jeremy Mitchell, *Marketing and the Consumer Movement* (London: McGraw-Hill, 1978), 4; David W. Cravens and Gerald E. Hills, "Consumerism: A Perspective for Business," in *Consumerism: The Eternal Triangle: Business, Government and Consumers,* ed. Barbara B. Murray (Pacific Palisades, CA: Goodyear Publishing, 1973), 234.

39. According to Abraham Maslow, our most base needs are physiological. Safety and belonging needs come next, followed by esteem needs and, ultimately, self-actualization. Abraham Maslow, "A Theory of Human Motivation," *Psychological Review* 50 (1943): 370–96.

40. Monroe Friedman, *Consumer Boycotts: Effecting Change through the Marketplace and the Media* (New York: Routledge, 1999), 218.

41. Ronald Inglehart, *Cultural Shift in Advanced Industrial Society* (Princeton: Princeton University Press, 1990), 68.

42. Amy Cortese, "Business; They Care about the World (and They Shop, Too)," *New York Times,* July 20, 2003, http://www.nytimes.com/2003/07/20/business/business-they-care-about-the-world-and-they-shop-too.html.

43. Ibid.

44. Manuel Castells, *Networks of Outrage and Hope: Social Movements in the Internet Age* (Cambridge, UK: Polity Press, 2012).

45. Tom Burns, "Holding Companies to Account in Cyberspace: The Threat Posed by Internet-Based, Anti-Corporate Campaigners," *International Review of Law, Computers & Technology* 21, no. 1 (2007): 39–57.

46. Castells, *Networks of Outrage and Hope.*

47. W. Lance Bennett, "The Internet and Global Activism," in *Contesting Media Power: Alternative Media in a Networked World*, ed. Nick Couldry and James Curran, 17–37 (New York: Rowman & Littlefield, 2003); Jeffrey S Juris, "The New Digital Media and Activist Networking within Anti-Corporate Globalization Movements," *Annals of the American Academy of Political and Social Science* 597, no. 1 (2005): 189–208; Craig Kanalley, "Occupy Wall Street: Social Media's Role in Social Change," Huffington Post, October 6, 2011, http://www.huffingtonpost.com/2011/10/06/occupy-wall-street-social-media_n_999178.html.

48. Castells, *Networks of Outrage and Hope*.

49. Pia A. Albinsson and B. Yasanthi Perera, "Putting the Roots Back in Grassroots: Consumer Activism through Social Media," in *NA: Advances in Consumer Research*, Vol. 38, ed. Darren W. Dahl, Gita V. Johar, and Stijn M. J. van Osselaer (Duluth, MN: Association for Consumer Research, 2011).

50. Catherine Boyle, "Lululemon Founder Steps Down as Chairman," CNBC, December 20, 2013, http://www.cnbc.com/2013/12/10/lululemon-founder-departs-after-criticizing-customers-figures.html.

51. Ibid.

52. Laura Seay, "Does Slacktivism Work?" *Washington Post*, March 12, 2014, http://www.washingtonpost.com/blogs/monkey-cage/wp/2014/03/12/does-slacktivism-work/; Evgeny Morozov, "Foreign Policy: Brave New World of Slacktivism," NPR, May 19, 2009, http://www.npr.org/templates/story/story.php?storyId=104302141.

53. For more information about the shift from collective to individual forms of political action, see Beck Ulrich, *What Is Globalization?* (Cambridge, UK: Polity Press, 2000); Lise Togeby, Jørgen Goul Andersen, Peter Munk Christiansen, Torben Beck Jørgensen, and Signild Vallgårda, *Power and Democracy in Denmark* (Aarhus, Denmark: Aarhus University Press, 2003).

54. For a further discussion of global citizenship, see Bennett and Entman, *Mediated Politics*.

55. Inglehart, *Modernization and Postmodernization*; Pippa Norris, *Democratic Phoenix: Reinventing Political Activism* (New York: Cambridge University Press, 2002).

56. Rob Harrison, "Secondary Effects of Consumer Boycotts: A Collaborative Project," Ethical Consumer Research Association, 1998, http://www.i-way.co.uk (accessed on December 23, 2001); Co-op America, "Boycott: An Effective Change Strategy." It is impossible track the number of boycott actions today given the diffusion of social media. However, we can draw general estimates from petition sites. Change.org, the online petition platform, lists over 1,500 boycott actions initiated in 2016. The actual number is many times higher given the plethora of petition sites available and the fact that many boycotts are shared on social media without an accompanying petition.

57. Benjamin J. Newman and Brandon L. Bartels, "Politics at the Checkout Line: Explaining Political Consumerism in the United States," *Political Research Quarterly* 64, no. 4 (2011): 803–17.

58. These data are drawn from Scott Keeter, Cliff Zukin, Molly Andolina, and Krista Jenkins, "The Civic and Political Health of a Nation: National Civic Engagement Survey I, Spring 2002," Center for Information & Research on Civic Learning and Engagement and the Pew Charitable Trusts, http://civicyouth.org/the-civic-and-political-health-of-the-nation-national-civic-engagement-survey-i-spring-2002/. This study is the most comprehensive assessment of political participation in the United States to date. The researchers tested for nineteen different types of participation, a new typology of activism that is now the standard in the field. The survey was administered to adults ages fifteen and older; 3,246 respondents were included in the final sample.

59. Scott Keeter, Cliff Zukin, Molly Andolina, and Krista Jenkins, *The Civic and Political Health of a Nation: A Generational Portrait* (College Park, MD: Center for Information & Research on Civic Learning and Engagement, 2002), 4.

60. Quoted in Lisa Heyamoto, "Buying as Political Message: Advocacy Consumerism Is Growing," *Seattle Times*, January 2, 2005, 1, http://www.seattletimes.com/seattle-news/buying-as-political-message-advocacy-consumerism-is-growing/.

61. Lance Bennett, cited ibid., 2.

62. For more information on the use of consumer activism by women, see Sandel, *Democracy's Discontent*; Monroe Friedman, "American Consumer Boycotts in Response to Rising Food Prices: Housewives' Protests at the Grassroots Level," *Journal of Consumer Policy* 18 (1995): 55–72; N. Craig Smith, *Morality and the Market: Consumer Pressure for Corporate Accountability* (London: Routledge 1990); Kathryn Kish Sklar, *Florence Kelley and the Nation's Work: The Rise of Women's Political Culture, 1830–1900* (New Haven: Yale University Press, 1995); Dana Frank, *Purchasing Power: Consumer Organizing, Gender, and the Seattle Labor Movement, 1919–1929* (Cambridge, UK: Cambridge University Press, 1994).

63. Friedman, "American Consumer Boycotts," 70.

64. For a breakdown of consumer activism by gender in Italy, see Francesca Forno and Luigi Ceccarini, "From the Street to the Shops: The Rise of New Forms of Political Action in Italy," *South European Society and Politics* 11, no. 2 (2006): 197–222. For more information on the British boycotting gender gap, see Charles Pattie, Patrick Seyd, and Paul Whiteley, *Citizens and Politics: Democracy and Participation in Twenty-First Century Britain* (Cambridge: Cambridge University Press, 2004). For a detailed assessment of female political participation in Japan, see Robin M. LeBlanc, *Bicycle Citizens: The Political World of the Japanese Housewife* (Berkeley: University of California Press, 1999). For more information on the gender gap with consumer activism in Denmark, see Goul Andersen and Mette Tobiasen, *Political Consumers and Political Investors: When Economic Agents Become Political* (Aalborg, Denmark: Aalborg Universitetsforlag, 2001).

65. For a thorough investigation of the resource model of political participation, see Sidney Verba, Kay Lehman Schlozman, and Harry E. Brady, *Voice and Equality: Civic Voluntarism in American Politics* (Cambridge, MA: Harvard University Press, 1996).

66. David Lazarus, "Black Buying Power Hits $1.1 Trillion. What Does It Mean?" Huffington Post, February 7, 2014, http://www.marketplace.org/topics/your-money/ask-carmen/black-buying-power-hits-11-trillion-what-does-it-mean.

67. As quoted in Smith, *Morality and the Market*, 199.

68. Stated on a *CBS News* broadcast, March 24, 2002.

69. Andersen and Tobiasen, *Political Consumers and Political Investors*.

70. Bill O'Reilly, website, http://www.billoreilly.com (accessed July 9, 2005).

71. "'Do Not Travel There': O'Reilly Calls for Boycott of Mexico," Fox News Insider, June 26, 2014, http://insider.foxnews.com/2014/06/26/watch-bill-oreilly-calls-boycott-mexico.

72. Adweek Staff, "Heinz in a Pickle Over Politics," *AdWeek*, April 12, 2004, http://www.adweek.com/brand-marketing/heinz-pickle-over-politics-71660/.

73. This finding is based on original data gathered from a random sample of Americans in 1999 for my dissertation. I completed 325 telephone interviews, for a response rate of 44 percent.

74. Newman and Bartels, "Politics at the Checkout Line."

75. Ibid., 811.

76. For more information on citizens' perception of the effectiveness of consumer activism, see Andersen and Tobiasen, *Political Consumers and Political Investors*.

77. As quoted in Heyamoto, "Buying as Political Message," 2.

78. Newman and Bartels, "Politics at the Checkout Line," 807.

79. Ibid.

80. Scott Keeter, Cliff Zukin, Molly Andolina, and Krista Jenkins, "Improving the Measurement of Political Participation," paper prepared for the annual meeting of the Midwest Political Science Association, Chicago, April 25–28, 2002, 2; Heldman, dissertation data, 1999.

81. Stephen W. Pruitt and Monroe Friedman, "Determining the Effectiveness of Consumer Boycotts: A Stock Price Analysis of Their Impact on Corporate Targets," *Journal of Consumer Policy* 9, no. 4 (1986): 375–87.

82. Friedman, "American Consumer Boycotts."

83. Larry Chavis and Phillip Leslie, "Consumer Boycotts: The Impact of the Iraq War on French Wine Sales in the U.S.," *Quantitative Marketing & Economics* 7, no. 1 (2009): 37–67.

84. Friedman, *Consumer Boycotts*; Brayden G. King, "A Political Mediation Model of Corporate Response to Social Movement Activism," *Administrative Science Quarterly* 53 (2008): 491–517.

85. King, "Political Mediation Model."

86. Ibid., 511.

87. IEG Sponsorship Report, "Sponsorship Spending Growth Slows in North American While Marketers Eye Newer Media and Marketing Options," January 7, 2014, http://www.sponsorship.com/iegsr/2014/01/07/Sponsorship-Spending-Growth-Slows-In-North-America.aspx?utm_source=twitter&utm_medium=referral&utm_content=tweet&utm_campaign=iegsrTweet#.UtBkbmRDscJ.

88. Cone Communications, "Consumer Behavior Study Confirms Cause-Related Marketing Can Exponentially Increase Sales," 2008, http://www.coneinc.com/content 1188 (accessed September 4, 2010).

89. Boston Consulting Group and Barkley, American Millennials: Deciphering the Enigma Generation, 2011, http://blog-barkleyus-com.s3.amazonaws.com/wp-content/uploads/2011/09/BarkleyMillennial-ResearchExecSummary.pdf.

90. Jayne O'Donnell, "Survey: Most Would Boycott Irresponsible Company," *USA Today*, May 21, 2013, http://www.usatoday.com/story/money/business/2013/05/21/consumers-boycott-companies-bad-behavior-gap-protests/2343619/.

91. Commonfund Institute, "From SRI to ESG: The Changing World of Responsible Investing," September 2013, https://www.commonfund.org/InvestorResources/Publications/White%20Papers/Whitepaper_SRI%20to%20ESG%202013%200901.pdf.

92. Social Investment Forum Foundation, "Report on Socially Responsible Investing Trends in the United States," 2010, http://ussif.org/resources/research/documents/2010TrendsES.pdf.

93. Ibid.

94. Thomas Berry and Joan C. Junkus, "Socially Responsible Investing: An Investor Perspective," *Journal of Business Ethics* 112, no. 4 (2013): 707–20.

95. Eng-Tuck Cheah, Dima Jamali, Johnnie E. V. Johnson, and Ming-Chien Sung, "Drivers of Corporate Social Responsibility Attitudes: The Demography of Socially Responsible Investors," *British Journal of Management* 22, no. 2 (2011): 305–23.

96. See Michael Connor, "Social and Environmental Shareholder Proposals Gain Traction," *Business Ethics,* May 20, 2011, http://business-ethics.com/2011/05/20/social-and-environmental-shareholder-proposalss-gain-traction/.

97. See Laura Brown, "Responsible Investing: Taking Stock against Corporate Irresponsibility," *Co-op America Quarterly*, no. 50, Spring 2000.

98. See Connor, "Social and Environmental Shareholder Proposals"; TriplePundit, "Record Number of Social and Environmental Shareholder Resolutions Filed in 2014," March 14, 2014, http://www.triplepundit.com/2014/03/record-number-social-environ mental-shareholder-resolutions-filed-2014/.

99. TriplePundit, "Record Number."

100. See Ernst & Young, *Six Growing Trends in Corporate Sustainability*, 2011, http:// www.ey.com/US/en/Services/Specialty-Services/Climate-Change-and-Sustainability-Ser vices/Six-growing-trends-in-corporate-sustainability_overview (accessed April 2, 2012).

101. Heidi Welshm "Unprecedented Investor Approval for 2010 Shareholder Resolutions," *Green Money Journal,* 2010, http://archives.greenmoneyjournal.com/article.mpl? newsletterid=53&articleid=769.

102. Cecelie Counts, "Divestment Was Just One Weapon in the Battle against Apartheid," *New York Times*, January 27, 2013, http://www.nytimes.com/roomforde bate/2013/01/27/is-divestment-an-effective-means-of-protest/divestment-was-just-one-weapon-in-battle-against-apartheid.

103. Arabella Advisors, "Measuring the Global Fossil Fuel Divestment Movement," 2014, http://www.arabellaadvisors.com/wp-content/uploads/2014/09/Measuring-the-Global-Divestment-Movement.pdf.

104. EY Global Consumer Products, "Global Corporate Divestment Study: Optimizing Your Portfolio of Brands," 2014, http://www.ey.com/Publication/vwLUAssets/EY-global-corporate-divestment-study-consumer-products/$FILE/EY-global-corpo rate-divestment-study-consumer-products.pdf.

105. Maureen Biharie, "Understanding Consumer Activism in the Age of Social Media: A Case Study," MA thesis, University of Amsterdam, 2012, http://dare.uva.nl/cgi/arno/show.cgi?fid=446662.

106. Simon Mainwaring, "The New Power of Consumers to Influence Brands," Forbes, September 7, 2011, http://www.forbes.com/sites/simonmainwaring/2011/09/07/the-new-power-of-consumers-to-influence-brands.

107. O'Donnell, "Survey."

108. Friedman, *Consumer Boycotts*, 266.

109. Brian D. Loader, "Social Movements and New Media," *Sociology Compass* 2, no. 6 (2008): 1920–33; Bennett, "Internet and Global Activism."

110. Janine Jackson, "Putting Consumers Back in Their Place," *Extra!* August 2012, http://www.fair.org/index.php?page=4588.

111. Jim Avila, "70 Percent of Ground Beef at Supermarkets Contains 'Pink Slime,'" *ABC News,* March 7, 2012, http://abcnews.go.com/blogs/headlines/2012/03/70-percent-of-ground-beef-at-supermarkets-contains-pink-slime/.

112. Change.org, "Tell USDA to STOP Using Pink Slime in School Food!" 2012, http://www.change.org/petitions/tell-usda-to-stop-using-pink-slime-in-school-food.

113. Norris, *Democratic Phoenix.*

114. Sigrid Baringhorst, "Political Protest on the Net," *German Policy Studies* 4, no. 4 (2008): 63–93.

115. Pippa Norris, "Democratic Phoenix Agencies, Repertoires, & Targets of Political Activism," paper delivered at the annual meeting of the American Political Science Association, Boston, August 28–September 1, 2002, 8; Peter Van Aelst and Stefaan Walgrave, "Who Is That (Wo)Man in the Street? From the Normalization of Protest to the Normalization of the Protester," *European Journal of Political Research* 39 (2001): 461–86.

116. Verba, Schlozman, and Brady, *Voice and Equality.* For information on voting decline, see Robert D. Putnam, *Bowling Alone: The Collapse and Revival of American Community* (New York: Simon and Schuster, 2001); Russell J. Dalton and Martin P. Wattenberg,

Parties without Partisans?: Political Change in Advanced Industrial Democracies (Oxford: Oxford University Press, 2000); Joseph A. DelReal, "Voter Turnout in 2014 Was the Lowest since WWII," *Washington Post*, November 10, 2014, http://www.washingtonpost.com/blogs/post-politics/wp/2014/11/10/voter-turnout-in-2014-was-the-lowest-since-wwii/.

117. *New York Times*, "The Worst Voter Turnout in 72 Years," November 11, 2014, http://www.nytimes.com/2014/11/12/opinion/the-worst-voter-turnout-in-72-years.html?_r=0.

118. Richard Brody, "The Puzzle of Participation in America," in *The New American System*, ed., Anthony King (Washington, DC: American Enterprise Institute, 1978), 287.

119. Paul R. Abramson and John H. Aldrich, "The Decline of Electoral Participation in the United States," *American Political Science Review*, no. 76 (1982), 502; Warren Miller, "The Puzzle Transformed: Explaining Declining Turnout," *Political Behavior* 14 (1992): 1–43. For more information on the role of political party decline in participatory decline, see Thomas Patterson, *The Vanishing Voter* (New York: Knopf, 2002). Putnam, *Bowling Alone*, 666.

120. Putnam, *Bowling Alone*, 665, quotation on 674.

121. Ibid., 674.

122. Bureau of Labor Statistics, "TED: The Economics Daily," U.S. Department of Labor, June 29, 2015, https://www.bls.gov/opub/ted/2015/time-spent-in-leisure-activities-in-2014-by-gender-age-and-educational-attainment.htm (accessed on February 18, 2017).

123. Cross, *All-Consuming Century*; Boyte, *Backyard Revolution*; Benjamin Barber, "Public Talk and Civic Action: Education for Participation in Strong Democracy," *Social Education* 53, no. 6 (1989): 355–70; Sandel, *Democracy's Discontent*.

124. See Boyte, *Backyard Revolution*; Barber, "Public Talk and Civic Action."

125. See James Nolan, *The Therapeutic State: Justifying Government at Century's End* (New York: New York University Press, 1998); Norris, *Democratic Phoenix*; Lance Bennett, "The UnCivic Culture: Communication, Identity, and the Rise of Lifestyle Politics," Ithiel de Sola Pool Lecture, American Political Science Association, *PS: Political Science and Politics* 31, no. 4 (1998): 41–61.

126. Samuel Barnes and Max Kaase, *Political Action: Mass Participation in Five Western Democracies* (Beverly Hills: Sage, 1979); Inglehart, *Cultural Shift in Advanced Industrial Society*. For more information about the shift from collective to individual forms of political action, see Ulrich, *What Is Globalization?*; Togeby et al., *Power and Democracy in Denmark*.

127. Norris, *Democratic Phoenix*, 5.

128. Albinsson and Perera, "Putting the Roots Back in Grassroots."

3. "WE ARE NOT A MASCOT"

1. See Susan Feriss, Ricardo Sandoval, and Diana Hembree, *The Fight in the Fields: Cesar Chávez and the Farmworkers Movement* (New York: Houghton Mifflin Harcourt, 1988).

2. Randy Shaw, *Beyond the Fields: Cesar Chávez, the UFW, and the Struggle for Justice in the 21st Century* (Berkeley: University of California Press, 2008).

3. Chávez made this reference in his 1986 Wrath of Grapes Boycott speech.

4. Melvin Oliver and Thomas M. Shapiro, *Black Wealth/White Wealth: A New Perspective on Racial Inequality,* 2nd ed. (New York: Routledge, 2006).

5. Jennifer Earl, Andrew Martin, Sarah A. Soule, and John McCarthy, "The Use of Newspaper Data in the Study of Collective Action," *Annual Review of Sociology* 30 (2004): 65–80.

6. Fred Hiatt, "Moving beyond the 'Imaginary Indian' Perception," *Washington Post*, September 21, 2014, http://www.washingtonpost.com/opinions/fred-hiatt-moving-beyond-the-imaginary-indians-perception/2014/09/21/ea1ee614-3f3b-11e4-9587-5da fd96295f0_story.html.

7. Associated Press, "Demonstrators Protest Use of American Indian Mascots," *New York Times*, January 27, 1992, https://news.google.com/newspapers?nid=1665&dat=1992 0127&id=iTMaAAAAIBAJ&sjid=ACYEAAAAIBAJ&pg=5240,6002498&hl=en.

8. Associated Press, "Native Americans Protest Redskins Name at Season Opener," ABC7.com, September 7, 2014, http://www.wjla.com/articles/2014/09/native-americans-protest-redskins-name-at-season-opener-106871.html.

9. Mike DeBonis, "With Name Vote on Tap, Redskins Urge Fans to Contact D.C. City Council Members," *Washington Post*, November 4, 2013, https://www.washington post.com/blogs/mike-debonis/wp/2013/11/04/with-name-vote-on-tap-redskins-urge-fans-to-contact-d-c-council-members/, Internet page 1.

10. Carl Setar, "Washington Redskins: Native American Tribe to Boycott FedEx Due to 'Redskin' Association," HNGN.com, September 25, 2014, http://www.hngn.com/articles/43669/20140925/washington-redskins-native-american-tribe-to-boycott-fedex-due-to-redskin-association.htm; Erik Brady, "Church Group Latest to Boycott Redskins over Name," *USA Today*, June 14, 2014, http://www.usatoday.com/story/sports/nfl/redskins/2014/06/14/church-of-christ-boycott-washington-redskins-name/10524269/.

11. Trillium Asset Management, "Shareholders Say Washington DC NFL Team Name Presents Heightened Reputational Risks to Stadium Sponsor FedEx," *Trillium News*, June 19, 2014, http://www.trilliuminvest.com/shareholders-say-washington-dc-nfl-team-name-presents-heightened-reputational-risks-stadium-sponsor-fedex/.

12. David Schulyer, "99% of FedEx Shareholders OK with 'Redskins' Relationship," *Milwaukee Business Journal*, September 30, 2014, http://www.bizjournals.com/milwau kee/news/2014/09/30/99-9-of-fedex-shareholders-ok-with-redskins.html.

13. John Woodrow Cox, Scott Clement, and Theresa Vargas, "New Poll Finds 9 in 10 Native Americans Aren't Offended by Redskins Name," *Washington Post*, May 19, 2016, https://www.washingtonpost.com/local/new-poll-finds-9-in-10-native-americans-arent-offended-by-redskins-name/2016/05/18/3ea11cfa-161a-11e6-924d-838753295f9a_story.html.

14. Kelly Rohrs, "Mt. Olive Boycott Ends after 5 Years," *Chronicle*, September 15, 2004, http://www.dukechronicle.com/articles/2004/09/16/mt-olive-boycott-ends-after-5-years#.VTq9byFViko.

15. As quoted in Steve Greenhouse, "Grower Group Signs the First Union Contract for Guest Workers," *New York Times*, September 17, 2004, http://www.nytimes.com/2004/09/17/national/17labor.html?_r=0.

16. Rose Parkman, *My Soul Has Rested* (Lulu Online Self-Publishing, 2013).

17. As quoted in David Slade and Jeff Hartsell, "Confederate Flag Controversy and NAACP Boycott Resurface amid Talk of Football Bowl Game in Charleston," *Post and Courier*, August 11, 2013, http://www.postandcourier.com/article/20130810/PC16/130819917.

18. Aviva Shen, "NAACP Ends 15-Year Boycott of South Carolina after Confederate Flag Is Removed," *Think Progress*, July 12, 2015, http://thinkprogress.org/economy/2015/07/12/3679565/ncaap-south-carolina-boycott-ends/.

19. Southern Patriot Group website (accessed July 7, 2009). This website is no longer functioning.

20. As quoted in Kay Steiger, "Meet the Fiercest Defenders of the Confederate Flag in South Carolina," *Think Progress*, June 22, 2015, http://thinkprogress.org/politics/2015/06/22/3672442/south-carolina-legislators-refused-take-confederate-flag-90s/.

21. Julianne Hing, "How to Make a Boycott Matter," Colorlines.com, May 20, 2010, http://www.colorlines.com/archives/2010/05/how_to_make_a_boycott_matter.html.

22. Evelyn Nieves, "Accord with Tomato Pickers Ends Boycott of Taco Bell," *Washington Post,* March 9, 2005, http://www.washingtonpost.com/wp-dyn/articles/A18187-2005Mar8.html.

23. Ibid.

24. Fairfood International, "Interview with Coalition of Immokalee Workers Co-Founder Lucas Benitez," October 18, 2015, http://www.fairfood.org/interview-with-coalition-of-immokalee-workers-co-founder-lucas-benitez/ (accessed February 23, 2016).

25. Selene Rivera, "Groups Call for 'a Day without an Immigrant,'" *Banderas News,* April 2006, http://www.banderasnews.com/0604/nw-adaywithout.htm.

26. Quoted ibid.

27. Jesse Diaz and Javier Rodriguez, "Undocumented in America," *New Left Review* 47 (2007), https://newleftreview.org/II/47/jesse-diaz-javier-rodriguez-undocumented-in-america.

28. Randal C. Archibold, "Immigrants Take to Streets in Show of Strength," *New York Times,* May 2, 2006, http://www.nytimes.com/2006/05/02/us/02immig.html?pagewanted=1&_r=2&ei=5094&en=e9b7414ed9b65b5f&hp&ex=1146542400&partner=homepage.

29. Ibid.

30. Robin Givhan, "Bubbly Boycott? Oh Please, Jay-Z, Just Chill," *Washington Post,* July 7, 2006, http://www.washingtonpost.com/wp-dyn/content/article/2006/07/06/AR2006070601667.html.

31. Associated Press, "Jay-Z Launches Cristal Bubbly Boycott," June 15, 2006, http://www.today.com/id/13350034/ns/today-today_entertainment/t/jay-z-launches-cristal-bubbly-boycott/#.VSrFwPnF_G8.

32. Douglas Century, "Jay-Z Puts a Cap on Cristal," *New York Times,* July 2, 2006, http://www.nytimes.com/2006/07/02/fashion/02cris.html?pagewanted=all; Beppi Crosariol, "Cristal Has the Last Laugh in Bubbly Bouhaha," *Globe and Mail,* October 12, 2010, http://www.theglobeandmail.com/life/cristal-has-the-last-laugh-in-bubbly-brouhaha/article1370285/.

33. Mark Caro, "Did Hindu Boycott Kill 'Love Guru'?" *Chicago Tribune,* July 30, 2008, http://featuresblogs.chicagotribune.com/entertainment_popmachine/2008/07/hindu-leaders-a.html.

34. AndhraNews.net, "Jewish Leader Calls for Boycott of the Movie 'The Love Guru,'" May 6, 2008, http://www.andhranews.net/Intl/2008/May/6/Jewish-leader-calls-43553.asp, Internet page 1.

35. Jeffrey Weiss, "'Love Guru' Movie May Be More Offensive to Fans of Humor than It Is to Hindus," *Dallas Morning News,* June 20, 2008, http://religionblog.dallasnews.com/2008/06/love-guru-movie-may-be-more-of.html/.

36. Jonathan Cooper, "Arizona Immigrant Law Target of Protest," NBCNews.com, April 26, 2010, http://www.nbcnews.com/id/36768649/#.VSlZOvnF_G8.

37. *CBC News,* "Arizona Immigration Law Sparks Huge Rallies," May 1, 2010, http://www.cbc.ca/news/world/arizona-immigration-law-sparks-huge-rallies-1.967969.

38. Randal C. Archibold, "In Wake of Immigration Laws, Calls for an Economic Boycott of Arizona," *New York Times,* April 26, 2010, http://www.nytimes.com/2010/04/27/us/27arizona.html?ref=us.

39. Betty Beard and Dawn Gilbertson, "Calls to Boycott Arizona Multiple on Social Media," April 27, 2010, http://archive.azcentral.com/business/articles/2010/04/27/20100427arizona-immigration-bill-boycott.html.

40. Barbara Hernandez, "Arizona's Boycott Goes Viral as State's Tourism Industry Tries to Fight Back," CBSNews.com, April 28, 2010, http://www.cbsnews.com/news/arizona-boycott-goes-viral-as-states-tourism-industry-tries-to-fight-back/.

41. Jane Babin, "Some Don't Buy Arizona Boycotts," Marketplace.org, May 18, 2010, http://www.marketplace.org/topics/world/some-dont-buy-arizona-boycotts.

42. Lucy Madison, "Poll: Most Americans Think Arizona Immigration Law is 'About Right,'" CBS News, December 14, 2012, http://www.cbsnews.com/news/poll-most-americans-think-arizona-immigration-law-is-about-right/.

43. Eric Kain, "Why Arizona's Controversial Immigration Law Is Bad for Business," *Forbes*, April 27, 2012, http://www.forbes.com/sites/erikkain/2012/04/27/why-arizonas-controversial-immigration-law-is-bad-for-business/.

44. Ashley Lutz, "Boycott over Arizona Immigration Law Costs $141 Million, Study Says," Boomberg.com, November 18, 2010, http://www.bloomberg.com/news/articles/2010-11-18/boycott-over-arizona-immigration-law-cost-state-141-million-study-shows.

45. Quoted in Kain, "Why Arizona's Controversial Immigration Law."

46. Mark Stevenson, "Study: 100,000 Hispanics Leave Arizona after Immigration Law Debated," NBCNews.com, November 11, 2010, http://www.nbcnews.com/id/40141843/ns/us_news-immigration_a_nation_divided/#.VSlnXfnF_G8.

47. Kain, "Why Arizona's Controversial Immigration Law."

48. John McWhorter, "'Shop and Frisk' Stokes Black Middle-Class Rage," *Time Magazine*, October 31, 2013, http://ideas.time.com/2013/10/31/shop-and-frisk-stokes-black-middle-class-rage/.

49. Curtis Skinner, "Boycott Threatened after Racial Profiling Claims at Macy's, Barneys," Reuters, November 4, 2013, http://www.reuters.com/article/2013/11/04/us-usa-newyork-barneys-macys-idUSBRE9A313Q20131104.

50. Brad Gerick and Stephen Rex Brown, "Jay-Z Feeling Heat over Barney's Fashion Line Deal," *New York Daily News*, October 24, 2013, http://www.nydailynews.com/new-york/jay-z-feeling-twitter-heat-barneys-deal-article-1.1495310.

51. Julia Lull, "'Treme' Actor Settles Racial Profiling Lawsuit against Macy's, NYC," CNN.com, July 19, 2014, http://www.cnn.com/2014/07/19/justice/hbo-star-lawsuit/.

52. Elisha Fieldstadt, "Michael Brown Protesters Urge Shoppers to Boycott Black Friday," NBCNews.com, November 29, 2014, http://www.nbcnews.com/storyline/michael-brown-shooting/michael-brown-protesters-urge-shoppers-boycott-black-friday-n257881.

53. Collier Myerson, "The Founders of Black Lives Matter: 'We Gave Tongue to Something We All Knew Was Happening,'" *Glamour*, November 1, 2016, http://www.glamour.com/story/women-of-the-year-black-lives-matter-founders.

54. Ibid.

55. Ibid.

56. Ibid.

57. For an account of the founding of #BlackLivesMatter and the erasure of queer women of color in the stories of its founding, see Alicia Garza, "A Herstory of the "BlackLivesMatter Movement," *Feminist Wire*, October 7, 2014, http://thefeministwire.com/2014/10/blacklivesmatter-2/.

58. Adam Sorensen, "ALEC: What It Does and Why Three Major Corporations Cut Ties," *Time Magazine*, April 9, 2012, http://swampland.time.com/2012/04/09/alec-what-it-does-and-why-three-major-corporations-cut-ties/.

59. Gabriel Rey-Goodlatte interview in John Hoffman, "ColorofChange.org and Advocacy: The ALEC Campaign," *Non-Profit Newswire*, May 1, 2012, https://nonprofitquarterly.org/policysocial-context/20238-success-in-advocacy-a-conversation-with-colorofchangeorgs-gabriel-rey-goodlatte.html.

60. Fieldstadt, "Michael Brown Protesters."

61. Ibid., 2.

62. Jazelle Hunt, "Black Lives Still Matter to Grassroots and Black Media," *Black Press USA*, January 13, 2015, http://www.blackpressusa.com/black-lives-still-matters-to-grassroots-and-black-media/#sthash.8MUa9r5t.dpbs.

63. Ibid.

64. Clare O'Connor, "Paula Deen Dumped by Home Depot and Diabetes Drug Company Novo Nordisk as Target, Sears, QVC Mull Next Move," *Forbes*, June 27, 2013, http://www.forbes.com/sites/clareoconnor/2013/06/27/paula-deen-dumped-by-home-depot-and-diabetes-drug-company-novo-nordisk-as-target-sears-qvc-mull-next-move/.

65. Jessica Chasmar, "Paula Deen Cookbooks Surge to Top Spots on Amazon Bestsellers," *Washington Times*, June 27, 2013, http://www.washingtontimes.com/news/2013/jun/27/paula-deen-cookbooks-surge-top-spots-amazon-best-s/.

66. Victoria Cavaliere, "Paula Deen Supporters Fire Up on Facebook," Vocativ.com, June 25, 2013, http://www.vocativ.com/culture/society/paula-deen-supporters-fire-up-on-facebook/.

67. Felix Gillette, "Since Dumping Paula Deen, Food Network's Ratings Have Continued to Slump," Bloomberg.com, October 9, 2013, http://www.bloomberg.com/bw/articles/2013-10-09/since-dumping-paula-deen-food-network-ratings-have-continued-to-slump.

68. Erik Semple, "Korean-Americans Seek Boycott after an Attack in a McDonald's in Queens," *New York Times*, December 30, 2014, http://www.nytimes.com/2014/12/31/nyregion/korean-americans-seek-boycott-after-an-attack-in-a-mcdonalds-in-queens.html.

69. Sarah Maslin Nir and Jiha Ham, "Korean Community Leaders Urge McDonald's Boycott," *New York Times*, January 16, 2014, http://www.nytimes.com/2014/01/17/nyregion/leaders-urge-customers-to-boycott-mcdonalds.html.

70. As quoted ibid.

71. Steven Greenhouse, "Labor Fight Ends in Win for Students," *New York Times*, November 17, 2009.

72. Ray Kwong, "Apple Faces Boycott over Worker Abuses in China. It's Not Crazy Talk," *Forbes*, February 9, 2012, http://www.forbes.com/sites/raykwong/2012/02/09/apple-faces-boycott-over-worker-abuses-in-china-its-not-crazy-talk/.

73. Charles Duhigg and David Barboza, "In China, Human Costs Are Built into an iPad," *New York Times*, January 25, 2014, http://www.nytimes.com/2012/01/26/business/ieconomy-apples-ipad-and-the-human-costs-for-workers-in-china.html?_r=1&pagewanted=all.

74. Alex King, "Sum of Us: Five Million Strong," *Huck Magazine*, August 27, 2014, http://www.huckmagazine.com/perspectives/activism-2/why-i-do-what-i-do-activism-2/sum-us/.

75. Sum of Us website, http://sumofus.org/about/ (accessed May 30, 2016).

76. Paul Harris, "Apple Hit by Boycott Call over Workers Abuses in China," *Guardian*, January 28, 2012, http://www.theguardian.com/technology/2012/jan/29/apple-faces-boycott-worker-abuses.

77. Joanna Stern, "Apple to Help Pay Costs of Improving Foxconn Factories," ABCNEws.com, May 10, 2012, http://abcnews.go.com/Technology/apple-pay-costs-improving-foxconn-factories/story?id=16320668.

78. Julfikar Ali Manik and Jim Yardley, "Bangladesh Finds Gross Negligence in Factory Fire," *New York Times*, December 17, 2012, http://www.nytimes.com/2012/12/18/world/asia/bangladesh-factory-fire-caused-by-gross-negligence.html?_r=1.

79. Aubrey Bloomfield, "Bangladesh Factory Collapse: Boycott the Gap or Primark, Not Bangladesh," PolicyMic.com, May 5, 2013, http://mic.com/articles/39519/bangladesh-factory-collapse-boycott-the-gap-or-primark-not-bangladesh.

80. Jim Yardley, "The Most Hated Bangladeshi, Toppled from a Shady Empire," *New York Times*, April 30, 2013, http://www.nytimes.com/2013/05/01/world/asia/bangladesh-garment-industry-reliant-on-flimsy-oversight.html?pagewanted=all.

81. Bruce Covert, "Walmart and Gap Announce Safety Plan with Less Accountability," ThinkProgress.com, July 11, 2013, http://thinkprogress.org/economy/2013/07/11/2281161/walmart-gap-bangladesh-safety-plan/.

82. M. Joy Hayes, "Should You Boycott Walmart or Gap over Factory Worker Safety?" DailyFinance.com, May 22, 2013, http://www.dailyfinance.com/2013/05/22/boycott-walmart-gap-factory-worker-safety/.

83. Covert, "Walmart and Gap Announce."

84. Jayne O'Donnell, "Survey: Most Would Boycott Irresponsible Company," *USA Today*, May 21, 2013, http://www.usatoday.com/story/money/business/2013/05/21/consumers-boycott-companies-bad-behavior-gap-protests/2343619/.

85. Rana Foroohar and Bill Saporito, "Made in the U.S.A.," *Time*, April 22, 2013, http://business.time.com/made-in-the-u-s-a/.

86. Yana Kunichoff, "One Year after Rana Plaza, Safety Issues in Walmart Supply Chain Persist," InTheseTimes.com, April 26, 2014, http://inthesetimes.com/working/entry/16613/one_year_after_rana_plaza_safety_issues_in_walmart_supply_chain_persist.

87. Kunichoff, "One Year after Rana Plaza."

88. William H. Flanagan, Nancy H. Zingale, Elizabeth A. Theiss-Morse, and Michael W. Wagner, *Political Behavior of the American Electorate,* 13th ed. (Washington, DC: Congressional Quarterly Press, 2014).

89. Robert J. Smith and Justin D. Levinson, "The Impact of Implicit Racial Bias on the Exercise of Prosecutorial Discretion," *Seattle University Law Review* 35 (2012): 795–826.

90. Joseph G. Altonji and Rebecca M. Blank, "Race and Gender in the Labor Market," in *Handbook of Labor Economics*, ed. Orley Ashenfelter and David Card, 3C: 3143–3259 (Amsterdam: Elsevier Science, 1999).

91. Trymaine Lee, "On State Level, a Flurry of Post-Ferguson Bills Fizzle," MSNBC.com, May 19, 2015, http://www.msnbc.com/msnbc/state-level-flurry-post-ferguson-bills-fizzle.

4. "600,000 BOSSES TELLING ME WHAT TO DO"

1. Monroe Friedman, *Consumer Boycotts: Effecting Change through the Marketplace and the Media* (New York: Routledge, 1999).

2. Earth Island Institute, "Questions and Answers about Earth Island Institute's Dolphin Safe Tuna Program," 2007, http://www.earthisland.org/immp/QandAdolphinSafe.html (accessed June 29, 2015).

3. Earth Island Institute, "Dolphin Safe Tuna Consumers," 2015, http://www.earthisland.org/dolphinSafeTuna/consumer/ (accessed June 29, 2015).

4. Lawrence Finson and Susan Finson, *The Animal Rights Movement in America: From Compassion to Respect* (Boston: Twayne Publishers, 1994).

5. Rebecca Rifkin, "In U.S., Many Say Animals Should Have Same Rights as People," Gallup Poll, 2015, http://www.gallup.com/poll/183275/say-animals-rights-people.aspx (accessed June 29, 2015); V between the Lines, "16 Million People in the U.S. Are Now Vegan or Vegetarian!" January 20, 2016, http://vbetweenthelines.com/index.php/2016/01/20/16-million-people-in-the-us-are-now-vegan-or-vegetarian-2/.

6. Mary Graham, *The Morning after Earth Day: Practical Environmental Politics* (Washington, DC: Brookings Institution Press and the Governance Institute, 1999).

7. Jeffrey Jones, "In U.S., Concerns about Environmental Threats Eases," Gallup Poll, 2015, www.gallup.com, http://www.gallup.com/poll/182105/concern-environmental-threats-eases.aspx (accessed June 29, 2015). People are most concerned about pollution of drinking water (55 percent) and the pollution of lakes and rivers (47 percent), although their levels of concern have declined in recent years.

8. Animal Liberation Front, "Mission Statement," 2015, http://www.animallibera tionfront.com/ALFront/mission_statement.htm (accessed June 29, 2015); Earth Libera tion Front, "Earth Liberation Front," 2015, http://www.earth-liberation-front.com/ (accessed June 29, 2015).

9. The first recorded act of ecoterrorism, a form of direct consumer activism, occurred in 1977 when a group of Greenpeace activists splintered off to form the Sea Shepherd Conservation Society, which targeted commercial fishing operations by cutting their nets. James Jarboe, Testimony before the House Resources Committee, Subcom mittee on Forests and Forest Health, the Federal Bureau of Investigations, Federal Bureau of Investigation, 2002, https://www.fbi.gov/news/testimony/the-threat-of-eco-terrorism (accessed June 29, 2015).

10. Phillip Andrew Smith, "An Axe without a Handle: An Exploratory Analysis of Eco-Terrorism and Its Relationships to U.S. Public Policy toward Terrorism: 1990–2010," PhD diss., Nova Southeastern University, 2014; Southern Poverty Law Center, "Eco-Violence: The Record," Southern Poverty Law Center Intelligence Report no. 107, fall 2002, http://www.splcenter.org/get-informed/intelligence-report/browse-all-issues/2002/fall/ from-push-to-shove/eco-violence-the-rec.

11. Jerry Markon, "FBI Probes Were Improper, Justice Says," *Washington Post*. Sep tember 20, 2010, http://www.washingtonpost.com/wp-dyn/content/article/2010/09/20/ AR2010092003100.html?hpid=topnews.

12. Tim Elfrink, "Campaign against Staples Comes to Columbia," *Maneater*, August 31, 2001, http://www.themaneater.com/stories/2001/8/31/campaign-against-staples-comes-columbia/.

13. Greg B. Walker and Stephen E. Daniels, "The Clinton Administration, the North west Forest Conference, and Managing Conflict When Talk and Structure Collide," *Soci ety & Natural Resources* 9, no. 1 (1996): 77–91.

14. Elfrink, "Campaign against Staples Comes to Columbia"; M. Tye Wolfe, "Activ ists Demand Office Supplier Staples Become More Environmentally Friendly," Behind Liberal Lines, 2001, http://www.freerepublic.com/focus/fr/579816/posts (accessed June 30, 2015).

15. Quoted in Wolfe, "Activists Demand Office Supplier."

16. Marianne Veach, "Pressure on the Paper Production Industry: Staples, Inc. & the Forest Stewardship Council," Graduate School of International Relations and Pacific Studies, University of California, San Diego, 2007, http://irps.ucsd.edu/assets/021/8434. pdf (accessed June 30, 2015).

17. Ibid., 5.

18. Ethical Consumer, "Kimberly-Clarke," March 2007, http://www.ethicalconsumer. org/commentanalysis/corporatewatch/kimberlyclark.aspx.

19. Greenpeace, "Greenpeace Activists Keep the Pressure on Kimberly-Clark," August 14, 2008, http://www.greenpeace.org/usa/en/news-and-blogs/news/greenpeace-activists-keep-the/.

20. Ylan Q. Mui, "More Than a Box of Kleenex," *Washington Post*. February 16, 2008, http://www.washingtonpost.com/wp-dyn/content/article/2008/02/15/AR20080215 03198.html.

21. Deborah Zabarenko, "Kimberly-Clark Joins Greenpeace to Protect Forests," Reuters, August 5, 2009, http://www.reuters.com/article/2009/08/05/us-kimberlyclark-idUSTRE5 745AM20090805?feedType=RSS&feedName=environmentNews.

22. Greenpeace, "Victory for the Boreal Forest! Kimberly-Clark Announces New Paper Policy," August 5, 2009, http://www.greenpeace.org/international/en/news/features/vic tory-for-the-boreal-forest/.

23. Ibid.

24. Felicity Barringer, "ExxonMobil Becomes Focus of Boycott," *New York Times*, July 12, 2005, http://www.nytimes.com/2005/07/12/politics/exxon-mobil-becomes-focus-of-a-boycott.html.

25. Chris Mooney, "Some Like It Hot," *Mother Jones*, May/June 2005, http://www.motherjones.com/environment/2005/05/some-it-hot.

26. Peter Overby, "Environmental Groups Launch Exxon Boycott," NPR, July 12, 2005, http://www.npr.org/templates/story/story.php?storyId=4749052.

27. Barringer, "ExxonMobil Becomes Focus of Boycott."

28. Kasaundra Tomlin, "Assessing the Efficacy of Consumer Boycotts: A Shareholder Analysis of Their Impact on U.S. Target Firms," Oakland University, School of Business Administration, 2007, http://www.webmeets.com/files/papers/EARIE/2007/384/EARIE_2007_Boycott.pdf (accessed June 30, 2015).

29. Terence O'Hara, "Oil Industry Seeks to Cast Huge Profits as No Big Deal," *Washington Post*, October 28, 2006, http://www.washingtonpost.com/wp-dyn/content/article/2005/10/27/AR2005102702399.html.

30. Tillerson reversed his position in 2012, acknowledging that climate change is real and caused by humans, but he still downplays the threat by asserting that humans will adapt as needed using technology.

31. Kai Tabacek, "Nestlé Stars in Smear Campaign over Indonesian Palm Oil," *Guardian*, March 18, 2010, http://www.theguardian.com/sustainable-business/nestle-indonesian-palm-oil.

32. Amrit Chaudhari, "Greenpeace, Nestlé, and the Palm Oil Controversy: Social Media Driving Change?" IBS Center for Management Research, 2011, http://www.bu.edu/goglobal/a/presentations/greenpeace_nestle_socialmedia.pdf (accessed June 30, 2015).

33. Aileen Ionescu-Somers and Albrecht Enders, "How Nestlé Dealt with a Social Media Campaign against It," *Financial Times*, December 3, 2012, http://www.ft.com/cms/s/0/90dbff8a-3aea-11e2-b3f0-00144feabdc0.html#axzz3eZbViGnq.

34. Ibid.

35. Campbell Robertson and Clifford Krauss, "Gulf Spill Is the Largest of Its Kind, Scientists Say," *New York Times*. August 2, 2010, http://www.nytimes.com/2010/08/03/us/03spill.html?_r=1&fta=y.

36. Kate Sheppard, "Should You Boycott BP?" *Mother Jones*, June 14, 2010, http://www.motherjones.com/blue-marble/2010/06/should-you-boycott-bp.

37. Diane Sawyer, "The Conversation: The Boycott BP Movement," ABC News, June 14, 2010, http://abcnews.go.com/WN/Media/boycott-bp-facebook-page-continues-grow/story?id=10909891.

38. Scott Neuman, "As BP Backlash Grows, So Do Calls for Boycott," NPR, May 25, 2010, http://www.npr.org/templates/story/story.php?storyId=127110643.

39. Krista Klaus, "Memorial Day Protest of BP Held at Clearwater Station," AP Florida, March 21, 2010, http://tbo.com/news/florida/memorial-day-protest-of-bp-held-at-clearwater-station-38905.

40. Derrick Ho, "BP Boycotts Hurt Local Stations; Gas Giant Offers Help," CNN, June 21, 2010, http://www.cnn.com/2010/US/06/12/bp.protest.atlanta/; *U.S. News and World Report*, "BP Giving Financial Help to Stations," June 29, 2010, http://www.usnews.com/news/articles/2010/06/29/bp-giving-financial-help-to-stations.

41. Emily Swanson, "Poll Finds BP Public Image Still Tarnished 3 Years after Gulf Spill," Huffington Post, April 20, 2013, http://www.huffingtonpost.com/2013/04/20/bp-poll_n_3111551.html.

42. Ibid.

43. Coral Davenport, "New Sea Drilling Rule Planned, 5 Years after BP Oil Spill," *New York Times,* April 10, 2015, http://www.nytimes.com/2015/04/11/us/new-sea-drilling-rule-planned-5-years-after-bp-oil-spill.html.

44. Naveena Sadasivam, "Drilling for Certainty: The Latest in Fracking Health Studies," ProRepublica, March 5, 2014, http://www.propublica.org/article/drilling-for-certainty-the-latest-in-fracking-health-studies.

45. Tom Zeller, "Yes, Fracking Can Be Directly Linked to Earthquakes," Forbes, January 6, 2015, http://www.forbes.com/sites/tomzeller/2015/01/06/yes-fracking-can-be-directly-linked-to-earthquakes/.

46. Paul Galley, "Why Andrew Cuomo Banned Fracking in New York," Huffington Post, December 29, 2014, http://www.huffingtonpost.com/paul-gallay/why-andrew-cuomo-banned-f_2_b_6388228.html.

47. Ad Crable, "Maryland Joins New York as Pennsylvania Border State Banning Fracking," Lancaster Online, June 10, 2015, http://lancasteronline.com/news/local/maryland-joins-new-york-as-pennsylvania-border-state-banning-fracking/article_adf682a8-0a3a-11e5-aac1-c777c5dd46fa.html; *Courier,* "New York Formalizes Ban on Fracking, Ending 7 Year Review," June 29, 2015, http://thecourier.com/ohio-news/2015/06/29/new-york-formalizes-ban-on-fracking-ending-7-year-review/.

48. Andrew Ba Tran, "Where Communities Have Banned Fracking," *Nation,* December 18, 2014, https://www.bostonglobe.com/news/nation/2014/12/18/where-communities-have-banned-fracking/05bzzqiCxBY2L5bE6Ph5iK/story.html.

49. Aleem Maqbool, "The Town of Texas That Banned Fracking (and Lost)," BBC News, June 16, 2015, http://www.bbc.com/news/world-us-canada-33140732.

50. 350.org, "What We Do," 2015, http://350.org/about/what-we-do/ (accessed July 1, 2015).

51. Fossil Free Indexes, "The Carbon Underground: The World's Top 200 Fossil Fuel Companies," 2015, www.Fossilfreeindexes.com. http://fossilfreeindexes.com/research/the-carbon-underground/.

52. David Gelles, "Fossil Fuel Divestment Movement Harnesses the Power of Shame," *New York Times,* June 13, 2015, http://www.nytimes.com/2015/06/14/business/energy-environment/fossil-fuel-divestment-movement-harnesses-the-power-of-shame.html; Dayana Morales Gomez, "Georgetown Becomes the Latest University to Divest from Fossil Fuels," Huffington Post, June 18, 2015, http://www.huffingtonpost.com/2015/06/08/georgetown-divestment-coal_n_7536724.html.

53. Tavia Grant, "Campaigns to Divest from Fossil Fuel Holdings Gain Steam," *Globe and Mail,* June 14, 2015, http://www.theglobeandmail.com/report-on-business/industry-news/energy-and-resources/campaigns-to-divest-from-fossil-fuel-holdings-gain-steam/article24953589/.

54. Gelles, "Fossil Fuel Divestment Movement."

55. Atif Ansar, Ben Caldecott, and James Tilbury, "Stranded Assets and the Fossil Fuel Divestment Campaign: What Does Divestment Mean for the Valuation of Fossil Fuel Assets?" Smith School of Enterprise and the Environment, 2013, http://www.smithschool.ox.ac.uk/research-programmes/stranded-assets/SAP-divestment-report-final.pdf (accessed July 1, 2015).

56. Melanie Warner, "Sharpton Joins with an Animal Rights Group in Calling for a Boycott of KFC," *New York Times,* February 2, 2005, http://www.nytimes.com/2005/02/02/business/sharpton-joins-with-an-animal-rights-group-in-calling-for-a-boycott-of-kfc.html?_r=0.

57. Quoted in Warner, "Sharpton Joins."

58. People for the Ethical Treatment of Animals, "Campaign Highlights," 2015, http://www.kentuckyfriedcruelty.com/h-campaign.asp (accessed July 1, 2015).

59. Ibid.

60. Humane Society of the United States, "Canadian Seafood Boycott Highlights," November 15, 2013, http://www.humanesociety.org/issues/seal_hunt/tips/boycott_high lights.html?referrer=https://www.google.com/.

61. Melissa Cronin, "How the U.S., Russia, and 32 Other Countries Are Saving Seals," TheDodo.com, May 22, 2014, https://www.thedodo.com/major-victory-34-countries-opp-561405503.html.

62. Sea Shepherd, "Canadian Boycott IS Hurting Newfoundland," October 11, 2006, http://www.seashepherd.org/news-and-media/2008/11/03/canadian-seafood-boycott-is-hurting-newfoundland-771.

63. Jamie Hartford, "Canadian Seafood Boycott," QSR Magazine, 2015, http://www2.qsrmagazine.com/articles/exclusives/0109/seals-1.phtml.

64. Cathy Kangas, "The Canadian Seal Slaughter—Again," Huffington Post, April 23, 2014, http://www.huffingtonpost.com/cathy-kangas/the-canadian-seal-slaughter_b_518 6675.html.

65. Belle Cushing, "Bourdain Calls Out 42 Chefs Who Signed Canadian Seafood Boycott," Grubstreet.com, October 28, 2013, http://www.grubstreet.com/2013/10/anthony-bourdain-seal-hunting-ban.html.

66. Cronin, "How the U.S."

67. Kangas, "Canadian Seal Slaughter."

68. Takepart.com, "About 'The Cove,'" 2015, http://www.takepart.com/cove (accessed July 2, 2015).

69. Samantha Cowan, "Activists Deliver to White House 1 Million Signatures Calling for End to Japan's Dolphin Slaughter," TakePart, April 18, 2015, http://www.takepart.com/article/2015/04/18/cove-dolphin-event.

70. Yoko Wakatsuki and Madison Park, "Japan Officials Defend Dolphin Hunting at Taiji Cove," CNN, January 22, 2014, http://www.cnn.com/2014/01/20/world/asia/japan-dolphin-hunt/.

71. Cowan, "Activists Deliver."

72. Associated Press, "All Things Animal in Southern California and Beyond," Los Angeles Times, September 15, 2009, http://latimesblogs.latimes.com/unleashed/2009/09/conservationists-say-70-dolphins-in-japan-released.html.

73. David Kirby, "Activists Debate the Results of The Cove Dolphin Hunt," TakePart, March 17, 2015, http://www.takepart.com/article/2015/03/17/record-low-num ber-dolphins-captured-killed-cove-japan.

74. Christopher Zara, "Following Animal Deaths, PETA Calls for Boycott of Peter Jackson's 'The Hobbit,'" International Business Times, November 19, 2012, http://www.ibtimes.com/following-animal-deaths-peta-calls-boycott-peter-jacksons-hobbit-890776.

75. Justine Ashley Constanza, "'The Hobbit' Premiere a Success Despite Controversy," International Business Times, November 28, 2012, http://www.ibtimes.com/hobbit-premiere-success-despite-controversy-905976.

76. Gary Baum, "No Animals Were Harmed," Hollywood Reporter, December 6, 2014, http://www.hollywoodreporter.com/feature/.

77. Constanza, "'The Hobbit' Premiere"; Madeline Boardman, "Weekend Box Office: 'The Hobbit' Sees a Record-Breaking Weekend," Huffington Post, December 16, 2012, http://www.huffingtonpost.com/2012/12/16/weekend-box-office-the-hobbit-record-breaking_n_2311695.html.

78. Michael Hewitt, "'Blackfish,' 'The Jinx' Leading Trend of Documentaries Hitting It Big on TV," Orange County Register, June 29, 2015, http://www.ocregister.com/articles/hbo-668989-documentaries-film.html.

79. Melissa Cronin, "Landmark Resolution: San Francisco Recognizes the Rights of Whales and Dolphins," TheDodo.com, October 22, 2014, https://www.thedodo.com/san-francisco-cetacean-rights-777140486.html.

80. Alan Duke, "Pat Benatar, Beach Boys Join 'Blackfish' Cancellation List," CNN, January 16, 2014, http://www.cnn.com/2014/01/16/showbiz/blackfish-busch-gardens-cancellations/.

81. Chris Palmeri, "SeaWorld Employee Masqueraded as Animal Activist, Says PETA," Bloomberg.com, July 14, 2015, http://www.bloomberg.com/news/articles/2015-07-14/seaworld-employee-posed-as-animal-activist-for-years-peta-says.

82. Tony McKay, "One Year Later, 'Blackfish" Finally Hit SeaWorld Where It Hurt," News.Mic, December 15, 2014, http://mic.com/articles/106528/one-year-later-black-fish-finally-hit-sea-world-where-it-hurts.

83. Colby Itkowitz, "After 'Blackfish,' SeaWorld Hurt Financially but Keeps Up Political Spending," *Washington Post,* August 19, 2014, http://www.washingtonpost.com/blogs/in-the-loop/wp/2014/08/19/after-blackfish-seaworld-hurt-financially-but-keeps-up-political-spending/.

84. Hugo Martin, "SeaWorld Entertainment Coming Back from 'Blackfish,'" *Los Angeles Times,* June 17, 2015, http://www.pressherald.com/2015/06/17/coming-back-from-blackfish/.

85. Rupert Neate, "SeaWorld Sees Profits Plunge 84% as Customers Desert Controversial Park," *Guardian,* August 6, 2015, http://www.theguardian.com/us-news/2015/aug/06/seaworld-profits-plunge-customers?CMP=share_btn_fb.

86. Joshua Berlinger, "SeaWorld's Orcas Will Be Last Generation at Parks," CNN International, March 17, 2016, http://www.cnn.com/2016/03/17/us/seaworld-last-generation-of-orcas/index.html.

87. SeaWorld, "Breaking News: The Last Generation of Orcas at SeaWorld," March 17, 2016, https://seaworldcares.com/2016/03/Breaking-News-The-Last-Generation-of-Orcas-at-SeaWorld/ (accessed March 21, 2016).

88. Anna Schecter, "Farm Workers in Undercover Video Charged with Animal Abuse," NBCNews, February 13, 2014, http://www.nbcnews.com/news/investigations/farm-workers-undercover-video-charged-animal-abuse-n29541.

89. Ibid.

90. Mercy for Animals, "Tell DiGigiorno Pizza to Stop Supporting Horrific Animal Cruelty," Change.org petition, 2014, https://www.change.org/p/tell-digiorno-pizza-to-stop-supporting-horrific-animal-cruelty (accessed July 2, 2015).

91. Erin Evans, "Constitutional Inclusion of Animal Rights in Germany and Switzerland: How Did Animal Protection Become an Issue of National Importance?" *Society and Animals* 18 (2010): 231–50.

92. Jon Cohen, "Behind the Numbers," *Washington Post.* June 10, 2010, http://voices.washingtonpost.com/behind-the-numbers/2010/06/poll_shows_negative_ratings_fo.html.

93. Dana Nuccitelli, "Climate Change Could Affect the Poor Much More than Previously Thought," *Guardian,* January 26, 2015, http://www.theguardian.com/environment/climate-consensus-97-per-cent/2015/jan/26/climate-change-could-impact-poor-much-more-than-previously-thought.

94. Rainforest Action Network, "Conflict Palm Oil: How U.S. Snack Food Brands Are Contributing to Orangutan Extinction, Climate Change and Human Rights Violations," 2013, https://d3n8a8pro7vhmx.cloudfront.net/rainforestactionnetwork/pages/2367/attachments/original/1405470759/conflict_palm_oil_lowres_(1).compressed.pdf?1405470759.

5. "STOP SERVING GAY CHICKENS"

1. Monroe Friedman, *Consumer Boycotts: Effecting Change through the Marketplace and the Media* (New York: Routledge, 1999).

2. Linda Greenhouse, "High Court to Rule on Colorado Law Barring Protection of Homosexuals against Bias., *New York Times*, February 22, 1995.

3. Steven Lysonski and Richard W. Polley, "Advertising Sexism Is Forgiven but Not Forgotten: Historic, Cross-Cultural, and Individual Differences in Criticism and Purchase Boycott Intentions," *International Journal of Advertising* 9 (1990): 317–29.

4. ERA Coalition, "Find Out More About the ERA," http://www.eracoalition.org/ (accessed on February 19, 2017).

5. The movement to ratify the ERA eventually failed in 1982 in the face of opposition from conservative women, newly elected President Ronald Reagan, and other conservative and religious leaders.

6. Jennifer Jackman, "Anatomy of a Feminist Victory: Winning the Transfer of RU 486 Patent Rights to the United States, 1988–1994," *Women & Politics* 24, no. 3 (2002): 81–99.

7. Suzanne Ferriss and Mallory Young, "Marie Antionette: Fashion, Third-Wave Feminism, and Chick Culture," *Literature Film Quarterly* 38, no. 2 (2010): 98–116, 99.

8. Political Studies Association, "Feminism: A Fourth Wave?," 2014, https://www.psa.ac.uk/insight-plus/feminism-fourth-wave (accessed July 19, 2015).

9. Friedman, *Consumer Boycotts.*

10. Media Matters for America, "Limbaugh: Sandra Fluke is 'Having So Much Sex, It's Amazing She Can Still Walk," March 1, 2012, http://mediamatters.org/video/2012/03/01/limbaugh-sandra-fluke-is-having-so-much-sex-its/155137.

11. Peter Grier, "New Anti-Rush Limbaugh Ad Campaign: Waste of Money or Coup de Grace?" *Christian Science Monitor*, March 22, 2012, http://www.csmonitor.com/USA/Elections/Vox-News/2012/0322/New-anti-Rush-Limbaugh-ad-campaign-Waste-of-money-or-coup-de-grace-video.

12. Media Matters for America website,: https://mediamatters.org/about (accessed May 30, 2016).

13. David Brock, "Confessions of a Right-Wing Hit Man," Esquire, July, 1997, http://classic.esquire.com/confessions-of-a-right-wing-hit-man/.

14. M. J. Lee, "Rush Limbaugh Loses 45 Advertisers," Politico.com, March 6, 2012, http://www.politico.com/news/stories/0312/73675.html.

15. Jack Mirkinson, "Rush Limbaugh Ad Boycott Cost Cumulus Radio 'Millions,' CEO Says," Huffington Post, May 9, 2012, http://www.huffingtonpost.com/2012/05/09/rush-limbaugh-cumulus-ad-boycott-millions_n_1502390.html; Darryl Parks, "The Business of Being Rush Limbaugh," PMedia, May 27, 2015, http://darrylparks.com/2015/05/27/the-business-of-being-rush-limbaugh/.

16. RadioInk, "DialGlobal Lost $98.6 Million in First Nine Months," November 16, 2012, http://www.radioink.com/article.asp?id=2575405&spid=24698.

17. Quoted in Angelo Carusone, "Rush Limbaugh Still Toxic for Advertisers One Year after Fluke Attacks," Media Matters for America. March 1, 2013, http://mediamatters.org/blog/2013/03/01/rush-limbaugh-still-toxic-for-advertisers-one-y/192865.

18. I appear as an expert in this film.

19. Kashmira Gander, "#NotBuyingIt: Feminist Group The Representation Project Launches App to Call Out Sexist Adverts," *Independent,* January 28, 2014, http://www.independent.co.uk/life-style/gadgets-and-tech/news/notbuyingit-feminist-group-the-representation-project-launches-app-to-call-out-sexist-adverts-9091243.html.

20. Quoted in Clare O'Connor, "New App Launched in Time for Super Bowl Lets You Call Out Brands for Sexist Ads," Forbes.com, January 27, 2014, http://www.forbes.com/sites/clareoconnor/2014/01/27/new-app-launched-in-time-for-super-bowl-lets-you-call-out-brands-for-sexist-ads/.

21. Quoted in Stephen Galloway and Chris Gardner, "Beverly Hills Hotel Boycott: How Will It End?" *Hollywood Reporter,* June 11, 2014, http://www.hollywoodreporter.com/news/beverly-hills-hotel-boycott-how-710692.

22. Jared Sichel, "What's a Boycott Worth?" *Jewish Journal,* May 21, 2014, http://www.jewishjournal.com/cover_story/article/what_the_beverly_hills_hotel_boycott_says_about_where_we_draw_our_lines_in.

23. Chris Heine, "Beverly Hills Hotel Boycott Gathers Steam," *Ad Week,* May 6, 2014, http://www.adweek.com/news/advertising-branding/beverly-hills-hotel-boycott-gathers-steam-157513.

24. Roger Friedman, "Beverly Hills Hotel Boycott Softening a Year Later: Russell Crow, Sean Penn among Those Who've Returned," Showbiz411.com, February 20, 2015, http://www.showbiz411.com/2015/02/20/beverly-hills-hotel-boycott-softening-a-year-later-russell-crowe-sean-penn-among-those-whove-returned.

25. Quoted in Ted Johnson, "Protesters Try to Keep Up Pressure in Beverly Hills Hotel Boycott," *Variety,* June 27, 2014, http://variety.com/2014/biz/news/beverly-hills-hotel-boycott-rally-against-sultan-1201253509/.

26. Ibid.

27. Michael Tracey, "It's Time to Start Boycotting the NFL," Vice.com, September 12, 2014, http://www.vice.com/read/its-officially-time-to-start-boycotting-the-nfl-912.

28. Drew Harnell, "Women Are Pro Football's Most Important Demographic. Will They Forgive the NFL?" *Washington Post,* September 12, 2014, http://www.washingtonpost.com/business/economy/women-are-pro-footballs-most-important-market-will-they-forgive-the-nfl/2014/09/12/d5ba8874-3a7f-11e4-9c9f-ebb47272e40e_story.html.

29. Quoted in Tracey, "It's Time."

30. Tasneem Nashrulla and Sapna Maheshwari, "Angry Customers Are Boycotting CoverGirl until It Drops NFL Sponsorship," Buzzfeed.com, September 18, 2014, http://www.buzzfeed.com/tasneemnashrulla/angry-covergirl-customers-are-boycotting-its-products-until#.cdBONMLQQ.

31. Quoted in Harnell, "Women."

32. Barry Petchesky, "So What's Actually New about the NFL's Domestic Violence Policy?" Deadspin.com, August 28, 2014, http://deadspin.com/so-whats-actually-new-about-the-nfls-new-domestic-viole-1628098179.

33. Janet Lee, "It's Not Just Hobby Lobby: These 71 Companies Don't Want to Cover Your Birth Control Either," *Mother Jones,* April 2, 2014, http://www.motherjones.com/politics/2014/04/hobby-lobby-sebelius-contraceptive-for-profit-lawsuits.

34. Daily Kos, "Sign the Pledge: Boycott Hobby Lobby," https://actionnetwork.org/petitions/sign-the-pledge-boycott-hobby-lobby?clear_id=true&source=widget (accessed on July 13, 2015).

35. Bristol Palin, "Join Me in Hobby Lobby Love Day—Thursday, July 3rd," *Patheos,* June 30, 2014, http://www.patheos.com/blogs/bristolpalin/2014/06/join-me-in-hobby-lobby-appreciation-day-thursday-july-3rd/.

36. Arselia Gales, "Fill the Cart of Boycott Hobby Lobby?" *Dallas Morning News,* July 3, 2014, http://www.dallasnews.com/business/retail/20140702-fill-the-cart-or-boycott-hobby-lobby.ece.

37. Megan McArdle, "Hobby Lobby Boycotters Aren't Crafty Enough," Blloombergview.com, July 1, 2014, http://www.bloombergview.com/articles/2014-07-01/hobby-lobby-s-boycotters-aren-t-crafty-enough.

38. Mike Swift, "Opponents of Gay Marriage Ban Ride Wave of Donations," *San Jose Mercury News,* October 24, 2008, http://www.mercurynews.com/localnewsheadlines/ci_10806730?nclick_check=1&forced=true.

39. Buddy Blankenfeld, "LDS Moms Hold Vigil against Proposition 8," Good 4Utah.com,November2,2008,http://www.good4utah.com/content/news/top%20stories/story/LDS-moms-hold-vigil-against-Prop-8/d/story/E81cQC526UaEWdX1G9N40A.

40. Jennifer Leaver "The State of Utah's Tourism, Travel and Recreation Industry," *Utah Economics and Business Review* 73, no. 4 (2014), https://bebr.business.utah.edu/sites/default/files/uebr2013no4.pdf.

41. Federal Highway Administration, "Summary of Travel Trends," 2009, http://nhts.ornl.gov/2009/pub/stt.pdf (accessed July 16, 2015).

42. Ben Sisario, "Lady Gaga Ends Deal with Target," *New York Times,* March 9, 2011.

43. Matthew Perpetua, "Lady Gaga Ends Deal with Target over Its Support of Anti-Gay Groups," *Rolling Stone,* March 9, 2011, http://www.rollingstone.com/music/news/lady-gaga-ends-deal-with-target-over-its-support-of-anti-gay-groups-20110309.

44. Adam Caparell, "Target Strikes Back at Lady Gaga, Criticizes Singer for Backing out of Deal over Gay Rights," *Daily News,* March 10, 2011, http://www.nydailynews.com/entertainment/gossip/target-strikes-back-lady-gaga-criticizes-singer-backing-deal-gay-rights-article-1.118005.

45. Quoted in Andrea Chang, "Target, Gay Rights Supporters at Odds over How to Settle Dispute," *Los Angeles Times,* April 8, 2011, http://articles.latimes.com/2011/apr/08/business/la-fi-target-gay-20110409.

46. Quoted in Matt Collier, "Chick-Fil-A President Says 'God's Judgment' Is Coming Because of Same-Sex Marriage," *Christian Post,* July 18, 2012, http://www.christianpost.com/news/chick-fil-a-president-says-gods-judgment-coming-because-of-same-sex-marriage-78485/#SUuZKIURo5MhCW2p.99.

47. Shane Windmeyer, "Op-Ed: Colleges Rally to Kick Chick-Fil-A off Campuses," *Advocate,* August 16, 2012, http://www.advocate.com/commentary/2012/08/16/campus-pride-says-college-students-will-protest-chick-fil.

48. Quoted in Andrew Ryan and Martine Powers, "Boston's Mayor Menino Clarifies Chick-Fil-A Stance," *Boston Globe,* July 27, 2012, https://www.bostonglobe.com/metro/2012/07/26/menino-clarifies-view-stance-against-chick-fil/S8zwf3nBeDUXKbWQ6TjExM/story.html.

49. Reuters, "Chick-Fil-A Kiss Day: Gay Rights Activists Hold Kiss-Ins at Restaurants Nationwide," Huffington Post, October 3, 2012, http://www.huffingtonpost.com/2012/08/03/chick-fil-a-kiss-day_n_1739850.html.

50. Matt Comer, "New Chick-Fil-A Filings Show Decrease in Anti-LGBT Funding," Qnotes.com, March 3, 2014, http://goqnotes.com/27860/new-chick-fil-a-filings-show-decrease-in-anti-lgbt-funding/.

51. See Rasmussen Reports, "61% Hold Favorable View of Chick-Fil-A," August 8, 2012, http://www.rasmussenreports.com/public_content/politics/general_politics/august_2012/61_hold_favorable_opinion_of_chick_fil_a.

52. Joe Satran, "Chick-Fil-A Sales Soar in 2012 Despite Bad PR," Huffington Post, January 31, 2013, http://www.huffingtonpost.com/2013/01/31/chick-fil-a-sales-2012_n_2590612.html.

53. Ibid.

54. Ted Marzilli, "Chick-Fil-A Takes a Hit with Fast Food Eaters," BrandIndex.com, July 27, 2012, http://www.brandindex.com/article/chick-fil-takes-hit-fast-food-eaters.

55. John Becker, "'Tolerate' Your Homophobia, Orson Scott Card? Um No," Huffington Post, July 10, 2013, http://www.huffingtonpost.com/john-becker/orson-scott-card-homophobia_b_3569146.html.

56. Ibid.

57. Carolyn Kellogg, "'Ender's Game' Studio Lionsgate Disavows Orson Scott Card's Views," *Los Angeles Times,* July 12, 2014, http://www.latimes.com/books/jacketcopy/la-et-jc-enders-game-studio-lionsgate-disavows-orson-scott-card-views-20130712-story.html.

58. Box Office Mojo, "Ender's Game," 2014,: http://www.boxofficemojo.com/movies/?id=endersgame.htm (accessed July 18, 2015).

59. *Variety,* "Hollywood's Biggest Box Office Flops of 2013," December 26, 2014, http://variety.com/gallery/box-office-disappointments-of-2013/#!2/enders-game/.

60. Joan Ryan, "Ender's Game Box Office v. Ender's Game Boycott: And the Winner Was . . . ," Eonline.com, November 4, 2013, http://www.eonline.com/news/477160/ender-s-game-box-office-vs-ender-s-game-boycott-and-the-winner-was.

61. Alex Luhn, "Russia Faces Vodka Boycott in Backlash against Anti-Gay Law," *Guardian,* July 26, 2013, http://www.theguardian.com/world/2013/jul/26/russia-vodka-boycott-gay-law.

62. Joshua Keating, "The Chilling Effects of Russia's Anti-Gay Law, One Year Later," Slate.com, October 9, 2014, http://www.slate.com/blogs/outward/2014/10/09/russian_lgbt_activists_on_the_effects_of_gay_propaganda_law.html.

63. Michelangelo Signorile, "Boycott the Olympics? Russian Vodka? NBC? Maybe—Here Are 5 Other Ripe Targets," Huffington Post, September 28, 2012, http://www.huffingtonpost.com/michelangelo-signorile/boycott-the-olympics-russ_b_3667829.html.

64. As quoted in Alexander Abad-Santos, "Here's Why Gay Men are Dumping Russian Vodka," *The Atlantic,* July 25, 2013, https://www.theatlantic.com/amp/article/312874/.

65. Alexander Abad-Santos, "The Russian Vodka Boycott Is Working, Whether You Like It or Not," *Atlantic Wire,* August 8, 2013, http://www.thewire.com/global/2013/08/russian-vodka-boycott-working-whether-you-it-or-not/68136/.

66. Associated Press, "Russian Vodka to be Dumped by NYC Bar Owners over Gay Issues," Huffington Post, August 5, 2013, http://www.huffingtonpost.com/2013/08/05/russia-vodka-nyc-bars_n_3709598.html.

67. Stephanie Mencimer, "Will Rick Santorum's 'Frothy' Google Problem Return?" *Mother Jones,* May 27, 2015, http://www.motherjones.com/politics/2015/05/rick-santorum-2016-dan-savage-google.

68. As quoted in Alec Luhn, "Russia Faces Vodka Boycott in Backlash against Anti-Gay Law," *Guardian,* July 26, 2013, https://www.theguardian.com/world/2013/jul/26/russia-vodka-boycott-gay-law.

69. Quoted in Emily Jane Fox, "Bars Worldwide Boycott Russian Vodka over Anti-Gay Laws," CNN, July 31, 2013, http://money.cnn.com/2013/07/31/news/russian-vodka-boycott/.

70. Jeremy Kinser, "Gay Bar Lifts Ban on Stoli Vodka, Boycott Ends," Queerty.com, February 7, 2014, https://www.queerty.com/chicagos-bar-sidetrack-lifts-boycott-of-stoli-vodka-20140207.

71. As quoted in Cavan Sieczkowski, "Barilla Pasta Won't Feature Gay Families in Ads, Says Critics can "Eat Another Brand of Pasta,'" Huffington Post, February 2, 2016, http://www.independent.co.uk/news/world/europe/i-would-never-use-homosexual-couples-in-my-adverts-barilla-pasta-bosss-anti-gay-comments-spark-8841902.html.

72. As quoted in Holly Richmond, "6 Tips from the Woman Leading the Barilla Protest," MoveOn.org, October 8, 2013, http://front.moveon.org/6-activist-tips-from-the-woman-leading-the-barilla-protest/#.V00MqJErLIU.

73. Sandhya Somashekhar, "Human Rights Campaign Says Barilla Has Turned around Its Policies on LGBT," *Washington Post,* November 19, 2014, http://www.washingtonpost.com/politics/human-rights-campaign-says-barilla-has-turned-around-its-policies-on-lgbt/2014/11/18/9866efde-6e92-11e4-8808-afaa1e3a33ef_story.html.

74. Karen Bosteels, "Barilla Buckles after Gay Protests," TheLoop.com, December 11, 2013, http://www.retaildetail.eu/en/eur-europe/eur-food/item/15455-barilla-buckles-after-gay-protests.

75. Somashekhar, "Human Rights Campaign."

76. As quoted in Laura Stampler, "Duck Dynasty Star Compares Gay People to 'Drunks,' 'Terrorists,' and 'Prostitutes," *Time*, December 18, 2013, http://entertainment. time.com/2013/12/18/duck-dynasty-star-compares-gay-people-to-drunks-terrorists-and-prostitutes/.

77. Clare O'Connor, "Duck Dynasty Star's Anti-Gay Rant: Is Walmart and A&E's $400 Million Empire at Stake?" 2013, Forbes.com, http://www.forbes.com/sites/clareo connor/2013/12/18/duck-dynasty-stars-anti-gay-rant-is-walmart-and-aes-400-million-retail-empire-at-stake/.

78. For further analysis, see ibid.

79. Amber Ray, "'Duck Dynasty' Patriarch Phil Robertson Once Again under Fire for Homophobic Comments," *Entertainment Weekly*, January 18, 2015, http://www.ew.com/ article/2014/05/23/duck-dynasty-phil-robertson-antigay-sermon-video.

80. Quoted in Clare O'Connor, "Cracker Barrel Chain Pulls Duck Dynasty Items amid Phil Robertson Gay Slur Scandal," Forbes.com, December 21, 2013, http:// www.forbes.com/sites/clareoconnor/2013/12/21/cracker-barrel-chain-pulls-duck-dynasty-items-amid-phil-robertson-gay-slur-scandal/?utm_source=huffingtonpost. com&utm_medium=partner&utm_campaign=duck+dynasty&partner=huffpo.

81. Chelsea Brasted, "'Duck Dynasty' Patriarch Phil Robertson Stirs Controversy Again; Imagines Gruesome Attack on Atheist Family," *Times-Picayune,* March 25, 2015, http://www.nola.com/entertainment/baton-rouge/index.ssf/2015/03/phil_robertson_rape_murder_ath.html.

82. Lauren C. Williams, "Mozilla's Anti-Gay CEO Steps Down after Boycotts and Protests," Think Progress, April 4, 2014, http://thinkprogress.org/lgbt/2014/04/03/3422 750/mozilla-ceo-steps-down-after-backlash/.

83. Rarebit, "Goodbye, Firefox Marketplace," Rarebit.com, March 24, 2014, http:// www.teamrarebit.com/blog/2014/03/24/goodbye_firefox_marketplace/.

84. Mozilla, "FAQ on CEO Resignation," Mozilla Blog, April 5, 2014, https://blog. mozilla.org/blog/2014/04/05/faq-on-ceo-resignation/.

85. Nate Anderson, "After Eich Resigns, Conservatives Slam Mozilla—and Call for a Boycott,"Arstechnica.com, April 4, 2014, http://arstechnica.com/tech-policy/2014/04/ after-eich-firing-conservatives-slam-mozilla-and-call-for-boycott/.

86. Brendan Bordelon, "Krauthammer Calls for Mozilla 'Counter-Boycott' after Company Fired Anti-Gay Marriage CEO," *Daily Caller,* April 4, 2014, http://dailycal ler.com/2014/04/04/krauthammer-calls-for-mozilla-counter-boycott-after-company-fired-anti-gay-marriage-ceo/.

87. Anderson, "After Eich Resigns."

88. Center for American Women and Politics, "Fact Sheet: Gender Differences in Voter Turnout," 2012, http://www.cawp.rutgers.edu/fast_facts/voters/documents/gender diff.pdf (accessed July 18, 2015); Vanessa Perez, "Political Participation of LGBT Americans," Project Vote Research Memo, June 20, 2014, https://inclusion.uoregon.edu/sites/ inclusion1.uoregon.edu/files/RESEARCH-MEMO-LGBT-PARTICIPATION-June-20-2014.pdf.

89. Kathy Lynn Grossman, "Poll Reveals Public Support for Contraception Mandate as Supreme Court Hobby Lobby Ruling Approaches," Huffington Post, June 23, 2014, http://www.huffingtonpost.com/2014/06/23/public-support-contraception-mandate_n_5521714.html.

90. Gallup Poll, "Marriage," 2015, http://www.gallup.com/poll/117328/marriage.aspx (accessed July 18, 2015).

91. Jonathan Clements, "Getting Married Has Its Financial Benefits," *Wall Street Journal*, May 25, 2014, http://www.wsj.com/articles/SB100014240527023046528045795719 31962914924.

92. Jennifer Lawless and Richard Fox, "Men Rule: The Continued Under-Representation of Women in U.S. Politics," Women and Politics Institute, School of Public Affairs, 2012, https://www.american.edu/spa/wpi/upload/2012-Men-Rule-Report-web.pdf.

6. "YES TO JESUS CHRIST, NO TO *JC*"

1. American Family Association, "About Us," http://www.afa.net/who-is-afa/about-us/ (accessed June 13, 2016).

2. As quoted on One Million Moms, "About Us," http://onemillionmoms.com/about-us/ (accessed July 27, 2015).

3. Paul Apostolidis, *Stations of the Cross Adorno and Christian Right Radio* (Durham: Duke University Press, 2000), 22.

4. James Dobson, *Dare to Discipline* (Carol Stream, IL: Tyndale House, 1970).

5. Joe Carter, "Should Christians Boycott Boycotting?" Gospel Coalition, February 20, 2012, http://www.thegospelcoalition.org/article/should-christians-boycott-boycotting.

6. Alan Noble, "Two Can Play at That: What Komen Can Teach Us about Boycotts," Christ and Pop Culture, February 7, 2012, http://christandpopculture.com/two-can-play-at-that-what-komen-can-teach-us-about-boycotts/.

7. CNN, "Southern Baptists Vote for Disney Boycott," June 18, 1997, http://www.cnn.com/US/9706/18/baptists.disney/.

8. B. A. Robinson, "Boycott of Walt Disney: By the Southern Baptists," Religioustolerance.org, updated January 13, 2003, http://www.religioustolerance.org/disney4.htm (accessed July 22,2015).

9. Associated Press, "Southern Baptists End 8-Year Disney Boycott," June 22, 2005, http://www.foxnews.com/story/2005/06/22/southern-baptists-end-8-year-disney-boycott.html.

10. CNN, "Conservatives Urge P&G Boycott," CNNMoney.com, September 17, 2004, http://money.cnn.com/2004/09/17/news/fortune500/pg_gay_rights/.

11. Katherine Phan, "Focus on the Family and AFA Call for Procter & Gamble Boycott," ChristianPost.com, September 17, 2004, http://www.christianpost.com/news/focus-on-the-family-and-afa-call-for-procter-gamble-boycott-20542/.

12. Quoted in Associated Press, "Conservatives Vow Procter & Gamble Boycott," FoxNews.com, September 26, 2004, http://www.foxnews.com/story/2004/10/26/conservatives-vow-procter-gamble-boycott.html.

13. David Kirkpatrick, "Conservatives Urge Boycott of Procter & Gamble," *New York Times*, September 17, 2004, http://www.nytimes.com/2004/09/17/national/17boycott.html?_r=0.

14. Associated Press, "Conservatives Vow Procter & Gamble Boycott."

15. Ibid.

16. Quoted in Yogita Patel, "Boycotts to Back Up Beliefs," Religion News Service, July 23, 2015, http://articles.orlandosentinel.com/2005-07-23/news/BOYCOTT23_1_wildmon-gay-games-boycott.

17. Curtis W. Wong, "Procter & Gamble Backs Gay Marriage," November 20, 2014, http://www.huffingtonpost.com/2014/11/20/procter-gamble-gay-marriage-_n_6192398.html.

18. Quoted in Frank Ahrens, "Gay-Marriage Opponents to Boycott McDonalds," *Washington Post*, July 4, 2008, http://www.washingtonpost.com/wp-dyn/content/article/2008/07/03/AR2008070303769.html.

19. Kathleen Gilbert, "Boycott Successful: McDonald's Abandons Homosexual Activism," October 10, 2008, https://www.lifesitenews.com/news/boycott-successful-mcdonalds-abandons-homosexual-activism.

20. Quoted ibid.

21. Janet I. Tu, "Controversy Sparked on Microsoft's Stance on Gay-Rights Bill," *Seattle Times,* April 22, 2005, http://www.seattletimes.com/seattle-news/controversy-sparked-on-microsofts-stance-on-gay-rights-bill/.

22. David Vise, "Microsoft Draws Fire for Shift on Gay Rights Bill," *Washington Post,* April 26, 2005, http://www.washingtonpost.com/wp-dyn/content/article/2005/04/25/AR2005042501266.html.

23. Christine Clarridge, "Former Seahawk, Pastor Ken Hutcherson, 61, Dies," *Seattle Times*, December 19, 2013, http://www.seattletimes.com/seattle-news/former-seahawk-pastor-ken-hutcherson-61-dies/.

24. Quoted in Julie Bosman, "Wal-Mart Resists Pressure in 'Brokeback' DVD Sales," *New York Times,* April 10, 2006, http://www.nytimes.com/2006/04/10/business/media/10walmart.html.

25. Faith2Action, "About Us," http://www.f2a.org/about.php (accessed May 31, 2015).

26. John Leland, "New Cultural Approach for Conservative Christians: Reviews, Not Protests," *New York Times,* December 26, 2005, http://www.nytimes.com/2005/12/26/movies/new-cultural-approach-for-conservative-christians-reviews-not-protests.html.

27. CBCalerts, "Wal-Mart Selling 'Brokeback' DVD Despite Anti-Gay Protest," April 6, 2006, http://www.cbc.ca/news/arts/wal-mart-selling-brokeback-dvd-despite-anti-gay-protest-1.595241.

28. Shan Lin, "Ellen DeGeneres Commercial for J.C. Penney Angers Christian Group," *Los Angeles Times,* December 7, 2012, http://articles.latimes.com/2012/dec/07/business/la-fi-mo-ellen-degeneres-20121207.

29. Ivan Volsky, "Ellen Responds to One Million Moms Boycott of J.C. Penney: 'My Haters Are My Motivators,'" Huffington Post, February 8, 2012, http://thinkprogress.org/lgbt/2012/02/08/421085/ellen-responds-to-one-million-moms-boycott-of-jc-penney-my-haters-are-my-motivators/.

30. Marc Snetiker, "Bill O'Reilly Defends Ellen DeGeneres in One Million Moms, J.C. Penney Controversy," *Entertainment Weekly,* February 8, 2012, http://www.ew.com/article/2012/02/08/bill-oreilly-ellen-degeneres.

31. Robert Mackey, "Murdoch Urges Irish to Boycott Guinness over Its Embrace of Gay Rights," *New York Times.* March 17, 2014, http://thelede.blogs.nytimes.com/2014/03/17/murdoch-urges-irish-to-boycott-guinness-over-its-embrace-of-gay-rights/.

32. Brownie Marie, "The Catholic League Expands Guinness Boycott," Christian Today.com, June 10, 2014, http://www.christiantoday.com/article/the.catholic.league.expands.guinness.boycott/37984.htm.

33. Catholic League, "Guinness Boycott Advances," March 18, 2014, http://www.catholicleague.org/guinness-boycott-advances/.

34. *Economist,* "It's No Longer Guinness Time," March 17, 2015, http://www.economist.com/news/business-and-finance/21646577-spite-its-st-patricks-day-marketing-sales-guinness-are-fallinglike-rest.

35. Quoted in Leonardo Blair, "NFL Team That Drafts Openly Gay Player Michael Sam Will Face Boycott, Says D.C. Lobbyist Seeking to Ban Gays from League," Christian Post.com, May 8, 2014, http://www.christianpost.com/news/nfl-team-that-drafts-openly-gay-player-michael-sam-will-face-boycott-says-d-c-lobbyist-seeking-to-ban-gays-from-league-119382/.

36. Quoted in Greg Price, "Michael Sam, Visa Boycott: Jack Burkman Starts Protest against NFL's First Openly Gay Player, Credit Card Giant," *International Business Times,* May 14, 2014, http://www.ibtimes.com/michael-sam-visa-boycott-jack-burkman-starts-protest-against-nfls-first-openly-gay-player-1584238.

37. Kashmira Gander, "Boycott Launched against Openly Gay St. Louis Rams Player Michael Sam, by Christian Lobbyist Jack Burkman," *Independent,* July 23, 2014, http://www.independent.co.uk/news/world/americas/boycott-launched-against-openly-gay-st-louis-rams-player-michael-sam-by-christian-lobbyist-jack-burkman-9365426.html.

38. Quoted in Lio Perron, "Michael Sam and the Fight against the Christian Right," Huffington Post, May 16, 2014, http://www.huffingtonpost.ca/lio-perron/michael-sam-gay-nfl_b_5331943.html.

39. Price, "Michael Sam, Visa Boycott."

40. Travis Gettys, "Conservative Christians Plan Protest, Boycott of Dallas Cowboys over Michael Sam Signing," RawStory.com, September 4, 2014, http://www.rawstory.com/2014/09/conservative-christians-plan-protest-boycott-of-dallas-cowboys-over-michael-sam-signing/.

41. Josh Voorhees, "Even the Conservative Lobbyist Hyping a Ban on Gay NFL Players Admits It's a PR Stunt," Slate.com, February 24, 2014, http://www.slate.com/blogs/the_slatest/2014/02/24/jack_burkman_michael_sam_gop_lobbyist_s_cynical_ploy_to_ban_gays_from_the.html.

42. Peter Paul, "New Hollywood Film 'Kinsey' Promotes Child Molester Who Launched 'Sexual Revolution,'" ChristianForums.com, September 15, 2004, http://www.christianforums.com/threads/kinsey-film-should-be-boycotted.1151419/.

43. Alan Cooperman, "Conservative Christians Protest Movie on Kinsey," *Washington Post,* November 22, 2004, http://www.washingtonpost.com/wp-dyn/articles/A2472-2004Nov21.html.

44. Quoted in *World News Daily,* "'Kinsey' Film Opens to Protest," November 12, 2004, http://www.wnd.com/2004/11/27510/.

45. Caleb Crain, "Alfred Kinsey: Liberator or Pervert?" *New York Times.* October 3, 2004. http://www.nytimes.com/2004/10/03/movies/03crai.html?pagewanted=print&position=.

46. Art Moore, "'Kinsey' Director Upset by Campaign," *World News Daily*, February 17, 2003, http://www.wnd.com/2003/02/17289/.

47. Cooperman, "Christian Conservatives Protest Movie on Kinsey."

48. Christina Larson, "The Joy of Sexology," Alternet, December 7, 2004, http://www.alternet.org/story/20692/the_joy_of_sexology.

49. Ibid.

50. Annys Shin, "Motrin Makers Feel Moms' Pain, Pull Babywearing Ad," *Washington Post*, November 18, 2008, http://www.washingtonpost.com/wp-dyn/content/story/2008/11/17/ST2008111703533.html.

51. Quoted ibid.

52. Josh Bernoff, "The Groundswell Gives Motrin a Headache," TypePad.com, November 17, 2008, http://forrester.typepad.com/groundswell/2008/11/the-groundswell.html.

53. Gardiner Harris and Pam Belluck, "Uproar as Breast Cancer Group Ends Partnership with Planned Parenthood," *New York Times.* February 1, 2012, http://www.nytimes.com/2012/02/02/us/uproar-as-komen-foundation-cuts-money-to-planned-parenthood.html.

54. Quoted in Austin Ruse, "How Planned Parenthood Outwitted Komen for the Cure," First Things, September 20, 2012, http://www.firstthings.com/web-exclusives/2012/09/how-planned-parenthood-outwitted-komen-for-the-cure.

55. Jennifer Preston, "Komen Split with Planned Parenthood Draws Fire Online," *New York Times,*. February 1, 2012, http://thelede.blogs.nytimes.com/2012/02/01/komen-split-with-planned-parenthood-draws-uproar-online/.

56. Ibid.

57. Laura Bassett, "Susan G. Komen Loses Support after Planned Parenthood Decision," Huffington Post, February 1, 2012, http://www.huffingtonpost.com/2012/02/01/susan-g-komen_n_1247262.html.

58. Michael Hilzik, "Susan G. Komen Foundation Discovers the Price of Playing Politics," Los Angeles Times, January 8, 2014, http://www.latimes.com/business/hiltzik/la-fi-mh-susan-g-komen-20140108-story.html.

59. Ruse, "How Planned Parenthood."

60. For example, see Steven Ertelt, "11 Komen for the Cure Affiliates Give Planned Parenthood Hundreds of Thousands in Donations," LifeNews.com, July 29, 2015, http://www.lifenews.com/2015/07/29/11-komen-for-the-cure-affiliates-give-planned-parenthood-hundreds-of-thousands-in-donations/.

61. Bruce Horovitz, "Urban Outfitters Holiday Catalog Gets Naughty," *USA Today,* December 11, 2012, http://www.usatoday.com/story/money/business/2012/12/11/urban-outfitters-christmas-catalog/1761971/.

62. As quoted ibid.

63. *World News Daily,* "Retailer Drops Dress-Up Jesus," March 24, 2004, http://www.wnd.com/2004/03/23862/.

64. Tim Nudd, "Kraft Salad Dressing Ad Gets Best Present Ever: A Slap from One Million Moms Fury over Zesty, Naked Picnic," *Ad Week,* June 17, 2013, http://www.adweek.com/adfreak/kraft-salad-dressing-ad-gets-best-present-ever-slap-one-million-moms-150412.

65. Kate Dries, "Kraft's Zesty Guy Is Back and You Can Thank One Million Moms for That," Jezebel.com, August 14, 2013, http://jezebel.com/krafts-zesty-guy-is-back-and-you-can-thank-one-million-1137856405.

66. Rene Lynch, "Kmart's 'Jingle Bells' Ad Goes Viral, Sparks One Million Mom Protest," *Los Angeles Times.* November 20, 2013, http://www.latimes.com/nation/la-sh-kmart-jingle-bells-commercial-20131120-story.html.

67. Jolie Lee, "Tweet Prompts Abortion Foes to Boycott Girl Scout Cookies," *USA Today,* February 19, 2014, http://www.usatoday.com/story/news/nation-now/2014/02/19/girl-scout-cookie-boycott-abortion/5609149/.

68. Ibid.

69. Steven Ertelt, "Pro-Life Groups Re-Launch Girl Scout Cookie Boycott after Group Honors Pro-Abortion Politician," LifeNews.com, February 27, 2015, http://www.lifenews.com/2015/02/27/pro-life-groups-re-launch-girl-scout-cookie-boycott-after-group-honors-pro-abortion-congresswoman/.

70. Emily Shire, "The Mothers behind the Girl Scout Cookie Boycott," *Daily Beast,* February 7, 2014, http://www.thedailybeast.com/articles/2014/02/07/the-mothers-behind-the-girl-scout-cookie-boycott.html.

71. Robin Marty, "The Cookiecott," *Politico,* March 10, 2014, http://www.politico.com/magazine/story/2014/03/girl-scout-cookies-boycott-conservatives-104487_full.html#.VbLWJflViko.

72. Ibid.

73. Austin Ruse, "Girl Scout Cookiecott Breaks Out All Over," Brietbart.com, February 6, 2014, http://www.breitbart.com/big-journalism/2014/02/06/girl-scout-cookie-cott-breaks-out-all-over/.

74. David Crary, "Girl Scouts Membership Drops Sharply," Associated Press, October 11, 2014, http://www.concordmonitor.com/news/work/business/13895318-95/girl-scouts-membership-drops-sharply.

75. Kristyn Hartman, "Low Cookie Sales Concerns Central Ohio Girl Scouts," 10TV. com, January 19, 2015, http://www.10tv.com/content/stories/2015/01/19/columbus-ohio-low-cookie-sales-concern-central-ohio-girl-scouts.html.

76. Marty, "Cookiecott."

77. Ertelt, "Pro-Life Groups."

78. Associated Press, "Vatican Calls for 'Da Vinci Code' Boycott," FoxNews.com, April 28, 2006, http://www.foxnews.com/story/2006/04/28/vatican-official-calls-for-da-vinci-code-boycott.html.

79. For example, activists protested outside a theater in Pittsburgh; KDTK2, "Locals Protest 'Da Vinci Code' Movie," May 19, 2006, http://web.archive.org/web/200712011 44832/http://kdka.com/local/The.Da.Vinci.2.383001.html.

80. For poor reviews of the film, see Liam Phillips, "Da Vinci Code Panned at Cannes," *Daily Mail*, May 16, 2006, http://www.dailymail.co.uk/travel/article-595036/Da-Vinci-Code-panned-Cannes.html. For box office returns, see Box Office Mojo, "The Da Vinci Code," 2010, http://www.boxofficemojo.com/movies/?id=davincicode. htm (accessed July 26, 2015).

81. Ben Child, "Vatican Weighs Calling for Boycott against Angels and Demons Film," *Guardian*, March 24, 2009, http://www.theguardian.com/film/2009/mar/24/vatican-weighs-boycott-against-angels-and-demons.

82. Dave Itzkoff, "Coalition Calls for Boycott of Comedy Central over Cartoon Depicting Jesus," *New York Times*, June 3, 2010, http://artsbeat.blogs.nytimes.com/2010/06/03/coalition-calls-for-boycott-of-comedy-central-over-cartoon-depicting-jesus/?_r=0.

83. As quoted in Matea Gold, "Comedy Central Cartoon Script on Jesus is Protested," *Washington Post*, June 3, 2010, http://www.washingtonpost.com/wp-dyn/content/article/2010/06/02/AR2010060204479.html.

84. Quoted in Hollie McKay, "Advocacy Group Protests Comedy Central's New 'Anti-Christian' Series," FoxNews.com, June 2, 2010, http://www.foxnews.com/enter tainment/2010/06/02/religious-advocacy-group-urge-advertising-boycott-comedy-centrals-new-anti/.

85. Itzkoff, "Coalition."

86. Media Research Center, "Unanimous: Comedy Central's 'JC' Has No Adver-tiser Support," June 22, 2010, http://www.mrc.org/press-releases/unanimous-comedy-centrals-jc-has-no-advertiser-support.

87. NBC News, "NRA Urges Members to Boycott Oil Giant," August 2, 2005, http://www.nbcnews.com/id/8796456/ns/us_news/t/nra-urges-members-boycott-oil-giant/#. VbUu5flViko.

88. Quoted ibid.

89. *New York Times*, "Guns in the Parking Lot," August 4, 2005, http://www.nytimes. com/2005/08/04/opinion/guns-in-the-parking-lot.html?_r=0.

90. Convenience Store News, "NRA Boycotts ConocoPhillips over Gun Policy," August 2, 2005. http://www.csnews.com/nra-boycotts-conocophillips-over-gun-policy.

91. Scott Gold, "NRA, Oil Company Clash over Guns," *Los Angeles Times*. August 2, 2005, http://articles.latimes.com/2005/aug/02/nation/na-nra2.

92. NewsOn6.com, "Court Upholds Workers' Right to Guns in Cars," February 19, 2009, http://www.newson6.com/story/9873937/court-upholds-workers-right-to-guns-in-cars.

93. Ken Dilanian and *USA Today*, "Rifle Maker Bounces Boss Who Supports Obama," ABC News, November 1, 2008, http://abcnews.go.com/Politics/story?id=6152085.

94. Quoted ibid.

95. Peter [no last name given], "An Open Letter to Dan Cooper," Firearms and Freedom, October 28, 2008, http://firearmsandfreedom.com/2008/10/28/an-open-letter-to-dan-cooper/ (accessed on August 3, 2015).

96. Nick Leiber, "Groupon Boycott: Reacting to Its Gun-Related Deals Suspension," Bloomberg News, January 23, 2013, http://www.bloomberg.com/bw/articles/2013-01-23/boycott-groupon-reacting-to-its-gun-related-deals-suspension.

97. As quoted in Brad Tuttle, "Boycotts, Petitions, Protests, Oh My: The Year in Consumer Outrage," *Time*, December 24, 2013, http://business.time.com/2013/12/24/boycotts-petitions-protests-oh-my-the-year-in-consumer-outrage/.

98. Claire Gordon, "He's a Democrat . . . and a Gun Shop Owner," Aol.com, January 16, 2013, http://www.aol.com/article/2013/01/16/confessions-of-a-gun-shop-owner/20426994/?jwp=1.

99. Quoted in Awr Hawkins, "Meet the Gay, Black Republican Selling Guns Online," Brietbart.com, March 10, 2014, http://www.breitbart.com/big-government/2014/03/10/gay-black-republican-selling-guns-online-for-bitcoin/.

100. As quoted in Eva Lorriane Molina, "Boycott Spurred in Texas Restores Gun Deals to Groupon," *Reporting Texas*, October 9, 2013, http://reportingtexas.com/boycott-spurred-in-texas-restores-gun-deals-to-groupon/.

101. Groupon, "Groupon Announces Second Quarter 2013 Results," Investor.groupon.com, August 7, 2013, http://investor.groupon.com/releasedetail.cfm?releaseid=783599.

102. Chris Crum, "Groupon Is Going to Offer Gun Deals Again," webpronews.com, July 1, 2013, http://www.webpronews.com/groupon-is-going-to-offer-gun-deals-again-2013-07.

103. Robert McChesney, "Global Media, Neoliberalism and Imperialism," *Monthly Review* 52, no. 10 (2001), http://monthlyreview.org/2001/03/01/global-media-neoliberalism-and-imperialism/.

104. Pew Research Center, "America's Changing Religious Landscape," May 12, 2015, http://www.pewforum.org/2015/05/12/americas-changing-religious-landscape/.

105. Rich Morin, "The Demographics and Politics of Gun-Owning Households," Pew Research Center, July 15, 2014, http://www.pewresearch.org/fact-tank/2014/07/15/the-demographics-and-politics-of-gun-owning-households/.

106. Gallup Poll, "Marriage," 2015, http://www.gallup.com/poll/117328/marriage.aspx (accessed July 18, 2015).

107. Gallup Poll, "Guns," 2014, http://www.gallup.com/poll/1645/guns.aspx (accessed July 27, 2015). To date, however, no poll has assessed public opinion on whether employers should be required to allow their employees to store guns in vehicles in the employer parking lots.

108. NBC News, "NRA Urges Members to Boycott Oil Giant," August 2, 2005, http://www.nbcnews.com/id/8796456/ns/us_news/t/nra-urges-members-boycott-oil-giant/#.VbUu5flViko.

109. Jon Shields, *The Democratic Virtues of the Christian Right* (Princeton: Princeton University Press, 2009).

110. Matt K. Lewis, "Caitlyn Jenner—and Why Conservatives Keep Losing Ground in the Culture War," *Daily Caller*, June 6, 2015, http://dailycaller.com/2015/06/05/caitlyn-jenner-and-why-conservatives-keep-losing-ground-in-the-culture-war/.

7. WHO RULES?

1. David Vogel, *Fluctuating Fortunes: The Political Power of Business in America* (Frederick, MD: Beard Books, 1989), 3.

2. Thomas Hartmann, *Unequal Protection: The Rise of Corporate Dominance and the Theft of Human Rights* (Emmaus, PA: Rodale Books, 2004).

3. Joel Bakan, *The Corporation: The Pathological Pursuit of Profit and Power* (New York: Free Press, 2005).

4. Naomi Klein, *The Shock Doctrine: The Rise of Disaster Capitalism* (New York: Picador, 2008).

5. Lynn Stout, *The Shareholder Myth: How Putting Shareholders First Harms Investors, Corporations, and the Public* (Oakland, CA: Berrett-Koehler, 2012).

6. Charles Lindblom, *Politics and Markets: The World's Political Economic Systems* (New York: Basic Books, 1977), 356.

7. David J. Rothkopf, *Power, Inc.: The Epic Rivalry between Big Business and Government—and the Reckoning That Lies Ahead* (New York: Farrar, Straus and Giroux, 2012).

8. Matt Grossmann, *The Not-So-Special Interests: Interest Groups, Public Representation, and American Governance* (Stanford: Stanford University Press, 2012).

9. William Greider, *Who Will Tell the People?: The Betrayal of American Democracy* (New York: Simon & Schuster, 1993).

10. David Vogel, *Kindred Strangers: The Uneasy Relationship between Politics and Business in America* (Princeton: Princeton University Press, 1996); Scott Bowman, *The Modern Corporation and American Political Thought: Law, Power, and Ideology* (University Park: Pennsylvania State University Press, 1996); Robert Mayer, *The Consumer Movement: Guardians of the Marketplace* (Boston: Twayne Publishers, 1989); Robert Dahl, "Governing the Giant Corporation," in *Corporate Power in America: Nader's Report Conference on Corporate Accountability*, ed. Ralph Nader and Mark Greed, 10–24 (New York: Grossman Publishers, 1973).

11. Lee Drutman, "How Corporate Lobbyists Conquered American Democracy," Atlantic, April 20, 2015, http://www.theatlantic.com/business/archive/2015/04/how-corporate-lobbyists-conquered-american-democracy/390822/.

12. Grossmann, *Not-So-Special Interests*.

13. Frank Baumgartner and Brian Jones, *Agendas and Instability in American Politics* (Chicago: University of Chicago Press, 1993); Erik Patashnik, "After the Public Interest Prevails: The Political Sustainability of Policy Reform," *Governance* 16, no. 2 (2003): 203–34.

14. Gregory Wawro, "A Panel Probit Analysis of Campaign Contributions and Roll-Call Votes," *American Journal of Political Science* 45, no. 3 (2001): 563–79; Grossmann, *Not-So-Special Interests*; Paul Burstein and April Linton, "The Impact of Political Parties, Interest Groups, and Social Movement Organizations on Public Policy: Some Recent Evidence and Theoretical Concerns," *Social Forces* 81, no. 2 (2002): 380–408; Frank R. Baumgartner and Beth L. Leech, *Basic Interests: The Importance of Groups in Politics and Political Science* (Princeton: Princeton University Press, 1998).

15. Richard L. Hall and Frank W. Wayman, "Buying Time: Moneyed Interests and the Mobilization of Bias in Congressional Committees," *American Political Science Review* 84, no. 3 (1990): 797–820.

16. John M. de Figueiredo and Brian S. Silverman, "Academic Earmarks and the Returns to Lobbying," *Journal of Law and Economics* 49, no. 2 (2006): 597–626; Mark A. Smith, *American Business and Political Power: Public Opinion, Elections, and Democracy* (Chicago: University of Chicago Press, 2000).

17. Frank J. Baumgartner, Jeffrey M. Berry, Marie Hojnacki, David C. Kimball, and Beth L. Leech, *Lobbying and Policy Change: Who Wins, Who Loses, and Why* (Chicago: University of Chicago Press, 2009); Jason Webb Yackee and Susan Webb Yackee, "A Bias toward Business? Assessing Interest Group Influence in the U.S. Bureaucracy," *Journal of Politics* 68, no. 1 (2005): 128–39; Marissa Martino Golden, "Interest Groups in the Rule-Making Process: Who Participates? Whose Voices Get Heard?" *Journal of Public Administration Research and Theory* 8, no. 2 (1998): 245–70.

18. Matt Grossmann, "Interest Group Influence on U.S. Policy Change: An Assessment Based on Policy History," *Interest Groups and Advocacy* 1, no. 2 (2012): 171–92.

19. Ibid.; Jeffrey Berry, *The New Liberalism: The Rising Power of Citizen Groups* (Washington DC: Brookings Institution Press, 1999); Loree Bykerk and Ardith Maney, *U.S. Consumer Interest Groups: Institutional Profiles* (Westport, CT: Greenwood Publishing, 1995).

20. Belén Balanyá, Ann Doherty, Olivier Hoedeman, Adam Ma'anit, and Erik Wesselius, *Europe Inc.: Regional & Global Restructuring and the Rise of Corporate Power,* 2nd ed. (London: Pluto Press, 2003); Daniel L. Levy and Daniel Egan, "Capital Contests: National and Transnational Channels of Corporate Influence on the Climate Change Negotiations," *Politics and Society* 26, no. 3 (1998): 337–61.

21. Martin Gilens and Benjamin I. Page, "Testing Theories of American Politics: Elites, Interests Groups, and Average Citizens," *Perspective on Politics* 12, no. 3 (2014): 564–81, 565.

22. Larry Bartels, "The Social Welfare Deficit: Public Opinion, Policy Responsiveness, and Political Inequality in Affluent Democracies," paper prepared for the 22nd International Conference of Europeanists, Paris, July 8–10, 2015, http://www.piketty.pse.ens.fr/files/Bartels2015.pdf.

23. Sarah Anderson and John Cavanagh, *Top 200: The Rise of Corporate Global Power* (Washington, DC: Institute for Policy Studies, 2000).

24. OpenSecrets.org, "Super PACs," Center for Responsive Politics, 2014, https://www.opensecrets.org/pacs/superpacs.php (accessed August 16, 2015) and OpenSecrets.org, "2016 Outside Spending, by Super PAC," Center for Responsive Politics, 2016, https://www.opensecrets.org/outsidespending/summ.php?chrt=V&type=S (accessed February 20, 2017).

25. OpenSecrets.org, "Political Nonprofits," Center for Responsive Politics, 2015, https://www.opensecrets.org/outsidespending/nonprof_summ.php (accessed August 16, 2015); Tom Kertscher, "Ten Times More 'Dark Money' Has Been Spent for 2016 Elections, U.S. Sen. Tammy Baldwin Says," November 5, 2015, Politifact, https://www.opensecrets.org/outsidespending/summ.php?chrt=V&type=S.

26. Mark E. Warren, "Citizen Participation and Democratic Deficits: Considerations from the Perspective of Democratic Theory," in *Activating the Citizen,* ed. Joan DeBardeleben and Jon Pammett, 17–40(New York: Palgave Macmillan 2009); Charles E. Lindblom, *The Market System: What It Is, How It Works, and What to Make of It* (New Haven: Yale University Press, 2002).

27. ALEC, "About ALEC," https://www.alec.org/about/ (accessed September 4, 2013.

28. Michael E. Kraft and Sheldon Kamieniecki, *Business and Environmental Policy: Corporate Interests in the American Political System* (Cambridge, MA: MIT Press, 2007); ALEC, "About ALEC."

29. Rebecca Cooper, Caroline Heldman, Alissa Ackerman, and Victoria Farrar-Myers, "Hidden Corporate Profits in the U.S. Prison System: The Unorthodox Policymaking of the American Legislative Exchange Council," *Contemporary Justice Review* 19, no. 3 (2016): 380–400.

30. Michelle Alexander, *The New Jim Crow* (New York: The New Press, 2012).

31. Steve Fraser, *The Age of Acquiescence: The Life and Death of American Resistance to Organized Wealth and Power* (New York: Little Brown & Co., 2015).

32. Greider, *Who Will Tell the People?*

33. Robert J. Brulle, "Institutionalizing Delay: Foundation Funding and the Creation of U.S. Climate Change Counter-Movement Organizations," *Climate Change* 122, no. 4 (2013): 681–94.

34. Lindblom, *Politics and Markets.*

35. National Priorities Project, "Fighting for a U.S. Federal Budget That Works for All Americans," 2016, https://www.nationalpriorities.org/campaigns/us-military-spending-vs-world/ (accessed May 28, 2016).

36. Dwight D. Eisenhower, "Military-Industrial Complex Speech," The Avalon Project, Yale University Law School, 1961 http://avalon.law.yale.edu/20th_century/eisenhower001.asp (accessed May 28, 2016).

37. John Gaventa, *Power and Powerlessness: Quiescence and Rebellion in an Appalachian Valley* (Chicago: University of Illinois Press, 1982), 18.

38. Ibid.

39. Crawford B. Macpherson, *Life and Times of Liberal Democracy* (Oxford: Oxford University Press, 1977); Carol Pateman, *Participation and Democratic Theory* (Cambridge, UK: Cambridge University Press, 1970).

40. Jane Mansbridge, *Beyond Adversary Democracy* (Chicago, University of Chicago Press, 1980).

41. Benjamin Barber, "Public Talk and Civic Action: Education for Participation in Strong Democracy," *Social Education* 53, no. 6 (1989): 353–70, quotation on 355.

42. Benjamin Barber, *Strong Democracy: Participatory Politics for a New Age* (Berkeley: University of California Press, 1984), xiv.

43. Jason Vick, "Participatory versus Radical Democracy in the 21st Century: Carole Pateman, Jacques Rancière, and Sheldon Wolin," *New Political Science* 37, no. 2 (2015): 204–23, quotation on 221.

44. Jeffrey D. Hilmer, "The State of Participatory Democratic Theory," *New Political Science* 32, no. 1 (2010): 43–63.

45. For a further exploration of the concept of imagined communities, see Benedict Anderson, *Imagined Communities and the Spread of Nationalism,* rev. ed. (New York: Verso, 2006).

46. Joseph Bessette, *The Mild Voice of Reason: Deliberative Democracy and American National Government* (Chicago: University of Chicago Press, 1997). Cass Sunstein, a constitutional scholar, popularized the idea of deliberative democracy in "Interest Group in American Public Law," *Stanford Law Review* 38, no. 1 (1985): 29–87). Jon Elster and Joshua Cohen made major contributions to further development of the theory: Jon Elster, ed., *Deliberative Democracy* (Cambridge, UK: Cambridge University Press, 1998); Joshua Cohen, *Philosophy, Politics, Democracy* (Cambridge, MA: Harvard University Press, 2009).

47. Bessette, *Mild Voice of Reason.*

48. Sunstein, "Interest Group in American Public Law."

49. James S. Fishkin and Robert C. Luskin, "Experimenting with a Democratic Ideal: Deliberative Polling and Public Opinion," *Acta Politica* 40 (2005): 284–98.

50. Jon Elster, "The Market and the Forum: Three Varieties of Political Theory," in *Deliberative Democracy: Essays in Reason and Politics,* ed. James Bohman and William Rehg, 3–34 Cambridge, MA: MIT Press, 1997).

51. Bernard Manin, "On Legitimacy and Political Deliberation," *Political Theory* 15, no. 3 (1987): 338–68.

52. Cohen, *Philosophy, Politics, Democracy.*

53. Iris Marion Young, *Inclusion and Democracy* (Oxford: Oxford University Press, 2000), 16.

54. Young, *Inclusion and Democracy*, 16.

55. See Jane Mansbridge, "Everyday Talk in the Deliberative System," in *Deliberative Politics: Essays on Democracy and Disagreement,* ed. Stephen Macedo, 211–42 (New York: Oxford University Press, 1999).

56. Jane Mansbridge, James Bohman, Simone Chambers, Thomas Christiano, Archon Fung, John Parkinson, Dennis F. Thompson, and Mark E. Warren, "A Systemic Approach to Deliberative Democracy," in *Deliberative Systems: Deliberative Democracy at the Large Scale*, ed. John Parkinson and Jane Mansbridge, 1–26 (Cambridge, UK: Cambridge University Press, 2013).

57. Nick Robins, "Loot: In Search of the East India Company, the World's First Transnational Corporation," *Environment and Urbanization* 14, no. 1 (2003): 79–88.

58. Pauline Maier, "The Revolutionary Origins of the American Corporation," *William and Mary Quarterly* 50, no. 1 (1993): 51–84.

59. David Ciepley, "Beyond Public and Private: A Political Theory of the Corporation," *American Political Science Review* 107, no. 1 (2013): 139–58, quotation on 140.

60. Ibid.

61. Robert Dahl, *A Preface to Economic Democracy* (Berkeley: University of California Press, 1986).

62. Richard Fry and Rakesh Kochhar, "America's Wealth Gap between Middle-Income and Upper-Income Families Is Widest on Record," Pew Research Center, December 17, 2014, http://www.pewresearch.org/fact-tank/2014/12/17/wealth-gap-upper-middle-income/.

63. Erik Olin Wright, *Envisioning Real Utopias* (New York: Verso Books, 2010).

64. Ibid., 367.

65. Karl Marx and Friedrich Engels, *The Communist Manifesto*, ed. David McLellan, trans. Samuel Moore (Oxford: Oxford University Press, 1992).

66. Tom Malleson, *After Occupy: Economic Democracy for the 21st Century* (New York: Oxford University Press, 2015).

67. As quoted ibid., 101.

68. Alexandra Bornkessel, "Unraveling the Myth of Slacktivism," Razoo Foundation, 2015, http://razoofoundation.org/2011/10/unraveling-the-myth-of-slacktivism/.

69. Georgetown University Center for Social Impact Communication, "Slactivists Doing More than Clicking in Support of Causes," November 28, 2011, http://csic.georgetown.edu/news/1308/slacktivists-doing-more-than-clicking-in-support-of-causes.

70. As quoted in Bornkessel, "Unraveling the Myth of Slacktivism."

71. Yu-Hao Lee and Gary Hsieh, "Does Slacktivism Hurt Activism?: The Effects of Moral Balancing and Consistency in Online Activism," *CHI '13: Proceedings of the SIGCHI Conference on Human Factors in Computing Systems*, Paris, France, April 27–May 2, 2013, 811–20, https://faculty.washington.edu/garyhs/docs/lee-chi2013-slacktivism.pdf.

72. Pablo Barberá, Ning Wang, Richard Bonneau, John T. Jost, Jonathan Nagler, Joshua Tucker, and Sandra González-Bailón, "The Critical Periphery in the Growth of Social Protests," PLoS ONE 10, no. 11 (2015): e0143611, doi:10.1371/journal.pone.0143611.

73. Juliet Eilperin, "Seeking to End Rape on Campus, White House Launches 'It's on Us,'" *Washington Post*, September 19, 2014, https://www.washingtonpost.com/news/post-politics/wp/2014/09/19/seeking-to-end-rape-on-campus-wh-launches-its-on-us/.

74. Clifford Kirkpatrick and Eugene Kanin, "Male Sex Aggression on a University Campus," *American Sociological Review* 22, no. 1 (1957): 52–58.

75. Mary Koss, "Date Rape: The Story of an Epidemic and Those Who Deny It," *Ms. Magazine*, October 1985.

76. Audre Lorde, "The Master's Tools Will Never Dismantle the Master's House," *Sister Outsider: Essays and Speeches*, rev. ed. (Berkeley: Crossing Press, 2007), 110–14.

77. Berry, *New Liberalism*; Andrew S. McFarland, "Interest Groups and Theories of Power in America," *British Journal of Political Science* 17, no. 2 (1987): 129–47.

78. Candice R. Hollenbeck and George M. Zinkhan, "Consumer Activism on the Internet: The Role of Anti-Brand Communities," *NA: Advances in Consumer Research*, Vol. 33, ed. Connie Pechmann and Linda Price, 479–85 (Duluth, MN: Association for Consumer Research, 2006).

79. OpenSecrets.org, "BP," Center for Responsive Politics, 2015, https://www.open secrets.org/orgs/summary.php?id=D000000091 (accessed August 16, 2015).

80. Thomas P. Lyon and John W. Maxwell, "Greenwash: Corporate Environmental Disclosure under Threat of Audit," *Journal of Economics & Management Strategy* 20 (2011): 3–41.

81. Thomas P. Lyon and A. Wren Montgomery, "The Means and Ends of Greenwash," *Organization & Environment* 28, no. 2 (2015): 223–49.

82. See Greenwashing Index, http://www.greenwashingindex.com.

83. Gallup Polls, "Trust in Government," http://www.gallup.com/poll/5392/trust-government.aspx (accessed February 5, 2013). For more information about Americans's psychological withdrawal from politics, see Robert D. Putnam, *Bowling Alone* (New York: Simon and Schuster, 2001).

84. David Moore, "Trust in Government Falls to Pre-9/11 Levels," Gallup, October 6, 2003, http://www.gallup.com/poll/9394/trust-government-falls-pre911-levels.aspx.

85. Ron Inglehart, "Postmodernism Erodes Respect for Authority, but Increases Support for Democracy," in *Critical Citizens: Global Support for Democratic Governance*, ed. Pippa Norris, 236–56 (Oxford: Oxford University Press, 1999); Dennis Thompson, *Ethics in Congress: From Individual to Institutional Corruption* (Washington, DC: Brookings Institution, 1995); David Vogel, *Lobbying the Corporation: Citizen Challenges to Business Authority* (New York: Basic Books, 1978), 9.

86. David Vogel presented this argument in 1978, during the heyday of the Consumer Movement, in *Lobbying the Corporation*. These sentiments are perhaps truer today than they were forty years ago because more citizens now choose to engage in everyday acts of consumer activism. For more recent publications on citizen power in the marketplace, see Margaret Scammell, "The Internet and Civic Engagement: The Age of the Citizen Consumer," *Political Communication* 17 (2000), 351–55; Nikolas Rosa, *Powers of Freedom* (New York: Cambridge University Press, 1999).

87. For a detailed discussion of consumer efficacy, see Stephen Brobeck, ed., *Encyclopedia of the Consumer Movement* (Santa Barbara: ABC-CLIO, 1997).

88. Wendy Brown, *Undoing the Demos: Neoliberalism's Stealth Revolution* (Cambridge, MA: Zone Books, 2015), 17.

89. Mark B. Brown, "The Civic Shaping of Technology: California's Electric Vehicle Program," *Science, Technology & Human Values* 26, no. 1 (2001): 56–81, quotation on 64.

90. As quoted in an interview with Wendy Brown by Timothy Shenk, "Booked #3: What Exactly Is Neoliberalism?" *Dissent*, April 2, 2015, https://www.dissentmagazine.org/blog/booked-3-what-exactly-is-neoliberalism-wendy-brown-undoing-the-demos.

CONCLUSION

1. Lance Bennett and Robert M. Entman, eds., *Mediated Politics: Communication in the Future of Democracy* (New York: Cambridge University Press, 2001), 2.

2. William Greider, *Who Will Tell the People: The Betrayal of American Democracy* (New York: Simon & Schuster, 1992).

3. Ibid.; Lizabeth Cohen, *A Consumers' Republic: The Politics of Mass Consumption in Postwar America* (New York: Alfred A. Knopf, 2003).

4. Lee Drutman, "How Corporate Lobbyists Conquered American Democracy," *Atlantic*, April 20, 2015, http://www.theatlantic.com/business/archive/2015/04/how-corporate-lobbyists-conquered-american-democracy/390822/. For a full explication of the

current state of corporate lobbying in the United States, see Lee Drutman, *The Business of America Is Lobbying: How Corporations Became Politicized and Politics Became More Corporate* (Oxford: Oxford University Press, 2015).

5. Timothy H. Breen, *The Marketplace of Revolution: How Consumer Politics Shaped American Independence* (New York: Oxford University Press, 2005).

6. Benjamin J. Newman and Brandon L. Bartels, "Politics at the Checkout Line: Explaining Political Consumerism in the United States," *Political Research Quarterly* 64, no. 4 (2011): 803–17.

7. Ibid.

8. Ronald Inglehart, *Modernization and Postmodernization: Cultural, Economic, and Political Change in 43 Societies* (Princeton: Princeton University Press, 1997); Scott Keeter, Cliff Zukin, Molly Andolina, and Krista Jenkins, "The Civic and Political Health of a Nation: National Civic Engagement Survey I, Spring 2002," Center for Information & Research on Civic Learning and Engagement and the Pew Charitable Trusts, http:// civicyouth.org/the-civic-and-political-health-of-the-nation-national-civic-engagement-survey-i-spring-2002/; Pippa Norris, *Democratic Phoenix: Reinventing Political Activism* (New York: Cambridge University Press, 2002); Olof Petersson, "Democracy the Swedish Way," Report from the SNS Democratic Audit, 1999, http://www.olofpetersson. se/_arkiv/dr/dr_1999_sns_audit.pdf; Goul Andersen, Jorgen and Mette Tobiasen, "Who Are These Political Consumers Anyway? Survey Evidence from Denmark," in *Politics, Products, and Markets: Exploring Political Consumerism Past and Present*, ed. Michele Micheletti, Andreas Follesdal and Dietlind Stolle, 203–21 (New Brunswick, NJ: Transaction Press, 2003).

9. Pia A. Albinsson and B. Yasanthi Perera, "Putting the Roots Back in Grassroots: Consumer Activism through Social Media," in *NA: Advances in Consumer Research*, Vol. 38, ed. Darren W. Dahl, Gita V. Johar, and Stijn M. J. van Osselaer, (Duluth, MN: Association for Consumer Research, 2011).

10. Norris, *Democratic Phoenix*. See also Ronald Inglehart, *Culture Shift in Advanced Industrial Society* (Princeton: Princeton University Press, 1990).

11. Naomi Klein, *No Logo*, 10th ed. (New York: Picador, 2009).

12. Stephen W. Pruitt and Monroe Friedman, "Determining the Effectiveness of Consumer Boycotts: A Stock Price Analysis of Their Impact on Corporate Targets," *Journal of Consumer Policy* 9, no. 4 (1986): 375–87.

13. Monroe Friedman, *Consumer Boycotts: Effecting Change through the Marketplace and the Media* (New York Routledge, 1999), 31.

14. Brayden G. King, "A Political Mediation Model of Corporate Response to Social Movement Activism," *Administrative Science Quarterly* 53 (2008): 395–421.

Index

Abercrombie & Fitch, 9
abolitionism, 21, 26, 30–32, 37, 53, 109, 217
abortion, 23, 136, 162, 167, 172–73, 176–77,
    185, 206, 219
Action Aid, 97
Adams, Samuel Hopkins, 36
Addams, Jane, 36
*After Occupy: Economic Democracy for the
    21st Century*, 205
Age of Acquiescence, The, 195–96
Agnew, Jean-Christophe, 37
Ahmed, Sharn, 208
All in the Family, 162
Allen, Beth, 151–52
Altria, 65
Amazon.com, 89
American Association of University Women
    (AAUW), 39
American Express, 66
American Family Association (AFA), 161–62,
    164–67
American Federation of Labor and Congress
    of Industrial Organizations (AFL-CIO),
    78
American Heritage Girls, 176–77
American Humane Association (AHA), 119,
    123
American Immigration Lawyers Association,
    86
American Legislative Exchange Council
    (ALEC), 88–89, 195
American Revolution activism, 25–30, 34, 45,
    50–51, 53, 57–58, 217, 225
Amin, Amirul Haque, 96
Anderson, Benedict, 200
Andrews, Larry, 119
Anglin, Andrew, 54
*Animal Liberation: A New Ethics for Our
    Treatment of Animals*, 106
animal rights activism
    American Humane Association (AHA),
        119, 123
    Animal Liberation Front (ALF), 107
    Arctic National Wildlife Refuge (ANWR),
        110–11, 130, 132

Blackfish, 123–25, 127, 129, 131, 223
    Canadian seafood campaign, 119–20,
        126–28, 223
    The Cove campaign, 120–23, 126–28, 223
    Defenders of Wildlife, 110
    democratic implications, 22, 107–8, 223
    DiGiorno Pizza campaign, 125–29, 223
    dolphin protection, 22, 106, 120–22, 129–31
    effectiveness measurements, 126–27
    Endangered Species Act, 107
    extreme measures, 107
    The Hobbit campaign, 122–23, 126–29
    Humane Society of the United States
        (HSUS), 119–20
    Kentucky Fried Cruelty campaign, 118–19,
        126–29, 223
    Mercy for Animals (MFA), 125–26
    Orca Welfare and Safety Act, 124
    People for the Ethical Treatment of Animals
        (PETA), 118–19, 122–24
    "pink slime" opposition, 70
    public support levels, 106–7
    seal protection, 119–20, 124, 127, 129–30
    Sea Shepherd Conservation Society, 122,
        124
    SeaWorld campaign, 123–29
    social media usage, 106, 118–19, 121, 123,
        130, 132–33
    Whale Wars, 124
Anti-Coolies Association, 32
Apartheid, 6–8, 68, 117
Apple Computers, 6, 66, 94–95, 98–100, 102–3,
    206, 222
Arab Spring, 1, 60, 208
Aravosis, John, 145
Arctic National Wildlife Refuge (ANWR),
    110–11, 130, 132
arson, 11, 106–7
Artists against Fracking (AAF), 114–16,
    126–31, 146, 223
Axtell, James, 27

Bakan, Joel, 190
Balanyá, Belén, 193
Bangladesh, 93, 95–99, 101–3, 206, 222

Bank of America, 8
Bank Transfer Day, 2
Baraka, Amiri, 44
Barber, Benjamin, 72, 197–98
Barberá, Pablo, 208
Barilla, Guido, 151–52, 159
Barilla Pasta, 151–52, 155–56
Barnes, Samuel, 19
Barnett, Allen, 151
Barneys, 87–88, 98–99, 101, 103–4, 222
Bartels, Brandon, 64
Bartels, Larry, 193
Battle in Seattle, 48–49, 51, 69
Baumgartner, Frank, 192
Ben & Jerry's, 7, 65
Benitez, Lucas, 81–82
Bennett, Lance, 56, 63
Berry, Jeffrey, 192–93, 211
Bessette, Joseph, 200
Beverly Hills Hotel, 139–40, 155–57, 159, 223
Beyer, Elizabeth W., 85
Biden, Joe, 122
Bill and Melinda Gates Foundation, 89
Billboard Liberation Front (BLF), 71
#BlackLivesMatter, 88–91, 98–104, 210, 219, 222
Black Bikers, 79
Black Friday, 88–90, 98
Black History Month, 177
Black Workers for Justice and Solidarity, 78
Blackfish, 123–25, 127, 129, 131, 223
blogs, 9, 50, 54–55, 60, 70, 87, 136, 143–45, 149–50, 171–72, 181, 185, 218. See also social media
Body Shop, 7
Bohlen, Jim, 109
Bolkiah, Hassanal, 139–40
Boot and Shoemakers White Labor League, 33
Boston Tea Party, 25, 29–30
Bourdain, Anthony, 120
Bowman, Scott, 21
Boxer, Barbara, 172
Boy Scouts of America, 46
boycotts
    American Legislative Exchange Council (ALEC), 88–89
    American Revolution activisim, 25–31, 34, 45, 53, 217
    Apple Computers, 94–95, 98–100, 102–3, 206, 222
    Bangladesh factory campaign, 95–99, 101–3, 206, 222
    Barilla Pasta, 151–52, 155–56

Beverly Hills Hotel, 139–40, 155–57, 159, 223
#BlackLivesMatter campaign, 88–91, 98–104, 222
Boycott Arizona campaign, 85–87, 98–104, 222
British Petroleum (BP), 70–71, 112–14, 126–31, 211, 219, 223
bus systems, 40–41, 43, 75
Campbell Soup Company, 77–78
Canadian seafood, 119–20, 223
Chick-Fil-A, 146–49, 155–57, 159, 162, 219, 223–24
Chinese exclusion efforts, 12, 19, 24, 26, 32–34, 51–52, 219, 224
Confederate flag campaigns, 79–81, 98–99, 101–3, 222
ConocoPhillips, 179–80, 182–84, 186
Consumer Movement activism, 26, 46–48, 59
Cooper Firearms, 180–84
counter-boycotts, 12, 33, 42, 79–80, 92, 134, 144, 148–49, 153–57, 162, 172–73, 219, 224
Cristal, 84, 98–100, 103
The Da Vinci Code, 178, 182–83, 185–86
demographic trends, 62–64
DiGiorno Pizza, 125–29, 223
Disney, 164, 182–85
Duck Dynasty, 152–53, 155–57, 219
Ender's Game, 149–50, 155–56, 158
ExxonMobil, 110–11, 126–28, 130, 132, 223
Food Network, 91–92, 98–99, 102–4
Gap, The, 96–97
Girl Scouts, 176–77, 182–83, 185
Global Justice Movement (GJM) activism, 26, 49
GoDaddy, 138–39, 155–58
grape industry, 74–75, 79
Great American Boycott, 83–84, 86, 98–99, 101, 104, 219
Groupon, 181–84, 225
Guinness, 168, 185
The Hobbit, 122–23, 126–29
Hobby Lobby, 142–44, 155–58, 219–20, 223
Japanese silk, 48–49
JC, 178–79, 182–83, 185–86, 224
J. C. Penney, 167–68, 185
Kentucky Fried Chicken (KFC), 118–19, 126–29, 223
Kimberly-Clark, 109–10, 126–28, 130, 223
Kinsey, 169–71, 182–83, 185
Kraft, 175, 182–83, 185–86, 224

Love Guru campaign, 85, 98–101, 103
Macy's/Barneys campaigns, 87–90, 96, 98–99, 101, 103–4
McDonald's, 82, 92–93, 98–99, 103–4, 165, 182–86, 222
Microsoft, 165–66, 182–87
Motrin, 171–72, 182–83, 185
Mozilla, 153–56, 224
Mt. Olive Pickle Company, 77–79, 98–101, 103–4, 206, 222
National Boycott Newsletter, 12
National Football League (NFL), 140–42, 155–56, 159, 168–69, 223
Nestlé, 6–7, 111–12, 126–28, 130, 132, 223
New Deal activism, 38–39
popularity, 4, 11–12, 47, 53, 62–65, 71, 73, 218, 220
post-September 11 terrorist attacks, 58, 64
Procter & Gamble, 164–65, 182–85
Progressive Movement activism, 34–37
religious objections, 12, 163
reputational damage, 9, 88, 92, 95, 120, 124
Roussel-Uclaf, 135–36
Rush Limbaugh, 137–38, 155–59
Russian vodka, 150–51, 155–56, 158
Sears, 161–62
SeaWorld, 123–29, 223
South Africa, 6–7
Staples, 108–9, 126–28, 130, 223
Susan G. Komen for the Cure, 172–73, 182–83, 185
Taco Bell, 81–83, 98–104, 206, 222
Target, 145–46, 155–57, 159, 162, 224
tuna industry, 106
Urban Outfitters, 173–74, 182–83, 185–86
Utah, 144–45, 155–57, 159
Visa, 169
Walmart, 96–97, 166–67
Warner Communications, 135
Washington Redskins, 76–77, 98–99, 101, 103
Boynton v. Virginia, 42
Boyte, Harry, 72
Bozell, L. Brent, 179
Bradley, James, 33
Brady, Harry E., 3
Brancheau, Dawn, 123
Brazil, 67, 205
Breen, Timothy H., 27–28, 51
British Petroleum (BP), 70–71, 112–14, 126–31, 211, 219, 223
Brock, David, 137
Brody, David, 71–72

Brokeback Mountain, 166–67, 182–83, 185
Brown, Dan, 178
Brown, Mark, 214
Brown, Michael, 88–89, 104
Brown, Rob, 87
Brown, Wendy, 214
Bryan, Bill, 78–79
Buckley v. Valeo, 194
Buffett, Warren, 93
Bumble Bee Seafoods, 106
Bundy, Ted, 162
Burger King, 82
Burkman, Jack, 168–69
Burtch, Bruce, 65
Bush, Aaron, 64
Bush, George W., 58
Buy Nothing Day, 1
buycotts
    alternate names, 6
    cause marketing partnerships, 7, 65–66
    Chick-Fil-A, 148–49
    civil rights activism, 40, 42, 44
    conservative groups usage, 30
    corporate accountability, 31–32
    defined, 4, 6
    demographic trends, 66
    Fair Trade tactics, 7
    Florida Gay Rights Buycott Campaign (FGRBC), 136
    Free Produce Movement, 7, 12, 26, 30–32
    government initiation, 20
    popularity, 4, 62, 64–66, 71, 73, 218
    price impact, 7, 66
    slavery opposition, 30–32
    smartphone technology role, 7
    socially responsible investing (SRI) participation, 67
Bykerk, Loree, 19

Caesars Entertainment, 91
California Anti-Chinese Non-Partisan Association, 32
Campbell, David, 14
Campbell Soup Company, 77–78
Campus Anti-Rape Movement (CARM), 209–10
Campus Pride, 147
Canada, 108–9, 117, 119–20, 124, 126–29, 223
Card, Orson Scott, 149, 159
Cargill, 84
Cargill, Michael, 181
Carson, Rachel, 45–46
Carter, Jimmy, 58, 82

Carter, Joe, 163
Castells, Manuel, 60
Castro, Manuel, 147
Catholic Family, 177
Catholic League, 168
Cathy, Daniel, 146–47, 149, 159
Catlin, Hampton, 154
cause marketing, 7, 9, 65–66, 211–12, 221
Central American Resource Center, 83
Change.org, 9, 70, 88, 92, 94–96, 120, 126, 151, 153
Charlie's Angels, 162
Chase, Stuart, 37
Chaudhary, Nita, 143
Chávez, Cesar, 74, 83
Chevron, 193
Chick-Fil-A, 146–49, 155–57, 159, 162, 219, 223–24
Chinese exclusion efforts, 12, 19, 24, 26, 32–34, 51–52, 217, 219, 224
Chipotle, 82
Christian, Trayon, 87
Ciepley, David, 203–4, 206
Citizens Against Religious Bigotry (CARB), 178–79
Citizens United v. FEC, 194, 226
Civil Rights Act, 44
Civil Rights Movement, 12, 26, 35, 40–45, 51–53, 161, 219
Civil War, 12, 91, 189, 219
Clay, Andrew Dice, 135
Clean Air Act, 107
Clean Water Act, 107
climate change, 68–69, 107, 110–11, 116–17, 127–28, 130, 196. *See also* environmental protection activism
Clinton, Bill, 108, 137, 164, 223
Coalition of Immokalee Workers (CIW), 81–83, 118
Coca-Cola, 89
Cohen, Joshua, 201–2
Cohen, Lizabeth, 26–27, 34, 38, 57–58, 216
Colligan, Christine, 92
Color of Change (COC), 63, 89
Colorado, 11, 134, 136
Colvin, Claudette, 40
Comedy Central, 178–79
Concerned Women of America (CWA), 169–70
Confederate flags, 79–81, 98–99, 101–3, 222
Conference of Catholic Bishops, 85
Congress of Racial Equality (CORE), 42
ConocoPhillips, 179–80, 182–84, 186

conservative group activism
    abortion opposition, 23, 136, 162, 167, 172–73, 176–77, 185
    American Family Association (AFA), 161–62, 164–67
    American Legislative Exchange Council (ALEC), 88–89, 195
    Brokeback Mountain campaign, 166–67, 182–83, 185
    Concerned Women of America (CWA), 169–70
    Confederate flag support, 81
    ConocoPhillips campaign, 179–80, 182–84, 186
    CookieCott campaign, 176–77, 182–83, 185
    Cooper Firearms campaign, 180–84, 219
    The Da Vinci Code campaign, 178, 182–83, 185–86
    democratic implications, 23–24, 183–88, 224
    Disney campaign, 164, 182–85
    Duck Dynasty counter-boycotts, 12, 153–57, 162, 219
    effectiveness measurements, 182–83
    Faith Driven Consumer, 153
    Faith2Action, 167
    Focus on the Family (FOTF), 161–62, 164, 167, 169–70
    Free Produce Movement, 30
    gender equality opposition, 169–77
    Groupon campaign, 181–84, 225
    Guinness campaign, 168, 185
    gun rights, 23, 69, 161, 163, 179–82, 184–85, 188, 206, 224
    JC campaign, 178–79, 182–83, 185–86, 224
    J. C. Penney campaign, 167–68, 185
    Kinsey campaign, 169–71, 182–83, 185
    lesbian, gay, bisexual, and transgender (LGBT) opposition, 12, 23, 148–49, 153, 162–69, 173, 183–88, 224
    McDonald's campaign, 165, 182–86
    Michael Sam campaign, 168–69, 182–83
    Microsoft campaign, 165–66, 182–87
    Motrin campaign, 171–72, 182–83, 185
    One Million Moms (OMM), 161–62, 167–68, 173–75
    Procter & Gamble campaign, 164–65, 182–85
    Pro-Life Waco (PLW), 176–77
    Republican Party connection, 12, 64, 111, 149, 162, 167–68, 170, 176, 179, 181, 184
    Shame on Kmart campaign, 176, 182–83, 185–86, 224

Shame on Kraft campaign, 175, 182–83, 185–86

social media usage, 163, 168, 172–73, 175–77, 179–81, 185, 188, 219–20

Susan G. Komen for the Cure campaign, 172–73, 182–83, 185

Traditional Values Coalition, 171

Urban Outfitters campaign, 173–74, 182–83, 185–86

Consumer Bill of Rights, 45

Consumer Federation of America (CFA), 45

Consumer Movement activism, 26, 45–48, 51–52, 59

Consumer Protection Agency, 47

Consumer Reports, 45

Consumers Union, 45

Cooper, Rebecca, 195

Cooper Firearms, 180–84, 219

Coppedge, Michael, 14–15

Cortese, Amy, 59

Coulter, Shannon, 54

Cove, The, 120–23, 126–28, 223

CoverGirl, 141–42

Coyne, Gary, 50

Cracker Barrel, 153, 156

Craven, Michael, 170

Crawford, John, 90

Cristal, 84, 98–100, 103

Cross, Gary, 56

Cullors, Patarisse, 88

culture jamming, 10, 61–62, 70–71

Cuomo, Andrew, 115

Da Vinci Code, The, 178, 182–83, 185–86

Dahl, Robert, 3, 16, 191, 204, 206

Dare to Discipline, 162

Dartmouth v. Woodward, 189

Dash, Stacey, 91

Davis, Wendy, 176

De la Rocha, Zack, 86

Dean, Howard, 112

Death in Custody Reporting Act, 90

Declaration of Independence, 26, 28, 42

Deen, Paula, 91–92, 98–99, 102–4

Defenders of Wildlife, 110

deforestation, 22, 108–12, 126–28, 130–31.
   See also environmental protection activism

DeGeneres, Ellen, 164, 167

democracy, 160
   American Revolution impact, 28–30, 51, 217, 225
   Apple Computers campaign contributions, 99–100, 102–3, 206, 222

Artists against Fracking campaign contributions, 128–31, 223

Bangladesh factory campaign contributions, 99, 101–3, 206, 222

Barilla Pasta campaign contributions, 156

Beverly Hills Hotel campaign contributions, 156–57, 159, 223

#BlackLivesMatter campaign contributions, 99–104, 222

Boycott Arizona campaign contributions, 99–104, 222

British Petroleum campaign contributions, 128–31, 211, 223

Brokeback Mountain campaign contributions, 183, 185

Canadian seafood campaign contributions, 128–29, 223

Chick-Fil-A campaign contributions, 156–57, 159, 223–24

Chinese exclusion impact, 19, 24, 33–34, 51–52, 217, 219, 224

Civil Rights Movement impact, 44–45, 51–53

Confederate flag campaign contributions, 99, 101–3, 222

ConocoPhillips campaign contributions, 183–84, 186

Consumer Movement impact, 47–48, 51

CookieCott campaign contributions, 183, 185

Cooper Firearms campaign contributions, 183–84

corporate accountability, 15–19, 22–24, 31–32, 36–37, 40, 45, 52, 103, 105, 128, 131, 133, 156, 158, 160, 186, 188, 207, 211, 217–18, 222–25

The Cove campaign contributions, 128, 223

Cristal campaign contributions, 99–100, 103

The Da Vinci Code campaign contributions, 183, 185–86

defined, 13–14, 17–18

deliberative models, 13–15, 23, 199–203, 206, 215

DiGiorno Pizza campaign contributions, 128–29, 223

Disney campaign contributions, 183–85

Duck Dynasty campaign contributions, 156–58

economic models, 13–15, 23, 203–6

Ender's Game campaign contributions, 156, 158

ExposeExxon campaign contributions, 128, 130, 132, 223

democracy (*continued*)
Flush Rush campaign contributions, 156–59
Food Network campaign contributions, 99, 102–4
Free Produce Movement impact, 31–32, 51
Global Justice Movement (GJM) impact, 50
Go Fossil Free campaign contributions, 128, 130–31
GoDaddy campaign contributions, 156–58
government accountability, 17, 19, 44–45, 103, 105, 131, 159, 186–88, 207, 218, 222, 225
Great American Boycott campaign contributions, 99, 101, 104
Groupon campaign contributions, 183–84, 225
Guinness campaign contributions, 185
The Hobbit campaign contributions, 128–29
Hobby Lobby campaign contributions, 156–58, 223
JC campaign contributions, 183, 185–86, 224
J. C. Penney campaign contributions, 185
Kentucky Fried Cruelty campaign contributions, 128–29, 223
Kinsey campaign contributions, 183, 185
Kleercut campaign contributions, 128, 130, 223
lobbying impact, 18, 100, 184, 192–95, 200, 210–11, 215–16
Love Guru campaign contributions, 99–101, 103
Macy's/Barneys campaigns contributions, 99, 101, 103–4, 222
McDonald's campaign contributions, 99, 101, 103–4, 183–86, 222
Michael Sam campaign contributions, 183
Microsoft campaign contributions, 183–87
Motrin campaign contributions, 183, 185
Mozilla campaign contributions, 156, 224
Mt. Olive Pickle Company campaign contributions, 99–101, 103–4, 206, 222
National Football League campaign contributions, 156, 159, 223
Nestlé palm oil campaign contributions, 128, 130, 132, 223
New Deal impact, 39–40, 51
participatory models, 13–15, 23, 197–200, 206
political equality, 13, 16–19, 28–34, 39, 44, 50–51, 101–3, 105, 129, 131, 157–58, 184–86, 201, 204, 214, 222
political participation, 3–4, 13–18, 28–34, 36–39, 44, 50–52, 71–73, 100–102, 105, 128–29, 156, 184, 188, 197–200, 215, 218, 222

popular sovereignty, 13, 15–17, 24, 32, 37, 40, 50, 53, 73, 194, 207, 212–15
Procter & Gamble campaign contributions, 183–85
Progressive Movement impact, 36–37, 51
Russell Athletics campaign contributions, 99, 103, 222
Russian vodka campaign contributions, 156, 158
SeaWorld campaign contributions, 128–29, 222
Shame on Kmart campaign contributions, 183, 185–86, 224
Shame on Kraft campaign contributions, 183, 185–86
social media impact, 15, 72, 105, 207–10
Stop Staples campaign contributions, 128, 130, 223
Susan G. Komen for the Cure campaign contributions, 183, 185
Taco Bell campaign contributions, 99–104, 206, 222
Target campaign contributions, 156–57, 159, 224
Urban Outfitters campaign contributions, 183, 185–86
Utah campaign contributions, 156–57, 159
voting rates, 17, 21, 71–72, 157
Washington Redskins campaign contributions, 99, 101, 103
Democracy for America, 112
Democracy Index, The, 14
Democratic Party, 34, 79, 112, 135, 145, 180–81
Democratic Phoenix, 72
Democratic Virtues of the Christian Right, The, 187
Denmark, 20, 63
Diaz, Jesse, 83
Dick's Sporting Goods, 93
DiGiorno Pizza, 125–29, 223
Direct Action Network (DAN), 49
Disney, 97, 164, 182–85
divestment activism, 7–9, 40, 52, 61, 67–69, 71, 73, 106, 111, 117, 131–32, 163
Dobson, James, 162, 164
Doctors Without Borders, 66
Dodge v. Woolsey, 189
Dogwood Alliance, 108
Dolphin Safe campaign, 106
Domhoff, William, 16
Domini, Amy, 8
Domini Social Investments, 8

Donohue, Kathleen, 37
Douglass, Frederick, 30
Duck Dynasty, 12, 152–58, 162, 219

Earth Island Institute (EII), 106
Earth Liberation Front (ELF), 11
East India Company (EIC), 30, 203
Easton, David, 2–3
Ecuador, 67, 97
Eich, Brandan, 153–54, 159
Eisenhower, Dwight D., 196
Eisner, Michael, 164
Ellis, Bret Easton, 135
Elster, Jon, 201–2
Emanuel African Methodist Episcopal
    Church, 81
End of Nature, The, 116
Endangered Species Act, 107
Endean, Steve, 139
Ender's Game, 149–50, 155–56, 158
Enron, 193
Entman, Robert, 56
environmental protection activism
    Artists against Fracking campaign, 114–16,
        126–31, 223
    British Petroleum campaign, 70–71, 112–14,
        126–31, 211, 219, 223
    Clean Air Act, 107
    Clean Water Act, 107
    climate change campaigns, 68–69, 107,
        110–11, 116–17, 127–28, 130, 196
    conservative group opposition, 111
    deforestation campaigns, 22, 108–12,
        126–28, 130–31
    Democracy for America, 112
    democratic implications, 22, 107–8, 223
    Dogwood Alliance, 108
    Earth Liberation Front (ELF), 11
    effectiveness measurements, 126–27
    environmental, social, and governance
        (ESG) investing, 67
    Environmental Liberation Front (ELF), 107
    ExposeExxon campaign, 110–11, 126–28,
        130, 132, 223
    extreme measures, 10–11, 107
    Forest Ethics, 108
    Forest Stewardship Council (FSC), 109–10
    Forest Trust, 111
    fracking opposition, 68–69, 114–16, 126–31,
        146, 195, 223
    Go Fossil Free campaign, 116–17, 126, 128,
        130–31
    greenhouse emissions, 111, 131
    Greenpeace involvement, 109–12, 124, 130
    Kleercut campaign, 109–10, 126–28, 130,
        223
    Natural Resources Defense Council, 110
    Nestlé palm oil campaign, 111–12, 126–28,
        130, 132, 223
    Public Citizen, 112–13
    public support levels, 107
    Sierra Club, 110, 112–13
    Silent Spring, 45–46
    social media usage, 111–13, 117, 132–33,
        219
    Stop Staples campaign, 108–9, 126–28, 130,
        223
    Water Defense, 115
Envisioning Real Utopias, 204–5
Equal Rights Amendment (ERA), 135
ExxonMobil, 110–11, 126–28, 130, 132, 223

Facebook, 2, 9, 60, 75, 84, 86, 88–89, 92, 94,
        96, 112–13, 141, 143, 145–47, 152, 172,
        175–77, 181, 209–10, 218, 221. *See also*
        social media
Fair Food Program, 82
Fair Labor Association, 95
Fair Trade Campaign, 7
Faith Driven Consumer, 153
Faith2Action, 167
Family Research Council, 178
Farm Labor Organizing Committee (FLOC),
        77–79
Farmer's Alliance, 33
Federal Bureau of Investigation (FBI), 107
FedEx, 77, 141
Feminine Mystique, The, 46
Feminist Majority Foundation (FMF), 136,
        139–40
Ferguson (Missouri), 88–89, 104
Ferraro, Linda, 151
Firearms and Freedom, 181
Fishkin, Jim, 200–201
Florida Gay Rights Buycott Campaign
        (FGRBC), 136
Fluke, Sandra, 137
Focus on the Family (FOTF), 161–62, 164, 167,
        169–70
Food, Drug, and Cosmetic Act, 39
Food Network, The, 91–92, 98–99, 102–4
Ford, Ezell, 90
Ford Motor Company, 6, 8
Forest Ethics, 108
Forest Stewardship Council (FSC), 109–10
Forest Trust, 111
fossil fuels, 9, 22, 68–69, 116–17. *See also*
        Go Fossil Free

Fox, Josh, 114–15
Fox News, 64, 149, 154, 162–63, 165, 167–68, 170
FoxConn, 94–95, 98–99, 206, 222
fracking, 68–69, 114–16, 126–31, 146, 195, 223. *See also* Artists against Fracking
France, 58, 64
Fraser, Steve, 196
Free Produce Movement, 7, 12, 26, 30–32, 38, 48, 51, 219
Freedom From Religion Foundation (FFRF), 143
Freedom House, 14
Freedom in the World Report, 14
Freedom Rides, 42–44
Friedan, Betty, 46, 170, 176
Friedman, Monroe, 9, 46–47, 53, 59, 65

Galbraith, John Kenneth, 56
Gap, The, 66, 96–97
Garcia, Mamerto Chaj, 78
Garner, Eric, 90
Garvey, Marcus, 38
Garza, Alicia, 88
Gasland, 114–15, 127, 129
Gaventa, John, 196–97, 201
Gay and Lesbian Alliance Against Defamation (GLAAD), 151–52
Gaylor, Anne Nicol, 143
Geeks OUT, 149–50
gender equality activism
    American Association of University Women (AAUW), 39
    Beverly Hills Hotel campaign, 139–40, 155–57, 159, 223
    conservative group opposition, 169–77
    Consumer Movement, 46–47, 52
    democratic implications, 36–37, 52, 156–60, 223–24
    effectiveness measurements, 154–56
    Equal Rights Amendment (ERA), 135
    Feminist Majority Foundation (FMF), 136, 139–40
    Florida Gay Rights Buycott Campaign (FGRBC), 136
    Flush Rush campaign, 137–38, 155–59
    Geeks OUT, 149–50
    GoDaddy campaign, 138–39, 155–58
    Hobby Lobby campaign, 142–44, 155–58, 219–20, 223
    Housewives League, 38–39
    Human Rights Campaign (HRC), 139–40, 151, 155
    League of Women Voters, 139

Media Matters for America (MMA), 137
    National Football League campaigns, 140–42, 155–56, 159, 223
    National League of Women Voters (NLWV), 39
    National Organization for Women (NOW), 46, 135, 139, 141
    New Deal, 38–40, 52
    Progressive Movement, 36–37, 52
    social media usage, 9, 135, 137–39, 141–43, 158
    UltraViolet, 143
    Women against Violence against Women (WAVAW), 135
General Motors (GM), 89, 193
Georgetown University, 10, 96, 117, 137, 168, 208
Gilens, Martin, 16, 193
Girl Scouts, 176–77, 182–83, 185
Glaser, Marcia, 119
Glickman, Lawrence, 5, 19, 21, 25–26, 28, 30–32, 34, 37
Global Fund, The, 66
Global Justice Movement (GJM) activism, 26, 48–51, 61, 217
Go Fossil Free, 116–17, 126, 128, 130–31
GoDaddy, 138–39, 155–58
Goldberg, Whoopi, 91
Gomez, Jewelle, 151
Goodell, Roger, 76, 141–42, 155, 159
Google+, 210
Gore, Al, 116–17
Gottlieb, Jessica, 171–72
Great American Boycott, 83–84, 86, 98–99, 101, 104, 219
Great Depression, 37–40
Green, Edith, 46–47
Green Century Equity Fund, 8
greenhouse emissions, 111, 131
Greenpeace, 109–12, 124, 130
Greider, William, 191, 196
Grijalva, Raúl, 86
Grossmann, Matt, 192–93
Group of 8 (G8), 48
Groupon, 181–84, 225
GrubHub, 54–55
Guatemala, 82
Guinness, 168, 185
gun rights, 23, 69, 161, 163, 179–82, 184–85, 188, 206, 224

H&M, 96
Haiti, 82, 146
Haldeman, Denny, 108

Hamer, Glenn, 87
Hansen, John Mark, 4
Harjo, Suzan Shown, 76
HarperCollins, 147
Harry, Jackée, 91
Hartmann, Thomas, 190
Hayne, Richard, 173
Heinz, 106
Heinze, Andrew, 35
Hill, Anita, 137
Hill, Julia Butterfly, 10–11
Hilmer, Jeffrey, 199
Hobbit, The, 122–23, 126–29
Hobby Lobby, 142–44, 155–58, 219–20, 223
Hoffman, Steven, 147
Holiday Inn, 79–80
Hollenbeck, Candice, 211
Holmes, Sarah, 147
Home Depot, 91
Home Owners Refinancing Act, 39
Honduras, 93–94, 99, 101, 222
Hooghe, Marc, 4
House Un-American Activities Committee (HUAC), 39
Housewives League, 38–39
Hsieh, Gary, 208
Huckabee, Mike, 149
Hum Lay et al. v. Baldwin, 33–34
Human Rights Campaign (HRC), 139–40, 151, 155
Human Rights Institute, 177
Humane Society of the United States (HSUS), 119–20
Hutcherson, Ken, 166

impact investing (II), 67
Inconvenient Truth, An, 116–17, 127
India Coal, 116
Indonesia, 61, 109, 111–12, 128, 132
Inglehart, Ronald, 59
Instagram, 60
Institute for Policy Studies, 193
International Monetary Fund (IMF), 48–49
Interstate Commerce Act, 36
Intuit, 89
Iraq, 49, 58, 64
Irving, Blake, 139
Italy, 20, 63, 151, 205

J. C. Penney, 96, 167–68, 185
Jackson, Darrell, 79
Jackson, Jesse, 63, 113
Jackson, Peter, 122–23
Japan, 33, 48–49, 63, 120–22, 129, 146

Jarrett, Jono, 149
Jay-Z, 84, 88
JC, 178–79, 182–83, 185–86, 224
Jim Crow laws, 35–37, 42, 44, 51, 217
Johnson, Lyndon B., 45
Johnson & Johnson, 171–72
Jones, Brian, 192
Jones, Helen, 119
Jones, Paula, 137
Jungle, The, 35

K. B. Homes, 8
Kaase, Max, 19
Kanin, Eugene, 209
Keeter, Scott, 19–20
Kelley, Florence, 36
Kelly, Robert Edwin, 49
Kennedy, John F., 43, 45, 57
Kennedy, Kathleen, 122
Kennedy, Ted, 6
Kentucky Fried Chicken (KFC), 118–19, 126–29, 223
Kerry, Theresa Heinz, 64
Khrushchev, Nikita, 57
Kimberly-Clark, 109–10, 126–28, 130, 223
King, Brayden, 65, 221
King Jr., Dr. Martin Luther, 41–42, 86, 113
Kinsey, 169–71, 182–83, 185
Kinsey, Alfred, 170–71
Kirkpatrick, Clifford, 209
Klein, Naomi, 9–10, 190
Kmart, 91, 176, 182–83, 185–86, 224
Kodak, 68
Kohl's, 96
Kolovakos, Gregory, 151
Korean American Business Council, 92
Korean Parents Association, 92
Koss, Mary, 209
Kraft, 89, 175, 182–83, 185–86, 224
Krauthammer, Charles, 154
Kroger, 78
Ku Klux Klan, 43, 45

Lady Gaga, 113, 145–46
LaHaye, Beverly, 169–70
LaPierre, Wayne, 180
Lasn, Kalle, 1
Lasswell, Harold, 3
League of Women Shoppers (LWS), 39
League of Women Voters, 139
Lears, Jackson, 56
Lee, Barbara, 177
Lee, Yu-Hao, 208
Lennon, Sean, 115

lesbian, gay, bisexual, and transgender (LGBT)
   activism
   Barilla Pasta campaign, 151–52, 155–56
   Campus Pride, 147
   Chick-Fil-A campaign, 146–49, 155–57, 159,
      219, 223–24
   Colorado campaign, 134, 136
   conservative group opposition, 12, 23,
      148–49, 153, 162–69, 173, 183–88, 224
   democratic implications, 19, 23, 156–60,
      223–24
   Duck Dynasty campaign, 152–53, 155–58
   effectiveness measurements, 154–56
   Ender's Game campaign, 149–50, 155–56, 158
   extreme measures, 147–48
   Gay and Lesbian Alliance Against
      Defamation (GLAAD), 151–52
   Human Rights Campaign (HRC), 139–40,
      146, 151
   media representation, 136
   Mozilla campaign, 153–56, 224
   National Gay and Lesbian Chamber of
      Commerce (NGLCC), 165
   National Same-Sex Kiss-In Day, 147–48
   Russian vodka campaign, 150–51, 155–56,
      158
   same-sex marriage, 23, 118, 136, 144–47,
      149, 151, 157–58, 160, 162–63, 165–66,
      182
   social media usage, 9, 135, 145, 149–53, 158
   Target campaign, 145–46, 155–57, 159, 224
   Utah campaign, 144–45, 155–57, 159
Levine, Matthew, 149
Lifestyles of Health and Sustainability
   (LOHAS), 59–60
Limbaugh, Rush, 137–38, 155–59, 166
Limehouse, Chip, 81
Lindblom, Charles, 191, 196
lobbying, 18, 45–47, 89, 100, 107, 111, 115,
   146–47, 179, 184, 192–95, 200, 210–11,
   215–16
Locke, John, 26
Lorde, Audre, 211
Loring-Albright, Heather, 90
Love Guru, The, 85, 98–101, 103
Lowell, Josephine, 36
Lucas, Billy, 151
Lululemon, 60–61
Lyon, Thomas, 212

MacPherson, Crawford B., 197
Macy's, 87–90, 96, 98–99, 101, 103–4, 222
Malleson, Tom, 205–6

Maloney, Matt, 54–55
Maney, Ardith, 19
Manin, Bernard, 201
Mansbridge, Jane, 197–98, 202
Marran, Keith, 149
Martin, Trayvon, 88–89, 104
Marxism, 203, 205
May Day, 83–84
Mayer, Robert, 34–35, 47
McComb, Paul, 124
McConnell, Glenn, 81
McDonald's, 8, 71, 82, 92–93, 98–99, 101,
   103–4, 127, 165, 182–86, 222
McFarland, Andrew, 211
McGehee, Carly, 147
McKee, Delber, 33
McKibben, Bill, 116
Meals on Wheels, 65
Meat Inspection Act, 35
Media Matters for America (MMA), 137
Mercy for Animals (MFA), 125–26
Mfume, Kweisi, 63
Micheletti, Michele, 4
Microsoft, 165–66, 182–87
Minutemen, 83
Missrepresentation, 138
Mitchell, Jeremy, 59
Mitsubishi, 8
Montgomery (Alabama), 40–41, 43, 75
Montgomery, A. Wren, 212
Mormon Church, 144–45, 149, 159
Morris, Aldon, 40
Motrin, 171–72, 182–83, 185
Mott, Lucretia, 30
Moveon.org, 77, 110, 143, 149
Mozilla, 153–56, 224
Mt. Olive Pickle Company, 77–79, 98–101,
   103–4, 206, 222
Murdoch, Rupert, 168, 182
Myers, Fred, 119
Myers, Mike, 85

Nader, Ralph, 46, 112
National Association for the Advancement
   of Colored People (NAACP), 41–42, 63,
   79–81
National Basketball Association (NBA), 10, 93
National Boycott Newsletter, 12
National Coalition for the Protection of
   Children & Families, 170
National Congress of American Indians
   (NCAI), 76
National Consumers League (NCL), 36, 39

National Council of Churches, 78, 82, 117
National Football League (NFL), 76–77,
    140–42, 155–56, 159, 166, 168–69, 223
National Garment Workers Federation of
    Bangladesh, 96
National Gay and Lesbian Chamber of
    Commerce (NGLCC), 165
National Highway Traffic Safety
    Administration, 46
National League of Women Voters (NLWV),
    39
National Organization for Marriage (NOM),
    149
National Organization for Women (NOW), 46,
    135, 139, 141
National Rifle Association (NRA), 179–80, 187
National Same-Sex Kiss-In Day, 147–48
Natural Resources Defense Council, 110
Nestlé, 6–7, 111–12, 126–28, 130, 132, 223
New Balance, 54
New Deal activism, 26, 37–40, 47, 51–52
New York Times, 12, 59, 69–70, 75, 92, 94, 165
Newkirk, Ingrid, 118
Newman, Benjamin, 64
Newsom, Jennifer Siebel, 138
Newsome, Bree, 81
Nicolosi, Barbara, 178
Nie, Norman, 3
Nike, 8, 10, 71
Nixon, Richard, 45, 57–58
No Logo, 10
Noble, Alan, 163
Nooyi, Indra, 55
Norris, Pippa, 17, 71–72
North Atlantic Free Trade Agreement
    (NAFTA), 48
NYPD Blue, 162

Obama, Barack, 81, 111, 114, 117, 122, 180,
    209, 219
O'Barry, Ric, 120–22
Occupy Wall Street (OWS), 1–2, 55, 60, 118,
    196, 208–9, 211
O'Connor, Sinead, 135
Olbermann, Keith, 141
Oliver, Jamie, 70
One Million Moms (OMM), 161–62, 167–68,
    173–75
Ono, Yoko, 115
Operation Backfire, 11
Orca Welfare and Safety Act, 124
O'Reilly, Bill, 64, 167–68
Ownby, Ted, 41–42

Pacheco, Alexander Fernando, 118
Pacific Lumber Company, 10–11
Paczynska, Agnieszka, 49
Page, Benjamin, 16, 193
Palin, Sarah, 144, 149
Palmer, Art, 87
Palmer, Janay, 140–41
Parents Television Council, 178
Parker, Dante, 90–91
Parks, Rosa, 40–41
Parnassus Fund, 8
*Participation in America: Political Democracy
    and Social Equality*, 3
Pateman, Carol, 197–99
Patrick, Danica, 138
Pattiz, Norman, 138
Peabody Energy, 117
Pearce, Russell, 86–87
People for the Ethical Treatment of Animals
    (PETA), 118–19, 122–24
People United to Serve Humanity (PUSH),
    63
PepsiCo, 55, 64, 141–42, 193
Peretti, Jonah, 71
Perkins, Lee, 113
Peterson, Esther, 45
petition platforms. *See* social media
Pfaelzer, Jean, 32
Phillips, Kaya, 87
picketing, 10, 52, 70, 97
Piscotti, John, 176
Planned Parenthood, 172–73, 176
Plessy v. Ferguson, 35–36
Polina, Billy, 140
Politics and Markets, 191
Populist Movement, 190
Porter, Janet, 167
Preface to Economic Democracy, A, 204
private prison systems, 16, 195
Procter & Gamble (P&G), 89, 164–65,
    182–85
Product Red, 66
Progressive Movement activism, 26, 34–38,
    47, 51–52, 56, 190, 217
Pro-Life Waco (PLW), 176–77
Proposition 8, 144–45, 149, 154, 157
Public Citizen, 46, 112–13
Pure Food and Drug Act, 35
Putin, Vladimir, 150
Putnam, Robert, 72

Quedraogo, Constant, 87
QVC, 91

racial equality activism
  abolitionism, 21, 26, 30–32, 37, 53, 109, 217
  Apartheid campaigns, 6–8, 68, 117
  Apple Computers campaign, 94–95, 98–100,
    102–3, 206, 222
  Bangladesh factory campaign, 95–99, 101–3,
    206, 222
  #BlackLivesMatter campaign, 88–91,
    98–104, 210, 219, 222
  Boycott Arizona campaign, 85–87, 98–104,
    222
  bus boycotts, 40–41, 43, 75
  Civil Rights Movement, 12, 26, 35, 40–45,
    51–53, 161, 219
  Color of Change (COC), 63, 89
  Confederate flag campaigns, 79–81, 98–99,
    101–3, 222
  Congress of Racial Equality (CORE), 42
  Cristal campaign, 84, 98–100, 103
  democratic implications, 44–45, 51–53, 76,
    99–105, 222–23
  effectiveness measurements, 97–99
  Food Network campaign, 91–92, 98–99,
    102–4
  Free Produce Movement, 30–32, 51, 219
  Freedom Rides, 42–44
  Great American Boycott, 83–84, 86, 98–99,
    101, 104, 219
  Love Guru campaign, 85, 98–101, 103
  lunch counter sit-ins, 40, 42–43
  Macy's/Barneys campaigns, 87–90, 96,
    98–99, 101, 103–4, 222
  Martin Luther King Jr., 41–42, 86, 113
  McDonald's campaign, 82, 92–93, 98–99,
    101, 103–4, 222
  Mt. Olive Pickle Company campaign, 77–79,
    98–101, 103–4, 206, 222
  NAACP involvement, 41–42, 63, 79–81
  New Deal, 38–40
  People United to Serve Humanity (PUSH),
    63
  Progressive Movement, 35–37
  Rainbow Coalition, 63
  Russell Athletics campaign, 93–94, 98–99,
    103, 222
  social media usage, 75–77, 79, 83–84, 86,
    88–89, 91, 102, 210, 219
  Student Non-Violent Coordination
    Committee (SNCC), 42
  Taco Bell campaign, 81–83, 98–104, 206, 222
  voter ID laws, 89, 195
  Washington Redskins nickname, 76–77,
    98–99, 101, 103
racial profiling, 65, 76, 85–88, 102, 104–5, 222

Rainbow Coalition, 63
Ramirez, Urbano, 78
Rana, Mohammad Sohel, 96
Rancière, Jacques, 199
Raymond, Lee R., 111
Reagan, Michele, 86
Reagan, Ronald, 47, 116, 135
Reddit, 137–38
Reid, Harry, 85
Reisman, Judith, 170–71
Representation Project, The (TRP), 138–39
Republican Party, 12, 64, 111, 149, 162,
    167–68, 170, 176, 179, 181, 184
Rey-Goodlatte, Gabriel, 89
Rice, Ray, 140–42, 155, 159
Rice, Tamir, 91
Rist, Darryl Yates, 151
Robertson, Phil, 12, 152–53, 159, 162, 219
Rockefeller Brothers Fund, 117
Rodriguez, Javier, 83–84
Rolling Jubilee, 2
Roof, Dylann, 81
Roosevelt, Franklin D., 37–38
Roosevelt, Theodore, 33
Rosenstone, Steven J., 4
Rothkopf, David, 191
Roussel-Uclaf, 135–36
Rouzaud, Frederic, 84
Ruffalo, Mark, 115
Runkle, Nathan, 125
Russell Athletics, 10, 93–94, 98–99, 103, 222
Russo, Vito, 151

Sainz, Fred, 146
Sajjad, Rooshi, 92
Sam, Michael, 168–69, 182–83
same-sex marriage, 23, 118, 136, 144–47, 149,
    151, 157–58, 160, 162–63, 165–66, 182,
    221, 223
Sand, Cielo, 108
Sandel, Michael, 34, 56–57
Sanders, Bernie, 196
Santa Clara County v. Southern Pacific
    Railroad, 190
Santorum, Rick, 150, 173
Sarandon, Susan, 115
Sasae, Kenichiro, 122
Savage, Dan, 150–51
SB 1070. See Boycott Arizona campaign
Schlessinger, Laura, 170
Schlink, Frederick J., 37
Schlozman, Kay Lehman, 3
Schor, Juliet, 56
Schultz, Howard, 55

Schumpeter, Joseph, 14
Scott, Walter, 91
Sea Shepherd Conservation Society, 122, 124
Sears, 91, 96, 161–62
SeaWorld, 123–29, 223
Second Treatise of Government, 26
Securities and Exchange Commission (SEC), 68
Seismological Society of America, 115
September 11 terrorist attacks, 11, 49, 58, 64, 213
Seventh Day Adventist Church, 79
shareholder activism, 7–8, 40, 61, 67–68, 71, 73, 76, 107, 110, 119, 128, 132, 217, 220
Sharpton, Al, 87, 91, 118
Sherman Anti-trust Act, 36
Shields, Jon, 187
Shock Doctrine, The, 190
Shue, Henry, 15
Siegel, Bettina Elias, 70
Siegel, Josh, 149
Sierra Club, 110, 112–13, 124
Silent Spring, 45–46
Silverman, Sarah, 173
Simmons, Russell, 118
Simpson, O.J., 91
Sinclair, Upton, 35
Singapore Airlines, 66
Singer, Peter, 106
sit-ins, 2, 10, 40, 42, 44, 52, 70, 75, 117
Sklar, Kathryn Kish, 36
Skype, 210
slacktivism, 207–10
Slager, Michael, 91
slavery, 7, 26, 28, 30–32, 51, 190, 202, 217
Small Business Saturday, 66
Smeal, Eleanor, 139
Smith, Jackie, 48
Snapchat, 210
Snyder, Dan, 76
social media
    animal rights activism, 106, 118–19, 121, 123, 130, 132–33
    blogs, 9, 50, 54–55, 60, 70, 87, 136, 143–45, 149–50, 171–72, 181, 185, 218
    cause marketing usage, 9–10
    Change.org, 9, 70, 77, 88, 92, 94–96, 120, 126, 153
    collective action role, 5, 60, 208–10
    conservative group activism, 163, 168, 172–73, 175–77, 179–81, 185, 188, 219–20
    corporate implementation, 15, 60–61, 66, 221
    democracy impact, 15, 72, 105, 207–10
    effectiveness, 1–2, 9, 15, 50, 60–61, 69–70, 73, 102, 207–8, 218–21
    environmental protection activism, 111–13, 117, 132–33, 219
    Facebook, 2, 9, 60, 75, 84, 86, 88–89, 92, 94, 96, 112–13, 141, 143, 145–47, 152, 172, 175–77, 181, 209–10, 218, 221
    gender equality activism, 9, 135, 137–39, 141–43, 158
    Global Justice Movement (GJM) usage, 48–50
    Instagram, 60
    lesbian, gay, bisexual, and transgender (LGBT) activism, 9, 135, 145, 149–53, 158
    Moveon.org, 77, 110, 143, 149
    origins, 62
    racial equality activism, 75–77, 79, 83–84, 86, 88–89, 91, 102, 210, 219
    reputational damage, 9–10, 52, 217, 219–21
    slacktivism, 207–10
    Snapchat, 210
    Tumblr, 60, 75, 89, 210
    Twitter, 9–10, 55, 60–61, 75, 84, 89, 91, 93, 120, 122, 141, 146, 151–52, 154, 168, 172–73, 176–77, 181, 185, 208–10, 218, 221
    Yelp, 138
socially responsible investing (SRI), 7–8, 40, 61, 67–68, 73
Solnit, Dan, 49
Sons of Confederate Veterans, 81
South Africa, 6–9, 68, 117
Southern Baptist Convention, 164, 172
Southern Patriot Group against Holiday Inn, 79–80
Special Assistant for Consumer Affairs, 45
Sports Authority, 93
Sprite, 59
Spurlock, Morgan, 127
Stamp Act, 27–30
Standard Oil Company, 35–36
Staples, 108–9, 126–28, 130, 223
Starbucks, 7, 55
Steinem, Gloria, 135, 176
Stern, Howard, 91
Stern, Joey, 149
Stinebrickner-Kauffman, Taren, 94
Stolle, Dietlind, 4
Stout, Lynn, 190
Stowe, Dorothy and Irving, 109
Stowe, Harriett Beecher, 30, 109
strikes, 38, 55, 74, 82
Student Non-Violent Coordination Committee (SNCC), 42

Subway, 82
Sum of Us, 94
Summit of the Americas, 48
Sunami, Chris, 26
Sunstein, Cass, 200
SuperSize Me, 127
Supreme Order of Caucasians, 32
Susan G. Komen for the Cure, 65–66, 172–73, 182–83, 185
sweatshops, 7, 10, 71, 93–94, 199

Taco Bell, 81–83, 98–104, 206, 222
Tahrir Square, 1
Takei, George, 143
Tarbell, Ida, 35–36
Target, 91, 96, 145–46, 155–57, 159, 162, 224
Tea Party, 86
Texaco, 193
Thomas, Shaunna, 143
Thompson, Liz, 172
Three's Company, 161–62
Till, Emmett, 41
Tillerson, Rex, 111
Tometi, Opal, 88
TOMS shoes, 7
Trader Joes, 120
Traditional Values Coalition, 171
Trump, Donald, 54–55, 111, 188, 219
Trump, Ivanka, 54
Tumblr, 60, 75, 89, 210
TV Turnoff Week, 1
Twitter, 9–10, 55, 60–61, 75, 84, 89, 91, 93, 120, 122, 141, 146, 151–52, 154, 168, 172–73, 176–77, 181, 185, 208–10, 218, 221. *See also* social media
Tyson Foods, 84

Uber, 55
UltraViolet, 143
Undoing the Demos, 214
Union of Concerned Scientists, 110
United Church of Christ (UCC), 77
United Farm Workers of America (UFW), 74–75, 82–83
United Methodist Church, 78
United Students against Sweatshops (USAS), 10, 93
Unsafe at Any Speed, 46
Urban Outfitters, 173–74, 182–83, 185–86
U. S. Public Interest Group, 110
Utah, 144–45, 155–57, 159

Valasquez, Baldamer, 77–79
Van de Kamp, 106
vandalism, 62, 70, 106–7, 113
Vanhanen's Index, 14
Verba, Sidney, 3
Vick, Jason, 198
Vidal, John, 49
Visa, 169
Vogel, David, 16, 52–53, 189, 191, 213
Voice and Equality: Civic Voluntarism in American Politics, 3
Volkswagen, 59
voter ID laws, 89, 195
Voting Rights Act, 44

Walden, Jeremy, 15
Walmart, 82, 89–91, 96–97, 152–53, 166–67
Walters, Barbara, 169–70
Warner Communications, 135
Warren, Mark, 2, 16–17, 194
Washington, Booker T., 38
Washington Post, 12, 75, 77
Washington Redskins, 76–77, 98–99, 101, 103
Water Defense, 115
Watson, Paul, 124
Wells, Ida B., 36
Wendy's, 89
West, Kanye, 86
Whale Wars, 124
White Label Campaign, 36
White Micah, 1
Whole Foods, 7, 82, 120
Wildmon, Donald, 161
Williams, Wendy, 91
Wilson, Chip, 60–61
Wilson, Darren, 88–89
Wilson, Joe, 81
Wilson, M. Chad, 147
Windmeyer, Shane, 147, 149
Wolin, Sheldon, 199
Women against Violence against Women (WAVAW), 135
Woolworth's, 42–43
Workingman's Party, 33
World Bank, 48–50
World Boxing Council, 86
World Social Forum, 48
World Trade Organization (WTO), 48–50, 120
World War II, 56–57, 213
WorldCom, 193
Wright, Erik Olin, 204–6

Yelp, 138
Yoplait, 65–66
Young, Iris Marion, 201–2
Your Money's Worth, 37
YouTube, 9
Yum! Brands, 82, 118–19

Zambrano, Angela, 83
Zed, Rajan, 85
Zimmerman, George, 88–89, 104
Zinkhan, George, 211
Zuccotti Park, 1–2, 118, 209. *See also* Occupy
    Wall Street (OWS)

CPSIA information can be obtained
at www.ICGtesting.com
Printed in the USA
LVOW07s0732071217
558966LV00001B/350/P